CRY OF THE PANTHER:

Quest of a Species

James P. McMullen

McGraw-Hill Book Company
New York St. Louis San Francisco Auckland Bogotá Guatemala
Hamburg Johannesburg Lisbon London Madrid Mexico
Montreal New Delhi Panama Paris San Juan São Paulo
Singapore Sydney Tokyo Toronto

First paperback edition, 1985

Published by arrangement with Pineapple Press, Inc.

1 2 3 4 5 6 7 8 9 A G A G 8 7 6 5

ISBN 0-07-045651-8

LIBRARY OF CONGRESS CATALOGING IN PUBLICATION DATA

McMullen, James P., 1934–
Cry of the panther.
1. Pumas.   2. Mammals—Florida—Everglades.
3. Everglades (Fla.) I. Title.
QL737.C23M383 1985   599.74'28 [B]   85-9998
ISBN 0-07-045651-8

For Janie and Ashley and Dana

CONTENTS

Book III SEARCHING

Book IV PAW PRINTS IN THE MUD

Book V STALKING

Book VI ULTIMATE CONCEALMENT

ACKNOWLEDGMENTS

I wish to thank the many generous people who have helped me in a vast number of ways and who, like the panther, were always there when I needed them. My thanks to Professor Lucien Stryke of Northern Illinois University; Frank Weed, Sr., Frank Weed, Jr., and Ellen Weed, internationally known feline breeders; John and Sue Smith; Jim Pergola of Naples, Florida; the Seminole and Miccosukee Indians of the Everglades; the staff of the Big Cypress Nature Center, Naples, Florida; Ed Roman, wildlife photographer; Phil and Natalie Fisher of the Endangered Species Research Foundation, Inc.; Harry Rudenshiold, publisher of the *Neapolitan,* Naples, Florida; and, the staff of the Audubon Corkscrew Sanctuary, Immokalee, Florida.

A special thanks to all the principals and teachers and students throughout Florida for their support. And I am deeply thankful to the many librarians and their staffs who assisted me in my "indoor" research; to Pat Tucker and her computer; and to June Cussen, my editor at Pineapple.

I would like to thank Governor Bob Graham of Florida and Representatives William Bankhead, Mary Ellen Hawkins, and Frank Mann for their support, and also Mary and Paul Kruse. Also special thanks go to Bill and Virginia Travers of London, England, and to Marjory Stoneman Douglas of Miami, Florida.

INTRODUCTION

Great Grassy Waters

As I write this I am in my canoe drifting in the Florida Everglades in search of the endangered panther. The layers of August heat not only beat down on me but creep across this wild land in waves. I watch the stillness seem to move as a breeze pushes the heat across water and sawgrass, shimmering, magnifying them, as though at any second they will melt. It's not so much the air temperature, 80 to 90 degrees, as it is the thick humidity. I need only to move to sweat. Vietnam was the same.

In the old days a person could paddle for hours in this part of the glades, going from hammock to hammock, never seeing any signs of man. Now it is different. Overhead a jet roars. In the distance an airboat drones. Trucks scream on Alligator Alley and Tamiami Trail. Swamp buggies sputter in mud.

Slowly parting the tips of sawgrass, my canoe sways. Around me hundreds of hammocks reveal that there is still life that walks, swims, crawls, or flies. You can find whitetail deer tracks. Maybe a black bear bedding. In the worst part of the summer these animals seem to disappear, mostly because of the high waterline. Old-timers say they run to the mangroves to the south and live in the shade and dampness.

To the outside world the Everglades might seem an impossible habitat for a heavy, furred cat. And yet the panther is here. He wanders. Ambushes prey. Drinks swamp water. Sleeps on high ground. Eludes man. He survives.

I pass over blue crabs in this vast place called the River of Grass. The nature of this watery wilderness was first named and best described by Marjorie Stoneman Douglas in her classic book, *The Everglades: River of Grass:*

There are no other Everglades in the world.

They are, they have always been, one of the unique regions of the earth, remote, never wholly known.

To experience the Everglades is to experience the panther. The glades are his home.

Still today a great deal more has to be discovered about this extraordinary predator. Researchers have neatly filed well-calculated data from a radio telemetry project that seemingly makes him out to be a different animal than he really is. The Florida panther is a cougar that has adapted to the subtropical environment of the Everglades.

The Seminole and Miccosukee Indians smile with their eyes, not their lips, when you mention a panther. They always have an open-ended explanation. The way cats act today doesn't mean they'll act that way tomorrow. They sometimes refer to the myths of their ancestors and the Calusa Indians, the original glades people, and this is the only time they do smile.

Swampmen don't smile when the subject of the big cat comes up over a campfire. They love to tell stories about him. But for the most part, they don't smile. Hunters no longer talk about the panther, probably because he is on the endangered species list and protected by state and federal law. Yet you can see the challenge and the thrill of just one more cat hunt in their eyes. Those hunters who talk about the panther through wisdom have mounted their rifles and shotguns and become conservationists. They are excited that this mysterious creature is still in the Everglades. Environmentalists use the panther's name with religious reverence and consider him to be the one great symbol of all wildlife in the swamps. Now that the panther is the official Florida state animal, politicians seize on him for votes through bio-politics. Land developers cringe at his very name, irritated that he still exists.

The swampies that live on the perimeter of the glades will call you a liar if you tell them you saw a panther, yet they can give you a vivid description of the cat. Some of them say he is black, or even white, and will try to steal your babies; that a person can tell the age and sex of a panther by the color of his or her fur and size; that he will come into your camp at night and sleep near your fire; that he is a menace and confined to the Everglades. None of this has ever been proven. Most of it is just plain wrong.

This book is about this magnificent cat and my lived-adventures tracking him in the Everglades, the eerie parallels to my Vietnam experiences, the swamp itself, and my quest to help save the cat from extinction—and also one man's journey to find himself. Eighty percent of it was written in the depths of the cypress swamps, custard apple sloughs, mangrove forests, slash pine woods, and the River of Grass—the very places the big cat roams. There is an overwhelming factor about this beautiful cat that sets him apart from the rest and puts his reproduction and survival in immediate peril: he is on the verge of extinction not only in Florida but in the Western Hemisphere.

Over the years many people have asked me why I bother with a big cat that is almost gone anyway.

Who knows his own motives? In writing this book I have begun to encounter a few of mine. Though I can't yet say exactly how or why, I am beginning to understand that going to Vietnam—and coming back—had a lot to do with why I have spent the last eight years tracking the panther in the part of the United States that is most like the Vietnam coastline and tropical jungle. Ironically, when I left Vietnam in 1967 I swore I would never go out in the forest again. I thought I hated it. A few years later I couldn't wait to get to the Everglades. Now I will never leave. I love them. Rather than being a grim, disheartening, empty place, they are infinitely fulfilling, still rich with vegetation, pulsing with animal life, abundant in beauty. Having been acclimated to the intense tropical climate in Vietnam made it easy for me to adapt to the climate of the Everglades.

For me the war was a time of cruel disillusionment beyond all conception. In my journey to manhood I participated in one of man's cruelest attempts at destroying half a country and thousands of people. Maybe I have taken on the personal responsibility of saving an endangered species on the verge of extinction because I found out first-hand what such a creature must feel like. Having been a part of destruction and death was a stepping stone to becoming an extreme preservationist. I was hunted by the Viet Cong, preyed upon, and finally almost killed. That I survived was a miracle.

I think miracles have a purpose. I know the miracle of my own survival is what brought me here. It's a miracle that any panthers have survived, too. And maybe the purpose of that miracle is to make us consider our own survival as a species. That will be the biggest miracle of all. It was the big cat that taught me peace, and a means of dealing with my life. The panther ultimately led me to God. Now I am never closer to Him than when I am in the swamp close to panthers. My long journey toward tracking panthers was a pilgrimage of the soul. The panther and I were conceived into this world to meet in the midst of the modern Everglades under siege by heavy development and over-population and biological politics that have no place in the swamp. Though the Florida panther and I were more than 15,000 miles apart at one point in our lives, circumstances eventually brought us together. I traveled a long, twisting trail to the panther. But sometimes I feel that it was the cat's cause to track me down. In our spirit territories we were seeking each other. Either way, our tryst was my wilderness rebirth as a human being into a new life, a life that offers itself as solid hope for the preservation of the Everglades, which has become the symbol of all wilderness throughout the world. It was the panther that poured into my consciousness an infinite, positive power that made me realize that this big cat is much, much more than a wild animal on the prowl for prey. He is a mysterious messenger.

In Vietnam I was not only the hunted but also the hunter. I carried an M14 rifle. My orders were to go out in support of other marine units, to search and destroy. When I came home with lead in my back as a partially disabled veteran, I felt compelled to hunt in a different way, though very likely for the same thing: myself, mankind.

So, why bother with a big cat that is almost gone anyway?

This book is my answer.

PROLOGUE

Swamp Lord

The Florida panther moves within the dark holes of the Everglades as though he is the shadows of trees. Carefully he chooses each step, and each time that he does, no sound is heard.

The panther turns, hesitates with one paw in the air, moves on, slows up, crouches, then sways his narrow body through the thick swamp. This cat knows exactly where he is going, for he has been over this territory hundreds of times.

Rarely is his gait broken, but when it happens there is a purpose. He pauses at the bleached bones of a deer, now half-buried in the swamp bog, an old kill he ambushed some months before.

The panther now moves swiftly on high ground, pivoting around small cypress trees and fallen logs. His movements are dominant, awesome.

This panther is a male, three years old. He is a dark fawn-gray, flecked with white on the back of the neck, creamy white under his stomach and chest. The swamp he is walking in is dense with second-growth cypress, red maple, oak, gumbo-limbo, strangler fig, and poisonwood. The trail he is on was first made by Seminole Indians living in the Everglades, then used by lumber companies hauling out as much of it as they could. Now the flowing water is wasting the trail away in some places.

It is April, an in-between month in the glades, raining occasionally, drying out more often. The panther has been alone for more than a year. Though he has not seen another cat, scent-markings have been left crossing his territory—a pile of droppings here, scrapes there.

But right now he is more concerned about meat, and since he set up his own territory almost a year before, prey has been plentiful.

Suddenly he stops dead in his tracks. There is scent of fresh blood in the air. Turning in the direction of the source, the panther, as though mesmerized by an invisible light, pursues the smell off the trail and into a deep slough. Not far in on a leaf island is a bobcat gorging himself on a freshly killed raccoon. Upwind, the panther suddenly crouches on his belly and slowly begins to creep closer and closer toward the unsuspecting bobcat. Ever so slowly, the panther draws his hind feet under his body, already extending his claws and baring his canines. In a burst of fury he springs forth, front legs and paws splayed out, pouncing heavily on the bobcat, engulfing it in his death grip.

Instantly his fangs sink into the back of the small cat's neck and crush the spinal cord. At the same time his claws dig deep and rip open long slashes on the side of the now dead bobcat.

The panther settles down to eat the raccoon and the hind quarters of the bobcat. Finished, he grooms himself, then moves back up to the trail and continues on.

This panther weighs one hundred and thirty-five pounds, measures eight feet from muzzle to tip of tail, and stands twenty-four inches high at the shoulders. His paws are huge, leaving paw prints in the mud three and three-quarters inches wide. During the cold months he walks with a slight limp, having been struck by a rattlesnake on the right hind leg four months ago. Now he stays away from all snakes.

Having fed, he will not kill again for two or maybe three days. He pauses long enough to lick some dirt, lap at the water, then goes on.

It is noon, the hot part of the day. He moves off the trail and finds a large shady bush where he can keep cool while he rests. As he moves in to lie down, a ring-necked snake slithers out of the way. A scorpion moves much more slowly, but manages to avoid the panther's heavy body as it rolls onto the ground.

After an hour he stirs, rises, and stretches out with forepaws dug into the mud, back arched, hind end raised toward the trees.

He roams once again. Two months from now he will be called in by a mating female, fight over her with an older male, win her, hunt with her, copulate, and father three panther cubs, though he will never know the cubs. The female will grow angry with him, they will fight, and he will leave long before the three-month gestation period is over.

Within two months after the birth the female will lose all three cubs, one to an indigo snake, another to a distemper fit, and the third to an alligator.

The male panther will kill two more deer during that time, but most of his food will be armadillo, opossum, raccoon, turkey, quail, and wading birds. He will have a close call at night on the highway when he is blinded by truck lights. He will also hear bullets whistle over his head.

He roams at the edge of a wet prairie now. The swamp seems different. It is overcast and the winds come up out of nowhere and then suddenly die. Soon there will be rains that fill up the swamp with deep water, and if it weren't for the man-made trails, there would be no high ground. He smells the thick scent of cypress and an occasional drowned animal. He sees snakes on the trail and up in the trees. He feels under his paws the spongy ground and soupy mud.

After every rain, he carefully retraces his territory and reestablishes his scent-markings.

In the years to come he will learn every sound, know every blade of grass, recognize every scent in his territory. Nothing will escape him. He will stalk and ambush opossum at play, try to slap fish out of a shallow pond, do battle with a young black bear and win, be run out of a portion of his territory by fire but return the following month. He will be chased by an airboat and run off by dogs.

And in the hot, blinding days of the summer he will

lounge under saw palmetto bushes and watch vultures soar silently overhead, while beneath his paws ox beetles will feed on moonflower petals.

CRY OF
THE
PANTHER

The only real revolutionary stance is that "nature" is the greatest convention of all. Perhaps there are no natures, no essence—only categories and paradigms that human beings mentally and politically impose on the flux of experience in order to produce illusions of certainty, definiteness, distinction, hierarchy. Apparently, human beings do not like a Heraclitan world; they want fixed points of reference in order not to fall into vertigo, nausea. Perhaps the idea of nature or essence is man's ultimate grasp for eternity. The full impact of the theory of evolution is thus still to come.

John Rodman
The Dolphin Papers

So all of us remain hunters to this day, either symbolic hunters or fantasy hunters, achieving ambitious goals and setting ourselves lofty targets. Little wonder that we are fascinated by the real hunters, belonging to other species, that have managed to survive on the scarred face of the globe that man has altered so radically in a few brief millennia.

Desmond Morris
Introduction to *The Hunter*

A long time ago when the Indians were emerging from the mountains, God spoke to the Panther clan and Wind clan when they were still like ten months old babies. God told them to come out of the mountain. So they dug and they dug and were the first of the forty-seven Seminole clans to come out. They were like brothers.

Panther clan followed Wind clan from the navel of the earth. Panther clan had a big head and couldn't get out. The Wind clan came out like a whirlwind. The Wind clan came out of one side of roots which grew on the mound, while the Panther clan members came out on the other side.

The trees grew up so fast that Panther was held down at first. Wind clan blew up the roots, and then Panther came out followed by Bird and Snake. They came out of the mound like babies.

Seminole Indian myth as told
to the author by a Seminole
of the Panther clan

Something hidden,
Go and find it.
Go look behind the ranges.
Something lost behind the ranges,
Lost and waiting for you,
Go.

Rudyard Kipling
The Explorer

Book I

Wilderness Obsession

And in himself
possess his own desire.
      —William Wordsworth

1

Sighting

Swamp notes—in the cypress
To enter the Everglades and experience the
haunts of the panther, to catch a fleeting
glimpse of this almost extinct cat is the ultimate gift for me. It gives me that rare
wilderness shock of power to accomplish the
impossible.

In the gentle embrace of this untamed world, deep in the
Everglades, I slowly crouched and ran my hands through the
swampgrass and water and into the cool, soft, wet, black peat,
letting it ooze between my fingers, smelling its thick swamp
scent. I had been on a furious search for the endangered
Florida panther in this region for more than three days straight,
and so far had not found any physical evidence that the cat
even existed. Questions and doubts, exhaustion and irritation
seeped into my thoughts like the slow-moving waters of the
River of Grass.

I splashed water on my face baptismal-like until my eyes
were clear. A shiver came up my arms and across my chest.
I stared at a coming wet dawn over an enormous prairie and
thick cypress swamp. In the growing gray light, my eyes detected on a moist blade of sawgrass a zebra butterfly awaiting
the warmth of the sun rays to dry its fragile wings for flight.
For a moment it appeared jittery.

At times like that I feel as though I am becoming part
of nature around me: the trees, mud, sky, water, birds—
everything. My soul seems to be cut in a million different
parts, all living and breathing in the same tempo of life. And
it is as real as the kiss of a single raindrop on the petal of a
wild orchid. Mankind began as energy to form a molecule,
and this power increased, and as it does, and probably will

do forever, the complexity of man will persist until he approaches sainthood.

Watching the butterfly, I could not help but think of what Rumi, a Persian philosopher in the twelfth century, said: "I died a mineral and became a plant. I died a plant and rose an animal. I died an animal and I was a man."

Flocks of white ibis passed over my head then and swirled in wide arches in elegant, careening uplifts, dissolving into the long pale streaks of a crimson-red sky. Distant gray thunder bursts, aglow with pulsing lightning, challenged daybreak and darkness and chased snowy egrets inland, their plumage looking like white flames dancing among blurred water souls. As the dusky rubric sun trembled halfway above a hardwood hammock, inches below and above a misty haze, the swampscape seemed to catch fire in a red-green heat wave that clutched, flushed and quivered the whole horizon. It all gleamed with an ancient polish as it moved in timeless languor.

Casting fragmented, dancing shadows on the swamp, four black vultures stalked air pockets high up with their wide sweeping wings and hovered and soared in wide swoops like mythical sky gods surveying their universe.

Far above them, haloed by a rainbow and epitomizing the power of flight, was the dark outline of the supreme bald eagle—gliding, holding position, rising, then gliding once again, proudly demonstrating that his species was still with us.

Within the thick cypress treeline, black holes revealed stirring anhingas, Louisiana herons and cattle egrets.

As the gilded haze of a swamp fog crept around me, harboring primeval ghosts of a forgotten time, my sixth sense, that inherent extrasensory psychic power linked to our ancestors at the dawn of time, warned me to be alert, tense, wary of something out there.

Something was stirring in the cypress trees some fifty yards out in front of me. Something that drew my spirit closer to the earth, closer to my own survival. I couldn't see anything, but I felt an animal presence. . . .

And suddenly a patch of gray-brown fur appeared in shadows between cypress trees. It might easily have been a white-tailed deer. Except the body seemed closer to the ground in a horizontal position, and it appeared to float a foot above the swamp as it moved, as stealthy as a—*cat*.

I breathed slowly, deeply, making every effort to hold sound in so as not to spook the animal whatever it was. For over six months I had been seeking and preparing for this moment. It was a moment of true excitement, maybe my only opportunity to be rewarded a sighting of this untamed, mis-understood creature.

Then, as abruptly as it had appeared, the fur was gone. My heart stopped. No, I cried inside. No, not now, not after so long. As the last words rolled across my mind, the fur was there once again. Then it melted into the shadows, reappeared, only to disappear once again. This happened three times, but still I had not had a glimpse of the entire animal.

Longing for a better position, I fought with myself not to move, for I knew that twitching even one muscle would have meant the animal would vanish forever. I remained a part of the swamp.

Then the movement stopped. It's seen me, I thought. And at that second, large paws sprang in a bolt of speed deeper into the slough. But I'd seen it, the whole cat, and it was like no other animal I had ever seen. It was furred power, gray-brown on top, creamy white underneath, and at the end of it, a magnificent, long J-shaped tail streaked in dawn light and swamp darkness like a retreating demon.

As though magnetized to the animal, I too jumped up and started running through the grass, pivoting into the cy-press, splashing into the swamp water, in pursuit of a Florida panther. Fumbling with my camera, I was trying to get it up to my eye, while maneuvering my body through the density, attempting to get him on film. Instead, I was getting tangled in vines and tripping over cypress knees. And yet I ran on, actually believing I could get within grasp of him. Most of the animals in the glades are quick when they have to be, but this panther was unearthly sudden.

He broadjumped cypress stumps and fallen logs with the grace of a finely conditioned Olympic athlete. Under that beautiful fur his shoulder and leg muscles flexed and rippled, and his whole body moved as though there weren't a bone in it. Even as I ran, it reminded me of the soft, silent motion of an ocean swell rising from the depth, rolling and forming into a single wave, then lowering into the depth once again, only to swell once more.

As this rarest of all rare cats faded into the glades, my mind burned with excitement. I kept on going, stumbling over oak logs, catching vines around my throat, passing frogs and turtles, and shattering the silence where lounging gators tore into the water for safety.

But it was no use. My legs felt like I was running in lead shoes, and my lungs heaved for oxygen. I slipped, gained my balance, then fell into the mud, detecting the last faint sounds of the big cat's paws slapping through a willow patch.

Lying there, gasping for air in a morning already hot and humid, I felt both elation and wonderment—not disappointment. In my mind I was by far the luckiest tracker on earth. I had searched out and found in a relatively short time a true panther without the help of hunters, park rangers, or anybody else. I hadn't used an airboat, swamp buggy, off-road vehicle, plane or helicopter. I had never once entertained the idea of using tranquilizers or a radio-telemetry collar. I had sighted a Florida panther roaming free in his natural habitat.

For some reason I felt I was going to get to know this panther quite well. So I decided to give him a name. He bounded through the swamp like a poem . . . like Shakespeare's poems, rhythmic, eloquent, stirring, and with a strength no other human being could hope to equal. So I named him Shakespeare.

Sitting there in the mud, panting heavily, tears of joy rolling down my cheeks, sweating, being bitten by mosquitoes, I suddenly knew that the panther and I were now intricately connected by an ancestral spiritual bond, or always had been. I needed only to recognize it. There he was roaming the Everglades as a symbol of my own soul crying out for survival, for liberty.

I knew then to understand fully this affinity, truly to feel it, I would have to immerse myself in the panther's world, to shatter the barriers between me and the panther and develop common ground.

It was at that moment I realized that wilderness, the big cat, all wildlife, the very breath of the wind, is everything holy to mankind. I vowed to track Shakespeare until I had proven beyond a shadow of a doubt that he truly existed. But I had no intention of catching him and putting him in a cage. I didn't have to. Instead, I would find the spoor—tracks, scat, scratch marks on trees, ambush sites, bush trails, old and new kills, maybe a log den.

I set out to protect, not to jeopardize his livelihood, and then to leave him to roam as he pleased, remaining untouched by man.

It became my wilderness obsession.

2

Going Home

> **Swamp notes—near a hammock**
> *Coming out here lets me relax. Trouble is when I relax too much now my mental defenses go slack and a lot of stuff that's been hiding behind them for years keeps surfacing. But it's OK somehow to let them take over my mind for a while out here. I'm finding that those memories hurt less if I think about them in the swamp.*

From my tent opening I saw in the Nam darkness the starlit phosphorescence that collected around rotted tree trunks in the stifling humidity. It pulsed and glowed over damp spots from a night rain in the gulley like haunting war souls still clinging to the divine principle of life. Belly lights, red and flashing, ascended slowly over the Chu Lai tent line, hovered, then passed into an obscurity dark as a panther's mouth. A

squadron of choppers on another night mission of mercy. I
heard distant thunderbolts and saw bursting lightning mixed
with muffled bomb thunder far out in the hills over the fetid
jungle. More war souls pulsed. The faint chatter of a machine
gun echoed from the north side of the perimeter near the
village in short intervals. A jerking in my gut at each round
put a sour taste in my mouth. Then the chatter was silenced
by a loud explosion. More war souls.

As the darkness melted into morning light, I finished
cramming the last of my gear into my sea bag and forced the
flaps over to snap on the shoulder strap. On the floor in the
corner was what was left of my last set of utilities—a mass of
green wet fabric, sleeves cut off, trousers torn. The smell of
Nam mixed with sweat from fourteen long eerie months exuded
from it. Red mud was caked on the helmet and decayed jungle
boots.

They didn't look like utilities any more, but like a dead,
misbegotten, bloody creature born of a bad dream, now dissolving back into that dream. I stood staring at that "creature"
for a moment, praying it wouldn't follow me as I picked up
my sea bag to leave. When I got to the tent door I looked
back to see if it had moved. It hadn't, and yet I felt it would
follow me for years to come.

I walked out into the night and slung the sea bag over
my shoulder. Everyone else had already gone down to the
mess tent for breakfast so it was a good time for me to disappear. I didn't want to remember last looks and warm hand-
shakes. I wanted to remember the guys as they were, continuing
on with life. I didn't want to read the casualty report in the
newspaper or get a letter that so and so went down hard, and
then think about the very last second I saw him when he said
good-bye and good luck. I didn't want any of that. I just
wanted to be gone from Nam without being noticed, to go
back to the World and try and forget it all. I had a spooky
feeling that wasn't going to happen.

A jeep was sitting on the muddy road at the base of the
hill when I got there, so I threw my sea bag in back and got
in. The driver was a new replacement and I didn't know him,
so we didn't talk, even when he said, "Well, marine, you're
short. You're so short I can't even see you."

When I didn't answer him, he looked at me peculiarly, then started up the jeep and we sputtered and slipped up the hill, over the top and down toward the corner to turn toward the airstrip.

I never looked back—not once. I didn't want to because I didn't want to be lured by the Nam syndrome—"acute environmental reaction," the corpsman had called it. As badly as I wanted to leave, to run from it all, I also wanted to stay, and the feeling was pulling at my back to stop the jeep, turn around and go back. But I squeezed my eyes tightly. I felt the job was unfinished, that I was abandoning my concepts. If I stayed I could do it all over again, but do it better, do it right. I turned to the driver and opened my mouth to tell him to turn around.

But my attention was diverted by a convoy of filthy trucks, tanks and jeeps with mud-covered weary marines inside and on top that barged around a corner and crowded us over to the side of the road. At the rear was a flatbed truck with a huge pile of rifles, camo-helmets, k-bars, backpacks, boots and a few .45-caliber pistol holsters. At a closer look I saw that the equipment was heavily stained with blood. Some of the packs had holes through them, and a number of the boots were blown apart. I turned and stretched and watched that flatbed until it was lost in the drab dawn and the red mud on the road. I clenched my teeth and sat deep in my seat all the way to the airstrip.

Suddenly the driver was saying, "You're on you're way, marine."

I looked up and saw the airstrip now glowing in front of me with the wavy morning humidity coming off the runway like ocean surf. I forced myself out of the jeep, grabbed my sea bag and walked over to a tent full of marines waiting for a C-130 to take us up to Da Nang for a jet to Okinawa. I sat in a corner, silent, staring at the sand, feeling depressed and wasted. When I looked up once, I was startled by how quiet it was in the tent. All I saw were tight-lipped mouths, empty eyes, hands rubbing nervously. There were cigarettes passed around. A lighter flared in one of the corners. But nobody seemed to have anything to say. Outside the airstrip buzzed with planes, sea bees running about, jeeps roaring past, orders yelled out. But inside our waiting tent it was like a dank sepulchre.

I sat there feeling even more depressed until finally a huge camouflaged C-130 transport plane slowly rolled up on the runway. We all picked up our sea bags and walked out to the ramp and filed in. The marine next to me stopped and turned around and said, "Shit. . . ."

I kept my eyes straight into the hull of the plane until I found a seat on the side and then I closed them until I heard the ramp clamp shut and the propellers splutter. Inside, the red light flushed over us and formed odd expressions on faces that used to be young, eyes that once were bright with anticipation, mouths that used to smile easily. Now all I saw were stone shadows across placid features that were empty.

At Da Nang I sat outside the huge warehouse terminal next to the strip, sweating in the sun, watching a mass of war energy steam off the runway in choppers, transport planes, jets, trucks loaded with marines. A battalion-size ARVN unit strung themselves out along the strip in a long green snake and boarded an assault brigade of Chinook helicopters. A Golden Continental jet landed and taxied to the warehouse and a straight line of clean marines walked down the steps. Their boots were spit-shined and they wore starched, pressed utilities and perfectly ironed covers. Each name above the breast pocket was aligned and in bold black ink. Falling into platoon formation, they marched off the runway over to the waiting buses. Raw, innocent replacements that, depending on where they ended up in Nam, would soon be warwise or dead. Behind them, gleaming in the sunlight, stacked coffins were being loaded onto a plane with a forklift.

I sat there like that, staring blankly at it all for hours until dark. Another Golden Continental jet landed. It was our ticket out of Nam. But then we found out that they had to call for another jet because the Viet Cong had ambushed this one as it was landing. Several holes were punched out in the left wing. Charlie, you got the last word in, I thought, you son-of-a-bitch. I stood there, looking at those holes; there was nothing I could do about it.

There was a lot of cursing from the others, and when finally another jet came in for us, we thought we were on our way. But when we lined up to get on that plane, one of the power units underneath the plane backfired and one of the guys went crazy and ran off, yelling, "Get down, get down! . . ."

I almost followed him because for a second I thought we were taking incoming rounds.

When the jet door opened and they put the stairs over to it, I looked around to see if anything else was going to happen. My legs were rubbery as I made it up those stairs. It was like climbing a mountain and when I got to my seat I collapsed in it and caught my breath. I had no idea what was going on to cause that. I could run five miles with a heavy pack. Why couldn't I climb a few stairs? This breathlessness and immobility would occur again and again in different situations in the World for the next five years. I was finally told that it was caused by anxiety bottled up inside. Though I was trying to be calm and cool getting out of Nam, inside my mind was battling as though in a firefight. The outward sign was immobility. I literally had to force my body to move, exhausting the attack in physical endeavor. It would happen when intense stress would build up concerning an incident in Nam I didn't want to think about, but was stimulated by some outward cause.

The jet took off and climbed fast, and throughout the plane the roar of yelps and hollers resounded against the walls. We were out. For the first time I looked back out the side of the window. At one end of the strip Da Nang was lit up with aerial illumination rounds in that pale floating glow. The outer perimeter was getting hit and jets were making night runs on the VC with rockets exploding and waves of orange tracers flashing through the night into nowhere. That was my last view of Vietnam.

We spent two days at Camp Butler, Okinawa, among fast orders and piles of paper. My uniform was cleaned, pressed and tailored to fit my one hundred and forty-five-pound body. (I had been one hundred and seventy when I hit Vietnam.) Once I walked off by myself and came onto a marine outside the barracks sitting on the sidewalk with a long banana knife that he was sharpening vigorously on the cement. He looked up at me with killer eyes, war-torn eyes, eyes that would never see happiness again. The blade gleamed and flashed as he pressed it into the cement and worked it back and forth. "I'm goin' back," he said to me, as though we were as close as any two marines could be in a war. "I'm goin' back and get me some gook hearts."

He had this fiendish expression on his face as he bent over and inspected the blade, then returned it to the cement. When I walked away I heard his low, growling laugh.

On the afternoon of the second day ninety-three marines boarded a jet at Okinawa bound for the States. I sat in the very back row staring at the blonde stewardess doing everything she could do to make us comfortable. I was ill at ease with her and had a hard time believing I was looking at a fresh, clean, light-skinned, beautiful American woman. All I wanted to do was touch her and when she brought the supper tray around with drinks, I made it a point to brush up against her fingers. Twelve hours later, at thirty thousand feet, and the third time around on the movie, we cruised over British Columbia, Canada. Then an announcement by the captain said we had just entered the United States on the west coast. I jerked a look out the window and couldn't see a thing.

The next time I looked out we were touching down at El Toro Marine Corps Air Force Base. At a deserted terminal taxis were waiting in a long line to take us to Los Angeles International Airport. I wasn't sure what to expect at El Toro, maybe a band playing, people on the fence waving at us, cheers. But instead there was a bright silent day, and not one person was there to greet us, just those taxis. I felt like I had been slapped in the face for something I didn't do.

There were five of us who got into one of the taxis. Four of us had purple hearts. One had a silver star. The fifth one acted like he didn't even want to be in the taxi with the rest of us and never said a word to any of us all the way to Los Angeles. It didn't make any difference because nobody was talking much anyway—not until we got close to the airport and were driving through road construction along one of the off ramps. Suddenly I heard machine-gun fire. I bent forward and hugged my neck. The marine next to me said, "Oh no, God no . . ."

The taxi driver slammed on his brakes and pulled over

to the side. "Hey, it's okay, man. You're in the States. It was a air jackhammer out there."

We looked up and saw the power tool pounding away on the curb cement, splitting it into fragments. Cars were honking at us to get out of the way. I never did calm down from that, not even when I got on the airplane headed for Chicago's O'Hare Airport. I kept my hands in my pockets and kept staring out the window so no one would see my eyes. All of the rush to get out of Nam, country-hopping, and the stress of going home had gotten the better part of my senses. I had never acted like that, not even in Nam. What was going on? What was the matter with me? The only answer I could come up with was that I didn't have a chance to decompress from the war. I had been simply and efficiently thrust back into an alien American population and expected to handle it. I guess I wasn't doing very well.

And to make things even more disorienting, I was suddenly deposited into Illinois at O'Hare in January at fifteen below zero in the middle of a snowstorm. Three days previous I had been in the middle of war-zone Nam, in the thick humidity, heat, sweat, rain, blood, death. Now by man's means of modern transportation, I had been plucked out of it and dropped twelve thousand miles away. All I can remember is seeing my sister standing at the gate trying her best to smile and at the same time wondering how to act toward me. We hugged, kissed and walked to the car. Because of the snowstorm we couldn't drive the three hours to Streator, so we stayed over and the next day we chanced it, arriving at night in a blizzard.

I got out of the car, walked up the porch steps to two people standing at the door I had sworn in Vietnam I would come back to. My dad shook my hand. My mother cried.

Days later I still didn't know where I was. My parents walked on egg shells the first week, never once asking questions about Nam, though my father was quite interested in seeing my wounds. I wandered, dazed, about town, as though my feet were about four feet off the ground, and my head was in a thick fog, a fog that didn't go away for a long time. I was still in Nam. In my bedroom I wanted to sit down on my foot locker and clean my rifle, reload a magazine. I wanted to volunteer for a convoy thunder run, security for a team going out on an operation. I wanted to go on patrol.

Nam was still with me: the roar of bulldozers, the whomp whomp of the choppers, tents blowing apart in a monsoon rain, the first time I heard enemy fire, the body bags on operation Deckhouse II, the wounded, the Cessna spotter plane going up in flames from a VC rocket, KIA's, MIA's, POW's, SIW's—I could still feel the round slam into me when I got wounded—ghosts, women and children screaming from their bus after it blew up from a VC mine, a young lieutenant fragged by his sergeant, a marine shooting himself in the foot to get out of a patrol, a wobbling chopper desperately trying to get to the LZ and missing our tents by inches before crashing near the medical center, another chopper with six of our guys in it which passed over us and out to sea and then suddenly lost altitude and plunged into the rough water. Later their bodies had washed up on Chu Lai's beach.

I wondered what all the guys were doing in Chu Lai. Were they okay? I would suddenly sit down and furiously write out a long detailed letter, then end up throwing it away. I still wanted to go back. I got drunk one night, packed my sea bag, wrote a note to my parents, got in the car and started driving to California. I ended up in a bar drinking all night, waking up the next day on the freeway sick and lost.

Though the guilt, the distrust of the American people, all the war-related stress and the eventual paranoia would surface more later, during those first months I was in a Kafka-esque existence. I had to keep almost all of my feelings covered up, even with my closest friends. They would look at me with strange eyes, ask about Vietnam and say something naive. "I heard Vietnam was a beautiful country."

By the time I could try to respond they were onto another conversation. From then on I began to drift away from them. They just did not have any conception of what Vietnam was really all about and what it had done to me inside. How could they? They were more concerned about insurance policies, buying a house, their careers.

What troubled me most of all about them was their reluctance to understand what was happening over there. I didn't know it at the time but I was one of thousands of Nam vets who were given the unpopular burden of the failure in Vietnam. It was almost as though they were embarrassed and ashamed of me.

From the United States to Vietnam and back to the United States again—all in a little over a year. I had been in a time warp. Nothing was for certain. Nothing was wholly real, except the discouraging reality of the war and people Stateside who acted like I wasn't around. I looked up my high school girlfriend, thinking I could resume our relationship. But when I saw her, she was different, distant, a little afraid of me, and then straightforwardly told me she was engaged to a Green Beret who was then in Nam at the Iron Triangle. I didn't see her much after that.

On the surface, I tried inventing the old Jim McMullen again—a nice guy, laughs a lot, carefree, doesn't take things too seriously. That meant never talking about Nam to anybody. I played that role pretty well for a while, thinking if I at least acted like him, eventually I would return to that person I left behind. But something was wrong with all of that. In the midst of minor problems or frustrations, I would suddenly jump into an uncontrolled rage, well out of proportion to the incident at hand. In cold sweat I would jerk up in the middle of the night from a Nam dream of being shot up and killed in an ambush. Instead of drinking moderately at a bar, I would shove down shot after shot of whiskey for half the night, then fall outside and vomit my guts out, have a terrible hangover the next day, get myself squared away and try to become that carefree person again—only to get drunk and go through the cycle all over again. It went on like that until one rainy day I swerved off a road and slammed my car into a telephone pole, leveling the pole and sending me into a cornfield. I laid off the booze for a while, but soon I was at it again. I job-jumped on construction work, tried to go back to college on the GI Bill and flunked out the first semester. I had no direction, no purpose.

One morning, in an icy wind, I walked down to the river where my grandfather had taught me to track raccoons. Like me, it had changed dramatically. I didn't like the way the river had changed. I didn't like how I had changed. I wondered what I was going to do with my life. I wondered if I ever was going to accept a true responsibility for living again.

3

Morning Star

Swamp notes—east side of Snaggle Tooth Creek

The signs panther/Shakespeare has left for me in his territory are among thousands of signs in his lifetime. They are among the oldest storytellers on earth, and are clear, undisputed evidence the big cat is here without ever seeing him. Up ahead he walks, occasionally leaving in the mud his mysterious trail, track by track, beckoning me to go on and turn the next page of his life. In my life right now there is nothing more difficult and at the same time more richly rewarding than tracking this glorious cat. At the very least, it has revealed a profound statement of myself, and hopefully, at the most, it will reveal a wilderness philosophy for Planet Earth.

After that first sighting, I wanted nothing more than to strike out on Shakespeare's trail then and there, to stay and feel his presence forever. But I was out of supplies and had exhausted myself in my search for the cat. So I went home for three days, rested and collected my thoughts, and decided to continue to track him as I had done before, revising my methods as I progressed.

I decided to look for books on how to track panthers, but there were none in the library. The book had yet to be written, it seemed. I tried to track Shakespeare in the entrails of the library and find what was there on his species. Scientific journals, history books, newspapers and magazines did give scanty evidence that he was in the glades. There was a mountain of information about the cougar elsewhere in the Western Hemisphere, but very little about the cougar in the Everglades. No one had bothered to compile a healthy volume of data on him. Apparently there had been little research on this particular cat. When mentioned at all, the panther roamed across the pages as mysteriously as he did in the swamp. An unknown animal. The scientific community had overlooked a rare subspecies. I couldn't rely on books for learning how to track this cat. I would have to rely on myself.

My grandfather, Grandpa Jim, greatly influenced my life because he was the man who had introduced me to my first animal paw print in the mud. He was a woodsman and had on occasion in his early days supported his family by hunting and fishing. He loved the wilds and it showed on him. He was lean, muscular, quiet, a strong man who talked with his eyes more than his mouth. And he always seemed to know what he was doing. When he took me fishing down to a river, I was sure he knew what he was doing.

One day when I was eleven years old, the fishing wasn't going very well and, sensing my restlessness, he thought it might be fun if we walked the riverbank a little.

Then he started doing some strange things—crouching, looking at the mud, standing up, walking slowly with his eyes to the ground, then straight ahead, then down at the ground again. Then he bent over and measured something with his finger. Peering at me with smiling eyes, he waved me over to him.

He was now staring at the riverbank into a pile of rocks and old logs. Putting his finger up to his lips he brought me forward, putting his arm around my shoulder and pointing into a hole. There in the darkness were several baby raccoons making strange sounds.

He then took me back to the mud and showed me tracks of the babies and the larger track of the mother. There were small paws perfectly imprinted in the soft earth that showed even the knuckled joint.

My grandfather had taught me my most needed lesson in tracking. First find the track and identify the animal, then follow it to its home. I began to learn how to place the correct animal in those tracks, forming a vivid mental picture of the color of fur for a mammal, length for a snake, size for a worm.

Although I had already learned how to push myself beyond my normal physical limits playing football, basketball and baseball from grade school through high school, my Marine Corps boot camp training at Parris Island, South Carolina, taught me that there are almost no limits to what a person can do physically as long as he's alive and determined. We marched double-time everywhere, did squat thrusts from morning until nightfall, and ran and ran and ran, and then ran some more. With full gear on, we carried buckets of sand up and down the parade deck until we dropped, then got up and did it again. We went through the obstacle course every day and did the confidence course until we had nightmares of it. Then we ran again, and ran . . . and ran. Gung Ho. Semper Fi. Push ups. Leg lifts. Chin ups. Sit ups. Squat thrusts . . . squat thrusts . . . and more squat thrusts. I was never in better physical shape than when I left boot camp.

All of this training put us in infantry training at Camp LeJeune, North Carolina. There we learned the art of seeing how far we could push ourselves after being in shape. Always with full pack, tent, sleeping bag and M-14 rifle, we were on the move. We ran in formation everywhere. During rain, cold spells and snow—it didn't matter. We learned the low crawl under machine gun fire, slow crawled during night maneuvers, set up L ambush sites, took gun emplacements on a dead run frontal assault, threw grenades, blew out pill boxes with flame throwers . . . and marched more than twenty miles a day, seven days a week, thirty days a month, for three months. From the halls of Montezuma . . . to the shores of Tripoli . . . as marines we were super-physically fit, knew how to handle our rifles, could move unseen in the forest in small fire teams setting up mock vantage points of observation. We were a crack outfit, and it showed on our confident faces. We felt we could do anything at any time anywhere. There was nothing that could

stop us, absolutely nothing. If there was one hard lesson I
learned during this time it was once you set your course on
a goal, no matter what, keep at it, don't quit, don't let anybody
tell you you can't do it. Keep on keeping on until you have
attained your goal.

That's what I fully intended to do in tracking Shakespeare. If I had to, and I figured I would have to, I would
invent new ways to track a cat, new means to verify his presence. I felt sure that methods would come to me if I would
just be there, in his territory, long enough. Somehow I would
accomplish an affinity with the panther. For it seemed to me
this would be the ultimate goal of any tracker, whatever animal
he is pursuing.

I had no idea yet what it meant to look upon the Morning Star, but I knew it would be the panther who could lead
me to the larger meaning in life, a life that had always held
the strong possibility of Enlightenment. And it was Grandpa
Jim and the U.S. Marine Corps who helped get me ready to
meet the panther.

For three days the elegant, blurred, bouncing shadow
of the cat roamed through my mind. When I was awake I
daydreamed of this creature. When I slept I had extraordinary
images of him stealing through the darkness of the Everglades,
carefully choosing each step, stopping, momentarily surveying
the region, then moving on, and each time he did his splendid
liquid stride merged with the swamp making him seem almost
invisible.

On the fourth day I could stand it no longer. Well before
daybreak I was up jamming supplies into my old Marine Corps
backpack, a constant companion, and speeding down Alligator Alley, dressed in a jungle camouflage suit splotched with
blends of green, brown, dull yellow and cat black. On my hip
I had a favorite hunting knife. I carried no other weapon and
I never would, no matter what.

Rolling down the highway that morning while the sun
was still below the flat horizon, I allowed my mind to dip back
into those torturous early months when I first got back from
Nam. I'd been opening myself to some of those memories
lately and they weren't as raw and bleeding as they used to

be. For a while I had felt naked without a rifle. I had been trained to polish, clean, and polish my weapon again in order to shoot, to kill. So, soon after I got home I bought a .22 bolt-action rifle with a scope and an old .45 pistol. For hours I would sit cleaning the rifle just as I had done with my M-14 in boot camp, in infantry training and in Nam. I cleaned the barrel with a rod and a drop of oil on a piece of cloth, again and again shoving the rod down into the depth, pulling it free and then ramming it in once more. It was pure ecstasy feeling the smooth metal slip around the rod and oil, and the faster I worked it the cleaner the barrel got. I took linseed oil and rubbed it across the butt, back and forth, back and forth, until the hard wood gleamed. I oiled the outside steel parts and re-blued the surface, took the bolt out and stroked it with oil until it slipped in and out of the bore with that sharp metallic click. I felt very much at home holding the rifle in my hands, snapping it up to my shoulder, dropping it to my hip, then back up to my shoulder.

I couldn't wait to get out in the woods to try it out. It was strange. All I wanted to do was hear the crack of the rifle, feel it pushing into my shoulder. I wanted to hear the round make that dull sound that means it hit something.

When I got out there I saw a blackbird on a bare limb. It was a mechanical, unthinking act for me to raise the rifle, aim and shoot. I shot that bird in half. Feathers and intestines flew everywhere in a small explosion. I rushed up to it and saw its guts spread out in the mud. Whatever it was that made me shoot that helpless bird left me as I vomited. It was the most repulsive, worst thing I had ever done in my entire life. I had zapped it for no reason, no reason at all. It messed me up. I stood crying, picking the poor thing up, trying to put the bird back together and let it fly away. I wanted so badly for it to be alive I was willing to die for it that second. "God, take me now but spare this bird," I sobbed.

I knelt down in the grass and let the blood run between my fingers, staining them. From then on I had blood on my hands. I prayed one day I could clean it off.

I picked up my rifle and pistol and hiked to a bridge over the river. Slamming the rifle furiously and repeatedly on the concrete, I splintered the butt and broke the bolt. Then

I took the pistol apart and threw the pieces into the river. When I kicked the last of the rifle fragments over the side, I felt like a heavy marble block was sliding off my back.

That had happened 16 years before and I had not picked up a weapon since. I knew I never would. That Everglades morning I reaffirmed my decision to rely totally on the 91st Psalm—"He who dwells in the shelter of the Most High, who abides in the Shadow of the Almighty, I will say unto the Lord, my refuge and my fortress: my God, in whom I trust" —and on the discipline and skills of survival learned in the Marine Corps and Vietnam, and on my own self-sufficiency, imagination, patience, wilderness resilience and endurance, will power, swamp lore, and most of all, my deep wilderness faith that Shakespeare and the Everglades would never shed blood from a man passionately devoted to saving them both.

It was turning into an unseasonably cool June morning, much like a fall day up North. Trees swayed in the wind. Dead oak leaves swirled in small tornadoes on islets of trembling water. False dawn was in the eastern sky before me, lit more by the fading stars than the moon, giving it a mysterious, surrealistic aura.

This particular morning I cherished this scene as much as the breath of life itself. It was fresh, pure, simple and immensely alive, maybe more than any other part of the day. The tourists and poets could have their fiery sunrises; for me the edge of light leading the sun at that moment over the glades was next to seeing the Greatest Naturalist of All.

As suddenly as an alligator tail slapping mud, I saw myself as I really was—a person possessed by an endangered wild animal, both of us now interlocked in a peculiar destiny we had very little control over. Although I knew I was doing something worthy for a noble cause most people had forgotten about, I could not see the outcome. I had no intimation that in the near future I would be heavily criticized and harassed for my work, jumped and beaten, my equipment stolen, my life threatened several times over the phone and on three separate occasions more tangibly, by a knife, by a double-barreled twelve-gauge shotgun at point-blank range, and by a high-powered rifle with a scope.

But I would also find praise and support for my work throughout the state of Florida from public officials, conservation organizations and the media. I would be officially recognized by the Florida legislature as "an acknowledged expert on the Florida panther."

In 1982, the Florida panther would be designated the official state animal in accordance with a vote by the school children of the state. In 1983 the governor would also see fit to declare an Endangered Species Awareness Week through the Endangered Species Research Foundation of Naples, Florida, which I would found in 1980. Even now, in 1984, it remains to be seen how much effect all this will have on whether or not the panther survives*.

But that morning, in the light of the Morning Star, the panther and I were on each other's trail, destined for affinity.

---

*Editor's note: In mid-1984, the official state count of Florida panthers is 30. However, the author claims the actual number is probably more like 60.

4

Embarking

> **Swamp notes—in prairie silence**
> I always know when I go out to track I will return home safely. But sometimes I'd rather not return. Sometimes I feel like turning my back on civilization and making my home in a forgotten slough. And yet, the more I blend my spirit with all living things, including people, the more I want to tell them. But I won't, at least not for a long time.

An hour later I was standing in the midst of that great prairie where I had first sighted Shakespeare, and all those wonderful feelings came back like water to a cypress slough on the first rains.

Sweating in the cool, gloomy dampness, my body—as well as my mind, heart and spirit-self—was charged with excitement, anticipation and a powerful commitment. So many times before I had failed to find the cat, but now here I was again embarking on an incredible journey into a primitive land tracking one on one, inch by inch, what is probably the ultimate, most elusive, super-efficient, highly developed mammal, besides man, on the face of the earth. My spirit quickened.

The single ear-piercing whistle of a southern loon echoed across the swamp and poured into my ears, a long, clear, sharp whistle that dominated all other sound, causing unseen birds to fly away.

I knelt in this prairie and stared at a distant, stationary cloud forest in the sky.

"Nam Yo Fara On," I whispered, closing my eyes and relaxing, feeling a stillness throughout my whole body. Then I directed my consciousness inward on the pleasant image of Shakespeare roaming, stalking, plotting his territory. Had trackers before me done this?

Just then I heard an unusual yet familiar quiet voice deep within me saying: *The swamp flows in the cat's veins. The animals are locked in his heart. All nature is reflected in his eyes. So look for the signs the big cat leaves. Go slow. Be patient. Concentrate. Feel the swamp. Let the swamp feel you. Track the way the cat tracks. Breathe his air. Eat his kills. Drink from his water. Sleep in his territory. Walk with the touch of a single breath from a newborn fawn. Feel his mysterious presence. Smell the fragrance of fresh scent. Live the cat's life. Be the cat.*

"Be the cat," I said aloud. I would miss nothing and find everything. As my breath crystallized in the cold air, mingling with swamp fog, I smiled, opened my eyes and read the wilds.

Before me lay the endless flat expanse of the Everglades, ravaged and rebuilt over and over again by time. Etched into a dark blue sky was the cypress swamp far out front. No creature moved.

Towering a hundred feet above the emergent layer, isolated in odd places in the sky, were the majestic giant royal palms—erect, robust patriarchs of the Everglades, standing motionless, hardy sentinels against all destruction. Living entities in flora form.

With only a little imagination I could see Vietnam around me. The direct parallels were striking, spooky, and brought back the eerie Nam feelings of death and destruction that were still very much a part of me.

The wet prairie I was in could well have been an abandoned rice paddy outside a village. Behind me were hammocks of hardwood. In Nam there were tree islands out in the middle of savanna grass prairies. There the jungle line was thick with bamboo, Japanese cedar, evergreen oak, rhododendron, mahogany, rosewood, ebony teak trees which compared to the cypress trees, water and live oak, maiden cane, maple and dogwood. Both in Vietnam and the Everglades, much of the forest had been leveled by heavy lumbering. Thus both were in second growth stages.

In Vietnam, bombing raids and defoliation campaigns had destroyed much of the natural vegetation. In the Everglades drought and fires during the dry season often wipe out a quarter of the vegetation.

My comparison went even further. South Vietnam and South Florida are warm the year-round due to the subtropical monsoon climate. A typical feature of Nam weather during the rainy season is morning cumulus cloud growing denser by afternoon when the rain begins falling. The same in the Everglades. Sometimes there are long overcast days in both parts of the world. Nam, like the Everglades, has some of the wettest areas on earth. Rainfall in Vietnam comes between April and October, close to eighty inches of it. Rain comes to the Everglades at the same time of year, averaging close to ninety inches. Temperature in Nam ranges from 80 to 100°; in the Everglades, 80 to 90°.

All of this was compelling enough, but one comparison that kept me up for nights thinking about it was Vietnam's list of endangered species. Most jungle wild animals are on the decline, but the douc langur, Asiatic wild dog, Asian elephant, brown antler deer, rhinoceros, buffalo, giant ibis, pheasant, river terrapin, crocodile and python are all endangered.

And Vietnam has two endangered predators on the verge of extinction: the Indochinese tiger and the clouded leopard, both big cats. Both, like the panther, are on the verge of extinction because of hunting, loss of habitat, and overdevelopment.

Up close to me several animal trails pushed through the high grass, forming an intricate map created by deer, bear, raccoon, opossum, armadillo, bobcat and very possibly Shakespeare. Never were there more vivid signs that a swamp was alive. In the distance I saw the silhouettes of black vultures motionless in the bare cypress trees. Could be a kill, I thought. Could be Shakespeare is still close by, maybe staring at me right this second.

I took out an old folded-up map and drew a 20-mile perimeter around my sighting location. In it was Shakespeare, and since he had run north I would go north as well—right toward the vultures.

Cold sweat was already pouring into my eyes, so I took a black bandanna out of my pocket, rolled it on my knee and tied it around my head. I picked up two handfuls of mud and smeared it on my face, neck and hands to camouflage me and knock my scent down. Adjusting my pack high on my shoulders, I took my first step forward—slowly, deliberately, silently, feeling as though I was leaving the earth itself. The chill of the water drowned my feet and a mild shock traveled through me.

I knew I had to get to the treeline before full light so I picked up my pace and crept swiftly forward, keeping my outline below the wet grass tips, causing the blades to squeak against my trousers like quail chicks. Dew drops flung off like glass spheres, then shattered and fell in microscopic rainstorms. Small green frogs, almost fluorescent in the morning grayness, bounced about spasmodically, their hind legs slapping in the water, applauding my pursuit.

How many more times before me had Shakespeare disturbed them?

Echoing cicadas rattled like an orchestra of castanets, building to a high crescendo, then trailing off. The sound rang in my ears long after they had stopped. Gently surrounding me, this beautiful prairie was a dense, luxuriant, waist-high paradise of faded brown, flaming yellow, and auburn grasses, with an incense as thick and spicy as if it had just been created in dawn's first light.

I had learned long ago that if there were not these prairies embracing the cypress swamp to act as a strong natural belt holding the nutrients inward, there would be no thick subtropical jungle where Shakespeare could take refuge, mate, and where females could raise their cubs. For it is the prairies that protect the soil from wind, sun and rain so that the water is held longer in the soil. Without them the moisture would evaporate from the surface leaving a desert. Then the swamp would crumble and erode. There would be no home for the panther.

I moved on, alone in my self-appointed solitude, independent of my own kind just as Shakespeare was, somewhere out there. Beneath my feet I felt slippery limestones, the bedrock of the Everglades. Far in front of me I could just make out the crisp outlines of several white ibis sitting statuelike in the trees, their curved beaks like commas on a page of swamp history. I knew these statues would soon come alive as the light stole into the dark shadows.

Morning always belongs to these wild birds. I stopped and didn't move so much as an eyelid. Still, it was impossible not to alarm them for they are nature's most sensitive signal to all the other animals that potential danger is near. As the ibis stirred, several fish crows shattered the silence with those loud, high-pitched calls to scold me for entering their territory, but the crows never showed themselves. Their calls started a flurry of activity. Then, slicing through the air between treelines, came a croaking anhinga looking like a finely sharpened black arrowhead against the dim light. I heard a clear sweet high-tilting whistle. Another. Then another. In the grass was a flitting meadowlark camouflaged with a black V crossing his bright yellow breast, the rest of him a light brown. Then several more appeared. An elusive male indigo bunting with a flash of glistening deep bluish-purple darted off in front of me so fast I wasn't sure I'd seen it at all.

Both the sound and the movement of these birds had told every animal in the area something was afoot. I checked the air and found I was downwind from the treeline for the present. As long as I didn't make any un-wild sounds, I was for all practical purposes another animal who had momentarily abused the silence, then moved on. I could have been a deer scampering for cover, a raccoon sloshing in shallow water after crawfish, a noisy wild pig rooting in the mud, or even a rattlesnake surprising a large rat on a dry leaf island.

But when these birds become nervous and scatter on the other side of a prairie, they also offer me the possibility that a panther is walking.

5

This Wild Swamp

Swamp notes—under dawn
It is always bitterness mixed with joy that I feel when I enter the swamp full of wild-life, knowing that no more than a few miles away development and destruction threaten the very water I am standing in.

Even more swiftly than before, I made my way to the trees as dawn rushed across the Everglades in a brilliant lemon glow, reflecting a hazy golden sun mixed with bright twilight under a clear place in the sky. It was a gentle soothing glow, bathing the glades in a serene, forever watery wilderness.

I was momentarily reluctant to turn from that scene, but as I did I stood awe-inspired in front of a thick 30-foot-high cypress treeline which looked like a fortress in an endless sheet of water. This was the exact spot I had sighted Shake-speare, and yet it appeared to have changed. It seemed as though each cypress tree was alive, a creature able to move about at will, inviting woodpeckers to clean its body of red ants, beetles and caterpillars, then returning to its original spot undetected. The smooth, wet, grayish bark resembled lizard skin. The crowns sprang out like giant brittle starfish, uneven and looking deceptively fragile because of the thin green needles and fernlike branches. But their straight sturdy trunks that swelled pear-shaped at the base, submerged in oily-looking water that reminded me of black ice, gave them a sense of strength and permanence.

This cypress swamp had possessed Shakespeare's most hidden secrets since his birth, and those of his ancestors before him. I had breached the wall of mystery with my sighting.

Holding my breath almost apprehensively, I stepped through the trees. The swamp swallowed me up, the lower branches of a small bush snapping back into place behind me like a heavy gate as though I had entered a timelock back into a prehistoric age. Human sound ceased. Things scuttled about in the foliage. I turned to the tall, waving prairie grass once more to reassure myself. Outside the sun looked like a half-submerged orange wafer in another world, a world I was no longer part of. A cool soft breeze, born somewhere deep in the swamp, embraced me, turned me toward it, and somehow went through me, making it sound as if the swamp were actually breathing. I was now caught in Shakespeare's stronghold as sure as if he had wrapped his powerful paws around me, and strangely I felt at home once again.

I accepted it and carefully scanned the region. Before me was a pouring forth of subtropical jungle, a rain-soaked insurgence of life, motionless in some places while in others it bent, twisted, skirted and twitched, dancing to unheard music. Every inch of ground was used, an overlay of moss, fungi, lichen and vines growing in every corner. It was a steamy, fog-haunted land, born millions of years ago. I felt I was in a great natural cathedral that ascended from the mud to the conical-shaped cypress knees, to the sword ferns, willow bushes, understory of smaller cypress, and then to the tall interlaced canopy of branches above. Unseen life flourished.

The tree roof was a pulsing ceiling with soft sunflecks and shafts of light filtering through gaps, constantly winking as a breeze blew and the sun moved up the sky, soaking into the veins of the leaves, a strange system of light and life leading to the heart of the swamp.

Woody branches, green briars, muscadine and deerhoof vines hopelessly tangled and snarled, forming giant bird nests. Some vines were as thick as a man's arm, others were more like looping cables. All resembled serpents.

Trees made way for more trees nobly clothed with soft skintight emerald moss, embellished here and there with stiff-leaved air plants that seemed to float in the gloom; they clustered so close together they looked like fur for protection against a flash of winter. Their long, red spike blossoms looked like painted oriental fingernails, like those which beckoned lonely soldiers in the streets of Da Nang and Saigon.

There was a bewildering, luminous, gray-green half-light hanging vapor-drenched over all the vegetation. The air had a thick sweet smell which mingled with decaying leaves, flowers, trees and animal waste that were becoming yet another layer of organic mud like those laid down for thousands of years to form the swamp.

In all of this I heard the swamp speak with a cascade of wild sounds, its own primeval language. Moonflower vines snapped off a tree. Palm fronds rubbed together, maple trunks creaked, wind hummed through willows. Wings whispered. A leaf softly rattled through others as it fell. A turtle plopped off a log into water. And just below the pitch of sound constant in this green silence was the steady drip, drip, drip of water off leaves and the violin sounds of lance-nosed mosquitoes. In every organism a heart pulsed.

Suddenly I felt very small, cut off from civilization. One man standing in the vast Everglades seeking the rarest creature in the swamp.

6

A Kill

Swamp notes—in the bush

It is a hideous sight to come onto a kill in the swamp, even a panther's. But that is nature's balance: a clean necessary death for the continuance of life.

With extremely slow steady motion, then, I proceeded through the water, sliding my feet on the bottom rather than picking them up and perhaps splashing, making ripples that went out to clap in short reports against the tree bases and continue forever.

With stealth and a growing sense of cunning and awareness, I crawled onto high ground, never once standing to expose my position, lowering my silhouette, spending as much time stopping and observing as I did moving.

Concealing every step, I crouched pantherlike, veering ever so carefully into each shadow, using the swamp's haunts, bending and weaving when I had to get under a low branch, twisting sideways between trees, looking all around at regular intervals—left flank, front, right flank, behind, all overlapping each other—almost motionless even when lifting my feet over submerged logs.

Slow motion, slow . . . motion.

Eyes alert, I shifted through the jungle density wondering what it would be like to stare into the eyes of Shakespeare. I imagined them to be pale goldengreen, icy lagoons of shimmering emotion, their depths plunging to his very soul. I wanted to experience the terror or tranquility of them, that rare moment of truth. But those eyes are almost impossible to detect in the swamp because of their natural camouflage. They have evolved for thousands of years to aid him in a specific dutiful act of predation. And with night-vision he can stalk prey 24 hours a day and easily elude man. Would I ever be fortunate enough to confront him?

On night patrol in Vietnam to reconnoiter the positions, strength and movements of the Viet Cong, we used goggles and a tube binocular with infrared capabilities that imitated the panther's vision. In fact they called this invention "cat eye."

I knew full well this great cat had a more intimate relationship with the Everglades than I could ever hope for—with every branch, leaf, blade of grass, bush and vine, the very shadows. In his territory he knew every sound, every rock, every animal, and if the slightest thing was altered, or anything new—like myself—was added, his attention was on it. He lived as a predator should, always on the lookout for prey or possible danger.

I had learned in Vietnam that letting my guard down for one moment—assuming everything was okay because I wanted it to be—not only gives prey a chance to escape, it gives the predator the moment of attack. I wondered which I was to Shakespeare: a threat or his next meal. More than ever I wanted to be aware of his presence first.

I looked far into the foliage, studying and analyzing every inch, every flickering movement. Male cardinals flitted overhead looking like passover flames in the green. In a bush inches away a black racer snake lounged. Vines clung to my waist and around my ankles like octopus tentacles, making me strain them to their utmost tension; they reluctantly gave way only to entwine me once again.

The insects demanded attention. There were countless species of butterflies, beetles, mantids, grasshoppers, bees, wasps, dragonflies, damselflies, ants and termites, and more. The swamp was alive with them, from the water to the trees, and underground as well. They droned and hummed until it seemed there was no sound at all. Insects might tell me something of Shakespeare's path. If he had gone this way, mosquitoes assaulting him as he passed through would bring squadrons of dragonflies to feed on the mosquitoes. In all of this I also looked for other clues Shakespeare might have left, clues that might easily go unnoticed. A broken branch fallen on high ground. Duckweed separated in the water. Mud sloshed up on a tree.

A strand of panther hair caught in a tree bark crevice, or on vine thorns, or lodged in leaves where he might have rested.

Then above me in a tree canopy opening I saw sixteen vultures gliding, circling, the same ones I had seen earlier. In formation they spun tightly together until their flight feathers almost touched. They were closing in on something dead. My stomach tightened. Noiselessly I made my way toward them. I didn't hurry, and I concentrated even harder on probing for better openings to slide through.

Now the vultures were spreading out, making wider circles, hanging in the air as though on puppet strings. One spiraled down and disappeared in the treetops, an arrow pointing to the kill site. I hurried along now, trying to keep my heavy breathing down as much as possible, knowing I was breaking the rules. Twice I climbed a tree to make sure I hadn't veered off course.

I rested, and a gust brought a strong odor that immediately turned into an unbearable stench. I didn't have to scent-read it to know what it was. When I got closer I slowed to a caterpillar crawl and scanned the region. Then I stopped inside the bushline and peered through a small hole, seeing several black and turkey vultures bouncing around a small clearing where a bloated brown bulk and antlers were spread out in high grass near a wax myrtle bush. Black flies swarmed in buzzing clouds. Thousands of maggots covered most of the flesh at the rear between the hind legs, clustered and shimmering like foam on a breaking salt water wave. The sound of the vultures tearing at the carcass was the sound of wet paper crumbling.

It had been a healthy, mature white-tail buck deer, a four-pointer. Now it was an old kill, a week old, maybe less, weighing about 140 pounds. I almost jumped up and screamed, not fully believing I had found such valuable evidence so soon. Surely, I thought, the cat is well gone, but nonetheless I decided not to expose myself. Two vultures sat nearby in a maple tree hunched in that sinister posture, staring at me with dead eyes, challenging me to walk toward their claimed prize.

Efficiently and with confident quickness, I swamp-read the site. What at first appeared to be brown paint speckled about the grass turned out to be dried blood baked in the sun and robbed of its bright color. Red ants scurried up and down the grass blades flaking off the blood. Some of the shorter grass had been eaten away to the roots. Around me were large dry clumps of sod turned over, twisted and thrown about. This must have been the ambush site where a short violent battle had been fought. From it a drag-trail led through the grass back into the cypress, probably made by Shakespeare pulling his kill to cover. Swamp floor debris was turned over and a long muscadine vine was pulled off a tree, likely snagged by the deer's antlers, probably momentarily frustrating the cat.

I followed the trail up onto high ground in the trees where piles of leaves were thrown about near a fallen sabal palm tree. I was sure Shakespeare had gorged himself here with close to ten pounds of fresh bloody venison, then covered his kill, urinated on it as a means of plotting his territory and claiming his kill, and gone off to rest nearby. But there were some peculiar circumstances beyond these facts. Another drag-trail led out from the cypress to where the dead buck lay. It would be highly unusual for the panther to do that. He would want to protect and hide his kill from other meat-eating animals.

With my hand over my nose I crept toward the carcass as close as I could without vomiting from the stench that made me belch. The vultures took off loudly, their wings spreading the stench even more. Among the maggots I found that the exposed hind quarters had been well eaten off and the cavity of the stomach cleaned out. These were clear signs of a panther kill. Small black beetles now massed there, climbing over each other for a morsel. Near the short white flag-tail was an old, uneven scar, deep but healed over, forming a spikelike figure. A wound from an old battle. It reminded me of a ranch brand, but this was a brand burned into the flesh from the rigors of wild living.

Dead silver eyes reflected a violent death. Parts of the nose were gone, the top of the neck was torn and mashed, the spine was crushed. Only a panther could have done that. Still embedded in the skin of the neck and inside the ears were ticks looking more like purple grapes than bloodsucking parasites. The chest and shoulders showed deep slash marks and four cleanly planted holes in the hide with fibers of dried muscle tissue hanging out of them—all pantherkill signs.

Several other parts of the carcass were chewed on or bitten off. Half of a foreleg was gone. A number of animals besides the panther and vultures had feasted on this kill. Perhaps a bear or bobcat had pulled it out into the clearing.

But the pure reality of Shakespeare stalking this buck stirred my imagination. I could see in my mind's eye the great cat creeping through the trees, head thrust forward and slightly down, ears rotating independently on every sound, eyes probing. Then he catches the deer's unmistakable strong, musky scent floating in the swamp air. Not far away the buck grazes casually in the open. Suddenly the antlered head darts up, the buck not sure if he has heard anything at all. Nothing happens. Nothing moves. No dangerous scent. The deer goes back to his grazing. Shakespeare creeps forward in the high grass almost thirty feet away on the buck's right flank. Again the buck suspects, nervously beats his hooves on the grass, and again, but this time even more warily, bends down to eat. In that split second Shakespeare streaks toward him in 20-foot leaps, claws and canines bared, body tensed to withstand the impact. The cat dives up into the air to pounce on the buck's back. The buck's reaction is instantaneous but too slow to save him from the cat. By the time he has pivoted to flee, the cat's stabbing fangs are already plunged into his neck, locking down on his spine to crush it. The claws of one paw are hooked underneath the buck's skin, while the other paw locks under the buck's chin and with a powerful jerk, snaps the neck back. The buck staggers, crumbles to his knees and falls over sideways. Then Shakespeare feeds.

Panthers are carnivores, getting their protein and salt from the muscle meats and skin of their prey. The fat is eaten for calories. Liver, colon, kidneys, heart, sexual organs and blood supply minerals, vitamins and liquid. The cat does not digest the bones, but rasps them with his tongue and crushes the fragments with his molars for the marrow and calcium.

After eating such a large quantity of meat, Shakespeare probably drank a great deal of water to avoid uremic poisoning.

There were many more questions to be answered, but I knew I could now be certain I was in Shakespeare's territory.

The certainty brought a slight tremor of fear. I took out a map and pinpointed the kill site by taking a bearing with my compass and marking the spot a little north of my sighting.

Two fantastic signs Shakespeare had now left. Two pages of his life verified. I was on him and would stay on him for the rest of our lives. I looked around almost expecting the cat to poke his head out.

Again I went over to the carcass. Braving the stench, I rubbed my hands on the thick hide and spread it on me. There was a remote chance the strong musk might draw the cat back to me. Then I took out my knife and sliced open a square of skin on the deer's chest and stared at the muscle still oozing with brown blood. I cut out a small portion and chopped it into even smaller sections which I put in my pocket to drop along the way in the hope they would help draw Shakespeare to me.

Then I cut a portion of the reddest part of the meat, stuck it on a stick and held a match to it until it burned to charcoal, let it cool and ate it. A communion of man, deer and cat.

Crouching to leave, I paused and stared for a short time at the buck. Soon he would dissolve into the earth. The swamp wastes nothing, not one ounce of matter, dead or alive. Soon after the onslaught of scavengers there would be no sign he had ever existed. Springtails, centipedes, mollusks and bacteria were already on their way to claiming their portion. The swamp floor was his grave, and for the moment, I was his mourner.

7

War Ghost

Swamp notes—next to buck
*Sometimes the green of the swamp is the
color of life, dappled with sunlight, glowing
with energy. Other times that same green
is the green of death, yellowed with thick
shafts of light, heavy with the dankness of
the past.*

Kneeling there over the rotting carcass of the buck, I felt an
intense memory coming on. When Nam memories come on
strong like that they always come whole. I lose control of time.
They are like dreams that can't be stopped just because they
get unpleasant; they have to be seen through to the end. I sat
on the ground and let the memory roll over me, take me.

I was standing on the deck of our ship in the humid
early morning darkness, staring at the vague outline of the
South Vietnamese coast spread out below the black silhouette
of hills lying like the hunched backs of sleeping demons.
During the night our ship convoy had silently slipped into a
huge lagoon just north of Tuy Hoa in the South China Sea,
a Viet Cong-controlled region. We were sitting defiantly at
anchor in the water waiting for daybreak when we would get
our operation under way. Farther out in the sea the black
outline of our aircraft carrier swayed in disturbed waters, its
flat top full of helicopters.

The region was quiet and peaceful, yet foreboding, the
kind of foreboding that reaches down into your guts and twists
them into a knot. A warm breeze brought the smell of the
sea and beach vegetation. I listened to the whispers of sailors
moving about in quick silent cadence.

We had been aboard ship for two months before we

finally got orders to hit Nam. We had convoyed toward this strange place all night. Not one of us in the entire battalion slept. Some guys acted like it, closing their eyes and rolling them under twitching lids, but more often there was tossing and turning in the bunks. In the hold near a light muttered curses punctuated an on-going card game. Other men were in the heads cleaning their rifles. A few compared pictures of girlfriends, remarking on breasts and legs and how often they got laid. One marine kissed his picture and put it in his shirt pocket over his heart.

Death's silent song stole into every marine's mind and showed itself in vacant stares, tension-filled jokes, unnatural laughter, nervous hands tightening backpack straps, and cigarettes lit with trembling flames. All through the battalion everyone knew that in the coming hours somebody was going to get killed.

Standing there, I stared down at the glowing fluorescent water and believed I could very well get wounded, maybe even lose an arm, foot or leg. But to die? That was hard to accept. Though I had no experience in combat, I kept trying to convince myself I was going to survive. There I was, poised for combat in America's teenage war that had been a fantasy on television until that moment. No matter how much training I'd had, no matter that I'd volunteered, the startling actuality of the moment was unnerving. Disembarking was minutes away and there was no turning back.

I found myself thinking about courage. Was the simple essence of courage being able to go on while knowing death could be just up ahead? But if I had no choice, was it still courage? At least I already understood that courage didn't mean having no fear. I knew it was fear that brought caution to the action. Controlling the fear so it wouldn't overwhelm me was the key. And I figured too that the real foundation of courage was calmness. With calm, the mind can keep thinking for ways to deal with the danger. I prayed all of this philosophy would hold up. Or was this all just prewar naivete?

The sun rose fast over the lagoon in a pale cloudless sky, revealing a coastline so beautiful that it was hard to believe it existed. The black hills were jungle-lined monuments as old as the sea we pitched and yawed in. The sea water changed from aqua-green to aqua-blue and reflected so brilliantly in the sun that it seemed to be made of submerged liquid prisms. The soft, thick, sandy beaches were protected by high sand dunes with salt grass for headdresses, and behind them was a treeline of tropical Australian pine. Farther to the right, nearer the hills, was the deep-green emergent layer of banana and palm trees standing like stone pillars. It was like Shangri-la. Hardly a place for a war. And yet South Vietnam was being torn apart by strife with American casualties mounting heavily.

Then that ugly war machine ground into full gear. Our company went over the side to board amtracs and landing craft, and before long we were fighting the morning waves as we circled, waiting for orders to go in. I was in the third wave with supplies and equipment, staring at the shoreline, tense, sweating freely. A chill went through me in that stifling heat and I felt sick.

The first wave of amtracs formed into frontal assault formation and headed toward the beachhead, creating their own waves. They looked like weird sea monsters contemplating the best place to creep up on the sand. I didn't know why but I wanted to be in the first wave, to be the first to set foot on virgin Viet Cong territory. I felt I was being deprived of a unique experience in my life.

Overhead three squadrons of helicopters carried other elements of our force inland. The rapid whomp, whomp, whack, whack of the rotor blades rang inside my helmet. Above them two silvery, flashing F-104 jets screamed toward the hills over the amtracs, then banked off to the right and disappeared. Then those sea monsters crawled onto the sand just ahead of the incoming tide, fanned out and opened their jawlike ramps to cough out marines.

I tensed even more. If they were going to get hit it would be at that second. I could feel my legs aching from the tension. I waited. I strained my eyes. But not so much as a round was fired. Were the VC there?

The first wave disappeared over the dunes while the second wave went in and moved north along the shore. And before long our third wave was on the beach bringing in supplies, tanks, ammunition, k-rations, etc. The sergeant threw out orders, "Over here, marine. Keep moving, keep alert. . . .

Hey, idiot stick, pick up your pack. . . . First squad, you're walking point. . . ."

We moved out to look for a good spot for a command post and perimeter guard on the beachhead. I put the butt of my rifle on my hip and trained it toward the sky as we swept over the dunes into the pine trees. The deep sand was boiling hot through my boot soles. I slipped and felt like I wasn't going anywhere.

"Keep your eyes on the sand. Good place for a mine," someone said. I felt sick again.

War noise was everywhere. Cobra choppers, looking like dragonflies, rushed over the trees creating sand storms. Tanks clanked and sputtered. Radios crackled with excited voices. "A, roger, that's a ten-four. . . . There's movement on the other side of the river. . . . Request permission to fire. . . . If you think it's the enemy, go ahead. . . . This is Red Devil. We have Bluebird in sight. . . . No VC here. . . ."

The heat was almost unbearable with full gear on— backpack, helmet, webbed cartridge belt full of ammo magazines, two canteens, grenades, and a flak jacket. The thick, salty, sandy sweat poured off my face in rivers, sticking my jungle utilities to my skin like wet paste. In fact the sun was so hot the steel of my rifle barrel burned my fingers. My eyes remained alert, roving out front and up among the hills, eyes that would soon grow old in a young body.

We got to the other side of the trees and saw a deserted semiprimitive village of plastered bamboo huts with palm frond roofs. Beyond it was a rice paddy, then a mud-colored river.

I was staring at the village, wiping my face, trying to catch my breath when it happened. Suddenly the guys were ducking, dropping to their knees, diving in the sand, crawling behind trees. I couldn't hear any rifle fire, but on the left flank the sand was shooting up as though someone were throwing rocks into it. We had made contact with the VC.

"Sniper fire!" a voice screamed.

Sniper fire, I thought, we're under fire. I didn't know what to do. Sniper fire! Goddarn. I should have been running for cover too, returning the fire, but I wasn't. I didn't know where to shoot. I just stood there dumbfounded. Twice I heard the intense hum and felt the wind of bullets just missing my head. When the third one passed I realized that if I had stepped forward one more foot I would have caught it square in the face. It snapped me out of the daze, out of my stupidity.

It was the spookiest feeling, knowing a Vietnamese was actually shooting at me—someone who had never laid eyes on me until that moment. I wondered how easy it was to shoot at me, at what I represented as an American invading his land.

Then we moved on in spite of the sniper fire, striding out, zigzagging, creating moving targets rather than sitting ducks. I crouched more, moved faster, zigzagged more often.

Tanks plowed through the trees and village, crossing the sand toward a hill. WHAM! The one that let off the round blurred in the sunlight from the recoil. Sand and smoke blew up on the hill. One of the tank gunners opened up with his .50-caliber where he thought he saw a VC. Small trees and bushes disintegrated.

Choppers were bringing in 105 howitzer cannons and dropping them in an open area near the village with their crews. Quickly we set up a perimeter around them.

I started digging a foxhole in the sand with my bare hands but the sand was so dry it poured right back into the hole. Two sniper rounds hit the sand pile I had just made. I jerked around at the hill. It was already getting to me and I hadn't been "in country" but half a day. Not knowing when or from where the next round might be coming was driving me crazy. I flinched at every crack of a rifle. I had not fired my weapon yet.

I now firmly believed in my own death, and I felt that sickness again. My heart drummed. I was moving robotlike. Another puff of sand went up in front of me.

The sergeant called for a patrol and I prayed our squad would not go. We lucked out.

But the hideous hum of a bullet came across my face once again. So this was the Vietnam war that Walter Cronkite talked about on the six o'clock news. Why did I volunteer to be in this God-forsaken place? Jesus, how stupid was I? What was I thinking about when I signed that paper? I asked myself over and over. It was everything I could do to keep my hands from shaking.

Suddenly a loud crackle of small arms fire rang out from

the village nearby where the patrol had gone. That was the first time I'd heard rifle fire that close. It was unnerving and I twitched at every sound.

Why didn't somebody do something? But nobody did. We just stayed in our foxholes and waited and stared at the village and waited. . . .

Then I saw marine helmets bobbing among the trees. When they got closer I could see two marines carrying a makeshift stretcher with a poncho over something. I let myself believe it was a wounded marine. But the person on the stretcher wasn't moving and the poncho was up almost over his head. I could see a light-colored, short-cropped head. I knew him; his nickname was Buck, an 18-year-old from the other platoon, a muscular light-skinned marine. They rushed into the perimeter with him and went over to the CP, gently placing the stretcher on the ground. Two corpsmen pulled the poncho down off his face, then slowly pulled it back up, shaking their heads.

The sergeant was talking to the lieutenant and shaking his head, too. Then he pointed out toward the village and back at the perimeter, then at the stretcher. Then he took off his helmet, went over to a tree and sat down rubbing his face.

One of the marines who had been on the patrol came over and slid down into my hole. His eyes were wide, glaring, and his forehead wrinkled as though he were on the verge of crying. "Buck's dead. . . ." he said. "Never knew what hit him."

He turned and looked back at the poncho. "Took . . . took a round at close range in the back. It went right through his flak jacket. When he fell . . . in front of me, he just grunted. . . . Shit, I can't believe I'm still alive. . . ."

He took a long breath. "All I want to do . . . is get outta here."

He dropped his rifle in the sand and buried his head in his hands.

I couldn't move. The word "dead" resounded through my consciousness with shock waves and I couldn't stop it. It kept repeating itself and growing stronger. Dead. Dead. Dead. DEAD!

Our first KIA—killed in action—and it sent a fear through

me I had never known before. It welded my body to the bottom of the foxhole, rendering me helpless. And it brought along a reverential fear of my own imminent death.

I stared out at the village and even though the 105 cannons were blasting away, I stared into nothingness.

Wham . . . wham . . . wham . . . wham. . . .

I began saying the Hail Mary and Our Father, blending one prayer into the next.

"McMullen! Get your head down!"

I heard a voice yell as it ran past me. Heavy boots hit the sand like elephant feet. It was the sergeant and he was running along the line slapping guys on their helmets, encouraging them.

I looked around at the hill. Sniper fire was coming in again. It brought me back. Back to the war. The Vietnam war. Death. Violent death. It was all something I could never have imagined or understood back in my hometown of Streator, Illinois, a peaceful community, as quiet as this little palm-thatched village had been before we landed.

Suddenly for some strange reason I had to see Buck close up, to face death head on. I grabbed my rifle, took a deep breath, sprang out of the hole and ran across the LZ. It was like I had never used my body until that moment. My legs were as light as feathers. When I rushed into the command post a great relief came over me. That intense physical activity washed away the energy that had been going into my fear.

"McMullen, what in the hell are you doing back here?" the sergeant asked.

I stared at him, gulped, trying to come up with an answer. "Aaaah . . . Sarg. Figured we needed more ammo."

The sergeant pointed to an opened box. "Get your ass back there."

I went over to the box and started pulling out ammo bandoliers and putting them on my shoulder. The med-evac helicopter appeared at the LZ to pick up Buck, and just then the wash from the blades blew the poncho off. A hideous gaping wound stared up at me. I turned away, but it had already imprinted itself on my mind forever. In the middle of his stomach, blood-soaked flesh was turned grotesquely outward in chunks. Parts of his shattered ribs were showing on the outside of his flak jacket. It was as if a thick jagged shaft had been plunged into his stomach, then jerked free taking everything with it.

But it wasn't just the wound that gripped me. It was his gray, bloodless face. His mouth was half open, his lips were a waxy, dull bluish-purple. Halflidded empty eyes that once held life seemed to be somewhere else. It was as though that dead body wasn't Buck at all, just a shell. An empty shell.

I stared at Death, that life-robber, and he stared back at me with a supernatural strength no human could ever challenge.

But what I expected to see in Buck's face wasn't there. I assumed there would be anguish, torment, an excruciating expression of pain. The bullet slamming through his body should have twisted his face in a mask of deep curved lines, squinting eyes, a gaping mouth caught in the act of screaming. There was none of this.

Instead, I saw peace in Buck's face. A peace I had trouble defining. What had he been thinking about as his body went limp, the round tearing his insides to pieces? Was he already glimpsing the "other world"?

And was that world a far better place than where I stood?

I put another bandolier of ammo over my shoulder and ran back to the line. All the glorious, glamorous motives of why I thought I had volunteered to come to Vietnam crumbled around me just like the sand in my hole. Patriotism. Saving the South Vietnamese from Communism. For God and country. Democracy. For my mother and father, brother and sisters. For my friends. For future generations. All of this youthful idealism meant absolutely nothing. I'd been in Nam one day and Death had wiped out all of my rationale. There was no glory in war.

For a while I even desperately clung to another reason. I had volunteered for myself. I had thought it was a self-gratifying act to volunteer to fight someone else's war. I had felt important. I was somebody in Streator, Illinois. I was going to perform that wondrous deed of self-righteousness so all could see. I was looked upon with awe by my parents and friends. In my eyes I was material for heroism. All of that rationale had worked beautifully in the States in the security of my hometown far away from the real war. But it had no meaning in Vietnam under fire with the strong possibility of getting killed. Self-gratification was a poor excuse for death.

From that point on, the only reason that made any sense to me was staying alive. Survival. Self-preservation was more powerful than all the rest of it. Even though there had been peace in Buck's face, he was still dead. And death I did not want. I wasn't ready for that other world. I was going to outlive the Vietnam war—somehow. I was going to do anything I needed to do to stay alive—but always with honor.

The Viet Cong out there were going to do anything they needed to do to stay alive, too. I could count on that. And that could easily include killing me as they had Buck.

Buck. I snapped out of my war reverie and saw that other dead buck lying before me. The panther also wanted to survive and would do what he needed to do to stay alive. And that could include killing me as he had this buck—though I knew even then that he never would. My mind was swimming back and forth between the necessity and the uselessness of death. But one thing was clear; the utter difference between the panther's clean and necessary kill and the filthy, needless waste of life in human war.

And yet I could feel, too, that the peace I had seen in Buck's dead face was the same peace I felt around me here, now, on this bright swamp morning. There is only one peace.

That other day after seeing Buck and resolving not to offer myself to total peace just yet, I had picked up my rifle, pulled open the bolt far enough to make sure there was a round in the chamber, gently closed it, looked out toward the village and begun to survey it for VC.

That day in the glades, after resolving to keep within me the swamp's peace, I picked up my backpack, adjusted the shoulder straps, retied the bandanna around my head, looked at the swamp and started toward it.

Book II

In the Gentle Embrace of the Untamed

For one who is fully aware of what is happening in every part of the wilds, nature's perennial show is fascinating to observe. That awareness comes generally through the mediums of sight, sound, and smell, and occasionally through touch.

—*Charles Elliot*
The Outdoor Eye

Book II

In the Gentle Embrace of the Damned

8

Swamp Eye

Swamp notes—Fern Island

I find myself using my eyes in a strange way here in the swamp. It is more like seeing inside of things. I look at a tree and see all the veins of all its leaves. I look at a bird sitting on the limb and see its intention to fly away. I look at a leaf and see the beetle crawling on the other side.

I struck out to the north. The water and liquid jelly were now up to my shins, and at each step there seemed to be no way through, though at the last second the swamp would suddenly open up. I had no idea which way Shakespeare had gone, but I was betting those vultures he was close, maybe even closer than I thought. More and more I began to see the wholeness of this creature. Truly he is a personification of beauty, freedom and wildness, ideally developed as a top predator in the Everglades food chain. He is a stabilizer in the drama of wilderness life, controlling the balance of population of all the other animals.

The farther I tracked the more exhilarated I became. I could think of no better life to lead than to be deep in cold water, my feet temporarily trapped by soft mud, snakes and turtles creeping about, flies and mosquitoes hovering around me, the sun streaking through the trees, the invisible world of the micros clinging to my skin, migratory birds overhead and the panther Shakespeare near. I felt I could wander like this among the wilds forever, searching and finding panthers, new earths every day.

Here there was no war, no human controversy. No boring hours. No thoughts of how to map out a future. There was no reason for ambition and tenseness. Here human morals had to fit into the larger scheme. The swamp has its own code of justice.

All around there was that undefined constant activity. Shadows seemed to be alive and walking with me, staring at me, yet never betraying their presence, stopping when I did, then continuing to move when I moved. Small mammal paths crisscrossed on leaf islands and under small bushes which formed foliage caves, offering cool shade from the sun in summer, warmth in the cool winter breeze.

With swamp eye, I calmly looked through the vegetation, the jungle, rather than at it, as far as my sight would penetrate, homing in on horizontal objects that held interest, passing over things that did not.

By taking Vitamin A, I had built up the chemical rhodopsin (visual purple) in my retinas so my eyes would be more sensitive to subdued light.

Rather than dart looks haphazardly, I scanned my eyes slowly 180 degrees without turning my head in the slightest, concentrating on the most extreme things I could see clearly. My intention was to see and interpret correctly every movement, every sign, and understand its meaning. The trick was to know if something was out of place.

Through trial and error, I had created a method of visually covering every inch of territory around me. Unless I saw something out of place or heard something to attract my attention, I kept to my scanning.

In reference to a compass I started at 270 degrees using peripheral vision and flashed my eyes across the swamp to 90 degrees . . . hold . . . back to 270 degrees . . . now slow . . . to zero degrees . . . hold . . . now to 90 degrees . . . hold . . . turn to the right to 90 degrees . . . peripheral hold on 90 degrees . . . flash to 180 degrees . . . peripheral hold on 180 degrees . . . flash to 270 degrees . . . hold . . . turn to 270 degrees . . . peripheral hold on 270 degrees . . . flash to zero degrees . . . hold . . . back to 270 degrees . . . hold . . . now slow to zero degrees . . . and begin again—until that part of the swamp was completely read with swamp eyes.

It has produced for me some of the rarest sights in the glades. Logs that had eyes, that cruised, then melted into swamp water film. A slow-crawling oleander caterpillar. The distant silhouette of a bald eagle, black, tipped with white on both ends. A huge banana spider with her long, threadlike legs, hanging in mid-air between two baby cypresses, looking like a yellow and black speckled African warrior's shield, her dew-strung spiral webs blending with the sun. Minute glimpses of fur passing through a quarter-inch hole in the wall of green. A largemouth bass rolling in the water. The smallest feather ruffled by a hummingbird.

Using swamp eye, I have spotted a fresh water river otter floating on his back, his face softened into that permanent smile. Creeping closer, I watched him crush apple snails with a limestone rock, gobble them down, then disappear to root on the muddy bottom among cattail stems. I continued to watch as he gracefully slipped up to the surface again, performing those undulating, buoyant movements with his powerful tail and webbed paws, seeming to swim for the sheer joy of it.

Using swamp eye, I have spotted a raccoon climbing across a low-hanging branch over a shallow rainwater pool, carrying a muddy rodent in his mouth as he scurried along toward me, his eyes to the ground. He was almost on top of me before he realized he had forgotten one of the main rules of survival: alertness. He was so surprised I was standing there when he looked up that for several seconds he didn't move at all. Then he rushed for the bushes.

My scanning has also shown me prisms of dazzling swamp colors, internally and eternally lit. Yellow primrose willow flowers lighting up bushes on the side of a forgotten jungle trail. Purple morning glories strung on walls of foliage and purple pickerel weed blossoms spread about in decorative fashion along streams and in shallow puddles. A light blue tree hopper, with orange patterns, flirting, jerking, then slowly crawling over, along and around an infinite maze of vegetation. And always the purple, green, tan and red dragonflies, zooming, hovering, then disappearing into the green air, reappearing, then becoming part of the invisible swamp world once again among the large, deadlike gumbo-limbo trees with trunks like elephant legs, the oily bark constantly peeling.

Swamp eye netted me numerous finds of Calusa and

Seminole Indian artifacts loose on high ground. When I stooped to pick them up I could almost hear the deep groans of those forgotten Indians seeping from the mud.

Swamp eye has searched out openings in what had seemed an impenetrable canopy of leaves and branches above me where I could watch swallowtail kites sharply ascending to stall speed, swooping, then gliding in long smooth sweeps. Truly, they are birds that dwell in rainbows.

Sometimes while using swamp eye on the lookout for Shakespeare, it would seem as if I were back on perimeter guard at Tuy Hoa. No barbed wire. Just a foxhole, sand, a treeline a little farther away, then the deserted village. Sitting. Looking. Waiting. Praying. It was head-wrecking. Out there somewhere a Viet Cong was going to squeeze off a sniper round and kill somebody, maybe even me. But if I was able to detect movement out there and call in a mortar on the position, it would let Charlie know we weren't sleeping. That's where I began to learn swamp eye. But it was different out there: more tense, more temporary.

Out here I could feel my head healing. Swamp balm. It was teaching me how to relax my mind while keeping my senses alert.

Would my swamp eyes hold? Would they net me the only sight that mattered to me now?

9

Dismal Apparition

Swamp notes—popash tree haven
Even the most glades-wise tracker can be fooled in broad daylight under a clear sky. Though I have trained all my senses to interpret the truth and put all my faith into them, still I find that I can be deceived by exhaustion, impatience and carelessness.

For hours I sat sight-reading the swamp around me. Sometimes for days I would go to the same spot and still-track for as long as I could keep awake. What I didn't know was my sense of sight, that one critical ability all else depends on, would be tested to its full limit and fail.

In this region I felt I knew every plant, animal, insect, the tiniest snail, the largest snake, the number of gators, even the amount of sunlight seeping into new shadows. But I was mistaken simply because I took for granted a developed and tested confidence that what my eyes told me was there actually was out there.

My sight was so sharpened that when black vultures flew over I knew where holes in the tree canopy would create instant trembling shadows off dahoon holly and Indian feather fern. I noticed the almost invisible flick of a kestrel's reddish-brown tail on pond surface film reflecting the camouflaged green on a bream's topside. Common houseflies landing on the inch-high tip of a gator's nose protruding out of water lettuce caught my attention. I saw an anole lizard caught in the razor teeth of a black racer snake next to grass fern.

With this intense kind of observation I was well overdue to be bitten by my own confidence. In my efforts to create means of detecting the unseen signs that would ensure Shakespeare's appearance, I had forgotten I was still a human being.

It was into the late afternoon. I was near a popash woods sharing ankle-deep water with terrestrial Guzmania air plants. My eyes began to water after more than ten hours of watching. High ground was out in front of me, and second-growth maple, cypress, and willow crowded the region like masses of people.

This section of Shakespeare's territory, probably two hundred yards long and a football field wide, offered prime cover for his night ambush of deer, raccoon and turkey. The whole area had scat and tracks spotting it like a three-dimensional map. I had found turkey tracks slicing the toe pads of Shakespeare's soft imprints several times, where he had neatly followed the scent of the turkey, stepping onto the bird's tracks to form a weird, unnamed animal spoor. In all probability, he had had an early Thanksgiving dinner.

My eyes had been irritated by sun and salty sweat earlier in the afternoon, but I felt they were still in good enough shape to carry me through till dark. I had been hearing some peculiar sounds out front and wanted to try for another sighting if at all possible. Those sounds, I suspected, were bear, bobcat, or Shakespeare. I had to check it out.

Now I was beginning to close my eyes, clear my vision, open, scan, hold, close once again, pause, look away, peer back, hold and re-scan the spot to make sure I wasn't seeing something that wasn't there.

But I was exhausted. To keep alert, I hung a vine of thorns around my neck so that when I closed my eyes and dropped my head, a thorn would prick my chin and wake me up. Then I would have to clear my eyes once more.

This went on until my concentration fuzzed away to almost nothing. As much as I wanted to stay, I decided I had had it, so I stood, stretched, yawned, and sighed heavily. Whatever silence I had created during the whole day was broken by a flurry of birds I disturbed. I even started to talk to myself out loud, mumbling something about the long hike back.

But the moment I turned my back on the high ground, it was as though, with my peripheral vision, my unconscious mind recorded a movement that required my conscious mind to catch up with it. I had already stepped into the water and was walking away when I gave it that last glance. First I saw jagged cypress stumps and smooth peeling cypress knees looking like just what they were called.

But, stopping dead in foot-deep mud, I stared at a sight I never thought possible up to that point with Shakespeare. The sleek, low, fawn-gray back of a panther was slowly floating through the small trees behind fallen logs, leaf mounds, and under Guzmania hanging from low branches, coming straight toward me.

Mary, mother of Jesus, I thought.

The very thing I wanted to happen in my destined affinity with Shakespeare was happening! I wanted him to come to me, to meet me halfway, and that's exactly what he was doing. But the way he was prowling told me he was stalking me as prey. Hardly a communion of spirits.

I knew there was no way I could run, and there was no way I could get to a high enough tree to climb. So, in a last effort to survive, I slipped down into the mud and water as far as I could, trying to erase my body from vision. I pushed up enough to see and peered at the big cat through the veil of floating duckweed that came up with my head.

He had noiselessly worked his way almost to the edge of the waterline, some twenty feet from where I was hiding. He was concealing himself magnificently because all I could see was his back and part of his foreleg.

He stopped, approached cautiously, moved closer, eased down behind a log, worked his way up to a half-crouched, half-lying position, stomach-crawled forward, and then, well out of character, stood straight up to expose a waving long brown tail that didn't quite fit the rest of his coloring.

I still could not see his head.

A steady strong wind came across the water and up the small embankment to Shakespeare. I expected to see his short soft fur undulating in that wind, but instead I witnessed a panther split up into long slender strands, reappear, then disintegrate altogether.

I blinked my eyes and threw water in my face, then got up to a kneeling position, ready to make a run for it. But when I looked at the spot where I had seen Shakespeare, there was nothing but a fallen, dry, brownish-gray sabal palm frond lying on a tree stump with the long leaf stalk almost touching the ground. Behind that frond was another one dangling low to the ground, hunched over a liana vine waving in the wind.

I really didn't know what to do with myself after I had checked out every inch of that spot for tracks, still half-believing that Shakespeare had been there and then gone off into the trees. But I finally had to admit to myself I had clearly experienced a very detailed wilderness sight mirage, an optical illusion brought on by overworking my senses and not knowing when to quit. When my brain tired, my conscious mind, nerves, and even my eye muscles had played tricks on me. My imagination had created a dismal apparition.

Walking back in the soft mud through a poison ivy patch and over several leaf islands surrounding second-growth cypress trees, I remembered dismal apparitions in Vietnam. Some of the guys were having sight mirages of a different kind. I remembered sitting in the USO near the beach drinking with a marine back from the bush, both of us staring at the bubbles in our glasses while we sipped the beer, savoring every swallow as though it were our last. I didn't know him until I sat down next to him, but it was not unusual out there to strike up a conversation with someone you didn't know. The only strangers out there were the Vietnamese. I noticed he was having a lot of trouble holding his glass still to drink, and when the edge of the glass hit his lips, he attacked the sip, dribbling beer down his chin.

He was an M-60 machine gunner and had been in Nam more than six months, wounded once when a chopper was shot out from under him up at Tam Ky. He said he had lain in a rice paddy for more than twelve hours playing dead until their back-up found them. In those six months he had participated in 15 operations already, running med-evac and supply runs to the DMZ. He was a combat vet and had almost been killed several times.

He kept bringing up his running buddy and how they would come into the USO and drink until their guts fell out. He talked about how his buddy had a Harley-Davidson motorcycle, and when they got back to the World they were going to get on it and ride all over the United States and start their own war on women.

Then he began to carry on about how his buddy was really crazy, always wanting to volunteer for the toughest runs, going in at night to pick up wounded during a fire-fight, refusing to take VC wounded, dropping right down into a battle to red-flare a VC position. Yeah, his buddy was crazy.

Then this marine got a far-off look in his eyes. He looked over at me with the strangest expression and said, "He protects me, you know. When I'm out there and we're bouncing off tree limbs and slicing through ridges, he's right there by my side helping me out, making sure things go my way." Then he took a long, dribbled drink.

I thought that was a bit peculiar, but I didn't put much into it. Maybe his buddy was making runs with him when he didn't have a mission.

The marine continued. "Thing is, he's been crowding me lately. Way too protective. I can handle myself out there . . . you know. He doesn't need to jump on my ass so much. . . ."

"Tell him about it," I said.

"I do, all the time. . . ."

As I looked at this marine, over his shoulder the marine on duty behind the bar was watching us with a grim look on his face, slightly shaking his head.

Then my new friend drank down the rest of his beer, stood up and walked away without saying a word.

The bartender came over to me. "You know him?"

I shook my head.

"The sorry bastard's been like that ever since his buddy got blown up by a VC rocket over Quang Tri."

"What! He just told me . . ."

"Yeah, I know. I heard him. He's been tellin' a lot of guys that in here. If I were the lieutenant I'd section-eight him. He's about to blow his cork anyway."

I looked out the plastic screen window and saw the marine lighting up a cigarette over near the generator. He staggered a little, dropped the cigarette on the ground, picked it up, cleaned it off and succeeded in lighting it again. As he turned to walk away, he waved somebody on behind him. But when I looked back toward the door of the USO, no one was there.

It gave me the willies knowing that sort of thing was

going on. I swore I'd never let it get to me that much, ever.
But I was mistaken. Later on I began to see giant snakes in
our squad tent. On guard duty one night I watched a spider
that was as big as the mess hall. And it wasn't until years later
that I finally admitted to myself that I had seen Buck back at
Chu Lai base camp walking up the muddy road with a towel
over his head as though he were going to the head.

10

Tracking Scent

Swamp notes—Bear Prairie

*Suspended in air currents, the scents from
glades creatures, vegetation and fish-filled
unnamed ponds hover, mix and churn in
an invisible cloud of natural chemicals forever changing. The panther's sense of smell
is infinitely more sensitive than mine. What
must this swamp smell like to him? Each
of its thousands of odors is clear, distinct,
unmistakable, a unit in his means of survival.*

I sat feeling black ants crawl up my leg, listening to a distant,
strange, humming song. I knew it was an ironhead woodstork
probing for food in a shallow pool. It was an unearthly hum
that echoed down through the nebulous wings of wind into
swamp tranquility.

Scent hung in the air like veiled aromas from another
realm, emitting just that amount of essence to tease Shakespeare back. Even with all my precautions to erase my human
scent—smearing mud on my face, staying wet with swamp
water—still my odor surely broke through those barriers to
whirl about and eventually alert his nostrils. But I was gam-

bling he was well aware of the various forms of human stench left in the swamp before I got there—the smell of gasoline, the smoke from a cigarette, the exhaust from a jeep—and so might not recognize mine as human.

My sense of smell was also set afire by this incessant world of odors, each one certain proof of some particular existence, even though it might remind my nose of something else: dry ferns about my legs smelling to me like burned cardboard; the intense vegetation smelling thick as wet dirt, pulling me toward it; a dead small blue heron floating with a heavy, fishy stench; water-soaked logs smelling like woody remains of an abandoned mullet boat. Other swamp smells came to be so unique in their familiarity that they smelled only like themselves: the wet bark of cypress and the fragrance of the blooming leaves, the strong odor of a rattlesnake as it wards off a predator, the smell of vast patches of wild coffee, willow submerged in rain-water, a dead skunk, the musk of a deer.

For me to scent-read Shakespeare's territory meant close-up observation of his signs. It meant smelling scat, old or new kills for urine deposits, scrapes where fresh urine had been left, and sniffing for possible den sites inside large hollow logs.

Every time I went back to civilization my nose was contaminated with car exhaust, foods, insecticides, perfumes. So each time back out in the swamp it had to readjust to the glades. Fortunately, I lived next to the swamp, so the swamp smells were always hovering nearby. I suspect our primeval forefathers' sense of smell was much more highly developed than ours and helped them locate food or warned them of danger. We have little use for this sense in modern society. Or do we?

I sat there, still as a slug, trying to pick out scents of interest. I had invented a system that helped me a lot.

Breathe in, nose only. Hold for five seconds. Breathe out, mouth only. Hold for five seconds. Empty lungs. Breathe in, nose only. Fill my brain. Blast it with scent. Hold. Breathe out, mouth only. Hold. Breathe in. Hold. Breathe out. Hold. Empty. Breathe in. Hold. Blast. Hold. Breathe out. Hold. And rest.

The smell of slash pine burning rushed into my nose.

·Ten minutes later smoke floated in like fog above the cypress. A burn-out downwind, far to the west, was leveling sedge grass, scorching pine bark, curling love vine into black nuggets which were then blown into oblivion by a gust of flames.

In all of this I smelled death and life changing positions according to the skills of living creatures. I smelled the misfortune of being a coontie plant rooted to sandy soil and limestone. I knew somewhere over there a red-shouldered hawk was taking advantage of the walking wall of fire which was exposing small rodents or marsh rabbits frantically scurrying for new cover.

For a few moments I allowed myself to imagine Shakespeare in command of the fire, running out in front of it as though directing its course, stopping, observing movement, then putting his nose in the air, and in a rush of excitement smelling a doe in flight heading for the edge of the burn-out to avoid being singed.

Then I was abruptly brought back to reality by a bream jumping in the water not more than a few feet away, disturbing water-scent.

I sat. I smelled. I yearned for the time when I would attune my nose to smell Shakespeare coming. Would that ever happen? How I was going to develop that skill I didn't know, but I was confident there was a way; I would at least try to find it.

I began to remember a sergeant in recon-marines in Vietnam who was a tracker with a German shepherd track dog. After his first year in Nam he claimed he could smell VC in spider holes and hooch floor hideaways before the dog could. He said it was easy, that Charlie had a smell that gave him away because when he spent so much time in a hiding place he would sit and smoke dope. A kind of sweet dry fragrance always came up out of the hole.

Once I went into one of those tunnels. I smelled human excrement and urine as I crawled right over a freshly made puddle of it. The odor of burned powder and stale water hovered in the turnaround crawl space. There was the distinct smell of tobacco and of wet vegetation that had been laid down for bedding, but there was no smell of dope.

There were so many smells in Vietnam that were wholly

Vietnam: fresh burning honey-buckets mixed with gasoline next to open latrines, jungles and the sides of hills aflame with napalm, my own sweat plastering my utilities against my body. And always, always that odor of dead things. It never left my nose. Not even when I went home. The smells of dying and dead flesh have a way of staying with you.

But I had retrained my sense of smell in Shakespeare's territory to detect the things that live around him, the unexpected things that intrude into his region. But to smell him I would have to figure out a way to keep a panther smell registered in my head. The trick was to smell, over and over again, a panther. Little did I know then that in the near future I would get more than my share of panther smell.

11

Green Silence

> **Swamp notes—Camouflaged**
> *Automatically, when it grows dark in the swamp, my ears take over. And now I am teaching my ears to maintain that alertness in full light.*

For a time I eased up on a fern leaf island just big enough for me, put fern leaves in my bandanna and sat Indian-style, still-tracking. Motionless as a spider, I listened. Maybe the cat would appear. Slowly I cupped my hand over the back of my ear and put a blade of grass between my lips and teeth and blew, producing a single distress call of a small animal.

Months before I had spent whole days concentrating only on wind sounds I had trained myself to perceive and distinguish. These were sounds not normally heard in the swamp until they became identifiable through conscious, consistent training.

Now, sitting there relaxed, I forgot about smelling and seeing, and just listened to the rhythm of the swamp. At first it sounded like a flood of incoherent noise. Then, languidly, there was an ever-increasing, cryptic, unnerving, green silence, suddenly shattered by the outburst of a crow's call.

Again, the unsettling silence.

Then, finally, I felt the swamp accept my presence. And as it did, this wild daytime concert seemed almost perfect in time and tone, a creation of graceful excellence. Would it reveal Shakespeare's sounds?

Birds cried, warbled, caroled, piped, trilled, twitted, cheeped, peeped and crowed. A woodpecker loudly drummed, dominating the air. A kestrel whistled, streaking through the trees.

Then the distinct slap of a snake tail as it slipped into the water.

Now, gaps of mellow silence.

A pig frog croaked. There was the splash-splash of a bird bathing. The quiet trickle of a stream. The "baa . . ." of a sheep frog. The eerie whistle of a nightcrying limpkin still looking for apple snails. Bream fish splashing. Solitary honks of alligators. Wading birds snatching small bass. A squirrel's chatter. Red-shouldered hawks screaming.

Then the distinct sound of a heavy body walking. I tensed. A cat would never make a sound like that. Was it a bear? A man? As quickly as I heard the sound it faded, and it was a long time before I breathed easily again.

In the Marine Corps I had been trained to combat surprise instantly with calmness. Under no circumstance did I give my position away with movement or sound. I sat still as hardened lava, cultivating patience, hoping someday the cat would come to me.

Then, suddenly, a deafening roar streaked overhead at treetop level.

"Christ!" I screamed, falling to the ground and pressing my hands over my ears. In Vietnam when that happened I would hug the bottom of the foxhole, praying to God the roar would go away.

And then as instantly as it had begun, it was gone. I sat up cautiously, my ears still vibrating with what I now recognized as the scream of a jet from Homestead Air Force Base flying a mock bombing run. In Nam it would have filled the side of a hill with napalm or blown out VC mortar emplacements in a barrage of rockets and machine gun bullets.

After that terrible intrusion swamp sounds vibrated for another hour, but there was nothing that would lead me to the cat.

As I sat there staring at the world, I imagined man wandering in it well before he ever used fire. I wondered if at that time he ever pondered his own destiny. Then, as now, he was a fragment of the natural world, a genetic expectation. Like the panther, man was a dawn creature, a predator with wild animal compulsions before he ever thought of progress. But he probably used those wild instincts initially for peaceful coexistence. They were used to gather food, provide shelter, protect others, and cherish those close to him. For the most part I see ancient man as a peaceful being in unison with nature, who, like the panther, killed cleanly, and only to survive. There must be some safe passage from the present back to the simplicity of swamp life without destroying everything along the way. If we could find it, then we could all return to that animal exploration, to those infinite instincts that so many call wild.

I sighed, dropped a piece of deer meat nearby, and moved farther north.

12

Ominous Whir

Swamp notes—on a leaf island
Some warning sounds are quieter than others. It's a good thing I can't hear them all as I track through the swamp, no doubt creating a high-frequency din of warning screams from every worm and beetle—maybe even every leaf and flower—as I intrude on their territories.

Up onto high ground, down into the water, up onto high ground, and back down into water. High ground. Water. Up. Down. This went on for some time until I eased up onto another island and rested.

I lay there allowing myself to be enveloped by the green silence. Suddenly it was ruptured by a faint, ominous, dry whir, distinctly and dangerously different from any insect sound. It put the hair up on the back of my neck, and even though I was on the verge of panic, I lay perfectly still, my eyes roving. From past swamp experience, I knew what I was looking for and I knew I would be far better off if I could spot it quickly. But I was also praying I would not see it, that my eyes would make liars of my ears.

But there on the edge of the island was a long, graceful chain of radiant, diamond-shaped, gray-green markings coiled up like a heap of ancient Indian jewelry, gleaming in the sunlight reflected from the water. An eastern diamondback rattlesnake, no more than ten feet away. I estimated his length at close to five feet. A queasy feeling gripped my stomach. Let fear have my stomach, I thought, I have to keep control of my head.

His head rose, and with his pits and a flicking red tongue sensitive to body heat, he probed the air for chemical clues to my exact location. Then the green eyes locked on mine. He recoiled the thickness of his body even tighter, the dry rattles whirring intensely, stopping, then whirring once again. This was one of his first-line defenses—a warning to me, not so much for my sake but for his own so that he would not need to waste his venom on something that would not make him a meal. I was praying that he wouldn't waste a drop of it, delivered by those tubular, hypodermic fangs with uncanny accuracy, lightning speed, and deadly results.

Now he lay stone still. Another defense. I could feel the tension vibrating between the two of us. One of the most poisonous snakes in North America sat feet away waiting for the exact second to strike, to plunge his fangs into soft flesh. For him it was survival. Me too. My tension was so great that besides sweating from the heat I was sweating from what was going to happen. If I moved a fraction of an inch, the shift of heat radiating from my body would trigger him to spring into action, his entire body moving as fast as his flicking tongue. I would have to be quicker. I wondered if I had a hidden reflex somewhere that would prove fast enough. But I also knew that if I escaped his venom on the first strike I was in even deeper jeopardy, for then he would be closer to me. And rattlers keep on striking as long as the body is there and moving. I might get hit three or four times within seconds. That would mean death.

Unfortunately I was in an awkward position, on my side with my arm folded under me. How long I could hold that position I didn't know.

The rattler kept his eyes on me all the time, as though daring me to move, confident he could get to me. His tongue shot out, and I saw his mouth open slightly. The fangs could just barely be seen, wet, halfway down from the upper jaw.

He was going to strike! His head moved toward me. I tensed every muscle in my body, held my breath, kept my eyes on him. I could feel fear streak through my body like a comet, that shocking bolt that rushes from the tip of your toes to the last hair on your head.

I couldn't believe what I was experiencing. I had thought all the worst dangers in my life were behind me. If it happened now, my life would be incomplete. I was in the middle of some significant discoveries about the panther. I was living my life full throttle again. I had unfinished business. Surely, destiny wasn't going to cut me short of my goal. Give me affinity with the panther, I prayed. Then take my soul. But not now, I whispered, please not yet.

In Vietnam I had prayed the same kind of prayer the first night on perimeter guard after the amphibious landing at Tuy Hoa. By then it was a killing zone. Alone in my foxhole, next to eight other marines strung out in foxholes, facing the village, I thought about Buck getting shot to death. And since his KIA we had had two wounded in action—WIA. We were sure VC had gone down into the hill inside those tunnels. How many we didn't know, but they were part of the killing zone.

After Buck, a strong fiber of tension had tightened along the perimeter and had been twisting itself into a grotesque knot as dusk settled in. Everybody seemed to be trying to stop the sun from going down.

Darkness was the ally of the VC. In it, he could move in and out of the village undetected. He was a professional guerilla, an insurgent who had dedicated his life to his cause of uniting his country. He lived with the people in the villages and educated them into communism, Ho Chi Minh style. And in the VC's mind, as far as we Americans were concerned, we could all go straight to hell. We had no business in his country. He was a patriot. We were invaders. We were the rich Americans who could buy whole countries—except Vietnam. With a committed attitude like that, the Viet Cong chopped away at us and in time drained us of the one important element we needed to survive: a good reason to be there in the first place. That was why it was so hard to keep a positive attitude when you were up against someone who is fighting for his country.

When night began to fall, my sixth sense told me we were going to get hit. It screamed deep within me to leave, to get away, but that was impossible. I would have been branded a coward for the rest of my life. It was an overwhelming feeling of terrible disaster coming over me, and even before the sun went all the way down, our forward observer had radioed that there was movement across the river toward our defense line.

I huddled in that foxhole, becoming part of it, my eyes wide, tired, peering over the loose, sandy edge, my finger on my rifle trigger, already pulling back the slack, making sure the barrel pointed out front. I could see the silhouette of my rifle muzzle throbbing in cadence to my quick heart beat.

It was my first night in South Vietnam in the middle of a killing zone surrounded by VC snipers. It was my first night, all right, and maybe my last, I thought. I prayed furiously that night. Not now, I don't want to die now. Please, not yet. Every time I felt a surge of insecurity, I rushed a prayer into it and tried to keep my mind on staying alive. That was the all-important goal. To stay alive. Figure out ways to stay alive. Become a genius in the art of survival. Survive. That word suddenly took on new meaning. I found out how badly I did want my life. I was willing to do anything to keep it—except run. That was where honor and pride came in. When I left Vietnam I still wanted to be able to live with myself, to say at least I tried to do the right thing. If I lost, then for that much it would have been worth it.

The VC probably knew we were fresh from the States, inexperienced in combat, and they were going to take full advantage of it. Their aim was to overrun us, have a field day scaring the shit out of us and then kill us all.

A month earlier, in Okinawa, I had talked with a marine combat vet who had been in on a lot of fire-fights. He told me about his first time under fire, and all the time he told the story his hands kept clenching. It had messed him up pretty badly. He talked about sitting all night on perimeter, just able to keep his eyes open. The whole line was half asleep, and he could hear some of the guys snoring. Suddenly, just before daybreak, hideous screams came from one side of the perimeter where black shadows were rushing into a hole in the defense, raking the inside with machine guns and throwing grenades. VC were running right through the whole perimeter, taking almost everybody by surprise, leveling marines as they stood up in shock.

The only marines shooting back were war vet sergeants.

A lot of guys hugged the ground and played dead. But when this marine saw his friend get zapped through the stomach and head, throwing him back against an embankment like a sack of dirt, he said he went crazy. He grabbed his rifle and started shooting wildly in the direction of the VC. Others joined in and cut down half the invading force. The next morning count showed that his outfit had taken sixty percent casualties. But the forty percent that had made it without a scratch suddenly became war-wise men out to save their asses.

As I lay in that foxhole I told myself I wouldn't go into shock. I would fire if fired upon. If I had to, I would kill. I had to do that or die myself.

The word came down the perimeter that the forward observer team was coming back in fast. They had seen enough movement to convince the lieutenant we were going to get hit. I could see their helmets coming up to the checkpoint. One rose and whispered the password. Then they all sprinted into the line, diving inside and rolling over out of the way of a .30-caliber machine gun emplacement camouflaged with a bush.

Then for over an hour it was deadly quiet. I had to keep moving my head back and forth to keep it from shaking and twitching. I was thirsty, but unwilling to let my rifle down so I could open the canteen and get a drink. My arms and shoulders were stiff, and the small of my back ached from being crammed into the hole and not moving.

Suddenly marines were whispering to each other, pointing out front. A couple of hundred meters out, shadows ducked into bushes, behind huts, alongside trees. We called in for an illumination round for light, but the lieutenant refused and told us to sit tight. What did he know? He was back at the CP, not right up in the middle of it. I had an illumination grenade and almost popped it and threw it out, but I could just hear the lieutenant yelling at me for disobeying an order. I decided to throw it anyway when the time seemed right. I reached for it and laid it next to me.

I kept watch out front toward the trees, staying perfectly still, barely breathing, playing dead to avoid death, just like I was doing now with that rattler, its hot venom promising death as sure as the hot VC lead.

Then I distinctly saw a man's body slip right across a five-foot clearing into the trees. His position was no more than 75 yards out front. If he moved again I would see him even more clearly because there was no cover other than those trees. Either he was a North Vietnamese regular and the officer in charge or a local VC pumped up on drugs and a belief in reincarnation. Like the rattler, this VC was ready to strike. He made that clear by taking the chance just to get there. And if I made a wrong move, he was probably going to kill me. If I got killed, I would have no one to blame but myself.

So I lay there and stared out, trying not to blink no matter how tired my eyes were. I told myself that at the very next movement I saw out there I was going to open up with the whole magazine. My only fire discipline was my will to stay alive.

The next movement came violently. It happened so fast that even after everything I had thought about, it still caught me by surprise. Small arms fire in blue tracers suddenly sprayed out from the village over my head. The VC had struck. I slammed my head down in the sand and I could hear the rounds humming over me. I put my rifle up over the sand and without shouldering it, pulled the trigger. My rifle jerked back in the hole and shot a round straight up in the air, then jammed. I had to put it between my legs and kick the bolt free of a crooked round that had come out of the magazine and lodged in the chamber. Jesus, why now? Why now?

Our whole perimeter opened up with war's noise and threw a blanket of death out over the VC. Two aerial illumination rounds burst with a popping sound in white light above us and exposed running shadows as I looked over the side. I began firing at the shadows, shoving magazine after magazine into my rifle.

The heavy scent of burned gun powder hovered in a foggy mist from our line, fading in the illumination round floating to the ground. I kept on shooting in the direction the shadows had gone and was sure no VC could have survived our return fire. Another illumination round popped in the air. Everybody sat up in their foxholes and looked at the free fire zone. Not one body lay dead out there—not one.

Voices from the line were surprised. "Where'd they

go? . . . Ain't no kills out there . . . Jesus, give me some more ammo . . . They might come back. . . ."

Twice more that night they did. They hit the right side of our perimeter with grenades and a machine gun. Toward morning a helicopter came in and dropped off c-rations, then ascended and toured the village for us. They caught a few rounds of sniper fire from the hill, but found nothing to indicate there was any sizable VC force holding out up there or in the village.

When the sun came up I breathed easy for the first time in more than twelve hours. The word came down the line to stay in our holes. A favorite trick of the VC was to leave a sniper behind to zap the first marine out at daybreak. So I lay back in my hole, exhausted. I had made it. The first heavy contact with the Viet Cong.

The rattler still had his mouth wide open, making sure I could see those fangs. He hadn't taken his eyes off me, and I didn't plan on looking away from him. Would I make it through this contact with another enemy I had volunteered to face? But this time my reasons for volunteering made sense to me, and besides, I had become convinced this rattler had decided not to be aggressive. He would probably remain on the defensive now. If he were going to be aggressive he would have been in my lap by now. No, he was holding his ground.

So, with a certain amount of risk, I waited him out until his mouth closed ever so slowly. Then, with luck on my side, I took the chance of easing off the leaf island inch by inch. After each movement, the rattler seemed to ease up too. So I dropped a morsel of deer meat, slid into the water, and put plenty of distance between us.

I was reminded of an old Seminole snake clan legend that explains why the Indian will never kill a snake if he can avoid it. The legend has it that in the beginning the rattlesnake had no teeth (fangs), but then an Indian happened onto a whole nest of snakes and killed the babies. The mother snake went to the chief and told him what had occurred. So the chief made teeth and put them in the snake's mouth and ordered her to bite the man next time.

13

Wind Words,
Water Voices

Swamp notes—on an Indian mound
*Swamp sounds: the high-pitched whistle of
a hawk, the deep solitary groan of a bull
gator, coots issuing their song on water weeds
the shrieks of a limpkin, the bright tea-kettle
notes of the Carolina wren, breezes bending
slim tree trunks, the wind in slash pine
trees. But are they all what they seem to
be?*

For eight days I moved about Shakespeare's territory looking
for the best cover where I could sit, listen, move only when
I had to. I had to find a place where I could blend into, maybe
merge with, the swamp enough to conceal my human form.
Saw palmettoes in deep sand sometimes worked well. For two
days I was a patch of maiden cane, constantly harassed by
bumble bees and paper wasps. Once, for six hours I was a
willow tree in black mud until dusk, blending into the thick
masses of short, knife-like leaves. When a breeze moved all
of the leaves, I moved with them, bending, leaning, then slowly
falling back into place.

In those days the swamp was accepting my ways. And
I was trying to accept the ways of the swamp. This meant
pushing all my senses beyond their previous limits. I was
developing swamp eye, and I had begun to pick up scents
unknown to me before. But hearing remained my weak point,
and I knew how vulnerable this left me.

My hearing had never been strong. As a child, I had
had ear problems, and in high school I once got my eardrum
popped playing basketball. In Marine Corps boot camp I was

on the rifle range when the blast of the rifle next to me on line put still another hole in my eardrum. It healed over, but with a small scar tissue that lessened my sensitivity to sound. Then in Vietnam while I was sleeping next to 105 cannons that were going off all night, it happened again. We were in support for extra fire power around a 105 howitzer emplacement next to an airstrip near Tam Key. A battle with North Vietnamese regulars was raging on the other side of a river to the east. We could sit and hear the rattle of rifle fire and the bomb thunder created by the 105's, even see some of the rounds hit the trees and the side of the hill.

I lay in a sand bag bunker right next to the ear-deafening blast of a 105 as it spat out the rounds all night and into the next morning. I was so exhausted that it was no problem for me to fall asleep, but each blast jerked me awake. The marine on duty next to me kept cursing each time a fire mission would come in. The radio would crackle, then the lead gunner would repeat the grids, and WHAM out would go the round. It happened so often that night I thought I would never get the sound out of my head. Late in the morning, I was caught by surprise as a round went out. I jerked up. The blast numbed my left ear, and suddenly I couldn't hear on that side. It was like being up in a jet at high altitude with the pressure so great that I thought my ears were going to blow out. Voices seemed far away.

I complained to the sergeant, who thought I was lying and didn't give me permission to go to the medical tent. He was a young sergeant, not even thirty years old yet, acting like he was headed toward general's stars. The difference between me and him was that he'd had six months more duty in Nam. So I wandered around Vietnam after that for a long time, during the rainy season, with two holes in my eardrums. They eventually healed over with thick scar tissue.

Out in the swamp, I knew that scar tissue would prevent certain sounds from ever reaching my consciousness. And yet I felt I could stretch the limits of even this limited hearing. Though my right ear was taking on a bigger load, I was determined to train my left to catch up. To accomplish that, I would set out to strain them both to new limits.

In the rare times of silence in the swamp I could still

surmise something was always moving, flying, crawling, stepping from dry ground to dry ground, up onto a log, down to rock, over to high grass. I would listen for those almost silent sounds, those wind words: limbs caressing each other, leaves crumbling under the paws of light-footed foxes, ripples on a pond.

I would close my eyes tight, block out all thoughts, put a white surface in front of my mind's eye and listen, hoping the distinct sound of Shakespeare would register, immediately putting his image on my white surface. When those sounds did finally emerge from the swamp again, it was more than two years later and quite by accident that I picked them up.

But now I was developing my swamp ears for other events, events that would lead me ever closer to my affinity with Shakespeare.

For another week, in the mornings and at evening hours, I sat and eavesdropped on the glades, cocking my ears toward every new sound, giving names to the fresh arrivals, mentally filing the old ones.

There were boring times when nothing happened. I longed to hear that highpitched scream of the panther, heard time and again on television in the Walt Disney wildlife movies, or in the old western shows where the mountain lion is jumping about the high rocks screaming, running from its pursuer.

Once in a zoo I heard the deep guttural moans of the lions just before feeding. I imagined Shakespeare slowly creeping about the swamp somewhere near me, hungry, in search of prey. I wondered if he would pick up my scent soon, if I would hear that same low moan.

But on this particular evening my imaginings were rewarded with at least the hint of a panther sound, something that put me a fraction closer to him. Weary and bored, I was making my way back to a trail that, after an hour of hiking, would bring me out on a long gravel road leading to my car. I made my way along the trail in high grass, side-stepping lazy water moccasins, a beautiful indigo and two small king snakes. Leopard frogs occasionally jumped into the grass at my approach, and a large gator sunning on the trail halted me in my stride. When he heard me coming, he turned in my direction, then as fast as he could, he scrambled off and plunged into the water like a falling timber.

It was not until I had passed that spot and walked several more feet down the trail that I heard someone else not far away from me in the swamp. Two men talking. At first I could hear only unintelligible gurgling, then the words started to come through the trees. They seemed to be laughing about something. I dropped to my knees and listened. They were off to my right and seemed to be heading south behind me. Oddly, I couldn't hear them going through the trees, though I knew they must be kicking up water, thrashing with their hands to open a way through bushes, probably letting go with a curse or two. But I could hear only occasional mumbling.

Then I picked out a few words. "Here, you carry . . ." The last words were lost. Then again, "You shot 'em. Your car . . ." More words lost.

Hunters, I thought.

"Well, shit, this here panther . . ."

My whole body went rigid. Poachers. And they'd killed a panther! Maybe Shakespeare. I shed my pack on the trail and slipped into the water off the trail and swam toward the sound. I had to stop several times to listen for more words. By the time I got right up behind them, I was astonished at how noisy they both were, and yet their words were still indistinct. I wondered if sensitizing my ears to the sounds of wildlife had left them less able to distinguish human sounds.

All I could think about was that if it was Shakespeare and he was dead, all that we had accomplished was shattered. By the bullet of a stupid hunter. A hunter who had now deprived us of our right to a wilderness affinity. Shot dead on the spot. And in that explosion of hot steel and panther flesh one of the last members of an endangered species had been wiped off planet earth.

I was enraged. I focused all of my senses on those hunters. I swam to the edge of a long trail above the waterline, covered over with baby maple trees, and checked up and down. I lay there for a while thinking I might have gotten there a little ahead of them. But no one came.

I crawled up on the trail, avoiding thorn vines, and looked again. The swamp was as quiet as a graveyard. I stood and listened. Then I heard the voices coming to me from down the trail to my left. Unintelligible gurglings again. I flashed a look. No one was there.

I crept slowly toward an old railroad bridge. Underneath it lay a bed of limestone rocks strewn about like the rocky walls of Jericho. Over the top, between the crevices, under clinging moss, water flowed from high to low ground. It gurgled, mumbled, sputtered and spat. I heard those mumbling voices right there in front of me, but there were no hunters. It was the language of running water, and from a distance it had mimicked the tones and inflections of the human voice. Where I had expected to see two two-legged, khaki-clad, gun-toting humans, I saw only rocks and water. I sat down on the bridge and stared at the water, the burnt orange rocks, and the moss strung out in the water like snake tails.

I had been fooled by water voices, and my imagination, prodded by weariness and boredom, had expanded on them. I had experienced an age-old wilderness phenomenon: a sound mirage. An acoustical illusion. So committed was I to developing super-hearing in spite of my disabilities that I had pushed myself over the limit too soon. Exhaustion is no barrier to destiny, but it can be a signal to back off and recheck, rethink what has already happened. Exhaustion can also be a protector by preventing you from being overwhelmed by the cause. This was something I was to learn too many times, from many causes—always for the sake of the same cause. And yet, at that moment, sitting there exhausted, I grinned at the water, grateful for its words, their sparkling innocence. Shakespeare was still out there somewhere. Our paths could still cross.

14

Wilderness Being

Swamp notes—Corkscrew Island

*To become a wilderness being is to be one
with the land and the plants and animals
that thrive on it. In the Everglades, the earth's
desperation for its human animals to become again wilderness beings is as real as
the dried, cracked mud around me.*

As the days and months passed, Shakespeare became my wilderness teacher. Through constant use, my skills of tracking
hovered on the edge of excellence, and yet I felt I could stretch
my limits a little further. I learned every inch of Shakespeare's
territory and could go to any part of it on any day and find
signs of the cat. I overlapped my own tracks, and it became
almost a game to see if I could guess where he was at that
moment.

Once my mind and body had acclimated to the subtropical environment, this cathedral swamp, Shakespeare's home
became my home. I felt myself evolving into a living, breathing
part of it.

By intense mental concentration and self-suggestion, I
trained myself to ignore weather, pain and other minor hard-
ships, just as I had done when I played football during the
hot months in high school and college, and as I had done in
boot camp, infantry training, and finally in Vietnam. It wasn't
until Vietnam, though, that this self-training really became
part of me. There it was a matter of survival, not a game. And
here too, now in the glades, it was a matter of survival—the
panther's.

In the winter, from November to June, the weather was
ideal for tracking. Cool days, insect-free nights. But in the

summer, late June to October, the sun was blistering and the air like a suffocating bath. So when I felt heat exhaustion and delirium coming on, I would slip into a cool water slough with the baby gators and vividly imagine I was in the Arctic Ocean among icebergs and seals, my body numbed purple from the freezing wind and water.

During those months inside the cypress swamps, the female mosquitoes, deer flies and gnats—jaws with wings, all —were buzzing or floating in clouds above stagnant water, ambushing every square inch of bare flesh on man or animal, crowding to get to warm blood. At night they covered the swamp like black fog. Many times I wished I had the fur, skin and resistance of Shakespeare.

But to combat them all, I developed my own defenses by staying away from suntan lotions and colognes and consuming large doses of natural thiamine, a B vitamin that causes the human skin to emit a strong, but yeastlike, odor which insects hate. I swore off sugar and ate raw fruits, yeast, green vegetables, grains and liver, other sources of thiamine, then supplemented my diet with ginseng root, wheat germ and wild honey. I learned from the Seminole Indians their ancient natural blend of citronella for candles. This is a combination of citric juices from wild oranges, grapefruits and key limes. I combined the candle wax with Deet oil and rubbed it on my skin to ward off the creatures.

In order to endure longer periods of time in the swamp, I built up my lung capacity and strengthened my feet and legs by jogging barefoot in slash pine forests, sprinting on sandy beaches, and running the wet prairies in ankle- and knee-deep water.

To withstand the torturous hours of pain in the crouched position while tracking, I duck-waddled up old trails with a packful of rocks until my thighs screamed at me to stop. I practiced the man-on-horse position of Kung Fu exercises, as if I were in the saddle, but without the horse. I used the cobra yoga posture to strengthen my back. Lying flat on my stomach, I would push myself up from the waist, head back, and hold that position as long as I could. The panther pose was an exercise I created, also to build up back muscles. Sitting on my ankles, spine erect, I would stretch out my arms, put my head to the sun and backwards as far as possible, and hold it as long as I could.

Later on I discovered yogametrics, a physical training program that, among other things, contracts muscles at the peak in their best angle of pull to develop maximum endurance. At one time this system of improving the body was a well-guarded secret of the yogis, and for thousands of years yogis have used it to increase their physical strength and endurance.

I was fascinated by the process, and searched out yoga exercises for my legs and back. I found that it also helped the rest of my body. By tensing my front thigh muscles fast and hard for five seconds ten times in a row, I was able to build up even more endurance for long tracking. I worked on my back and shoulders with an exercise called wing swing, and with the upward eagle spread which meant clasping my hands behind my back, elbows straight, and pulling them upward as far as I could.

I learned to live off the land when I had to, studying the edible plants like cattails, fire flags, muscadine vine and strangler fig fruits. I carried a hook and line and caught bream, bass and small catfish with grubworms and dragonflies, filleted and cooked them over a small fire. Later I learned to eat chunks of raw fish dipped in soya sauce. I carried nuts and honey in a small pouch on my belt and mixed them with pennywort for a swamp salad, and always drank the fresh moving swamp water.

In the beginning I had no idea how much my wilderness obsession with Shakespeare would consume and dominate my life. He came to be always on my mind, ruling my thoughts and desires, just as he reigned over prey. I was under his spell, possessed by his mystique, and it eventually became a ruling passion bordering on a curse.

When I found no sign of Shakespeare, I worried terribly. And when I wasn't in the wilds tracking him, I was frustrated, irritable, and constantly plagued by his desperate plight to survive. I harbored this dreadful, vivid nightmare that some idiot would hunt him down and murder him.

I checked and rechecked fragments of evidence trying

to detect man-movements. I looked for a machete trail through thick willow, a man's boot print in slough mud, beer cans, jeep tracks, warm doused campfires, cigarette butts. There's an old swamp saying that man is the only species who fouls his nest. It is easy to track a man.

I began taking days off from my part-time jobs and always spent my weekends tracking. I would call in sick for a hundred different reasons until it became embarrassing, and then would quit or be fired.

Through it all, in order to keep to my vow of never revealing Shakespeare's existence, I spent a great deal of time and effort devising clever alibis to cover my tracking time. I became a master of concealment in civilization. I would wander off in the early evening, then end up in Shakespeare's territory at a spot where I had stashed my gear in a garbage bag. When I went canoeing or camping with friends in state parks, I acted like I didn't know much. In conversations about the Everglades and the panther at parties, I fell silent or changed the subject. I was living many lives.

I longed to tell my wife everything, for she was my anchor to civilization. She was helping me more than I can ever thank her for. She is an elementary school teacher and if she hadn't been working, our bills would never have been paid. Just as important, she knew, though I never had to tell her, that ever since I got back from the war something had been eating at me, something I had to have a lot of time on my own to work out. I wondered many times if she thought I was seeing someone else. Shakespeare was probably the most peculiar swamp mistress anyone could find.

Sometimes I strongly suspected she knew what I was doing, but at the brink of discussing it I would always stop short. I tried it out once to myself, and it came out ridiculous, but more important, I felt that betrayal to the cat once again. So I remained silent.

A few years before, I'd read a brief article in a Chicago newspaper that said there were no more Florida panthers in the Everglades. I had promptly drawn a sharp black line on the map from Illinois to the middle of the Everglades and then just packed up the old maverick car and followed that line. I drove all those hours down the road with no idea what

I'd find at the end of it. After three days of nonstop driving, half of it in the rain, I arrived in Florida and drove all the way down to Everglades City, the last town on the west coast before the Everglades takes over. I remember getting out of the car and walking right into a small grocery store there and asking if there were any Florida panthers left. An old man in a shadow by the door had said in a cracked, tired voice, "Shoot, not long ago I saw one of them there critters up close to the highway 'bout half way 'cross to Miami."

I took him at his word. Now it was up to me to find the cat.

After I'd been tracking for more than a year, trying to hold onto part-time jobs, I did manage to get and hold onto a worthwhile job, a position with Big Cypress Nature Center in Naples, Florida. It was a rare opportunity for me to learn the Everglades in even greater depth. I was hired on as an assistant naturalist and rapidly developed into an environmental education teacher, wildlife lecturer and researcher.

My first year's salary at the nature center was paid by the United States government through the CETA program. The fact that I was a veteran of a foreign war had put me right up at the top of the list for the job to begin with. I was fortunate, indeed, though I was the only one who knew the extent of my luck. The ironies piled up. It was the same government with their ideas of "foreign war" that sent me off to this swamp in the first place. Now they helped me get hired here to care for and teach about the environment after they had taught me to burn and blast it in Vietnam.

Even during my career as a naturalist with the nature center I didn't tell anyone on the staff what I was doing in my spare time. To them I was a novice in the swamp, theirs my only education in its ways.

Through it all I never talked about the panther, my obsession, my tracking. I practiced a basic principle I learned from Shakespeare. He was elusive, secretive, and had outsmarted man time and again. I would be like the panther. He had managed to elude man for years. Only his elusiveness could save him now. He had kept his secret. I would keep mine and his.

Book III
Searching

Attempt the end, and never stand to doubt;
Nothing's so hard, but search will find it
out.

—*Robert Herrick*

15

Slough Creature

Swamp notes—in water
Swamp animals help protect each other from
their greatest enemy—people. And they can
do it based on sheer reputation. For example, the panther's reputation keeps people out of his territory. They can also do it
with just sound. For example, the screech
of the smallest owl can make human blood
run cold and human legs run away.

I came across a glossy slough lit by a brilliant sun creating a
glow within fog, making the slough look like something out
of a dream. Giant cattail blades danced like tongues of cold
greenish flames in a breeze. The delicate slender images of
cypress trees in the water, their needles threading the water
beneath the surface like stitches on embroidered silk, created
two swamps, each as alive as the other. A weak wind skimmed
this water, now softly waltzing, shattering a mirrored cypress,
then putting it back together again.

Parts of the slough bottom were arranged with soaked
red maple leaves and drowned duckweed, flashing colors back
too deep to be their own. Other parts of the slough were
black, deep, maybe even bottomless.

It teemed with mosquito fish, feeding on mosquito larvae. When I dipped my finger into the thickest concentration
of the larvae, they clung to it, wiggling frantically, peering at
me with over-sized eyes that gave them the look of creatures
from outer space.

A brown Brazilian tree frog sat perfectly still on a branch,
looking like a bump, and would have gladly gone unnoticed.
I crawled past him looking for signs of Shakespeare. Carefully
I lifted fallen leaves, picked up broken branches and inspected

them, then put them back in the exact same spot. I observed small limestone pebbles to see if they had been pressed into the mud by a great weight. But there was nothing. If he had come through, how could he not have left at least one track?

I went back to the pool, knelt down, cupped my hands and took a long drink of water, wiped my face and looked up at the sky, then down at my watch. I had been in the swamp not more than six hours, though it felt like much longer. Time, I thought, has no place here. So I took my watch off and dropped it in the deep end, watching as it sank slowly into a dark shadow out of sight. That's what time is all about anyway, I thought. With a long quiet sigh, I sat back on my heels, took out a portion of deer meat and placed it in the mud.

At that moment, within the density, something moved. I gazed at the swamp. Another movement rustled branches.

Had Shakespeare been there all the time, studying my every move, smelling the trail of deer meat, calculating the exact moment to attack? Had he been waiting in ambush all this time? Had the balance of nature finally put me directly in his path? Suddenly I felt empty, defenseless, yet tensing my thighs as if believing I might actually spring up out of the swamp to safety. But at the same time, though I didn't stand a chance of survival in combat with the cat, I was strangely intrigued to be so close to such a wild creature on the prowl for prey.

My hands shook, wet with sweat. I swallowed hard. I could feel the muscles in my neck quivering. A burning, striking pain rushed across my solar plexus. I felt dizzy and fought disorientation.

I had had that same feeling in Vietnam every time I walked through a village on patrol wondering if a rifle was sticking out of a hut window aimed at my back. I would jerk around looking for that rifle, almost expecting to see the flash from the barrel, then feel the explosion in my back or face. I never got used to walking through villages. I never got used to anything in Vietnam. Not even the long, boring times at Chu Lai Base Camp, months on end of doing nothing. Then suddenly an operation would form and we would be off on a truck convoy to Tam Key, choppered into Outpost Fourteen, or strung out on perimeter guard.

God, if I am to die in this swamp, I thought, by what better means than the panther? If he is to be my executioner, then so be it. I will fight him to the last breath, but I welcome this means of death. It would be quick, beautiful, worthy, necessary. In Nam, no death was necessary or beautiful, though it was often quick. I had prepared myself for this a long time ago. It gave me the edge on danger.

There was another movement and the density parted slightly. Now I did want to run, as fast and hard and as far away as I could get. But that defiant element of facing danger stopped me. The next sight would be a hunched cat, eyes aflame, fangs bared.

But to my utter amazement a small, round, red eye with a black dot in the middle appeared in the green. Panthers don't have eyes like that!

Then a brilliance in full nuptial plumage side-slipped out into the open water. I squinted to make sure I wasn't hallucinating. It was a drake wood duck. His gaudy array of colors shone in the sun and contrasted against the green from which he had emerged. His head and crest were an iridescent greenish-purple. White streaks ran over and behind his eyes to the back of his head. He had a beautiful white throat with two up-pointed bars extending to the sides of his head, almost as though they had been painted there with smooth, long brush strokes. Chestnut plumage went down his neck, giving way to black and white crescents in front of his wings. Yellowish-gray buffy sides blended with white underneath.

Like all wild animals who have been around men, he seemed shy, wary of my presence and quickly paddled back into the cattails.

I felt both relief and disappointment. I had been spared, of course, but yet I was dissatisfied that the cat had not been there. He could easily have torn me apart in seconds, left me like the deer to disintegrate in the oozing mud. And yet I felt even that would have lent something to the saving of the panther.

Slowly I rose to a crouched posture and backed out of

sight, listening to the wood duck's feet and wingtips scampering and slapping across the water to full flight.

16

Resting Site

> **Swamp notes—next to a strangler fig**
> *Shakespeare leaves so many signs in this wondrous swamp. I long to know them all, but I suspect I have already walked past more than I have noticed—those that are so small that only another panther would be able to find them.*

Soon I spotted an old cypress wood cabin almost completely lost in the entwining clutches of a thick quilt of vines. They climbed up on the roof and hung over the sides, making the cabin look like a cave on stilts. The crumbling cypress stilts, which once had held it above the waterline, now caused the cabin to sit lopsided like a shipwreck.

On the doorway frame and extending down to a small porch was a strangler fig tree, its thick tentacle roots giving it the appearance of a deep-sea squid wrapped around prey. The door itself hung loose on rusty beer cans flattened out and nailed on. A pulsating column of red ants marched up and down the center, while a sulphur butterfly momentarily rested on the handle.

This might be a resting site for Shakespeare in daylight hours, a place for him to find refuge from anything or anyone who wished harm to him. It might also be a perfect place for him from which to observe game and ambush prey.

I moved forward as slowly as a slug, not ruling out the possibility he might be inside. I listened for the slightest creak of a great weight on worn wood or the splashing of water behind the cabin and riveted my eyes on the door in case he suddenly bolted out. My sixth sense told me to be cautious. But there was no sound, no movement, only that undefined jungle stillness.

This cabin reminded me of the hooches in villages in Vietnam. At Tuy Hoa we eventually had to check out every one of them to make sure the VC hadn't sneaked in during the night. It was brain-racking coming up to them because it was so easy for a VC to shoot out of one of the open windows before we could detect him.

I remembered the first time I went out on patrol into the village walking out front of a squad, my eyelids glued to my forehead, darting looks at every hooch, every open window, every door. If the doors were closed, I was more worried. The dark window opening could be framing a rifle farther inside the hooch. The grass roof could be hiding a sniper willing to sacrifice his life for a close, clean shot at an American, and I was the first target he would see. I carried my M-14 cowboy-style on my hip. I had switched it over to rock and roll (automatic fire) and I kept the barrel moving back and forth all over the hooch, my finger on the trigger, wishfully thinking I would somehow get the first shot off, giving me enough time to fall to the ground and get out of the line of fire from the squad behind me.

That first hooch I checked out was the worst one. They were never easy after that, but the first one was the one that gave me a lesson on how to keep my head under that kind of war pressure.

It was three days into the operation, and I already felt war-wise with Buck's death and that first fire-fight swallowed down hard into me somewhere. Charlie had shown us he was not in the least afraid of us and had even offered us the chance to fight back to see who was going to come out on top. This was one of those head wars, too. Psyche-outsville. The VC were playing with our nerves, stretching and twisting them with sporadic sniper fire from the hill. They boldly walked out in front of our perimeter line near the river out of range of our rifles, taunting us to shoot at them. They pushed their children out in front of them to see if we would fire on them.

They sent their women into the village to pick up supplies, acting as though we weren't even there. They wired up their hooch doors with trip wires, but no explosives at the other end. They dug holes at their doorways and filled them with pungi stakes, with human excrement on the tips. They left live ammunition in key places that looked as though they had accidentally dropped it. They even left us a barrelful of peanuts. The corpsmen checked it out and told us there was dried urine all over them.

So by the time I had reached the center of the village, having dodged every suspicious pile or hole in the sand in order to miss land mines they might have put in the night before, my mind was already exhausted. Word came from the lieutenant that he wanted the other side of the village checked out thoroughly—inside hooches, down in the ditches leading to the rice paddies, and along a wide treeline that could be good cover at night for VC infiltration.

The first hooch I came onto was a well-constructed, plastered, bamboo-walled, thatched hut with a single open door. From the angle I was looking at it, I could see a stone patio in back with an animal stall on the far side. It must have been for a water buffalo because of the large dried patties on the ground. On the side next to me was a strange-looking structure that looked like a cage. But for what I didn't know. It was too big for a bird and too small for a man.

The door went into a main room. Two windows were on each side of the opening. I stared at the left window, then at the door, then at the right window, then back at the left window. I was wishing hard that I had three eyes that could look at all three locations at the same time for movement—something that might indicate hostile action. But there was nothing.

Out of reaction rather than thought, I ran up to the right window, slammed against the side, and slowly turned and peered in, almost expecting to get my face blown off from a bullet fired at point-blank range. After being in the sun, it was hard to adjust my eyes to the darkness inside, but I did the best I could, breathing hard, glancing back at the squad who were now all hiding behind trees and the stone well in the middle of the village.

I ran my hand down to a fragmentation grenade in my pouch, contemplating pulling the pin, dunking it into the window and being done with the whole thing. But the lieutenant wanted it checked out. He didn't say search and destroy, or give us permission for a temporary free-fire zone. So I looked in again. And when I did my heart jumped and I lost my breath. A shadow dashed across the back wall behind a clay stove. I jerked my head away from the window, then signaled to the squad with a hand motion to stay down.

My hand went back down to the grenade, hesitated, then took it out. I stared down at the pin and put my finger through it. But I couldn't pull it. What if that shadow belonged to a small, frightened child that had somehow been misplaced by his mother in the shuffle to get out of the village when we came in, and had been hiding out in that hooch all this time, hungry, thirsty, maybe even whimpering?

But what if it was a jungle-trained, Viet Cong sapper taking his chances of using that hooch to hide in during the day and creeping around our lines at night collecting data for a VC mortar team not far off in the hills? Maybe I was up against a seasoned Charlie guerilla, one who knew night tactics like the back of his hand, and who for kicks tried to see how close he could get to our perimeter without being detected. For even though I had been trained for it, I wasn't looking for hand-to-hand combat with somebody like that—not just yet, and, I hoped, never. How many Americans had that VC killed already? How many notches had he carved into the banana knife tucked in his black pajamas? Was he carrying American ears around his neck? And was he carrying an intense hate for all Americans because his family had been bombed out in a B-52 air raid? I decided I better throw that grenade in fast, stick my rifle in behind the explosion and fill it with a magazine of 7.62-mm. bullets to ensure I would not have to tangle with this killer . . . if he was there. That was the safest way if I wanted to be around a little longer.

So I drew the grenade up to my chest and began pulling the pin when I heard a faint squeak from inside. A child, I thought. It had to be a child. I put the grenade back into my pouch, crouched, and went under the window to the door, quickly looked in, then boldly walked through the doorway and looked over at the clay oven. What I saw staring back at me left my hands limp, my legs turning to jelly, my stomach tightening so hard it ached, and my throat feeling like a thick steel pipe.

At that second I could have been sliced right in half by a VC machine gun, never knowing what had hit me. At that second I could have been run through with a machete pinning me right onto the bamboo wall, my face draining of the blood that would drip onto the dirt beneath me. I was trapped, and there wasn't a thing I could do about it. I almost wanted to turn my own rifle on myself for being so stupid to have put myself in such a vulnerable position.

The keeper of that shadow, the keeper of that squeak was one of the largest, darkest, ugliest creatures I had ever seen: a giant hump-backed jungle rat with a long bare tail that swept back and forth on the dusty floor. Crooked teeth snarled at me as this gutter animal went up on his hind feet and probed the air with a narrow, wet nose that sat in the center of his long whiskers. There I stood with a high-powered rifle and grenade, spellbound by this garbage robber. I could have blown him away in seconds by simply lowering my barrel and cranking off one round, but in those seconds I couldn't even breathe. All that time I had been holding my breath and then I found myself backing up into the sunlight. Finally I reacted and opened up on the rat, sending flesh, blood and chunks of bone all over the inside of the hooch. I looked down at my jungle trousers and there were bits of black hair on them, and on the toes of my boots dusty blood soaked the leather.

That rat stayed with me in nightmares for a long time. I kept seeing legs on it and hands holding a rifle, a sneer from a VC face. Then, just before the bullet ripped into me the scene would change and the VC would turn into a tiny child huddled in the corner, squeaking, the picture of innocence except for the long bare tail that emerged from his body and swept back and forth on the dirt floor.

Now, going up to the doorway of this cabin in the swamp, I carefully peered inside, working hard to pay heed to all of my six senses, and working just as hard to ignore the irrational flashes of hooch-searching memories that were trying to swamp my mind. At the far corner, a sword of sunlight sliced through thick dust onto a puddle of water where the swamp had seeped in. Pieces of wood floated about on surface film, acting as life rafts for ants, water spiders and weary mosquitoes. A green water snake coiled in the shade of a corner. Wrens, nesting in the rafters, chattered and flew out of a window, then returned with another fury of protest. The air smelled of wet spongy wood, damp vegetation and stagnant water. What dry floor was left was covered with old raccoon scat full of crawfish shells and muscadine berry seeds.

When I went inside, the wrens protested once again, then left me to my investigation. At first my glance landed in the corner near the door where the sun would never reach. There layers of dust and dirt had been swept about to leave a cleared area where an animal might have lain down.

But there was something else, something that stunned me. Scraped deep across the planks were long, wide claw marks. And even more important and shocking, this wood scraping was new!

The cypress had been opened up maybe a day ago. I could just see Shakespeare stretching out, extending his posterior upwards, then gouging his extended claws into the wood, pulling them towards his body again and again, the wood splintering as his claws dug into it.

I sat on my calves staring at the deep scratches. How close I felt to him. How close he was to me.

My immediate thought was to sit it out in the bushline and wait for his return. Surely he would come back to this superb hiding place. But then I figured he wouldn't be back here for quite a while. I had just contaminated the site. My very presence had left an invisible, human scent to warn him of foreign encroachment.

It seemed a reasonable conclusion that I now had a resting site. On my map I plotted and designated it. This was the third page of my life with Shakespeare.

When I left, I felt I had left part of my self there just as Shakespeare had done. His scent. My scent. His spirit. My spirit.

17

Seminole

Swamp notes—under ghost orchids
The Indians are the real owners of the swamp
as they have always been. They know how
to live with the land instead of against it,
to take what they need for survival, then
replace it. The Indians know what it will
take to save the panther. Their good med-
icine may be the only answer.

I had suspected for a long time that someone was nearby, but when he appeared on the strand, the shock of seeing another human being there in a wild part of the swamp where I thought no one else ever went rocked me.

He was a young Seminole Indian and seemed to be carved out of the raw material of the swamp. Close to six feet tall, lean, strong, he was as slim as a deer, and his streamlined muscles flexed as though at any second he could instantly sprint off into the swamp like Shakespeare.

Wearing only blue jean cut-offs, his almost naked body glistened a copper-bronze tinted with red under a narrow ribbon of sunlight. His shiny black hair flowed to his shoulders, straight, long and thick.

Extremely remote, deep-set, mistrusting eyes under a lofty brow gave him a stern, closed face which was nevertheless broad and handsome. Those eyes coldly gazed into mine with fibers of fierce independence inseparable from the sacred earth. I stared back at him.

He seemed like an earth man, the epitome of all the Indians who ever lived in the glades, emerging from the wilds, part of them, standing vigil, carrying in him the ancient secrets of survival, and yet, like the panther, an endangered species.

Almost annihilated by the white men who had pushed

them farther and farther south, his tribe had ended up in the Everglades and quickly adapted to the environment and made it their home. But again they were preyed upon, their numbers lowered to a few hundred. But they are still with us today, standing witness to life in harmony with the swamp.

I wanted to approach this Indian, somehow to tell him of our common purpose, our brotherhood. I wanted his blood to be my blood. I wanted to touch him, to symbolize our affinity, to feel his strength as mine, to know I could turn to him for help. I wanted to merge our souls for the slightest second, just as I wanted to do with Shakespeare. And in so doing gain earth power.

But that would never be. The look in his eyes was not friendship. It was mistrust. And close behind that there seemed to be anger near the threshold of attack. And that's exactly what I thought he was going to do.

I quickly calculated my options: fight or run. As for the first, I had no desire to meet this man in combat—though it might have been an even match, my muscles and reflexes as hardened and quickened as his from years in the swamp. I prepared to sprint.

But instead of moving toward me, he just stood there staring, causing me to look away. His anger at the white man was stronger than my desire for affinity. Maybe it was open hatred. Maybe he thought I was a direct threat to him. But still I tried to absorb that anger and thought nothing less of him. He had the right. Look at what we have done to his home. What would we do if he ran a bulldozer through our living room?

I was sure now I was treading on Seminole land, or at the very least a part of the swamp the Indians considered theirs. Should I have sought him out and gotten permission? How long had he been watching me before he showed himself? Did he know I was tracking panther? Would he now leave me alone?

For a while he stood staring. Then he moved forward toward me in a fluid motion, the water hardly disturbed. Halting to glance at a flickering warbler, he came closer and stopped. I prepared for the worst.

Abruptly, he turned his back on me and eased back

into the swamp until only a small foam trail was left in the water. What did that mean?

I had a naive impulse to run after him and find out. But that would have been stupid. After a lot of contemplation, I decided that if he had wanted me out of the swamp he would have run me out. But by not speaking and leaving me there with my tongue hanging out, he had given me two roads to take. I could get out and never come back. Or, as long as I didn't bother or destroy anything, I could do what I had to do, then leave the glades untouched. I couldn't leave, now or ever. I would have to hope he offered that second option and just see what I could do about extending my time allowance.

In his strange Indian way he may have been helping me to save the panther. Though I may never see him again, he may be out there at my side in the next hammock, on the next river, in a cypress swamp, or far south in the mangroves, maybe even on one of the wild beaches. He may never show himself again, but then he may know what I'm doing and help me in his own way. Just by being there.

Nam Yo Fara On.

18

Devil's Pool

Swamp notes—feeling eternal mercy
I had been close to death many times in my life before I made peace with my Maker. Now, though I will fight with claw and fang to stay alive, I feel death is strange but not something evil, not something that can hurt me. Sometimes I feel I can never die.

I went on through the swamp, dwelling on that Indian, his presence. He was so much at one with the wilds, so close to the animals. Being like him would be almost like being Shakespeare. What would it take? How could I accomplish that, I wondered. My mind was lost in that question, turned in on itself, looking for that one thread of creativity that would lead me to Shakespeare's soul—when suddenly my feet dropped out from under me and I plunged underwater into a hidden, suffocating abyss of cold, black swamp water.

I was completely disoriented and within seconds oxygen was sucked out of my lungs. All I could see were shapeless, vibrating air bubbles floating up to a fading narrow hole above me.

My backpack had become a wet cement block, and I realized I wasn't coming up. Death's hands were pulling at my feet. I began kicking and thrashing, trying to swim upward, to somehow pull my way to that rapidly disappearing narrow opening, but it wasn't working and I kept going down. I tore the pack off my back. My lungs aching for air, I opened my mouth to keep from breathing the water in, but swallowed water instead. I was about to let go of my pack when my other hand hit the rocky side of the hole. I frantically started grabbing at those rocks, catching hold, desperately climbing up, gasping water, and using my feet to stop myself from sinking back down.

I stared up through the black churning water at a bright, quivering hole above, and with all my strength, all the energy I could muster up from the deepest inside of my guts, I clawed my way up to that brightness, still hanging on to my pack. In a last surging attempt, I broke free to the surface, gasping for air, hanging on to the rock side with bleeding fingers, vomiting, my heart pounding against my chest in long thumps as though on the verge of exploding.

Every time I vomited water I swallowed hard, breathing in longer and harder. I lay there for a long time, weak, shaken, still disoriented, trying to figure out why this thing ever happened.

I had learned yet another lesson in the glades: make a mistake, lose my concentration, and it would mean my life, a one-way trip to what the Seminoles called the Land-of-the-Big-Pahokee. This rare, wild swamp was as dangerous as it was beautiful, and it could as easily destroy me—with terrifying suddenness—as protect me. Truly there was eternal mercy here—but also death in its rawest form and in ways I was not yet aware of. I had forgotten myself and made a stupid mistake by stumbling into what the Indians called a devil's pool. A mistake seldom, if ever, repeated.

I meditated on that for a long time and it reminded me of an even worse mistake, a deadly, perverted mistake in Vietnam that had also left me weak and shaken. But in Nam there was no eternal mercy—only death, the kind of unnecessary death that has no business in any war but occurs in every one of them. It was a stupid error that could have been prevented if we had just checked things out a little further. But we hadn't.

Two weeks into our first operation we all began to feel war-wise. We had been shot at continuously, been in a furious firefight and won, looked into the belly of death and so far had survived, had gone on numerous patrols and even night recon for VC infiltration from across the river, even taunted the VC snipers by standing up in our foxholes and drawing their fire, then laying a salvo of 105 rounds in their laps to blow them to hell and back.

Our bodies were sunburned and blistered, heads frying under our helmets, eyes weak by the end of the day from the intense brightness of the sun and sand. We'd all lost water weight—the sweat drying on our skin as quickly as it formed. But we all felt pretty good and figured we were going to make the operation with a low casualty ratio. So far we had dealt Charlie the worse hand. But our confidence gradually slipped over to aloofness, and we lost our concentration. It is the worst mistake ever to make in a war. It gave an opening for danger and death to creep in. It gave us a lesson from the devil we didn't want or need. But then, death was always lurking about looking for that opening.

One of our guys from communications platoon had gone out in front of the perimeter on our right flank just below the hill where we had taken a lot of incoming rounds. We figured the whole hill was honeycombed with VC tunnel networks dug years ago for just such a war. It was nothing for VC to pop up out of a hole behind a bush, crank off a belt of ammo, and before we could zero in on him, pop back down only to come up somewhere else on the hill with a fresh belt of ammo ready to go at it again. We called it "Harassment Hill" and concluded that if we bombed it for a week there would still be VC popping up out of new holes. So we put up with it.

The reason the communication marine went out there at dusk was to reset firing line stakes and trip wires for claymore mines. But as the scoop came down to us later, he had failed to tell the perimeter guard where he was going, why, and how long it would take him to get back. It was even said that he had gone out too late when the sun was already going down, making it hard to see the hill. Where during the day we saw bushes, now we saw shadows that formed, crept about, slid through the vegetation like snakes, and sometimes jumped from rock to rock. From the edge of the hill to the perimeter measured only fifty meters. A VC could easily sneak up and throw a grenade over the barbed wire and sand wall and escape before he got cut down. The guys over there were all going squirreling anyway, shooting at those shadows, calling in a fire mission to blow rocks to bits, even calling for white light before it was dark. And being on one hundred percent watch 24 hours a day was enough to put us all on edge.

I was sitting in my foxhole cursing at the turkey in my c-ration can, trying to stomach it, and at the same time looking out at the village which was beginning to look like a typhoon had gutted out the center of it. In the past two weeks it had taken hundreds of mortar and cannon rounds. Pockmarked and charcoaled in places, it was on its way to total destruction.

I remember forcing a spoonful of turkey into my mouth, then spitting it out on the hot sand, watching it ooze down the side of the hole in the sweltering heat, then throwing the whole can out, when suddenly the chatter of M-14 rifle fire on rock and roll clattered across the perimeter from the right flank. That burst was followed by several more semi-automatic rounds, then stale and smoky silence. A cry came from the hill and I thought for sure the guys finally zapped a VC there. Then there was that spooky silence again. We all waited for the word to come down the lines about what exactly had happened. When the word came, it was predictable. A VC had ventured in too close, found himself exposed to the perimeter and got zapped pure and simple. When morning came, a patrol would be sent out to pick up the body and the count would be called in to the CP aboard ship. One VC dead, another million to go.

But when morning came there was one marine unaccounted for. A communication marine. A marine who had gone out at dusk to set the stakes and trip wires. Nobody seemed to know where he was. Had he gone out on the last chopper? Or was he at the other side of the perimeter with somebody else? He could not be found anywhere inside the perimeter. The captain was worried. He sent a patrol out along the hill's edge in front of the right flank's line.

Minutes later the patrol carried a body back in and over to the CP. It was the communication marine with 14 bullet holes in him. When the right flank had thought a VC was sneaking around out there, they had made a mistake. A costly mistake. The captain called it "death by friendly fire." I gagged. How could any death in war from bullets be called death by "friendly" fire, whether the fire was from the enemy or our own guys?

The marine who had opened up first threw his rifle out of the perimeter and refused to go get it. He even gave the lieutenant the finger and screamed that if he ever picked up his rifle again he would shoot himself. The lieutenant jumped on him and wrestled him to the ground, calmed him as much as possible, and med-evaced him out to the ship.

I sat there shuddering. I didn't go see that KIA. I didn't have to. I was feeling as bad as the marine who shot him first. That war-wisdom we had all valiantly demonstrated floated away above the sand and the waves of heat. In a very direct sense we all shared that shooting, even those of us who had not pulled a trigger. When training for a war, and then fighting that war in units of platoon and battalion size, the troops begin to think and feel alike. Moods sweep over a unit like waves. If there was joy, even ecstasy, from success in a maneuver, all of us felt it together. It was like one mind was thinking, one body reacting, one soul. Each one of us took on the mass attitude, whatever it was at the time. If there was confidence, we all shared it. When a 105 barrage leveled a part of the hill and silenced a VC sniper, we all jumped for joy as though we all had run over to the cannons and pulled the wires ourselves. All of it came from the same war machine, a destructive power plant invented, developed, perfected over centuries. We were just the most recent embodiment of it.

And when death by "friendly" fire struck one of us down, then we all felt remorse. We were all responsible.

It was a long time before I picked up my pack and set out again, carefully skirting that devil's pool. In fact, it had been a long time in my life before I was able to shed a lot of guilt that KIA brought on. All I could see were his parents staring out at nothing and asking why. But out here in the glades I had given birth to a whole new attitude—to live on my own terms, terms that I would set up as an individual, and terms that would save this big cat.

I moved on through the water, glancing back at where the bottomless pit was lurking, and smiled. To me it was just a reminder to keep alert and never lose my concentration. No more mistakes on my way to the cat.

19

Scat

Swamp notes—inspecting spoor
Each time I find a shred of evidence of
Shakespeare's life it puts me closer to him.
My heart pounds. I look off into the swamp
and smile.

Every piece of evidence I had found so far had drawn me closer to Shakespeare, and him to me. Was he, in his animal way, seeking me as feverishly as I was seeking him? Could we really merge our spirits in a suspended second of truce—and truth—between man and animal? This I prayed for.

Through waist-deep water I separated floating bladder-worts. A green heron, crown feathers spread up in anger, flew off in front of me on the trail which looked like an old swollen scar between the low places.

When I got to the trail I found poison ivy vines stretched across it between sabal palms. No man had walked this trail for a long time. There were no human paths, only those vague arterials made by small paws.

I crept along for more than an hour, studying every fraction of ground. I passed an alligator slide well cleared out and used often. The skeletal remains of a small snake were strewn about over cypress needles. I came across the carcass of a rat, newly killed by a hawk which I was sure I spooked just minutes before. The rat's hind legs still twitched, head torn open by the hooked beak of his slayer.

The eeriest thing I saw was an old human skull under shallow water, the head and eye sockets peering out of black mud. My curiosity almost made me jump into the water and dig it out, but my respect for swamp law stopped me. No one in his right mind touches the remains of a human in the depth of the swamp. There's an old swamp legend that if you do, you release an evil spirit to roam the glades in search of dead things. I wasn't about to put my hands on that skull.

Twice I stumbled over cypress knees just pushing up to the surface, hidden under the carpet of thick leaves and palm fronds. The third time I tripped I stared down at what I thought was a small pile of white rocks, a marker for a lost hunter. What caught my eye was how neatly they were placed on the leaves. But when I picked up a pebble, it crumbled and fragments of bone fell from it to the ground.

It was a nice pile of scat, bleached out and hardened by sun, weather and time. I knelt over it and measured the longest plug. Eight inches. But what was even more significant was the circumference. More than three inches. No bobcat had dropped this.

Not more that a few feet away was another pile of scat, just as large and bleached out. No doubt about it. Both were Shakespeare's.

With a naturalist's eye I inspected it all. After his meal, the big cat's intestines had operated quite efficiently. This scat showed teeth and claws well packed inside the long, thick, densely compacted plug of thick hair evenly distributed and easily protecting the intestinal walls as it was excreted. Grass threaded through the plug and not having been digested, had acted in soft, cleansing sweeps across the walls, gently ridding them of bacteria and debris.

I broke open another plug and smelled the dry, stale odor. I examined the hair. On the outside it was gray-white. An opossum. In another plug was brownish hair mixed in with long fawn-gray strands. The gray hair was from a rabbit, marsh or cottontail. The brown hair from a deer. The dead buck in the clearing ran across my mind and almost like an invisible white beam of light I felt the two connect. Like all the evidence so far, I plotted it on my map and left it in its exact spot. This was the fourth page in my life with Shakespeare.

20

Survival Food

> **Swamp notes—deep in**
> The swamp is my mother and will provide anything I need to survive. In this primeval place are some of the most nourishing foods man could ever want to stay healthy. I seek them out, relish their taste, take them into my body, cherish their nutrients, laugh at those who find them repulsive.

I took a break to catch a young dragonfly and put him on my hook. Before long I had a small, slippery catfish. I cleaned it quickly and wrapped it in a section of sabal palm frond and added pickerel weed seeds for seasoning. I found some branches dry enough to start a fire and then put a small log over it and put the fish on top.

Then I started food gathering. My senses were always my best guide in picking out good wilderness food. Also, I had studied and tested wildlife foods with other naturalists, park rangers and swampmen. If it looked clean, fresh and healthy, and smelled fairly decent with no foul scent, and wasn't poisonous, and then didn't taste bitter or sour, it was good to eat.

The swamp is a produce, meat, fish and poultry market anyway, so I had plenty to choose from.

Fresh water was the first priority. There had been no recent rains, so I went to the edge of a gator hole and gathered two handfuls of small limestone rocks. I took off my bandanna and placed the rocks in it, then dug a small hole and lined it with palm fronds. I dipped my bandanna into the water and strained the water through the rocks into the palm-lined hole to filter out any large bacterial growth that might have formed from contamination by a dead animal.

Then I dug a finger-size ditch from the small hole down an incline and, putting a portion of my shirt over my empty canteen mouth to strain it once again, let the water run into the canteen. Tying a thin vine around its neck to secure it, I dropped the canteen into the gator hole to keep the water cool.

Next a wilderness salad. All of the plant life in the swamp is organically grown with natural minerals in the swamp muck, so it would all be nutritious. But plants must be chosen very carefully because some, like the rosary bead and the Brazilian pepper heads, are poisonous.

On the logs near the water in a low part of the swamp were green coin-shaped plants called pennyworts. I picked a handful of the youngest and most tender, then found a mus-cadine vine and picked some of its tender young leaves. Then I went to the water's edge and pulled up four cattail plants. I cut off the stems and laid them aside. Pulling open the white bases, I got to the tender hearts of the cattails, cut them out, and laid them aside as well. These I would eat like onions. Tender, juicy grass roots were cut up and sprinkled over the muscadine leaves and pennywort. With a little honey added, it turned into an inviting salad.

When I looked about the ground, trees, bushes, flowers, and deep into the mud, I found another choice food product. I dug my hands into the mud and let these creatures run about my fingers. In the air, they sped past me and on top of the water they darted like tiny buffaloes. Insects. Eating them is not so vile as consuming some of the junk foods found on the grocery shelves these days. In fact insects are far more nutritious.

I was first introduced to insects as a steady diet for people when I was in the Philippines on Mindoro Island. There I watched the people relish the large brown cockroach for breakfast, dinner and supper. They were also quite fond of a very colorful long worm they found in abundance under dead logs and in the sides of hills.

At the time, I was repulsed by the sight of a freshly caught beetle being quickly browned in a pan and then gobbled up by the children, but later I found this was like a rare T-bone steak to them. For those people it was a delicacy.

I have been told there are African tribes that crave termites, eating them greedily, as we do popcorn. And I have since been told there are people in the Southern United States who consider it a rare treat when they get chocolate-covered black ants for an appetizer.

Insects have been with us as long as plants have, and all through the ages animals and man have eaten them for survival. They are loaded with calories, crammed full of vitamins, and high on the list for protein content. It seems evident now that they would be a very good choice for an alternative food for those millions of people who are now starving. Without too much trouble, insects could be introduced into our diets without our even being aware of it.

I located three good-sized black cockroaches, wrapped them in with the catfish, and put them all closer to the fire.

The thought of freshwater shrimp coupled with willow bush leaves made my mouth water. I looked for shrimp, but instead found several large apple snails in the mud near the water. I wrapped the apple snails, fish and willow leaves inside strangler fig leaves, tied the bundle together with vines, and placed it on the coals that had dropped off the log. I dug a small hole and put all of this in it, then covered the hole with branches and a little mud and added more coals on top.

Sitting Indian-style close by, I relaxed as I sipped the water and wove a square plate out of the cattail stems.

Soon the aroma made me so hungry I couldn't stand it any longer. I uncovered the hole and peeled the fronds from the steaming fish, snails and roaches. I put them on my plate and gorged myself. When I finished, I sought out some strangler fig fruits for dessert.

Hunger satisfied, my urge to move on and track Shakespeare revived. And that I did with the strength of the swamp within me.

21

White Eagle

> **Swamp notes—under a solitary cypress**
> I am always pleasantly surprised by seeing
> something new in the swamp, something
> different, something that stirs my soul to go
> on with even more vitality. I relish the thrill
> of creeping up on animals and observing,
> unnoticed. I wonder how often they have
> crept up on me and observed, unnoticed.

I was about to move when my sixth sense told me I was being watched. I read the wilds. My eyes moved in long curves above and below the treeline, on the ground, through swamp fern, along the waterline, over a stump, among stiff-leaved air plants. Then they came across a high branch on a solitary cypress near where I was lying. Large, hooked talons grasped the bark with a strength unknown to man, unknown to the prey population until those talons had plunged through thick fur, and then it was too late.

There perched on the thick branch, was a creature that almost stopped my heart. So close was he to me that the only thing I could do was stand rigid, unnaturally so, and plead inwardly to nature to give me the power not to startle him.

My eyes went up sturdy limbs and onto a full chest of black-brown feathers, then onto the bird fully. I couldn't believe it. Right there, not more than twenty feet up, was an endangered Southern bald eagle. He had to be at least two-and-a-half feet tall. He demonstrated his enormous wing-spread as he balanced himself in a breeze, then settled his wings again carefully around his body, folding each feather perfectly into place. Those feathers and the snow white plumage on his head blended with the shadows and sky to make him seem almost transparent. His hooked, yellow beak glowed like gold in white light. I could see straight into his alert, yellow eyes, eyes that roved about the wilds with an intense stare, diligently inspecting this swamp, looking skyward, then down into the maze of trees.

There has been so much written about this national bird as a symbol of liberty and justice, more than any other bird in the Western Hemisphere; and yet, like Shakespeare, he is on both the state and federal lists of species on the verge of extinction, yet still hunted, still poisoned, still on the way out of existence. It has taken nature so long to perfect this animal, so long to mold it into a top link in the food chain. Does man have the right to destroy it in a few short years? It is a sad commentary that a nation of people who believe in freedom—and who will quickly send young men to foreign countries to battle for freedom for others—would deny this homeland symbol, a symbol of freedom, his own rightful place on earth.

How many times had I stood in formation at attention staring at the eagle above the American flag on a proud pole during roll call at Chu Lai Base Camp, while in the far distance alongside a hill the curling white smoke of mortars exploding bordered this great bird's wings? Later, at a medical center near a chopper landing zone, flat on my side because I couldn't stand or sit up, I had spent weeks lying there staring at that same eagle set atop a grass-roofed church. While other marines around me died in their sleep, I lay there healing from wounds taken in a VC ambush—all under the sign of the eagle.

I remembered too, when I first came back to the States, staring into the tearful eyes of a mother who had recently lost her son in Vietnam, and then staring at the medals he had won. She had them all carefully placed on a flag with the eagle standing proudly above it.

I remembered dreams of the eagle, sometimes dreadful nightmares. Always he was a fantasy, a solid statue clutching branches.

But now I stood there in the midst of the Everglades, spellbound, watching this great bird look down at me, his eyes probing mine more deeply than mine probed his. What was he seeing in me? Did he detect just another man? Or was he as absorbed in me as I was in him? Did he care I was even there?

I kept my eyes open wide, looking for some sign of recognition. But so intense was he about keeping his eyes on mine that I ended up looking away twice, each time returning to that stare.

Suddenly, in a graceful silent ascent, he dove from the tree, flapped his wings and rose above the swamp, catching the wind, floating up in it, dissolving into the brightness of the sun as though a huge veil had opened up. But against that brilliance I did not see just a bird disappearing. What I saw was the distinct outline of a transfiguration vanishing in an ascension toward the land of wild things untamed forever. What I saw was the timeless symbol of mankind that would never go extinct. What I saw was a white eagle, the Great White Eagle, that deep in the heart everyone sees.

It was no revelation to understand what was happening with this eagle. For it happens with all who dare to probe the mysteries of the wilds. The Great White Eagle is in all of us, in every soul, every cell, every thought. The White Eagle is mankind's supreme spiritual victory over himself. Anyone can look at an eagle, but those who dare to look within, to probe that eagle's soul, find their own souls.

I looked to the north, toward my affinity with Shakespeare, putting one foot in front of the other, smiling, feeling deeply the message of the eagle, knowing as long as I did put one foot in front of the other I would attain my objective.

Book IV

Paw Prints in the Mud

The mystery leaves itself like a trail of breadcrumbs, and by the time your mind has eaten its way to the maker of the tracks, the mystery is inside you, part of you forever. The tracks of every mystery you have ever swallowed move inside your own tracks.
—*Tom Brown, Jr., Tracker*

22

Carnage

Swamp notes—in a dead swamp
Heartache for what we have already lost of the Everglades is a good sign. But that emotion must soon evolve into action not only to save what is left, but to try to replant the seedlings of what has been lost.

I pushed forward, slowly sinking into the tender bosom of this deep green corridor that wound through the swamp in a perpetual maze. Now willow bushes, maple, and cypress trees crowded the ground. Brown water snakes and snapping turtles poked their heads out of the water alongside.

I felt my wilderness obsession pushing me to go on a little farther, around the next curve, past a royal palm tree, up over a patch of love vine, and down into mud myriads once again.

When I finally emerged from this corridor, I stared disbelieving at a strange scene. At first it reminded me of a bombing site in Vietnam. Huge fallen cypress trees, some at least a thousand years old, lay strewn about. Some were half-submerged in the filmy black water, covered with birdnest fern and moss; others were floating about, stripped naked; while others still pushed out their edges in the water like half-buried bodies. The large tree stumps, perfectly cut across, sat like unmarked gravestones. The whole area was a decrepit, forgotten cemetery for a once magnificent giant cypress forest now slaughtered.

I felt something leave me as I scanned this horrid example of how mankind had performed premeditated rape and carnage on the only Everglades in the world. No wonder the panther was on the verge of extinction.

From the 1920's to the 1950's, and to some extent still

today, lumber companies leveled the cypress swamps of all the monarchs. Even more tragic, a great many of the trees cut down were never used. Wasted, they have been lying in the swamp all these years, their juices draining from them like blood from wounded soldiers on a battlefield.

A small bird's song sounded like a sob, and my sorrow for this unnecessary act of violence seeped into the swamp as well. I knew my sudden surge of anguish was not only for this terrible scene. It was also for the first village in Vietnam we were ordered to search and destroy. "Level it," was the order that had come through stiff lips from the CP.

Six patrols of ten marines each were sent out into the village. Every hooch that was left standing had to go. We took in C-4 plastic explosives and whole sacks of concussion grenades. Everybody carried two throw-away rocket launchers. One by one, we started blowing out all of the bomb shelters the villagers had made next to their homes. Then we started on the tunnels underneath the hooches that led out to the rice paddies and hills, not bothering to look and see if anybody was inside.

Explosion after explosion shook the ground. If there were any cries coming from the tunnels, we didn't hear them.

Then we started burning the hooches. With Zippo lighter fluid, matches and cigarette lighters we started fires on the grass roofs, inside on the furniture, out on wood piles next to the back doors. Blazes began to fill the village with snapping sheets of flame. Trees caught fire and swept large branches back and forth like great fiery paws of some flaming, writhing animal. We worked at it all morning, sweating until we were exhausted, until the entire village was aflame and blowing in the hot wind.

It was early in the game of war for me, and even though we had caught a lot of fire from the VC, had lost guys and taken wounded, we had already won this particular battle. Was it all that necessary to destroy the village so completely?

But the captain wanted it off the face of the earth, and even called in to Command to see if they could chopper out barrels of gasoline so we could fill the rice paddy fields and burn them out too. He wanted nothing left over for the VC to come back to.

So then we brought in bulldozers, and what had already burned down was then plowed up and buried by the machines' sharp blades. They tore into huts that had been smokehouses for fish, leveled the play areas for small children near the village square, smashed a stone well and filled it in. Water buffalo, spooked by all of this, ran for the river, but were cut down by an M-60 machine gun before they reached the tree-line.

The F-104's had a field day on the side of the hill and the old road winding around it. On run after run they hit it until the road was pocked with large holes and the hill looked like the side of an erupted volcano.

I remember sitting down against a tree, dazed from the heat, pulling my helmet off, my body screaming for fluid and salt. Eyes blinded by the sun, I took my canteen and poured it over my face. Then I heard a whimpering noise that grew louder and louder. I wiped my face and cleared my eyes and looked off at the south side of the village where the sound was coming from.

There I saw at least twenty women and children crowded together, some squatted down, some down on their knees with their heads in the sand and dirt. They were staring at their burning village, crying, bewildered at what we were doing. I had never before heard such a piercing, constant wail of sorrow. I jerked looks around at their village: roofs falling into the remains of the hooches, the bulldozers gouging out freshly planted gardens, marines running after dogs, the lieutenant shouting out orders to go back to the perimeter.

I looked back at the villagers and then at the ground. How would I have felt if a foreign government had sent a fighting force into my hometown and done this? I picked up my helmet and canteen and started walking away. Then I remembered I had left my rifle by the tree. When I turned to pick it up I was forced to look at those people again, especially the small children who had nothing to do with this strange war.

Standing in the swamp, I still remembered every one of those faces. They were staring at me from the cypress carnage spread out in front of me. As best I could, I collected my spirit and tried to contemplate what use all this might be to Shakespeare.

Finally I got my mind going. How would Shakespeare react to this part of his environment? At the least, he might have gone through it on his territorial rounds. Though he could swim when he had to, he probably walked and jumped from log to log, stump to stump, until he found solid ground again. The logs were certainly big enough to hold his weight.

So I started calculating a route through it all, picking out what the big cat might decide were the best logs to give him a safe passage. After mapping a path, I began leaping from log to log—in spite of the alligators gliding about like submarines—figuring that the clues to Shakespeare's passage I would most likely to find would be slash marks on the soft rotting wood.

As I moved ever so cautiously, I ran my hand across the tree trunks, almost hearing the whine of the huge saws as they ripped into the virgin wood. Twice I rested on immense logs forty feet long. I was sure a Seminole Indian on the Big Cypress reservation would have loved to have found those logs to make dugouts. Small cottonmouth moccasins kept me off ideal stepping logs. Once the slippery moss and clusters of fungus caused me to slam to a sitting position muffling a cry of pain. I was sure my testicles had turned blue.

The smell of this dead forest was like nothing civilized, distinctly its own, unwild, unnatural. It was of rich mold, wet, woody, brought on by a teeming swamp abyss of hiding, crawling wonders, stifling year-round humidity, heavy summer rainfall, winter draught, intense heat, and perhaps a million different wild organisms passing through it. How easy it was for Shakespeare to hide his scent in such a place.

I carefully stepped over snails curled into gold nuggets, a frog's leg bone bleached and fragmented, colonies of termites, camouflaged thorn bugs, an enormous, oval-shaped Australian cockroach, centipedes, and a small ring-necked snake.

I stopped abruptly more than once and held on for dear life when an alligator of any size approached too close. The only way I kept them uninterested was to throw clumps of wood into the water well away from me, causing them to streak swiftly toward the splashes probably thinking they were made by prey like garfish or bass.

Plump wood spiders dashed up my trousers. Anole lizards gobbled flies foolish enough to land on their logs, then skittered off for cover in the crevices.

Finally, though, I did make it to high ground on the other side. I was exhausted as I parted the bushes and found myself on still another unused trail. Or it may have been the same one I was on before, circling this cypress slough and coming around on the other side. Closer investigation proved this to be the case.

As I hit the high ground again, dizzied by the leaping and circling, it seemed for just a moment that I had just made it through a bombed-out Vietnamese village, bamboo posts strewn like cypress logs. But the moment passed and I knew that the carnage I had just waded through was an older wound. I asked myself if either would ever fully heal.

23

Bear

Swamp notes—on bear hammock
I saw death in Nam, looked it in the face, beat it at its own game; but sometimes in the glades I never know how close I am to that ultimate menace until the incident is over.

No sooner had I sat down on a fallen tree than the silence was pierced by the noise of air rushing through large nostrils. This snort, followed by several more, created a stranger silence, only to be broken by another snort.

It came from far down the trail to the south. As my heart skipped a beat, I quickly looked in that direction, intent on seeing the animal that made that hideous sound. In the distance I saw a large, black, wobbling object, periodically stopping to root, then continuing down the trail toward me. More snorts told me it was a wild boar, and I wasn't about to stay around and shake tusks with him. Boars have been known to run a man down and kill him.

I knew when he detected me because of the way he stopped and centered his gaze. But then the animal stood up on his haunches. There were round ears up and attentive, a thin Roman nose sniffing everything in the air. His fur was shaggy and the sunlight painted brown around his eyes and nose making him look like a man in a fur coat. It was no boar.

It was a black bear standing close to six feet tall and weighing probably three hundred pounds. It was now senseless for me to run. Hungry enough, that critter could easily track me down, even if I ran up a tree. So, like a mud turtle, I slipped back into the water neck-deep and probed my way out a good hundred feet to the longest, largest floating log, lily pads wrapping around my neck as I pushed my way through water hyacinth. I leaned against the log. The water kept rippling into my mouth and nose, but my profile and scent were literally washed out of the swamp, while my head and face were assaulted by a swarm of mosquitoes.

I lay in the water stiff as an oak tree, hoping the bear would choose to go the other way. Something brushed across my legs underwater, a creature long, soft and wiggly. Still I didn't move. Still I prayed the bear would go the other way.

But he didn't. I could hear him brush through the trees, snort, breathe heavily. He even opened up a small sabal palm tree and ate the heart. And I was sure I heard him lean on a larger palm tree, felling it, then moving on.

He was close now, and a big bear indeed. Coming along the treeline, he paused several times, looking through the vegetation as though he knew I was there but couldn't quite locate me. Each time he glanced I went underwater, holding for seconds, then slowly coming up to eye-level. Mosquitoes landed on my eye lashes. I could feel them crawling in my hair.

At the exact spot where I had gone into the water the bear stopped and sniffed around the ground. How I wished Shakespeare was between me and that bear. Panthers always have been known to stand up to a bear when confronted by one, and even win a battle.

The bear stepped into the water, then suddenly backed off and stared right into my eyes with his black eyes. Now he was sure I was there, and I couldn't look at him for very long. He stepped into the water toward me once again.

This is it, I thought. He's coming in after me. I was turning to swim away into even deeper water when I heard him splash up onto high ground. When I looked back he was already wobbling down the trail.

I couldn't imagine what made him lose interest, but to be on the safe side I stayed in the water next to that log for another half hour. Then, weary, I made my way back to the trail.

The bear's behavior was still playing on my mind, but I sighed and casually looked back at the log I had hidden behind. The blood left my face. My legs turned to rubber and my mouth became as dry as sand at low tide under a summer sun. On the other side of that log, not more than three feet away from it, was a ten-foot alligator.

24

Zen

> **Swamp notes—on Turkey Trail**
> I like to feel something surprising or un-
> expected is going to happen in the swamp
> each time I go out. Most of the time some-
> thing does.

For hours, days, weeks and months I tracked Shakespeare. Each time out was another step closer. Our relationship was maturing far beyond my first calculations.

That morning I was on Turkey Trail, the favorite haunt of Shakespeare. Though I had never found a fresh turkey kill, several times I had found feathers in clumps, ambush sites in high grass or near oak trees, and on one small island I did find a turkey skeleton with the skull.

I was moving slowly on all fours next to the trail near the treeline, constantly checking for lounging snakes. Shakespeare hadn't been in there for a long time. Earlier in the week I had found even older signs and was now concluding he had gone to the north end of his territory where there was more water and prey. In fact, Turkey Trail seemed void of all wildlife.

I stood up and walked out on the trail itself, ate a salt tablet, picked some muscadine berries nearby, ate them, and turned south.

Suddenly, to my left, swamp grass and wax myrtle bushes exploded like muffled concussion grenades. My entire body turned to gelatin melting in the humid sunlight. It was as though my mind instantly left my body, creating a momentary void in my life. A fragment of reality passed in front of me in the form of a brownish-gray mass of hide and fur leaping up and out, then down in the grass on spindle legs. It riveted me motionless to the ground.

I had let my guard down and had to pay the price. In Vietnam I would have been dead. In the Everglades I was rewarded with another wilderness rarity.

Still somewhat disoriented, I stared at the creature before me, not more than ten feet away. Large, liquid, dark bluish-brown eyes stared intensely back at me. They were strange, human-like eyes that portrayed fear, anticipation, and also more history of the glades than could ever be recorded. They were wild, yet gentle. Probing. And at the same time distant.

A mature white-tail doe.

As long as I stood perfectly still—because all deer are colorblind—I had at least a slim chance of experiencing contact with an animal that was constantly on the lookout for Shakespeare. She was his prey, this elegant lady standing upright, head high, proud.

With her independently twisting ears she used her keen sense of hearing to examine every sound. Her eyes were just as alert. In quick glances, she even turned her head backwards, but at the blink of my eyes her eyes were back on me.

She put her nose to the air and tried to pick up my scent. When she licked her muzzle several times, I knew she was picking up my odors, and as I stood there sweating, that was no problem to her.

I couldn't figure out why she hadn't turned and run off. There was nothing stopping her. She was in command. She could even have run over to me slashing me to bits with those sharp, spike-like hooves. Yet she chose to stand there and stare at me, just as I was staring at her. I was totally fascinated at being so close to this wild creature so at one with the swamp.

I asked myself how far I could carry the encounter and what degree of communication we could attain. Could I merge my spirit with hers, and in so doing, prove it could be done with Shakespeare? It was a worthy experiment. I at least had to try.

I kept looking deeply into her eyes. When she would glance about to make sure nothing was around to threaten her, the sun reflected out of her pupils like white fire tossed upon wandering dark oceans. I began to swim in those oceans, now diligently looking for an opening to her soul. Strangely, she began to look at me in a different way, possibly realizing I wasn't going to hurt her.

Like a praying mantis on foliage, I ever so slowly picked up my foot and moved it forward, carefully setting it on the ground, avoiding noise.

She saw the movement and even looked down at my foot. And still she did not run.

Always I kept my eyes on hers. Or was she keeping hers on mine?

Physical nearness, I thought, would bring communication. Man. Animal. Both from the earth. Both destined back to the earth. I braved another step forward. Instantly her whole body tensed. But she didn't bolt. Instead her tail went up straight and exposed that cotton white, a signal for other deer to be alert. Maybe it was telling me not to venture closer. So I stood for what seemed to be an eternity until she relaxed. Then I sneaked one more step, and I was eight feet away.

The swamp around us seemed to obliterate itself into a creamy yellow-white light, as though all of the trees had fallen away to expose some other kind of a world behind the wild world. I longed to blink and look around, to bring myself out of this state, and yet I was lured on by its eccentricity.

I moved one more step, and as suddenly as she had appeared, this lady turned, left the ground and in three long bounds was off into the trees, immediately swallowed by the swamp. My experiment came crashing down around me.

All of the elements were there, but I had moved too fast. Overanxious, I had crossed her danger perimeter without assuring her I was friendly. And yet I felt I had attained something quite interesting. What would it have taken to get her to come to me? A handful of apples? Sweet cornmeal?

If I could get that close to a deer, wary of every smell, every movement, every sound, could I do the same with Shakespeare? What means would it take to finally draw him to my arms? What door must I open to see his soul?

25

Slash Marks on a Log

> *Swamp notes—sitting on a rotten log*
> *As Shakespeare leads me through the swamp*
> *within his territory leaving the scanty re-*
> *mains of his presence, he is teaching me*
> *lessons of his habitat. I never pass a log, or*
> *even a leaf, without looking it over thor-*
> *oughly. It is my ongoing wilderness edu-*
> *cation into the depths of his spirit.*

In the prime of that swamp day, noonlit and rich, I knew something was strange. With such a clearly defined wet season/dry season cycle, the Everglades become the scene of unique combinations in the wilds. The rain gives blossom to rare orchids, bright flowers springing suddenly from brown, drooping plants. The dry season becomes a host for migratory birds from all over the world, their foreign songs creating an ornithological Tower of Babel in the air over the drying swamp. There are times in this wild swamp when I wonder if the word mystery was not created here.

In the dry season, earth, fire, air and water seem to rearrange themselves in such a way as to defy the normal pulses of nature, and within this negative power what is created is an abstract denial of the web of productivity. The panther, all wildlife, nature itself, our great earth, the universe, infinity have always offered us wilderness mysteries. The Everglades always hold true to these forces even if what is in front of our eyes seems to deny it.

I have been fooled many times by these mysteries, unsolved, untouched, and for the most part, unnoticed. But sometimes I stand alone among these untamed elements and am treated to a pure, primitive glimpse of an all-encompassing event that these swamp lords choose to show me. I wonder if Shakespeare sees them all the time.

The second I entered that day, I felt drawn deep in, and I felt the swamp was . . . different. I didn't know why at first, and was wondering if my senses were merely deceiving me once again. But there was something about this particular part of Shakespeare's territory that was odd. It seemed as fertile and spiritual as always and there was that usual feeling of pleasure, freedom, security. That day, as every other, on entering I had instantly taken on the swamp rapport born from the first time I came into the glades. I always welcomed the solid fragility. And yet in all of this, mirrored in small strands and pools, was that mystery.

During the rainy season the glades are wet, with deep greens reflecting themselves from every exploding bit of vegetation. There seems to be, then, an infinitely thin film of green air and fog, and the sounds of wildlife play through this enthralling emerald atmosphere as though born from the greenness. I wear forest-green camouflage then, becoming this swamp, becoming a tree, a bush, a bunch of vines, high grass, green water.

During the dry season the swamp is still green, but more gray with dark shadows. The cypress are bare and the growth cycle slows. Prairies turn yellow. Water seeps away to hidden caverns and the sloughs are vacant of nature's images. I become a dark shadow without scent then. From head to foot, I conceal my every step in blackness.

But on this day I stuck out in the swamp like a flashing light in darkness. Though I was black-hooded, the skin around my eyes blackened, my body dressed in tight black, my hands in black gloves and my feet in black boots, I might as well have been naked in the middle of a congested street in New York City. I felt totally exposed to the smallest spider eyes, and probably to Shakespeare himself. What was going on?

Having been outsmarted so many times by Shakespeare and the glades, I felt the best thing I could do was analyze the physical surroundings.

Even though there had been plenty of rainfall the season past, the ground I was standing on, although low, seemed dry. The swamp around me was an entanglement of bizarrely-formed scrub cypress where stiff-leaved wild pine bromeliads had descended from their arboreal homes to the ground, and where solution holes pockmarked the swamp floor. Spike moss and hand fern clustered near hoary bromeliads, and the red oval fruits of the understory of wild coffee shrub offered food for birds, small mammals and rodents. The paradise tree stood thick and solid next to a young gumbo-limbo.

The oddest thing about this place was that there was no water in it—not a drop—which was unusual even in the dry season. I checked for natural dikes, but there were none around to keep the water out. There wasn't even high ground around me, and yet, not more than a few yards to the north, water drained to the east. Somehow this section of the swamp refused waterflow and chose to remain dry. In effect, it was like a dry, sunken plateau, within a huge pond of water but untouched by that water. Odd indeed.

This mysterious place displayed an unusual number of fallen cypress and oak trees. Some had fallen naturally through age, others had been sliced off at their bases, plunging them into the soft dirt covered with cypress needles that crushed underfoot. Some of the more recently fallen logs hosted resurrection fern, which in this dry place looked dead, curled up in grayish formations that reminded me of small crippled hands. It was hard to remember that rain would bring it to new green life.

I slowly scanned the entire region, eyes riveted to the ground, surveying every inch. I came upon several black crickets at the edges of logs, their armored backs shining in fragments of light. Inspecting them closely, I was fascinated to observe their ears, which are located on their front legs. These insects are fierce fighters. I have seen them take on creatures twice their size and win. On an oak log I found a black and buff walking stick. I knew she was a female because the males are much, much smaller. Holding her up close, I smelled the foul odor emitted from her back leg glands to ward off her enemies and quickly placed her back on the log. I found a web-spinner inside its webbed home in the bark of a cypress log. I assumed it was a female tending her eggs. Catbirds were shy as usual, flying off, giving out their catlike calls with squeaks attached to the endings. I suspected they were after the insects and wild coffee fruits, and I had disturbed their lunch. But in all of this, to my frustration, I still couldn't figure out what was wrong. So I stood up, concentrating on other elements.

At noonday, there was a glowing pinkish color in the air that held on to the swamp like a virgin clinging to her first lover. As I stood there I realized that for the time being most of the shadows I could hide in were gone. The sun at high noon sat at exactly the right angle to suck up those shadows. But in the sky were rolling thunderheads. Suddenly blocking the sun, they dissolved that pinkish glow, giving the swamp not an ashen color but an intense bright lemon yellow hue. The whole swamp was bathed in this yellow, and that included the wildlife as well. At first I thought an unnatural fog had somehow worked itself off the water and swept into this area, but as far as I could see through the swamp, it was all entrapped by this yellow light. I looked down at my hands and they looked yellow, as did the catbirds that were flying to high limbs. I went over to a log and rubbed my hands on it, and though it should have been that drab gray, it too was yellow.

What had I stumbled onto here? By what turn of fate was I shown this phenomenon? And why? And if I told anybody about it would they believe me? I doubted it. But then I remembered a Seminole Indian medicine man I had once

met, and I was willing to bet he knew of this strange glades
light and could explain it. He knew of the harmony of man
and the Great Spirit, of thunder, lightning and rainbows, of
things unexplained in the glades. But I doubted he would
ever tell me, a white man.

For some time I sat in this yellow air and accepted it
for what it was—a swamp mystery. To further complicate
things I found on my clothing and skin a thin film of yellow,
and when I rubbed it or scratched my arm, it glowed like
fluorescent organisms do in the surf.

I was so enchanted by all of this I had all but forgotten
why I had gone into this section to begin with. To find evidence Shakespeare had been here. Sensitive as I was to what
was happening, I had a strange confidence I was going to find
something even more worthwhile. In all that yellow earth and
wild woods, I had found no paw prints, no signs he had so
much as stepped one paw there. But because of the mystery
of the place and Shakespeare, and the fact it was dry ground,
it seemed like a good place for a cat, a place he might very
well seek out to rest and muse over his next meal.

I went over to one of the logs, somewhat irritated that
I hadn't found any tracks, sighed deeply, and lay back on the
log. As I gazed up through the bare cypress, it struck me that
I should check out each log, for on one might be that rare
sight—slash marks left by Shakespeare. It was probably the
best concealed sign left by a panther in his constant quest
to plot territory, the places where he scratched his claws to
strengthen his claw ligaments and sharpen the claws themselves.

If ever there was a place to leave these signs it was here.
Hundreds of logs lay about, many of them soft and rotting.
I let my eyes rove over each of them, one by one. Then I
stood back and looked from a distance. Then I went up close
and ran my hands over them.

I found raccoon scat, dried out and held together by
crawfish shells; a small brown water snake; and what appeared
to be scat from a small frog. My search brought me to what
was left of a rotted-out cypress log, opened up, with woody
chunks thrown about. At the very edge of the log where the
wood was still hard were long, uneven grooves stretching
down into the soft, spongy wood. The grooves were more

than four and a half inches wide. There were three on the side near me and a fourth on the opposite side. Slash marks!

Shakespeare had indeed visited this place, left his sign, then moved on. My heart was pumping wildly.

I went back over my tracks through the whole region once again in a concentrated effort to find his tracks. Surely they were there. Surely his heavy body would leave traces in this earth. There was no way he could fail to. And yet I found none.

I went back to the rotted log with the slash marks. They were fresh marks all right. Maybe less than a week old. In time this log would disintegrate, but for now it held a definite sign the big cat was deep into his territory, doing the things all big cats do to survive. And for a few moments he had lingered at this log, and with the power born in him from the swamp, slashed open the wood.

And as he had done that, he had exposed a vibrating micro-life within the confines of the log, maybe even had licked some of the creatures off with his long rough tongue: cockroaches, ants, termites—all held nutrients for his powerful body. The remains of the algae, moss and mushrooms had been thrown about. Chambers made by carpenter ants had not only provided a home for the ants but after them for other insects like centipedes.

This rotted log was so necessary to the swamp, to Shakespeare, to me, that in the final analysis it was not wasted at all. It would become swamp earth, provide high ground for Shakespeare, and eventually help build up the swamp to hide him, to hide his secrets from all who might wish to destroy him.

I was satisfied that I had gained still another thread of knowledge about this great cat. Overhead the now gray clouds moved over the swamp, and if it rained, the water would help to dissolve that log, to dissolve all the logs in the swamp.

Every living thing, every seemingly dead thing, is filled with the chemical energy to produce once again a solid link in the food chain. There lies the hint of infinity. Was I to believe that if Shakespeare was shot tomorrow or slammed into by a truck on the highway, or run out of his home by overdevelopment, that he would never exist again? Even though his body would decompose and become part of the chemical world, in some mysterious way he would live again in some other form, and maybe even closer to mankind than people would want to believe. And believing this kept my optimism alive, even though I wanted him to remain as that magnificent panther.

But there was something more to consider in this episode. The odd place and the mysterious yellow air. Dame Nature may have been helping more than I realized. By riveting me to that spot in the middle of the glades, causing me to check out the area thoroughly, she had opened another page in Shakespeare's history for me. The oddness of the place and then the yellow air filling my lungs, intriguing me, leading me, kept me there and led me to Shakespeare's signs. Maybe that is why I felt so at home in the swamp among the wilds. Maybe I was being led by that gracious lady, Dame Nature. Many times I have thought: when I die I will still always be in the glades. Generations from now I will be tracking panthers, and though my body, like Shakespeare's, will dissolve into the chemical world to become something else, my soul will track closer and closer to my true meaning of infinity.

26

Storm Prisoner

> **Swamp notes—Otter Bay**
> Rain is Shakespeare's means of disappearing. It is that single element that dissolves all physical signs that he exists. It makes him more spiritual than I sometimes want to admit, for it gives him not only elusiveness but complete invisibility.

There was the deep bass muttering of thunder and overhead, through the leafy windows in the tree canopy, a huge whirling lake of gray clouds came in like unknown flowers swelling out of sky pods.

A fine mist sprayed across my face, mingling with the wind, disintegrating brilliant rainbows as they appeared. Vapor, air, water, the thick smell of vegetation—all signaled a summer storm.

Birds flew for cover—in the tree branches, under large leaves and in old cabin roofs. Gators submerged. Mammals dashed into hollow logs. Deer streaked under tree overhangs. Caterpillars crawled beneath fallen trees. Insects burrowed, flew to the underside of leaves. Spiders clung to their webs. And the swamp seemed to open its woody arms to embrace this necessary tempest.

Gradually the mist turned to large cold drops, liquid pearls, splattering onto the mud, churning it, setting the soil in motion to dissolve minerals. Small flash floods started everywhere. Dry regions began to submerge.

Battering fragile flowers, reviving buried fish eggs, pattering palm fronds, collecting seedlings from the air and planting them, the rain never wasted a drop.

Split-second flashes of lightning rivaled sunbursts. They could have ripped me apart and swept me away with but a mere flick of the wind. But instead they riveted me to the spot, letting me witness a rare spectacle of nature at work in one of her most intense moments.

There we stood: one man, one swamp, one panther, one earth. And around and in us a torrential storm raged, producing rainlight coming into the swamp in surrealistic sheets, blurring everything around me until I felt I was a storm prisoner.

I stood with my face to the clouds, feeling the sting of every drop. I reached out and filled my palms with the purest water on earth, drank it and revived my spirit.

Again and again, the rain caressed me, comforted me.

The roars of thousands of gallons of water rushing from this reservoir rang in my ears. It was as though this wild swamp was shouting it could still thrive, still spread across the land, still save itself from destruction.

I stroked the trees around me and watched rivulets of water stream down the bark almost as though the trees were weeping.

Then slowly, ever so slowly, the rain receded until a calm, drenched, wild world stood around me. The fresh smell of wet exposed wood hovered like sweet honey. And everything seemed to be an exaggeration of itself—much sharper outlines, deeper colors, waxy.

Still I stood silent, drenched, drained of emotion, staring at the swamp, accepted.

Then the swamp came alive once again. Birds took flight. Small pools in what was left of animal tracks glistened. Snakes made their way to high ground. And I was sure Shakespeare emerged from a dry spot, shook his fur and went on.

27

Firetrap

Swamp notes—in a burn-out
A burn-out can be very beneficial in the Everglades. Fire has always provided nature a means of reestablishing new land, cultivating fresh earth fertilizer, opening up the tree canopy to let sunlight reach seedlings, ridding the region of dead vegetation. But now that the glades have become an extremely sensitive environment on the verge of extinction, fire can be a serious threat to their survival. Ironically, burn-outs during the dry season actually help Shakespeare.

Tracking Shakespeare during the dry season wasn't easy. Normally he confined himself to high ground surrounded by water, but now he was able to move about at will within a huge range, crisscrossing his territory for prey, water, shade or the best hiding place.

On this particular morning the open khaki sawgrass pressed down by the puritanically clear blue sky was aflame with a mile-long cliff of fire. Above the flames and below the skyline a thick, blurred veil of gray-white smoke erupted from the flames like newborn clouds. Though each tried desperately to hold onto life as an individual cloud, the wind stirred them into a shapeless gray muddle between sky and flame.

At this time of the glades year, the pendulum swings in a wide arc and a time of drought begins. Higher land dries out, lower muddy ravines dry out and crack in a maze of arteries. Brown sawgrass begins to look like wheatfields, and fallen pine needles in the pine forest mat the ground. Egrets, herons, and even sandhill cranes survey the hardwood hammocks for wetter habitats. Deer, raccoon, opossum and panther are forced to roam the dry marshes in search of water. Flower buds lift toward the sky, pleading for moisture. But the scorching sun answers with blinding heat. Leafless dwarf-cypress trees cluster in wild pines. A nest of baby anhingas sit statuelike in dry moss.

Suddenly a flash, a single speck in the night, disturbs the silence. Crackling white and red tongues dance and spread across the swamp like ocean waves. In a moment the swamp is a raging torrent of flame. Saw palmetto leaves curl like frightened panther cubs. Trees become black toothpicks. White rocks turn to cinders. Belches of smoke rumble like herds of elephants. Alligators dig into what is left of the pools of mud. Rabbits and rodents scurry about in frantic attempts to escape.

I stared at the long shimmering fire line as it begged for a wind, received it, then bent wildly in the opposite direction. The flames sprang back and engulfed each other in their own combustion, feeding on each other's fuel, throwing fiery sparks out into the air like sunbursts.

Suddenly I was seeing a barrage of jellied gasoline na- palm bouncing across a rice paddy in Nam and then walking its way to a river's edge like a firedrake born out of hell, only to be swallowed up by the clay mud of the river, leaving behind total destruction of a summer crop.

I found myself hurrying toward the glades fire eagerly, drawn to it by some innate fascination with one of nature's basic components, the one that promised excitement. But as in Vietnam, this fire was deadly and unforgettable. Along the way, in hot ashes and blackened pebbles, I found some of its results. A small rattlesnake was fire-cured black, still cooking, its skin curling away from exposed charcoaled meat. Strangely, its mouth was open as though it had turned in the direction of the onrushing fire to strike at the heat. I put my thumb on the top of its head and pressed, and it crumbled into a heap of ghastly cinders.

Next to what had been a good hiding place of small sticks a small rabbit was sprawled out grotesquely. All of his fur and skin had been burned away, leaving bare muscles, tendons and bones to be barbequed. It seemed as though he had been in full flight when the rushing wave of fire caught up with and raced over him before he even knew what hit him. There must have been a desperate attempt at finding oxygen, suffocation, then death, all in a matter of seconds. I couldn't bear to look at the rabbit for long. As he lay there with no fur or skin, his legs splayed out and one of his paws over his eyes, he looked like a human infant. He looked as though he was going to turn over and plead with me to save him.

I forgot about the fire, Shakespeare, tracking, and sank to my knees next to this creature. I heard a faint popping sound, felt a void, then saw small Vietnamese children running out in front of our perimeter, trying to get out of the village. We had set fire to their houses, burned their rice barrels and piles of firewood. With C-4 plastic explosives, hand grenades, and Zippo lighter fluid we had blown up their bomb shelters and village square.

Suddenly marines were screaming about a baby left in one of the houses. I wanted to drop my rifle and run to the houses, but the lieutenant wouldn't let us off the line. He ran out and into a house and came back out empty-handed. He wasn't even sure he was in the right house. Others ran out and began checking the houses they could get into. But it was no use. The hooches were crumbling under the flames.

Later, as the bulldozer knocked down the remains, the charcoaled infant was put in a small bag and choppered out.

Suddenly I was back in the Everglades, opening my eyes, clearing my vision, seeing the firetrap dance around me. I could feel the heat closing in on me, and as I stood and surveyed the area, walking up as close as I could to the flames, feeling their intensity as though they wanted to get at me, I could see my boot soles smoking from the hot pebbles. I wasn't in any great danger yet, but if I didn't get out soon I could be cut off, and cooked like that rabbit. Luckily the fire was burning away from instead of toward me.

There I stood watching the ten-foot flames perform their vigorous, sensuous dance, flicking their disappearing, pointed crowns at me, taunting me. I wasn't about to rush through them to the other side to complete safety. I would stay calm and wait until it burned itself farther west close to a canal and then I would wade across the canal to high ground.

The flashback kept dominating my thoughts and interfering with my full concentration on the fire. I was amazed at how real it had been, at the power of my mind to relive the past. I knew it was my baptism into a closely guarded secret, one that had been haunting me without showing itself. Now I'd seen it, been back through it, shed its guilt. And it was Shakespeare who had led me to it. For what reason I had no idea. That cat. That grand cat. He is mankind's guide to safety.

Now the fire had worked its way far to the west. I walked with it, totally drenched with sweat from the fire's heat and the sun and my own emotions. And within minutes I was in the canal and on the other side looking back, looking back at a smoking acre in the glades that had brought me closer to myself.

28

Tracks

Swamp notes—on his tracks
The power or force that drives me can only
be measured by my attempts to accomplish
my goal. Sometimes I feel even death will
not stop me. I imagine my ghost wandering
through the glades in search of the panther's
tracks and maybe never finding them. Maybe
that ghost will haunt Shakespeare's territory
and become a legend.

I pressed on, carving my way through the soft walls of this
perennial, liquid-green vale of wilderness. Leaves sliced across
my face and neck like razor blades. The trail seemed endless,
a startling symbol of infinity. A yellow-crowned night heron
sprang off a branch to high trees, looking for a better place
to sleep. My thoughts were punctuated by crackle calls and
kingfisher croaks, and I could smell the now insistent heat
rather than feel it. It hung in the air like death's last breath.
Whispers commanded me to search on for one of the most
mysterious signs the big cat could possibly leave. Tracks. Paw
prints in the mud. They would tell a true story, and would
ignite an even deeper, more intimate relationship between us.

I imagined what the print would look like in the mud,
constructing it in its finest detail. It would be large—as big
as a man's palm—deep, distinct, with oval toe pads the size
of bird eggs, evenly separated and arched above a heel pad
that had three lobes on the bottom. I was mesmerized by the
idea of it and vowed never to leave until I had proven Shakespeare existed by finding it.

This magnificent cat had taken on a whole new meaning.
In his most wild state he was mysteriously reaching out and

touching me. I was not just tracking a panther. I was tracking one of mankind's last hopes for survival on planet earth. I was putting one foot in front of the other toward a lasting relationship between man and the wilderness, man and wildlife, man and himself. Save the panther, I thought, and we have saved our children's children. Annihilate him and man has written his own epitaph.

My eyes scanned, studied, memorized, halted, and then scanned again, using my method. I walked and crawled on the trail, smiling widely, possessed by the chance Shakespeare had softly padded down it earlier. I took off my moccasins and went barefoot, feeling every leaf, every pebble, even the smallest branch, just as Shakespeare did. It was a sense of touch that went beyond normal feeling. Not only was I able to see, hear and smell, but this wild swamp was now letting me feel it in every detail.

I avoided fallen dry branches, moved past palm tree fronds ever so slowly, for they hung across the trail like large dead hands, almost stretching out to catch my hair, arms, or shoulders, trying to strangle me. I stopped, looked ahead, turned and looked back down the trail, then made a complete circle and continued forward, trying to improve my method even more. This I did many times lest Shakespeare creep across the path behind me undetected.

It would have made no difference if a hurricane threatened, a flash flood suddenly rushed into the swamp, a forest fire engulfed me, or even if I was challenged by a crazed maniac escaped from an asylum with a high-powered machine gun. Finding the track was my all-important goal. For that first true track would give life to an endangered animal, would mean there still was a chance to save him.

I would find it. I was sure I would find it. Over and over again I said to myself: I'll find it now, I'll find it now, on the next turn, at the next sabal palm, maybe near a limestone rock. But I'll find it.

Nam Yo Fara On.

The wealth of the swamp was within me, an abundance that would carry me through any hardship, weeks and months of tracking. I searched, probed, walked dead center on the trail, veered left, then right, then turned around and back-tracked thirty yards, constantly overlapping and rechecking the area in the opposite direction.

Up ahead I saw a glistening tea-colored stream cutting across and tumbling over rocks, mud and leaves. I hurried to it, knelt and examined the mud on the edge closely, pains-takingly, anticipating a track of Shakespeare. But still there was none.

As I went on I leaned and rested on trees when I could, squatted behind bushes whenever I heard movement, always peering up and down the trail whether I was sitting in soft mud or half-lying in cut grass. The trail curved and turned in the swamp as though a monstrous snake had silently crawled through toward a prehistoric mating ground only hours be-fore.

It was a strange time in my life. Things were happening around me that probably would be exciting for any naturalist, and yet I could not have cared less. I could think of nothing but that paw print. My eyes were glued to the ground, sweep-ing back and forth momentarily halting on the slightest in-dentation.

Suddenly I stopped. The obvious slapped me in the face as a gust might do before a rainstorm. I was standing in the midst of a bush trail. Was it Shakespeare's? I got down on all fours and crawled back, studying every fraction of the earth. And there it was: the vague shadow of what appeared to be a print. Had I made it with my own feet minutes before? I wasn't sure. But the mud spread around into the shape of a small bird egg. Just the size of a toe pad. Or was I talking myself into all of this?

At that second I was willing to give up ten years of my life for it to be Shakespeare's print. I sprang to my feet and strode down the trail, eyes riveted to the ground in search of still another fragment of evidence. I was going far too fast, breaking one of the most basic laws of concealment, but I was out of control and anxious, and before I could catch myself, my foot landed on another shadowy imprint. I almost screamed at the top of my lungs for being so stupid.

I took a deep breath and closed my eyes. I was on the

verge of a rare experience in my life that might never come along again. And I wasn't going to blow it.

I looked down the trail, focusing on a muddy blotch surrounded by green ooze. Like a magnet drawing a key to a locked door, the blotch drew me forward. The closer I got the more uncontrolled I became until I was trotting, jogging, then running. Swelling inside of me was a feeling of actually seeing my first fresh track of an endangered animal on the verge of extinction.

When I stopped over it, what my eyes beheld in the glittering soft mud left me breathless.

Like rare uncut diamonds lodged in thick earth were Shakespeare's tracks. Not one. Not two. Not three. I counted 37 large, beautiful paw prints, each one so well defined and carefully placed it was as if Shakespeare had contemplated just exactly how he would compose this one chapter of his life—and mine—on this historical swamp page.

How many times I had dreamt of that moment! How many times I had been disappointed. Now I had before me a volume of knowledge, a place in this wild swamp where the treasure began and ended in the midst of a fragile substance that at any moment could crumble, wash away, be wiped clean of any physical evidence by weather, other animals or man.

I stared at the tracks for a long time. My sighting of Shakespeare was clear-cut evidence he existed, but only for me, for I was the only one who saw him. On the other hand, what lay before me was hard-core fact. Undeniable. Plaster casts of these tracks immediately put a whole different light on Shakespeare. He was now a living, breathing animal to anyone I wanted to convince. I sat staring at those tracks and strangely I felt I had betrayed Shakespeare.

Reluctantly and reverently, I began to study each track. The round edges of each toe and heel were definite, solid. Small crumbs of mud around them were still wet. That meant Shakespeare had walked through there probably that morning. I was much, much closer to him than I had realized.

Along the edge of the mudhole I paced off 33-1/2 feet. Plenty of room for him to soak his weary paws in the soft, cool mud. In the middle he had stopped, stepped over to the left edge of the hole as though he had been attracted by something in the water, then returned to the middle and proceeded to walk out. Up on dry land were several wet, muddy crumbs trailing into high grass. On each side of the crumb trail were more crumbs where he had stopped to shake mud off his paws. In the middle of the trail and at the edge of the grass I found deep narrow claw prints with crisp edges, evidence he had sprung into a run, extending his paws for traction.

I went back to the tracks. The sets were all clearly stated: fore paw, hind paw close behind and to the right, then a gap of approximately 24 inches between sets, then fore paw with a hind paw closer in but still to the right, 24-inch gap, then fore paw, hind paw now directly behind, 24 inches distance, and so on until he stopped in the middle. Each set of tracks was staggered. At the stopping point the two fore paws were in line next to each other, as were the hind paws. The distance between the fore paws and hind paws went 35 inches. That meant, with an approximate tail length of three feet and a distance from nose to shoulder of one foot, this was no yarn-ball-pushing kitty. If my measurements were even close, he had a total length of seven feet and a conservative guess at his weight would be 100 to 130 pounds.

I slowly rocked back on my heels, keeping a watchful eye on the swamp. Popular opinion among students of the panther put the female at full growth somewhere in the 90 to 100 pound range. The adult male panther is usually larger than the female, and should go well over that.

Containing my excitement as best I could, I went on with my work. Each track had to be examined individually because any of a million possible impulsive movements would make each one different. Whether or not I could detect the differences was an interesting question.

Closer inspection of the first fore paw print that went into the mud revealed he might have been testing the footing to see how solid it was. There was half a print, then a fraction forward of it he had pushed all the way down two and a half inches. Inside the track a glob of mud was pulled out, exposing part of a limestone rock.

The length of the fore paw was an eighth of an inch

under four inches, and the width at the toe pad went close to four inches. I allowed a little for the mud spreading when he stepped in, but the measurements were still impressive. The appearance of the whole track sent my blood racing. There were absolutely no claw marks anywhere in the soft mud. The very sight of it showed strength and force.

The physical design of the paw that made those tracks explained how the big cat had adapted so well to the Everglades. The toes and heel were well muscled, heavily boned, thickly padded and calloused from the years of roaming the swamps, even though some of his roaming was in water. The paws, spread out as they were, told me they were perfectly able to carry the weight of such a big body, and they were well developed for clasping prey.

At the point where Shakespeare had stopped and then gone on again I noticed only fore paw prints. No hind paw prints. That wasn't especially peculiar, but when I got closer to the track I could see that there were five toe prints. No panther I had ever heard of had five toes in a track; a panther does possess a fifth toe, but it is on the middle and inside of the foreleg. Then I understood the reason for the five toes in a track: Shakespeare had made the going easier for himself by carefully and efficiently placing his hind paw in almost the same track as the fore paw where the mud had been pushed open by the fore paw. He also had another reason for doing this. When a panther is stalking prey he picks out the softest, quietest place to step on the ground with his fore paw, and of course that will also be the softest, quietest place place for the hind paw.

I went to where Shakespeare had left claw marks for me to study and estimated the depth of those marks at about an inch. They were hardly dog tracks. In fact a dog's track is so vastly different from a panther's I find it puzzling that anyone can see similarities.

I was sighing, ready to quit but at the same time feeling there was much more I could learn from those tracks, when I saw something strange behind two tracks at the deepest point in the mud. It looked like someone had taken an average-size paint brush and passed it back and forth lightly over the mud. I stared for several minutes, trying to fathom what could have made those marks. Then the explanation jumped out at me: Shakespeare's tail. As he had gone through the mud he had sunk down to the point where his tail dragged slightly on the wet surface, just enough to leave an imprint of hair leading in the same direction as the paw prints.

I knew the more I thought about this rare page of Shakespeare's history in the mud the more important information I would gain, but what I had already evaluated had imprinted his tracks in my mind forever, like welded spots connecting my life with his. I had come so very far in understanding his existence. I had proven he was still in the Everglades. But I was far from being satisfied. I had not merged my spirit fully with his. I still had not felt that . . . affinity.

Again the question rose in my mind: had I now betrayed Shakespeare? Should I have ever set out to prove he was still in the swamps? For years after the hunting had stopped he had managed to conceal his movements, to roam the glades undetected. What right did I have to prove his existence? And yet, even then I knew it was our destiny to meet like this.

I opened my pack and took out a plastic sack of plaster of Paris, opened a canteen of water and began mixing it into a creamy thick liquid. As the plaster swirled in the cup I kept glancing at the tracks. I picked out the best one and crawled over to it. As I poured the plaster into it, the track filled up and the plaster spilled over the sides. When the plaster dried it would be solid evidence that panthers still roam the cypress swamps. The public would know. Anyone interested in the big cat would know. It would bring people out of the walls to the swamps to catch a glimpse of him. What right did I have to betray Shakespeare's secret? No one on the face of the earth knew I was tracking panthers. Not my wife, not my friends, not my parents. To my knowledge no one knew I even had this intention, let alone an intense obsession. So I, one man, must decide whether or not the information I had so far gathered should be made public. As long as he was a secret he was safe. Then and there, I made a vow to Dame Nature, the Supreme Preserver, never to reveal Shakespeare's presence to the general public.

I slammed my foot into the plaster and threw the sack into the water. Then I walked up and down in the mud until

I had completely blotted out all of those tracks, even the claw marks, even the crumbs. I took out my map and burned it, and watched the ashes float up into the air and disappear.

I was no longer troubled. I felt secure in my decision. I was again at peace with the Everglades, myself, and most importantly, with Shakespeare.

If I left the swamp for a week, a month, a year, I could always return to him. He was mine, and mine alone. He was my cat, my possession, and this hinged on the fact that I found him first and was willing to sacrifice anything to protect him. But I was his possession as well, for I was now his direct connection to mankind.

Book V
Stalking

He went back through the wet wild woods
and walked by his lone.
But he never told anybody.
                          —*Rudyard Kipling*

29

Dead Man's Slough

*Swamp notes—surrounded by ancient
ghosts*

*For many more adventuresome months I
have tracked Shakespeare. The more I do,
the more I am consumed by him, his habits,
his elusiveness, his spirit. Track for track, I
have obtained a kinship with him I never
thought possible with a wild animal, let
alone a predator.*

Nam Yo Fara On.

It was the time of yellow grass, when moths glide toward
the moon, that I was deep in Shakespeare's territory. A silver
sun sat high over the glades like a cold white day-star, searching out openings in the tree awnings, finding them, then being
sucked out of existence by this dark wild abyss. The milky
yet ethereal sky domed over the swamp with but a single cloud
in the shape of a dove with oversized wings, holding its form,
then melting into the brightness like a wandering ghost unable
to speak.

The cypress trees were bare and their tops quivered as
dawn wind dusted across them. Midway up their boughs,
sugar maples painted irregular crimson aprons with autumn-
colored leaves that seemed to belong in a far north forest.
The dry air stank of decayed vegetation, swamp fire smoke,
and stale unmoving water. This unsweet air had been created
by the Breathmaker, the Seminole term for God. This was
the air that had given Shakespeare his life, and life to me to
track him. Both of us were at the Breathmaker's mercy.

It was well into the dry season, and the swamp had
drained frightfully, causing the animals to seek out the few
remaining water holes. I was headed toward one hole that I

knew was used by deer. Time and again I had found Shakespeare's tracks around it.

I knelt in cold winter water, leaned against giant cypress knees, and painted my face with ink-black and forest-green camouflage cream, doing the best I could to depict the stems of water plants. Then I took what mud there was and packed it on my head. I pulled out several nearby fire flag stems and stuck them in it. Wearing camouflaged utilities (torn, worn and re-dyed in some places) and yet another pair of moccasins (the latest pair had rotted off my feet two days before), I took the glades to my heart. Licking the dried salt on my lips, I meditated on Shakespeare. We had come so far, and yet I had so far to go. The more I learned about this ghost-walker the more ignorant I felt. He seemed to be an infinite species.

From the beginning I knew physical evidence would never be enough to explain his presence. My obsession had already carried me beyond that. But it was still unknown to me exactly what jungle corridor I would go down to touch the soul of the great cat. It meant my soul had to become one with the glades, and that I was still developing. I had no more fear of anything in the swamp. I felt joined to it. The feeling would sometimes slip off when I left the swamp and reentered civilization, but I always regained it the second I stepped into the swamp once more.

I sometimes asked myself if I was on the trail of death. If an outsider heard about what I had done so far and considered my background, the obvious answer was yes. But whenever I entered the glades I felt I was going home. They would always bloom with beautiful light, deeply set colors of joy, happiness. Never had I had to dodge the scythe of Death nor look deep into the grim, pale, dreamless face of Hell, or the serene slumber of the all-merciful God. In Vietnam I had been forced to confront, to step over, to run from the litter of Death's earthly ravages. But in the Everglades the panther had already led me to kind nature's signal of retreat, to God. I craved His presence, felt empty when He seemed far, but worked with the confident assurance that He would never forsake the cause. Man's cause. The panther's cause. And He never did.

He is Always. Ever. Here.

Just like sunlight to water, flashing back radiant, in union
with the garden of bliss and planet Earth, from east to west,
following the predestined path, I longed to do the same, to
be guided beyond all limits to that one ultimate goal, which
is in me, though still as secretive as Shakespeare, my panther,
my life.

I moved inward with every breeze, stood still in quiet.
After an hour I slipped into a jungle-rimmed liquid garden
sunk deep in fresh humus in the midst of the cypress head,
hidden, protected. It was a primordial custard apple tree swamp
called Dead Man's Slough. All this time I kept a sharp swamp
eye out for Shakespeare in this strange place on earth. This
is where the Seminole Indians lured Union soldiers, harassed
them to the point of exhaustion, and sent them to a violent
death. Knowing that this is also where the white man had
pushed those Indians—as far south as they could be pushed—
by equal harassment and violence did not give the place any
more of an aura of balance or peace. An eye for an eye only
brings blindness.

But its eeriness at least served to keep this place a wilderness. Few people ventured here and I was glad, for it gave
Shakespeare his liberty. It also gave me the edge in tracking
him. I wasn't afraid in the least and had spent many a night
in the middle of it. There were moans and sounds that could
tear your heart out. But also God-given peace that prevailed
over all.

Slow motion . . . slow motion. . . . I slipped into neck-
deep black water, and as wary as a fish below the surface, I
advanced into and surrounded myself with giant quavering
fire flags on the edge of the slough. Entering this cold water
was like getting into a tub of ice. It bit to the bone in this
subtropical zone where winter's 40 degrees feels like 40 below.
Dissolving my scent under fog, I arranged a vantage point
that gave me good cover and a view of an open spot near an
oak tree on the other side. It was high ground and a good
place for animals to water. Shakespeare's tracks were there
more often than not.

A Cooper's hawk proudly sat erect on the very top of
a dead cypress above the treeline darting those intense, quick
and erratic looks into the swamp below. Detecting movement,

he suddenly dropped off the tree to circle in a wide arc, then rifled down into the green shrouds, his slate-gray plumage turning into a blurred streak. I suspected a rodent would never see another dawn.

This daytime hunter, the epitome of sudden death from the sky, was probably already ripping its prey apart with its hooked talons, the pointed beak snapping at the flesh.

A fox squirrel, member of another endangered species, raced awkwardly along a thick limb high up, perhaps toward a mate, cheeks full of food, his long, bushy, orange tail flitting as he moved. Largest of his kind, he truly did look like a small red fox. This is the same squirrel that can be sighted in a black color phase with a white face and tail tip. What was so different about this particular fox squirrel was that he was dwelling in the depth of the swamp. Normally, fox squirrels take to the open woodlands where they have more opportunity to sun themselves.

My eyes went back to the slough.

Originally it had been nothing more than a gator hole, carved out of the thick mud many years ago by powerful, scaly tails to create low ground for water run-off to protect this prehistoric reptile from the dry season. It offered a place for females to nest, babies to grow. It provided habitat for mammals, birds, amphibians, fish, insects and arachnids.

Then over many more years its perimeter, slowly, in nature's own time, thickened with a rare grove of custard apple trees, their seeds brought in by the wind, birds, fur-bearing animals, in the excretion of gators. As the trees matured, each one began to look like a sleeping giant tarantula turned upside down. Their arching boughs and low branches hold wartlike lumps which look like the long hairy legs tangling upward and about. Soft, dark brown bark, grotesquely twisted around the buttresses and limbs, forms weird lava-flow patterns. Elliptical leaves, smooth and thick, cluster heavily around the fleshy, pear-shaped, seedy yellow apples that contain an aromatic substance used for medicine.

I felt transfigured into something unreal in this unreal place.

Each tree was loaded with epiphytes—bromeliads, Spanish moss, old man's beard, and extremely rare orchids found nowhere else on the face of the earth—all gently clinging to the bark, nonparasitic, receiving their nourishment from the air and rain.

Orchids. They suggest grace, elegance, possibly divine sanctification. They are flowering plants that have evolved into something wholly their own. They cross-pollinate, bloom almost to the day at certain times of the year, are food for insects, even imitate insects to draw them in, and yet can conceal themselves and blossom for weeks. The ghost orchid is the most mysterious. Like the panther, it has adapted to a wild, watery environment. And like Shakespeare, it is endangered. In full bloom, its broad snowy white petals paint a floating ghost shape in the inky green dampness.

Amidst all of this a large female alligator, ten feet long, highly protective of several babies, cruised under a sheet of dusty surface film in pursuit of garfish. There would be a sudden movement and an explosion of water from her mighty tail, then that all-engulfing silence. On occasion she would pass close by me, wary of my presence. She could easily have submerged, come under me and pulled me under to drown, but instead she chose to reestablish her distance.

A large black horsefly flew around me, its loud buzz sounding like sniper rounds. Near the edge of the water a small blue heron snatched a small-mouth bass. Love bugs, glued together at their tails in copulation, landed on a stem and were trapped by a raft spider that rushed upon them from beneath the water. Pig frogs bounced off exotic hydrilla water weed, trying to escape a young anhinga trailing them underwater at the edge of the weed bed. Zebra, victory, and yellow sulphur butterflies fluttered. And that black horsefly slammed right into my face, dropped in the water next to my mouth, went crazy trying to regain flight, only to fly upside-down in the water on his wings until he lodged under a piece of log and algae.

As I waited there for Shakespeare, submerged, my mind reeled back in time to when the Everglades emerged from the sea, bombarded by the climate constantly changing from ice to fire, cold to heat, for hundreds of thousands of years. Then this dense, subtropical rain forest began to be caressed by the warm waters of the Gulf of Mexico on the west and cooled by the Atlantic Ocean on the east. Silently, then, this wild swamp was finally and fully formed during the last glaciation period about ten thousand years ago.

Lake Okeechobee, that great shallow, freshwater lake, eventually spilled its water over its banks and flowed south through the river-of-grass into the cypress swamps, producing a natural watershed. And in this wild swamp where fertile mud and cooled water merged, the panther wandered, known only to the ancient Indians. I could imagine the intense feeling the Indian must have had when he first sighted this big cat. It must have been a spectacular event. The panther, stalking a young animal in the early morning; the man beholding the magnificent furred creature, its existence hitting him with full force. Terrified, fascinated, awe-struck, the man flees, his lips trembling, his heart skipping beats, his legs like rubber. What did he call the panther? No one will ever know. But that same Indian sitting that night around the tribal fire anxiously telling his story, maybe even drawing the outline of the cat in the dirt by the light of the flickering flames, produced a subject for fact and fiction that has lasted up to this minute.

That minute there I was, submerged to my neck in a swamp, face streaked with paint, plants and mud on my head— all to catch a glimpse of that same cat, to feel the same terror, fascination and awe as that first man who saw him. Given patience by my training, I let my mind wander back again, back to the panther's very beginning.

I'd spent a lot of time reading about how scientists thought the panther came to be the cat he is, and I'd discovered it's true that if you put ten mammalian paleontologists in a room to discuss the evolution of the panther, you'll get ten different theories on the exact course of his ancestry. But after sifting through all the theories I could find, I had managed to satisfy myself with a simple, straightforward version of nature's formula for producing this magnificent creature.

It took a very long time for the panther to evolve as the most highly developed cat in the Western Hemisphere. Evidence of his earliest ancestor dates back to the Mesozoic era, about 75 million years ago. This was a time when giant reptiles like Triceratops and Gorgosaurus wandered about the earth, a time when coniferous trees, ferns, cycads, and gingkoes grew on the marshy ground.

The fossil evidence from this period shows a small shrew-like creature with rows of sharp teeth used for feeding on insects. It was born with a placenta and was clearly a mammal rather than a reptile. It scooted about hidden in the under-brush and therefore went unnoticed by the giant reptiles.

At the end of the Mesozoic era most of the reptiles disappeared and the age of mammals began about 65 million years ago. This is known as the Cenozoic era. During this interval some of the animals that survived from the Mesozoic era continued to prey on insects, but others began feeding on plants. Some of the plant-eaters evolved into hooved mammals that later became horses and hogs.

The insect-eating mammals began to grow larger than most of the plant-eaters and started hunting plant-eating animals for food. These early meat-eaters (carnivores) have been la-beled Creodonta because they developed nonretractable claws on their toes, and 44 close-rooted teeth including canines for holding their prey. But the Creodonta had three physical drawbacks—a long body, short legs, and a small brain. This configuration made it extremely hard for them to chase ani-mals any great distance. Presumably they employed the am-bush technique, probably from trees, rock ledges, bushes, and the like.

As the Creodonta continued to evolve, they acquired large molars with cutting edges similar to those of the panther today. But for reasons that can only be speculated about, even this mammal declined and eventually faded away about forty million years ago.

It is widely believed that evolving from the Creodonta was another animal with a larger brain. This animal, also short-legged and long-bodied, was about the size of a skunk and had a long bushy tail. It was labeled Miacis, a forest and swamp creature which developed meat-eating shearing teeth located in the rear of its jaws, forerunners of the molars and pre-molars. The Miacis became an extremely fast and specialized animal, evolving into a civet cat.

In comparison to the Miacis, the civet had long legs

which made it easier for him to chase and run down prey, a long J-shaped tail, and retractable claws useful for holding onto prey once caught. And, of course, he had the fangs and meat-shearing teeth.

Approximately thirty million years ago the civet cat evolved into what we term a true cat. Up to this point none of these animals looked much like the cat as we know it today. Within the cat family, then, some grew big while others remained small; some acquired spots while others had stripes; still others had only one predominate color. Over a few more millions of years they became tree climbers and leapers, and hunted with power and stealth.

Out of all this my mind constructed a simple formula: tiny insect-eater—Creodonta—Miacis—civet—true cat—panther.

I could not entirely ignore the school of thought that contends the panther evolved from the famous saber-tooth tiger, that ferocious, hairy monster with long sparkling sword-like canines. There is weak and scanty evidence, chronological and physical, that points to some sort of ancestral line from the saber-tooth tiger to the panther, but what can be interpreted from this evidence is that the panther has no relation to the saber-tooth tiger other than the fact that they are both cats on separate branches of the same cat family tree.

Elusive and secretive as he has always been, the panther has been able to wander in and out of history, covering his tracks as he ventured from one time zone to another. While hundreds upon hundreds of other animals over millions of years have come and gone, still the panther survives. In competition with man, he has outsmarted us time and again. This alone may be the reason why man has openly tried to destroy him. A supposedly inferior animal is not supposed to make man look like an idiot, and yet throughout the history of man and panther, the panther has done just that, many times and with the utmost efficiency.

Thinking about all of this, I kept my eyes on the far bank of the pond and on the gator close by. My bones ached from the chill of the water. My muscles twitched. I knew by now my skin had begun to shrivel and that even though I had only been in the water a day, I had a long way to go on this

vigil. At the very least I would stay the night and the following
day.

Shakespeare hadn't come. Not even a deer had come
to that water hole that day. Just me, the gator and her babies,
the other wildlife, and my prehistoric reveries.

Shakespeare hadn't come in the flesh, but my brain had
brought his spirit to Dead Man's Slough. That is the first step
in stalking.

30

Nighthawking

> **Swamp notes—in the grip of the night**
> As a nighthawker I sit in cold water, listen
> for a movement, the sound of a paw pushing
> down in mud. As a nighthawker I pan my
> eyes back and forth, up and down, over and
> under, every inch in front and back. To be
> a nighthawker is to be someone who is on
> guard for all the rest, the ones who are
> sleeping. I nighthawk for you now, all of
> you who are asleep to the call of wilderness.
> But pretty soon you will have to wake up
> too.

The gray hood of owl-light slowly impressed a nighttide glow
around Dead Man's Slough, giving it an obscure overshadow-
ing. The moving, yellowish-green lumination of the fireflies in
the trees and lower in the bushes dotted this darksome shade
like flashing teardrops. One last cry of a hawk accented the
nocturnal cricket chirps, and a retreating migratory wood stork
flew low overhead destined for a mate and nest deeper in on
a cypress tree. The slough, the trees, everything seemed to

halt momentarily in the leaden silence, as though paying homage to a great ruler. I paused too, for it was my aspiration to feel that natural union of day to night, as night took over.

Spending a night in the swamp is like nothing else. Under camouflage in neck-deep water, unable to change positions, I had devised a way to exercise my stiff muscles and frozen bone joints. I tensed my leg muscles as a ballerina might do in warm-up exercise, pulling up my calf and thigh muscles to their highest degree, then holding for five seconds, relaxing, then doing it again for five more repetitions until I felt a warmness flush my legs. Standing on one foot in the water, I bent my leg, grabbed hold of the ankle and stretched it up behind me, holding for five seconds, then repeating the process five times with each leg. It was all in slow motion so as not to disturb the water and give my position away. This wilderness exercise routine I did throughout the night to keep warm and also to keep myself awake.

I sucked in my stomach, held, released, sucked in, held, released, sucked in, held, and released to keep those muscles alive. With my arms I did the same movement I did with my legs. Stretching out all the way, I straightened my arms to the fullest, then tensed my muscles, biceps and triceps, holding for five seconds, then repeated it five times.

It was impossible to eat anything under those conditions, so I did without, listening to my stomach growl underwater until finally it realized no food would be coming.

It was going to take a little while, but eventually I would drop into a half-asleep, half-awake state. My senses were alert to sight and sound, but it was an attempt to rest my body without going to sleep. In the water, for the most part, my body was weightless, so it was easy to get tired. At that point I needed something to keep my eyes open. Under my chin was the answer: water. I simply submerged my head whenever I felt drowsy, raised up, cleared my eyes, and down again. And the water was cold, oh so cold. It would keep anything alive awake. Also, to my advantage, I was periodically assaulted by a swarm of mosquitoes that bit at my cheeks and forehead. When I had had enough of them I eased down underwater and washed them off.

I kept this up throughout the night. What it brought

me was a strange solitude. There I was more than forty miles into the Everglades, completely cut off from society, not interested in what was going on in the city among people so far away from my way of thinking, who would have a great deal of trouble understanding why I was there in the slough in the first place, stalking a panther for no more reason than to save it. Who, in all the population of the state of Florida, or the United States for that matter, would stand alongside of me there in the icy water for a day and a night and a day? I could think of no one who would care to volunteer. That gave me a solitude no other man could touch. That gave me a hermetic, splendid detachment from the human race that put me purely in the grip of Dame Nature to do as she pleased with me. With little choice, I had surrendered myself to her, her ways and her modes of survival. In this wanted isolation, I could create a means of death or life. I had my hands deep into the living flesh of the earth, and I let it ooze and crawl about my body, my spirit. Maybe it was the only reason I was alive to begin with. It gave me a sense of motivation to try to do something no one else could. Maybe that was another reason why I was tracking panthers.

In a very direct sense as a Vietnam veteran I had shunned society and chosen to live in the wilds close to the panther. From what I had learned in the Marine Corps and Vietnam and through my own imagination, I had chosen the swamp instead of the city. I had chosen for the most part to be away from people. I was like a "trip-wire vet."

A trip wire is a deadly trap the Viet Cong laid in the bushes alongside and across paths to blow up marines on patrol. This term was also applied to the marines who were able to sniff those trip wires out and then defuse the mine. I had not been a "trip-wire," but now I knew how they did it, now that I knew how to sniff out a spider web that had been displaced in the swamp.

As I stood in the water, now a liquid form of the black sky above it, I began to think about all the so-called "jungle vets" that I'd heard were hiding out in the wildernesses of America. These were guys like me who had come home and, unable to fit into the unforgiving society they found here, just disappeared into the wild and lonely places of our continent.

I guess they were trying to sort it all out—the war, the killing, the guilt, the alienation—and they had to do it alone, living by the skills they had learned in Nam. I guessed I was like them in a lot of ways.

I had chosen to disappear into the swamp. To be left alone to deal just with the wilds and not people. For days at a time I could leave society behind, and when I returned to people I always knew the swamp, Shakespeare, would welcome me back. Maybe that was another reason why I was tracking Shakespeare. But even more, maybe I was attempting to prove to myself there really was the existence of God in Nature, and not just something invented by but separate from man. Nature surely had to be part of every man's soul. And when Nature is destroyed, man destroys part of himself, little by little, until nothing is left of himself, only the bare dead bones turning to dust and blowing away in the wind of the night.

But nighthawking would change all of that. Just the feel of the water I was in convinced me of it. To nighthawk Shakespeare meant proving he existed. Once I'd done that I would somehow relay that truth to other people to set the record straight and to let Shakespeare point the way toward a new way of living that would include his ethics of survival—utterly natural, utterly normal.

I stood there in that cold black water, listening. I heard baby gators, flitting insects, mammals moving over on the dry land. I heard cottonmouth moccasins attacking frogs and cruising bass snapping at the defenseless bait on the water's top. Twice I saw deer come to the edge and drink, and once the vague, wobbling outline of an opossum.

But in all those hours through the night, there was not the slightest sign Shakespeare was around.

In the face of that disappointment, I smiled. In that seed of failure was success, and I would find it. I was determined to sit it out all the next day regardless of the constant ache I had in the small of my back where a piece of lead sat lodged in a body casing next to my spine. That ache served always as my personal reminder that when things got hard I could figure a way through.

When light finally did flush over the swamp, I eased down

in the water, cleared my vision, and prepared myself for another day's vigil.

31

Ambushed

> **Swamp notes—in the water**
> *I am worn out and my eyes are gone. My body has taken a real beating from the cold water all day and night. But I have to revive myself somehow. Keep alert. Never let my guard down. Even now as I think of all of this, my concentration is gone. But I have pledged myself to stay another whole day.*

Shortly before noon the alligator attacked. It was jet-swift and swamp-necessary. With a turn of her ten-foot length and vise-jaws, she dove into the water, lashed out and was gone. Only the small footprints of a soft-shell turtle remained on the bank.

A purple gallinule sang in a henlike cackle on the far side of the pond, exposing his bright red bill that looked like a large drop of blood in the green. I tried not to be distracted by this lily pad walker, and tried as best I could to keep what attention I had left on the surrounding jungle. The small blue heron from the previous day came back to feed, and I saw a water moccasin ease into the water off one of the hanging limbs of a custard apple tree, submerge, surface, then disappear in the hydrilla water weed.

I warily peered through a swamp silence no one could possibly understand unless he has been enraptured by its timeless, invisible wisdom. But this silence was an uneasy empty pause, soon ruptured by wild desperate outcries, the temporary image of death or timely birth. Silence settled back over us, the swamp and me. And time passed over sugar maple trees as the sun mutely wandered toward the west. It was in this uncivilized quietude that I heard the faintest sound of a small dry twig cracking under a heavy weight. I ducked my face into the water and washed away the night's cobwebs from my mind.

The swamp hushed as though all sound had suddenly been sucked out of it by the eye of a hurricane. My chest thumped. Goose bumps swelled on my waterlogged arms. My sixth sense was telling me something. I was happy to know it was still alert. On the other side of the pond was an animal. An animal that had just broken that ancient wilderness code of silence.

Slowly I took out a piece of deer meat, raised my hands above the water and smeared it on them, then opened them to the air. It was a long shot, but I hoped, after I'd dropped it all over the swamp all these months, the scent would float over the water to the animal's nostrils. And if it was Shakespeare, it would be a familiar scent that had been teasing him, and prompt him to move a little closer to find a hidden dead deer. Or, all this time it had meant nothing to him.

I waited.

Oak leaves rattled in a breeze. I strained to listen. A space of time slowly passed through the swamp. At the end of it the quick sucking sound of a large paw pulling out of the mud was instantly swallowed up. A bear? Whatever animal it was didn't know I was there. I couldn't see him, but I was amazed how careless he was being. Maybe it was Shakespeare. Maybe this time my ordeal in the pond, coupled with patience, had outsmarted him. Maybe I had learned a valuable lesson here that I had been overlooking: to sit and wait for him.

"Let it be Shakespeare," I whispered.

I began to move slowly, inch by inch along the fire flags toward the sound, body in the water, head floating between the stems, silent as a snake, looking always at the opposite side of the pond where the sound had come from. I lifted my feet over logs at the bottom in the mud, ducked underwater beneath a fallen tree and eased past an old humped alligator nest, moving finally into another fire flag patch. There I waited.

Then I heard a bush branch slowly sweep across what

seemed to be a long body and snap back into place. If it was Shakespeare, maybe he had fed well the last couple of days and now, his stomach full, didn't care whether or not he made any noise that might scare prey away. Or maybe it was really a bear lumbering through the swamp in search of fruits to stoke up his body with energy. I smiled and the black water seeped into my mouth. I could feel mosquito fish play on my tongue.

Whatever animal it was then moved around still another bush farther away from the water. But even then it was hard to pinpoint the exact location of the sound. Bird song interrupted. And yet with my faithful sixth sense I could feel the animal moving.

What was it?

I started moving again, maybe a bit too fast because I was beginning to make ripples in the water. But I kept my head down as low as possible to keep the water movement to a minimum. Then at the edge of the pond, where mud met wet leaves and water, snakelike I slid out on my stomach about halfway up the bank. I let the water drain from my camouflaged utilities, then ever so quietly pulled a camouflaged hood over my head and pushed myself up on my feet and crouched. Being in water for so long left my legs stiff and aching. And even with adrenalin pumping into my being, I couldn't get oriented. My eyes were a lot more tired than I had believed, and it reminded me of when I had that dismal apparition. I felt dizzy and sick to my stomach. This abrupt change from water to land shocked my body into illness. My legs shook and the back of my neck ached. All of my concentration was gone. I sank to the mud exhausted, suffering from loss of body heat in the icy water. My hands and feet, the tops of my ears, were numb. Two days submerged in the water had left me helpless on land. I couldn't hold myself in the crouched position and collapsed in the mud. Even the mud was cold on my face.

And just as suddenly as the realization of dehydro-freezing hit me, an explosion of bushes a few feet away destroyed all that was silent in the swamp. In my delirium I truly expected to be annihilated by some swamp gaboon monster. As everything was falling apart, I felt myself struggling to get back into the water, diving headfirst and going under. It was the worst thing I could have done. But at least I knew what I was up against in the water.

"Saints of God, save me," I gurgled.

I stayed down as long as I could, and when I came up I saw blurred brown fur disappearing into the bushes. At that point I didn't care what was on the bank. Safe or not, I slopped to the bank and pulled out once again. Checking the bushes where I had seen the fur, I crawled forward, and there, staring up at me, were deer tracks up and down across a single line of raccoon scat and tracks. I had spooked a deer. All the time I had been struggling to revive myself a deer was nearby. I didn't know whether to laugh or cry, but it seemed I was doing both.

I lay there for a long time staring at the sun burning fog off the treetops with the wet winter swamp breeze blowing on me, unaware I was still losing body heat and putting myself closer to death. I had to react soon or Shakespeare might have another fresh meal to eat.

32

Red in Tooth and Claw

> **Swamp notes—next to a fire**
> I no longer fear death for myself. But I do for Shakespeare. I wonder if it all has to do with him, or with myself as well, or maybe even with all of mankind. Maybe a book about the panther with his true identity revealed will turn man's thoughts to preservation.

I got up on dry ground and, using waterproof matches, started a fire with sabal palm tree fronds, dry sticks and a thick log.

I built a log heat-shield on one side of the fire, then wrapped myself around the flames. As my utilities began to dry, I opened them up and turned my backside to the fire, took off my boots and socks and put them near the fire. I ate ginseng and energol capsules from my pack, and slowly began to revive.

Lying there smiling at death-passed, I thought of Shakespeare. What a smart and beautiful cat he is. How could anybody in his right mind ever raise a rifle to such a creature? And yet hunting was one of the most basic historical reasons why he was an endangered species.

In the old days hunting was the norm. And there were no conservationists to point out the niceties of the difference between hunting a plentiful species to provide food and hunting an endangered species for sport. But early in the century the panther did not seem to be endangered. The panther numbered in the thousands in the United States then, competing for food with the bobcat, lynx, bear and bird of prey. To man, he was nothing more than a varmint to be eliminated as fast and efficiently as possible. Hunters from all over the world came to the Everglades and stalked the panther. Like the tiger in India, the lion in Africa, he was a prized trophy for the wall.

These brave hunters in all their glory and with the experience of a lifetime of tracking in the bush, came to the swamps with well trained "panther dogs" that could tree a big cat within minutes. And when their dogs caught the scent of a female with cubs, the hunters didn't give much attention when the dogs ran down the cubs and killed them as they stood defenseless screaming to their mother for help. In fact in some cases the cubs were a reward to the dogs for their valiant efforts to please the hunter. What better meal for a dog on the chase than the soft tender flesh of three-month-old panther cub? In the winter months the swamps had been filled with the echoes of barks and the occasional crack of a rifle.

Lying there in Shakespeare's territory, still shivering, I could almost see the dogs sprinting through the swamp, plunging into the water in close pursuit of a panther not more than a few yards ahead. Then behind them come the hunters, rifles waving above their heads, hooting and hollering at the dogs to run harder. I could see the hunters' sweating faces smiling, even sometimes laughing, at the possibility of actually bagging a panther. Suddenly the dogs crowd around a big oak, jumping up on the tree, barking in that crazy yelp as though they believe they can get a bite out of the hide of the panther. Up high in the camouflage of the oak the panther is clinging to a limb, peering down at the chaos, snarling with that horrifying expression, spitting, even lashing out with a paw.

Then the hunter in all his glory, shoulders squared, chin out, head high in the courageous stance of a coming victory, steps under the tree, slips his rifle up to his shoulder, tightens his grip and settles his cheek against the butt. Squinting over the sight, he picks out that one-inch space slightly above and between the panther's eyes, holding the position as the cat turns his head. Then, finally, the panther looks right down the barrel. The hunter slowly takes up the slack of his trigger, holds it, and then ever so gently but with a strength steady and firm, squeezes the trigger. Instantly an explosion in the swamp tears off half the panther's forehead, skin and fur and skull bone spraying out in all directions, fresh blood dampening the bark on the tree. The cat never knows what hit him. Maybe there is that instant pain of the bullet splitting through his skull before turning his brain to mush. But flinging backwards, his body falls hard in a heap into the water, his blood mixing with the tannic acid to form a muddy crimson and leaving a dank stench in the swamp above the regular smells.

There is an uproar from the hunters and a lot of back slapping and congratulations, maybe even a pint of whiskey pulled out of a back pocket and passed around. The dogs are contained on leashes while the panther is hoisted onto the hefty shoulders of the biggest man to be carried out like so many pounds of butchered meat. In fact during the Depression, panther steak was a substitute for pork, which gave Everglades hunters even more incentive to track the cats. Word was the broiled meat tasted like pork or greasy chicken, tender, but with a wild smell to it.

I shivered again. The thought of eating a panther, maybe even Shakespeare, repulsed me. That was one way I would never attain an affinity with him. I put a few more logs on the fire, took off all my clothes and lay naked, feeling the intense warmth. My utilities were almost dry and I felt a lot better. I felt I could go on for the rest of the day until dark. I had to go farther and farther into the swamp after him, and deeper and deeper into my own reasons for being there.

Because of where Shakespeare's territory was located, I had a recurring fear that would sometimes wake me up in the middle of the night. It was the nightmare that Shakespeare was being hunted down for no more reason than to become a rug on a den floor.

It always made me wake up sweating, vowing that I would somehow make people understand the value of his presence and make the efforts necessary to save him. But I also feared my efforts might just remind some wowie hunter that this particular panther was still around, and then he might decide to bag just one more panther. Shakespeare.

I prayed it would never happen. That my nightmare was not a premonition. But hunting season was due to begin soon, that time of year when the government issues a piece of paper for a price that says you can carry a gun and shoot at certain animals. And these trigger-happy swampers would be coming out to shoot at whatever happened to move.

33

WIA

Swamp notes—in a slough
I've managed to fence my worst war thoughts into a corner of my mind. But whenever one of them breaks loose to roam and ravage, chasing it down takes more out of me than three days' tracking in the swamp.

During this day in hunting season, inside the killing zone, I wandered off the trail and down into a small slough, then through more trees and up close to a weather-destroyed cabin. Far in the distance a rifle cracked in the wind, then echoed. I snapped a look into the swamp as though I could see the round, prevent it from hitting a deer, or possibly Shakespeare.

I was going to cut across another slough to get up on another trail and make it out to the main road in search of more hunters when the distinct sound of a bullet rushed through the air. WHACK! A branch not far from me shattered from the force. Another round strayed up into the trees. And a third sliced through the low bushes along the back side of the cabin. All three rounds went off in different directions, and I knew none were meant for me, but it was that sound of rifle fire close to me, the projectile speeding overhead, that instantly triggered the overwhelming memory of the intense moment in my life when I was wounded in Nam. I slid down alongside the cabin wall, hidden from anybody or anything. Tears welled up in my eyes, ran down my face. My hands shook and my throat was dry. My stomach ached. All those haunting emotions were still with me. That quick heart beat. Cries of pain echoing. I could feel death's dreadful wave of darkness coming toward me. And the shattering of hope that I'd be going home alive. I could taste thick sticky blood on my face. Smell open flesh. Then those agonizing cries once again from the other wounded. Those torturous feelings have never left me. They were then, and are now, and probably always will be a part of my soul forever, a part of my spirit-self that is in constant battle for enlightenment.

It was in 1966, south of Chu Lai Base Camp, when my moment of credence overtook me. I was with eight other marines, two of them radio men we were escorting to the Seventh Marines dug in on Snaggle Tooth Island. These guys were going to be used as support communications on an operation kicking off the following day on the island. Everybody knew it. So we were sure the VC knew it too.

Snaggle Tooth Island was called that by the Marine Corps because from a distance it did look like a snaggletooth grown way out of proportion. Jagged rocks among thick jungle blended and climbed skyward to a very irregular point.

Since the Seventh had been there, harassment from the VC, night attacks and a couple of battles had taken place.

The general was fed up. He ordered a search and destroy mission to root out every gook on the island.

We sped along the beach in a heavy monsoon rainstorm in a PC pickup truck and jeep crammed full of PR-6 radios, batteries, backpacks and ammunition, headed toward the edge of a narrow channel separating the island from the mainland by about a hundred yards. There a Navy landing craft would ferry us across.

I sat at the back end of the truck, staring out at the South China Sea, drenched, my flak jacket waterlogged, rifle cradled in my lap coated with wet sand and rusting around the barrel, the sand splattering up in my face whenever the tires slipped and spun in place.

Huge black waves farther out in the sea churned, chopped and rolled, forming ever-changing jagged mountain ridges and deep valleys, seeming to move independently of the earth. And this raging storm fought that sea, leveled it in fleeting seconds in pockets of foam that dissolved instantly, an uncontrollable fragment of nature gone wild. And yet, for me, it was a desperate peace in this crazy war. Looking at it stole me a few seconds of solitude. Gray river clouds and gray, spooky rain haze swirled overhead, creating a ghost-ridden light and a dismal view of an endless sea.

Miles to the east, the edge of the storm was abruptly cut off by white light and a sun frantically looking for its place in the sky, forever being challenged by this tempest—and losing. To the north the famous Chu Lai seawall stood bravely absorbing the intense shock of a south gale that pounded it with those waves, the white caps punching it with knuckled fists. But the hundred-foot cliffs, straight up, black, smooth, looking more like marble than rock, seemed unaffected. At their base were immense boulders like chunks of uncut black jade. On top of the seawall, entrenched in a small valley the size of a football stadium, was our First Shore Party Battalion Camp. It was barely visible in the storm, the tents flapping like bat wings and the small lights in the mess tent swinging in the grayness like fading beacons.

Directly over the top of us a whole squadron of Huey helicopters passed out to sea, their open slide-back side doors showing mud-covered grunts sprawled on the floor and hanging out the wide opening, their zombielike eyes staring out at me. The rapid whack-whack-whack, whomp-whomp-whomp of the rotor blades as they throttled overhead sliced through the rain. And above them a screaming F-104 jet fighter broke from a formation of four and lost itself in oblivion, only to appear again ahead of a sonic boom at the other end of the beachhead above the island, leaving behind it a furrowing red wall of flames from a single napalm drop.

Our truck and jeep raced down the beach, occasionally hitting headlong into a rush of incoming waves, sliding out of control, then gaining stability once again.

Soaking wet, we huddled around a cassette recorder, listening to a tape of the Mamas and Papas blasting into the rain like rifle fire. I had heard that tape so many times I could sing the song backwards. "Monday, Monday . . . can't help that day . . . Every other day of the week is fine, yeah, Monday, Monday. . . ." It was one of those strong fibers of sanity I held onto that reminded me there was a Real World back in the States. It seemed to push aside that constant pliant reality of death, getting wounded, going crazy from boredom that plagued us all.

A wave of rain slapped me in the face. Glancing back at the island in the grip of the storm, next to turmoil in the sea, action in the war in front of us, surrounding us, I was again struck with a fatalistic feeling. Many times before an operation, or even in the anticipation that we were going to be close to contact, I had felt this emotion tighten my stomach. Insecurity and a failing attitude toward survival could put me in a vulnerable position. And that was bad. I always tried to practice optimism, but under these conditions it was very hard. A fatalistic atmosphere covered all of South Vietnam like a thick canvas soaked in oil.

"When your time is up, your time is up," I'd heard many marines say, just as I had told myself over and over. It didn't seem to make any sense, but it was a way of dealing with getting blown away by some warmongering VC. Believing in fatalism would release me from the responsibility of living. Death was going to happen no matter what I did. I looked around at the rest of the guys. It was amazing the way our faces had changed over the months. We were young, but old.

There was something deep in our eyes that had changed, something that had made us all old.

We came to the edge of the beach where the narrow channel stretched across to Snaggle Tooth like a dead snake. The silent tide eased inland and slowly cut away some of the beach. Vietnamese children from the local village on the other side of the sand dunes came up to us for candy, cigarettes, k-rations, or anything else they could get from us. With their black hair slicked down from the rain, skinny legs sticking out from baggy shorts, and with those pleading, large dark eyes, they smiled at us with crooked teeth.

"Maline, numba wun," they shouted with one finger in the air.

I smiled back, guarded, but pretty sure none of them had a grenade hidden in his shirt. But where were all the teenagers, adult men and young women? All I saw were children, older people, and the crippled ones of the village. It was a bad omen, but I paid little attention. After all, I wasn't going on the operation. Before nightfall I would be back on the seawall having chow.

There was a young Vietnamese girl-child in the group who had unsmiling eyes, deep-set, with unusually thick lips and a scar under her left ear. She hobbled toward us on a crudely made bamboo crutch. Both of her legs were mangled grotesquely, with only one doing the work. Half of one foot was gone, and as she leaned on the crutch near me her blouse was open and I could see more scars. She was trying to talk in English, but the words came out of a mouth that couldn't open all the way.

One of the boys came up to me and said, "Amelican malines kill her father, and throw bomb on her." The boy said it matter-of-factly.

I looked at those unsmiling eyes, then took out a Hershey bar, unwrapped it and walked toward her.

She immediately turned and tried to run on that crutch, falling, picking herself up and hobbling away from me. When she was sure she had a good distance between us, she stopped and looked around. Now those eyes were staring at me with a hateful intensity I never thought possible in a child. They burned at mine, and I couldn't look back at her. I dropped the Hershey bar in the sand and rain and walked over to the truck.

The Navy landing boat was coming across the channel, so we started our motors and drove to the very edge of the beach where the ramp would drop. When the boat hit the beach, I waved at the children, and they waved back, with no smiles. They were all empty-handed.

"This place is going to be a hell hole tomorrow," a sailor said as he looked at the kids, "and they're going to be part of it."

I surveyed the beach as we pulled away, my eyes finally finding the young girl. Odd that she would look at me or pay any attention at all, but she did. It was as though she was trying to kill me with those eyes. I couldn't blame her.

Before we hit Snaggle Tooth beach, the Navy lieutenant on deck, barechested with red-blond hair and enormous biceps, told us to keep going full speed until we got to the Seventh Marines perimeter checkpoint on the newly cut road that led through a VC ambush site. "These people are already hostile. Don't give them an excuse to shoot at you now."

I let my bolt go home and unclicked my safety. Looking across the channel, I saw two hooches, open-walled, with several older South Vietnamese women standing in them next to a counter. They all wore those black pajamas, were barefoot, and had their hair pulled back tightly in buns. Two had beetle-nut in their mouths, chewing it slowly, savoring every drop of the juice that made their mouths and teeth look full of blood.

When we hit the beach our truck drove off into wet, soft sand. Our tires spun, dug in, and then caught solidly enough to spring us up onto higher ground. The women yelled at us in those high-pitched whining voices to come over, buy a beer, a coke. They waved Korean Tiger beer bottles in the air. All the time looking at us with stony glares of bitterness. It was as though they knew something was wrong, something deadly was going to happen. I had no idea I would be directly involved in it, and yet I carefully looked down at my rifle bolt to make sure I had let it go home.

The marine next to me laughed, and I laughed too— maybe a little too hard, but it seemed to relieve the nervous-

ness that was causing my neck to twitch. What was wrong?
I could always handle it before. Why a problem now? I felt
naked, vulnerable, unsure of my every move. I could usually
cover those feelings with a ridiculous dirty joke or a smart
remark, but this time I didn't. This time I stared out at the
jungle and black rock speeding past as our truck went down
the road.

Coming around a short bend, we saw painted on the
slab of the rocky embankment the words, GO HOME AMER-
ICAN IMPERIALIST. I resented the slogan. Here we were
trying to help these people, and at the same time the VC had
infiltrated their minds, infested them with communism, and
had for the most part turned the people against us. I almost
fired a round at the rock. The sign must have been put on
recently because the paint was still dripping and mixing with
a drizzle of rain.

"This is where the Navy lieutenant said the VC ambush
site was," the marine across from me shouted over the roar
of the truck.

For some reason it was funny, and we both laughed
again, except we all kind of crouched in our small seats and
pointed our rifles outside toward the rock and jungle.

Just then the sun broke through the thunderheads and
flushed the whole area with deep, wet, green air. It was great
to see the sun take away some of the gloom, some of the
anxiety in the pit of my stomach. The marine across from me
made me put my safety back on.

"There ain't no VC 'round here," he said with confidence. "Look." He pointed out of the truck down a small
valley where several people were taking in their rice crop.

I pointed too. "They're VC."

The marine shrugged his shoulders. "How long you
been in this country?" I asked.

"Three weeks."

I rolled my eyes up. Suddenly, thankfully, we drove up
to Seventh Marines perimeter checkpoint, then sped over to
the Command Post tent. The perimeter was a beehive of
activity. Tanks were moving into position. Marines changed
guard, slung rifles over their shoulders, and ate cans of rations
on the move. Choppers dropped out of the gray sky, unloading

equipment, picking up squads of marines. Young second lieutenants scurried about, shirtless, carrying .45 pistols on their hips, issuing orders to reluctant, tired grunts who were not interested in getting out of their poncho-covered foxholes to do anything.

Oddly, I felt detached from all of it. There I was, seven months in-country without so much as a scratch on my hand, having gone through four operations before that, one at the DMZ, in the middle of a hundred percent perimeter watch, gearing up for a search and destroy operation that would finally meet the Viet Cong face to face, and I felt like I wasn't a part of it. That made me feel even more vulnerable. What the captain at the CP said suddenly snapped me out of that trance.

"I want you to take the lieutenant here out to the first perimeter east."

Our driver complained. "But sir, I've got to get the truck back to battalion."

"Marine, do it," the captain ordered.

In a rush, a young, fair-haired lieutenant, sunburned and still wearing his bars, jumped into the truck and sat down across from me. He was a ninety-day wonder going out on his first operation. He was smiling and making jokes, excited, as if we were going to a college football game.

We looked at each other and rolled our eyes.

We started off down the road, our truck taking point, the jeep behind us. The storm was now behind us and blue sky and sun in front of us. We rolled up the canvas on the sides of the truck and let the wind cool us off, but I still sweated as though wet from the rain.

Maybe it wasn't so bad after all. Maybe there were no VC around. Surely inside Seventh Marines perimeter as we were, there would be no VC. We had it made. We all leaned back on our seats and relaxed. It wasn't such a bad day after all. The faces I had seen earlier meant nothing now. The sign on the black rock had no meaning either. Thick green mounds of bushes passed my vision as we slid along the red clay road. I definitely felt better. The unnerving feeling of vulnerability was gone, replaced by conversation and smiles. It really wasn't a bad day after all.

One of the communications marines was talking about how it was his last operation. Thirteen in all. He didn't have to go out any more to combat, to a killing zone.

Killing zone, killing zone, killing zone. . . . The words echoed in my mind. Killing zone, killing zone, killing zone. . . . The words were screaming at me like a high-pitched voice against plate glass. I didn't know what it meant at first, but suddenly I knew something was wrong. Something was telling me something bad was going to happen. My sixth sense was desperately telling me to look out for danger. I felt I had to get out of there, run like hell, put as much distance between me and that road as I could. Get out of there . . . get out of there . . . get out of there. . . . Those words began to echo too.

Suddenly a terrific, muffled explosion underneath the front of our truck blew up mud and metal and slammed the truck up and then back on the road. The marine riding shotgun in front next to the driver screamed out in pain. We were thrown back and forth against all of the supplies and equipment. I tried to grab my rifle but it flew out of my hands onto the floor. The truck bounced and slid off the road into the bushes, rammed a mud mound and stopped. Smoke steamed from the remains of the hood, now contorted and bent into crazy shapes. A sick whistling sound issued from the radiator. We had driven over a buried VC land mine.

We all looked at each other. Then suddenly the lieutenant, without saying a word, jumped out of the truck and disappeared into the bushline. And suddenly bullets were tearing through the canvas top in a chatter of small arms fire from our right flank in the bushes, with a noise like balloons popping. I jerked a look over my shoulder and saw smoke floating up from rifle barrels in the leaves.

The marine next to me yelled, "Ambush! Ambush!" His mouth was thick with saliva and his lips were twisted over a cigarette that blew out of his mouth.

The VC were right next to us, yards away, filling the truck with bullets. I dove headfirst down into the equipment on the floor. But the marine sitting directly across from me was a second too slow. A machine gun clattered from the bushes and raked the back side of the truck, blasting right over my head. I could hear the repulsive sound of bullets splitting and splattering flesh. When I looked up I stared into glazed vacant eyes, eyes that now held half death, half life. Eyes that stared at me for years to come in nightmares, on street corners, at parties, when making love, when getting so drunk I was sick for days after.

The left side of his head was slashed open wide, a chunk of his skull missing, and gray liquid mixed with watery blood and matter slid down his head.

Then I stared at blood spurting out of the side of his neck like a fountain of water all over the canvas and the marine next to him. Half of his neck had been blown off by the machine gun. He tried to turn and bend toward me, making a horrifying gurgling sound and pointing at his rifle.

The marine next to me grabbed him and threw him down on me. I put my arm around his waist and tried to get him under me, but there was no room. Another burst of bullets went over us. Warm, thick blood poured all over my face, back and arms. Still another burst of rifle fire tore into the truck and dropped the other communications marine toward the back of the truck. He had taken rounds in both hands and across his back. He was trying to get to one of the radios, which were smashed.

A voice yelled out over my head, "Grenade!"

At first I thought one of our guys had thrown one out. But a VC had lobbed one over the bushes. Just missing the inside of our truck, it blew up outside against it. Hot spraying metal pieces snapped through the side of the truck like a shotgun blast. My head slammed down on the floor, and I felt sick, my head dizzy as though someone had hit me as hard as he could on the back of the neck with a rabbit punch. The little finger on my left hand was numb, opened up and bleeding, the bone sticking out of the flesh. I tried to push it back in.

Then the VC opened up on us still again and pinned us down completely. All we could do was pray. I remember saying, "God, if you get me outta here, I'll never volunteer to come out here again."

Then suddenly I was thinking about my father and being home in Streator, Illinois. I wanted to be with him so much just then. I wanted to sit with him and talk, tell him my desires, and all the things sons and fathers talk about.

Then suddenly I felt like someone had kicked me as hard as he could in the back. At first there was no pain, just a dull numbness, a tingling sensation that traveled up and down my back and legs. In the next second an excruciating, striking pain went all over my back as though it were splitting apart. I couldn't move.

God, God, I thought, I'm paralyzed.

I could hear the communications man trying to get one of the radios working, but his hands were all bloody and he couldn't move the dials.

"Son of a bitch," the marine next to me said, then jumped up and started firing into the bushes. He had a look of hate on his face I had seen before in others.

Though dazed, as though half of me wasn't there, I quickly made up my mind to move, refusing to believe I was paralyzed. When I thought that thought and lifted up my arm I could move. I moved every part of my body, even though my head, hand and back were aching with pain. I was wounded all right. Badly. But not as bad as the others. My legs were okay and I could move around. I took the marine who was on top of me and gently laid him him down on the floor. His face was gray and the grotesque wound in his neck was more horrible now than ever. I grabbed a tourniquet and did the best I could to put it around his neck, but it wasn't doing much good. The blood still poured out of his neck in a river. He was dying right in front of me and there was nothing I could do for him.

The marine who was firing at the bushes stopped firing. "They're running," he said, then jerked around. I have never seen anybody move so fast. Within seconds he had bandaged the communications marine, grabbed his rifle and started firing again.

I grabbed my rifle and pointed it out the back of the truck at the bushes moving as the VC rushed for cover. They were trying to get out of our sight. But my rifle wouldn't fire, and when I looked at it I saw that the barrel was bent over.

"McMullen, no radio . . ." the communications marine lying against the radio was saying over and over.

I looked at him, his fist rolled up in tourniquets like white boxing gloves.

"You guys gotta go for help," he said.

I looked up at the cab of the truck and could see that the driver and shotgun were still alive. Through it all they had ducked down and were spared. The shotgun's hand was all bloody, but that was his only wound.

I picked up a rifle and without hesitation jumped out of the truck, looked at the bushes where the ambush had come from and started running back up the road.

I kept thinking, where's the jeep? Where did those guys go? Where was the lieutenant? I looked into the bushes as if to find the jeep blown up too, but it wasn't.

Suddenly the lieutenant jumped out of the bushes waving his .45 pistol, wearing a red face and a look of horror.

"We gotta get help," I said to the lieutenant. "They're down there dying."

Without waiting for his reaction I started running up the road again, and when I got to the top of a small hill I saw our jeep coming my way. They had gotten out when the mine went, and were now coming back to help. I leaped and shouted and pointed down the road to the truck. They raced past me with rifles in the air.

Then I turned toward the right flank and looked off in the bushes and up to a small hill about two hundred yards away. I saw a Viet Cong wearing a red head band disappear over it. At that instant an ugly primitive feeling swept over me. I wasn't angry. Or even mad. What I felt was the worst kind of hate. I wanted to kill and kill again. I wanted that VC. I wanted to jam a knife right into his heart, again and again. I could feel my face twisted in this hatred, as I pointed my rifle at the fleeing VC, but the rifle I had wouldn't fire. There were no more rounds in the magazine. I ran toward the thick bushline and plowed into it, darting my entire body around in every direction. Then I started running toward the hill.

"Marine!" a voice said behind me. When I turned I saw the lieutenant staring at me strangely. "Let them take care of the sweep." He pointed to a truck full of marines jumping out and putting helmets on. He grabbed my arm and pulled me free of the bushes. "You're wounded. Give me your rifle."

I knelt down, weak, spent, drained of all energy and

emotion. I looked up and saw our jeep speeding past headed for the CP with the two communications marines in it. Both were still alive.

Another jeep came up and the lieutenant put me in it and we too raced back to the medical tent at the CP. When I walked in they had the marine with the torn-out neck on the operating table under lights pushing tubes into his neck. His chest was heaving.

"Over here, marine," a corpsman said, putting me on a stretcher. He laid me down on my stomach and took a flashlight and looked down the hole in my back. "Yep, you took a round in your back. It's a fourth of an inch from your spine. And your head's opened up in the back with grenade fragments. Nothing to worry though."

"Shit," I said, "nothing to worry about? . . ."

"Hey, man, you're alive aren't you?" He walked away. "Let's get a chopper in here on med-evac to Chu Lai."

On board the helicopter, vibrating over the island then out to sea and along the beach, I stared at the unreal world in Nam as it passed by, then at our wounded, then out to sea into the drab outline of heavy mist that blocked out the Real World thousands of miles away. Uncontrollably I dropped my head in my hands, wiped my eyes, and stared up at the gunner of the chopper, who was wearing tiger utilities and a helmet and goggles that made him look like death. He leaned on his machine gun, which was sticking out in the rain, and looked down at me through those goggles, looked out at the water below, then at me and winked.

It scared me, and the only way I stopped myself from blacking out was to cling to the trousers of the marine who had taken those rounds across his neck.

34

Panther Power

Swamp notes—beyond dedication
*Energy is never created nor destroyed, we're
told. Maybe so. I know that when one form
of evil energy is destroyed, a strong and
positive power rushes in to take its place.*

I'd been sitting against that cabin wall for a long time, how
long I couldn't tell, but I felt weak from the memory that had
overtaken me. When it finally released me back to the present—this cabin, this swamp—I gradually gathered my energies
to make one last effort at tracking Shakespeare that day.

It was the first time I had relived getting wounded in
every detail. Other times I had desperately tried to block it
out with long pulls from a whiskey bottle, later finding myself
with a spinning head staring up at a dark sky in an alley, on
a back street, pulled off the side of the road with vomit on
my chest. A few times I had black eyes and a bloody nose,
not even remembering the fight or the opponent. Once I woke
up sprawled out on the carpet in a strange apartment along
with half a dozen half-naked other burned-out looking people
I'd never seen before.

But Shakespeare's swamp had carefully brought it to
the surface, bared it in every detail so that I could finally look
at it for what it really was. I knew then why it had bothered
me so much over the years. I had carried with me a guilt that
I could have done more to help those guys getting busted up
in the ambush. The marine across from me who was a second
slower ducking had taken the rounds I thought were meant
for me. The communications man at the other end of the
truck had tried desperately to tell me how to work the radio
to call for help, and I didn't know how to get it started.

And there was one more critical moment in that ambush, a split-second decision just before I jumped out of the back of that truck. Had I truly been going for help, or was I trying to save my own ass, leaving all those wounded behind to bleed to death? No, my pure and simple motive was to get help. I smiled out into the swamp in all its glory, into God's glory. All these years I never wanted to face up to that. I never had wanted to stare it straight in the face. But looking at it in every minute detail as I had just done left me with no other conclusion. No other marine in the entire corps would have done better. Somebody had to run back up that road and at least try to get help. There was no other way. But when I found the lieutenant, then the guys in the jeep coming down the road toward me, and another truckload of marines from the perimeter, something had snapped off in my mind.

Oh, I had gotten wounded all right, just like the rest. But I was still on my feet, still able to fight. Maybe it was the very idea of running away from the ambush, something that is unheard of in the Marines. But I hadn't done that until the VC had broken contact and fled. So there was no coward-born feeling there. I now wondered if I would ever have another flashback on that ambush. I doubted it.

I felt revitalized and wanted to track Shakespeare more now than ever. I moved out onto the high ground and pursued tracks. My efforts were immediately rewarded. Farther into the bush were fresh tracks. Panther tracks. Shakespeare's tracks. Two fore paws. One hind paw on the left side. All distinguishable enough to prove they were his. And even though they were not hard-crusted—in fact they were pretty fresh—in this dirt they looked fossilized. Examining them close up in the light, I could even detect the toe print crevices calloused time and again in Shakespeare's life as a predator.

I knew I was a lot closer to him now than ever before. Maybe he had grown used to me after all this time, accepted my crazy ways and preferred not to worry about me. That closeness made me feel very good. But it also brought on a fear that dropped in my stomach because the hunters in the swamp were close to him now, too. That thought made me move swiftly in the direction Shakespeare had taken. I tried to close the gap between us just a few strides, and when I did, I noticed more tracks in the mud. So fresh were they that I noticed blades of grass just springing back up into place.

Could it be? I wondered. Could it be he is just up ahead?

I moved on, and as I did I had the eerie feeling Shakespeare was leading me to a remote place in the swamp only he knew where, a place untouched by humans.

Then I heard paws dash ahead. He really *was* just ahead of me. My heart stopped and began again with each step I took forward. What had I accomplished? Was I the first? Those paws hitting mud were pivoting trees and bushes, digging into more mud, leaves, swamp bog, and striding out. And all the time I stayed close to him. I was directly on the track of Shakespeare, behind him by yards, now fully in the gentle embrace of the untamed, more than ever in my life. My body seemed to be guided in, about, sideways and under the trees and vines, expertly. As though possessed by some great power. His power. Panther power!

I was staying with a panther, on his scent without dogs, without any radio telemetry equipment, relying on my physical senses, reasoning, perception, concentration. And my sixth sense—I knew that was operating full-power too. I wondered how long I could do it, how long I could match him stride for stride. If I could conceive in my mind to stay with him always or for as long as I liked, then truly, affinity was no dream. I prayed there were no hunters sitting in tree stands, looking for the brown fur of deer who by mistake might shoot Shakespeare, destroying this rare moment of ours forever.

I was so excited I wanted to dash up and grab his tail, but I contained myself. I never broke stride. My body continued to move forward in the direction it saw fit, and more tracks showed up.

Then I heard rifle fire far in the distance. I stopped dead in my tracks, listened, then carefully moved on. Suddenly his trail seemed to fade into divinity, and I felt Shakespeare go away like my soul leaving my body.

Those rifle shots were not meant for Shakespeare but they had spooked him and me. I was spent emotionally and physically, and knew I needed to go back home, collect my thoughts, organize my mind, revel in what I had just done.

In all my tracking of this great cat I had relied upon searching out the physical evidence he was leaving in his territory: kills, resting sites, scat, slash marks on trees, tracks. My sighting had been but a fleeting glimpse. But what I had done now opened up a whole new chapter in my quest. Could I do it again? The key really was to *be* a panther. Think, act, react, somehow to become Shakespeare. Do what he does in the swamp. Be the cat, be the cat, be the cat. They were just words. But to become the panther and stalk panthers was the real feat. At that point I didn't know how. But God had cracked open the door just a sliver to show me it was possible for it to happen.

35

Defeated

> **Swamp notes—winter months**
> *I long for another glimpse of Shakespeare. Maybe to reassure myself he wasn't a ghost or a figment of my imagination. Elusive and secretive are weak words when describing this creature of the shadows. It is now dry winter, and I too have become a shadow.*

Now I was among cypress, cold black water, hyacinth, clusters of pepperomia, vines of poison ivy with wet red leaves sweating resin. Immature white ibis in their brown plumage stepped back into the leaves to hide. An aggressive pair of red-bellied woodpeckers knocked on dead wood as they sang their distinct chiv-chiv. I disturbed a nighthawk from a small dry mound of mud and leaves. I slid through it all.

My eyes drank in every leaf, every tree, every movement, looking for a floating, deep, dark shadow moving in the dim light. When shadows did move, I stopped and did not blink an eye until I saw the animal. Most of the time it was a raccoon on a log, an owl in a tree, a snake in the water, a gator in the weeds, a turtle plopping, or one of the numerous warblers and starlings in the bushes.

It went like this for hours. Up on the high ground, and now in the soft mud of a drained water hole, I looked for the large paw prints. Even thinking about it made me excited as I crept about. If it were not for some encouragement, some smallest thing that would spur me on, I wondered how long I would stay out there. These little nuggets of will would crop up out of nowhere, just when my interest was dropping off.

On this trek it was getting close to evening, and I now felt I had lost Shakespeare altogether. I decided I would go to another part of his territory the following day. But strangely I felt a presence, as though something were watching me not far off. The feeling didn't last long, but it was the way my whole body trembled, telling me something was afoot. That sixth sense again.

Without seeing the animal yet, I knew it was Shakespeare. A chill went up my spine, that great feeling, and just as I smiled, it vanished. I went to the treeline and sure enough, after a little searching, I found paw prints perfectly shaped in the leaves and mud. It was the only place he could have been standing because it was the only high ground anywhere around that led off into a trail.

I began to follow the prints on that trail, passing through shadows and sheets of light, inching around logs and under bushes. Several times I lost the tracks and had to wander until I found them again, feeling confident the great cat could roam the swamps for the rest of his life and always I would be behind in close pursuit. Nothing would stop me. Somehow, I thought, I must figure out a way to see him once more. But no matter how slowly I crept forward, I didn't see so much as an ear.

Shakespeare was living up to his reputation. Then it dawned on me I should pick up my pace, maybe even run after him. It was worth a try. Surely he would have to rest. So, with my eyes to the tracks, I started to trot, then run, until I was striding out in full speed and still keeping on the trail. But the cat might as well have been a million miles away, no matter how fast I ran. I pushed on nonetheless. Finally my legs got weak and crumbled beneath me, sending me rolling into the mud and bushes.

As many times as I tried to push myself past that barrier on that day, I never seemed to have the strength to withstand the agony. Running as close to the tracks as I could, building up speed, then striding across small clearings, attempting to shift all of my power and strength into my legs, heart and lungs, swinging my arms close to my body, and then trying to stretch out even more, imagining Shakespeare doing the same and thinking I could match it. I expertly dashed through the thickest part of the swamp on high ground directly behind the big cat's trail. But could I keep it up long enough to outlast the cat? My legs were already getting heavy again, my heart pumping.

Just because Shakespeare was a sprinter, short-winded and unable to run long distance, didn't mean I could catch up to him in a dead run, or even tree him. But I actually thought I could, until again I stumbled and fell. I lay there, puffing, sucking for air, sweating heavily in the sun. Maybe, I thought, the trick is to try and get around him. I noticed I was traveling a huge broken circle, probably the cat's complete territory. Knowing it as well as I did gave me an advantage.

So I tried again, only this time I cut across the swamp in an attempt to head him off. I made a forty-five degree turn, made it across high grass and slipped into the trees. I was defying all the usual professional ways of tracking. Instead I was trying to turn the tables on Shakespeare, outsmart him, just for another glimpse. Not far away I figured I would run right into the great cat. A smile turned to laughter.

But as quickly as my elation surfaced it dissolved in the weakness of my body. It simply would not keep up with my desires. I was physically limited. I again stumbled to the swamp floor, close to heat exhaustion. I vomited and I was dizzy and saw flashes of red and purple stars.

That scared me to death. I remembered in Vietnam during the hottest part of the summer one time when we were on a sweep through two villages on an old unused road alongside hills filled with VC spider holes. From those holes, on occasion, a rifle muzzle would appear and a sniper round would missile past somebody's nose. It wasn't funny. We were wearing full gear, flak jackets, packs, helmets. I was in a free sweat and my utilities were soaked against my body. Guys were falling, searching for shade, pouring the last of their canteen water over their faces, staring off into the distance with a blank, dead expression, their faces turning to plastic. Heatstroke not only took several guys out of Nam but also some of them out of existence. Their brains were fried in the heat and they became vegetables. I remember one marine screaming at the top of his lungs, holding his head and slamming it against a tree. It took two corpsmen to rope him down and carry him to a med-evac chopper.

Now, in the swamp, my head was pounding violently. I was having hallucinations of giant snakes crawling onto the trail. A big ugly bird sat peering at me from a tree with something wet and slimy slipping out of its mouth.

Then the Nam hallucinations started, surrounding me with frightening images I never wanted to see again. Olive faces were staring at me from the bushes. Narrow, brown, upward-slanted eyes crowded shadows. Small round faces with crying eyes shot out at me from the cypress. Then rifles were pushed through vines, and foreheads with red and black bandannas filled more shadows. Bare feet and muscular legs were moving around me, surrounding me.

I kept jerking around looking for a way out. I struggled to my feet, eyes blurry, and began running aimlessly through the trees, slipping and falling, desperately trying to get to my feet, running through mud and vines entangling me. I tore them off, fell backwards over a log, my back slamming onto sharp cypress knees, got to my feet, stumbled, and began crawling on my hands and knees in the water. And all around me trees turned into VC—some dead, some wounded and bloody, some with no arms or legs, others pointing rifles and pistols at me. Small children pointed accusing fingers and held hand grenades.

"No-o-o-o! . . ." I screamed.

I was deep into a Nam war-panic and couldn't control my mind, couldn't stop it from reeling aimlessly through Vietnam. I got to my feet, gasping for air, my lungs heaving in the thick humidity.

Farther and farther I pushed myself, trying to escape those war souls who had it in for me, who wanted to destroy one more American life for their cause. I was their prime target because I did not have to participate in the Great Atrocity. I could have easily sat it out in my hometown oblivious to the destruction, drawing a check from one of the factories. But I didn't. I volunteered. I picked up an M-14 rifle and headed for Nam. I filled my magazine with 7.62-mm. bullets and blasted away at the night, filling a hooch full of lead. I was the guy out there setting up trip wires, loading ammunition dumps, destroying rice crops, shooting at children, beating up VC prisoners for information. I was even the guy who shoved my rifle barrel at a Buddhist monk's temple, searching him for weapons. His saffron robe hid nothing except his thinly fleshed bones.

And now I was paying the price for having sacrificed my own morals and sense of good judgment to an American cause that had no meaning.

I ran and ran and ran, not even looking where I was going, hoping that maybe my heart would explode and it would be over. All the guilt would fall into the black swamp water and wash away in a rain storm and I would be free. It would be over. And so I pushed myself harder yet. But my legs were no longer moving and I stopped and flopped headfirst into the water. "Shoot me! . . . Go ahead, shoot me! . . . Do it! Get it over with! Pleeeeeease!"

I staggered to my feet and bared my chest. But no bullets tore into my body.

Instead when I opened my eyes I saw only a peaceful swamp. I collapsed and pulled myself toward deeper water, fell in, melting into the cool savior.

When I'd stayed underwater as long as I could, I came up for air, drank small amounts of water, then slipped down under once again. I did that over and over until the pounding stopped. My heart was still racing and I couldn't seem to get relaxed. My legs seemed severed from my body, floating about on their own. Yet I could feel the deep pain in my hamstrings and calves. I had pushed myself way too far, too soon, and I was paying the price.

Oddly enough I felt there were two of me there, one in the water, another watching. Yet I was more conscious of me in the water. I felt sick again, as though somebody had jammed a hose down my throat and poured tar into my stomach. A bile taste hung in my mouth and I vomited once again, only this time it was the dry heaves. Hot stinking air came out, and that made me all the sicker.

When finally my body cooled, I lay there thinking how ridiculous it was ever to entertain the idea I could run Shakespeare down. Yet the thought lingered.

I pulled myself out of the water and rested on the embankment. Exhausted, I felt myself drift off.

When I came around, the sounds of frogs and night insects filled the hot, humid, quiet air of the swamp. Ants crawled over my still body. Mosquitoes bit harder than ever. My legs were sore and stiff and my aching head roared with defeat, disappointment, failure. It would have been so easy for me to leave my body for dead there for the ants, beetles, crows and vultures. Maybe even Shakespeare. As I lay there in the wilderness of creepy crawly things, in the tranquility of wildlife, a strange feeling came over me. It was something I didn't want to accept, but it was staring me in the face this time and very hard to avoid.

I was nothing more than a human being—just another element in the balance of nature. Accept it, I thought. I am like all the rest of the human race. If I had been meant to track panther and attain an affinity, then I would be a panther. I wasn't. I was nothing more than a man. Only a man. Just a man. Nothing more, nothing less. I belonged back in society, working nine to five at a stupid job. And in search of . . . nothing.

Who cares about Shakespeare? A panther. An endangered species, supposedly almost extinct. So what?

I got up and stretched long and hard and slowly started to walk out. After a while, once I got a halfway decent job, paid off all the bills, things would be better. Maybe after a year or so I would establish a way of thinking like the rest of society, settle down, have children, get fat, drink beer, watch boring football games on TV, go bowling, play golf. Be a human being, be a grandfather, and eventually die. I felt pretty good. I had just made another very important decision in my life. I was going to disband the whole project and forget about panthers. I told myself I was very grateful for the opportunity I had had to see how I could develop tracking skills with all of my service background. I had at least attempted to track the most elusive mammal on earth, and that was good enough.

But all of that was behind me now. I was finished with it. Oh, maybe I would make it a hobby just for the fun of it. But for the most part, it was over. I kept telling myself I was nothing but a mere human being—a good one, but just the same like all the rest. A man is a man wherever he may roam in this world. Ordinary. Nothing special. I would now give it my best to be like the rest.

So, quite weary from my tracking, I plodded through the swamp, setting a course for home. Head down. Eyes forward. Looking for the main road. All in all, I felt pretty good inside. What the heck was so bad about being an everyday human being? Nothing bad about that, I guess. Anyway, it was better than the madness of chasing panthers around a swamp—which wasn't all that far from the madness of Nam. Hadn't I just experienced how the one had so easily taken me back to all the horror of the other?

With this thinking I made a gallant effort to splinter the bridge of thought I had had with this obsession to attain affinity with the panther. It felt really good not having a challenge, a challenge that hardly could be attained. To be free of the burden of succeeding at something no man could ever hope to imagine really felt super good. It didn't make any difference now. I felt better at that moment than I had ever felt in my life.

It was an unusually cool night and a black breeze went through the dark swamp. My arms gently brushed against the tall grass on the old trail I was now following out of the swamp.

Yes, it's good. It's going to be a much better life now, I thought. I realized that my heart, lungs and legs were not built for long-distance tracking. Or any tracking, for that matter. I went home.

36

Man and Panther

Swamp notes—at home
*I have devised every means possible to free
myself from Shakespeare, from my wilderness obsession. Besides, if anyone found out
what I've been doing, they would cart me
off. I am determined to become "normal."*

I did go home, got a part-time job, and for a long time forgot
about Shakespeare. My life did unfold to a degree and I was
happy for that.

But I couldn't hold on to the job. It was boring, boring,
boring. And eventually I was fired. Oddly, when I walked out
I felt calm, collected. Not angry. Not bitter. I began to believe
that what I truly needed in my life was a large degree of
uncertainty, independence, some chaos. Every day different
from the one before. That's when I was happy. There had to
be adventure, a mystery. What was I doing with a white shirt
and tie on, with shined shoes? I needed the wet wild mud of
the swamp on my skin. I needed wildness. Craved it.

I needed Shakespeare far worse than I knew.

I had trained myself to track day in and day out. How
had I managed to do that? By what force of nature was I able
to produce even that? The forces of nature. That thought
crammed itself into my mind constantly. Somehow the forces
of nature had to get my mind, body, heart and spirit-self to
work together. The words rang in my ears. That would be a
great deal more than the force of nature. That would be the
force of . . . super-nature.

Finally the first chance I got, even though it was night,
I sped out to the swamp, rushed into the trees, and screamed
at the top of my lungs.

"Shakespeare! Shakespeare!"

Dropping to my knees, I pleaded with him to come rushing out of the bushes and slam into my chest, wrestle me to the ground, maybe even go for my throat. I opened my watery eyes and stared up at the night sky. Then, as softly as I could utter, I whispered, "God, from here on out, I commit myself to you. My body, heart and spirit-self. I do this so that someday I can teach others."

At that second a strange thing happened. Even though the sky still held clusters of stars, a large cloud appeared overhead and bathed the swamp and me in a purifying rush of cold rain.

All I could do was kneel there, cry, and thank God for such a sign.

I had, through a spiritual revelation, broken through still another barrier, probably the most important one of my life: the barrier of belief in something I had never seen, something far greater than man, greater than the panther.

Now, as I knelt there, face cradled in my thighs, I envisioned Shakespeare once again. Every hair, every twitch of his muscle. My first sighting. His tracks, scat, ambush sites, kills. The very presence of his scent. His godly eyes. I envisioned myself staring into those eyes, face to face, in a final wilderness meeting between man and panther. Affinity. Our souls locked. There was a way for that to happen. And a very special reason why it should happen. I knew it would benefit mankind. Change our way of thinking. Change the course of events of destruction. If I could attain it, then all men could. Spirit to spirit. Man to panther. Life to death. Death to life. From the inside outward it would have to come.

37

Essence of Freedom

> *Swamp notes—a clearing in the trees*
> *It is as though I am being lifted. The Ever-*
> *glades are taking on a whole new meaning*
> *for me. Shakespeare is more than just a pan-*
> *ther. In the end I know that all mankind*
> *should be panthers.*

Early the following day I went back and looked for a clearing in the trees. When I found an open prairie, I started slowly walking through the high grass in the dim gold of the pale sky. Then I stretched out in a full stride, moving swiftly, warming up, but containing myself to only walking, stalking. I blended with the shadows, becoming those shadows momentarily, contributing to the blackness in them. Inwardly I felt as though I were in a radiant light, a protective light with a higher power pushing me onward.

I tracked harder and harder, longer and longer. I thought positively, of successful tracking, of only Shakespeare. I mixed faith with desire, God with each step. The cool air brushed across my face. Mosquitoes hovered around my eyes and ears.

Soon I was in waist-deep water, and after a while it was almost impossible to lift my knees up. But I forced myself onward, until my body was thrown into super-glide. I was refreshed with new energy, new vitality. I smiled, rejoicing in my wilderness recognition of the forces of super-nature. I wondered how far and long I could track. How long it would take me to be at Shakespeare's side.

I was on the lookout for him. I forgot completely about the ordinary, unchallenging, human existence I had resigned myself to earlier. That vanished in the shadows of the swamp. I could never be fair to myself now if I went back to that life, and I knew I could never turn back anyway. My commitment and revelation had thrust me into a higher realm and I was determined to attain still another goal in my life. Getting closer to Shakespeare was a far better step toward perfection than anything else in my life had ever been.

I knew there would be no more boredom, no more questions of what I should be doing with my life. I felt complete in my goal. Now it was time to find Shakespeare. I was ready.

Days and weeks passed. At dawn one morning, as red-shouldered hawks dove for rabbits, I stopped and rested for only the second time in six hours of tracking. I was exhausted. As the sun passed over the trees and high grass far off I noticed a large brown shadow in full flight.

I sprang to my feet. In the path of that sunlight, the shadow floated through the grass, parting the blades softly, effortlessly, but with the force of a power bordering on supernature. It was the very essence of wildness rolled up into one panther. So excited was I that I had been awarded still another fleeting glimpse of the great cat Shakespeare that it rekindled and in seconds inflamed my burning desire to reach out even harder for our affinity.

I tracked toward that shimmering shadow with zeal and power. Even though I had had little sleep for days I never felt more alive than at that moment. My entire body shook both from elation and from the realization that I truly could be like Shakespeare. It was that last barrier I had to break through. . . .

As though on a thin, straight, white light, I tracked through shallow sloughs, then across the grassy waters, staying directly in line with Shakespeare. What was once a brown shadow up ahead, now turned into a distinct outline of a large cat. The swamp seemed to beckon him forward, obeying his commands, parting at his every movement. It was one with him, in him, and for him. He was the rarest creature the Everglades would ever give birth to, and it made no mistake in its recognition of the great cat. He was the essence of freedom. And it was my quest to merge my spirit-self with that essence. A communion. An intimate marriage of man-to-animal-to-super-nature.

Even though I was in the midst of the swamp, my eyes

glued on him at every stride, I still felt in another realm. He was like wind come alive, pure power, happiness transformed into a spirit. Then, at a forty-five degree angle, he rushed into the cypress trees, twisting and pivoting in that acrobatic wildness. Then he was gone.

When I got to the exact same spot, I entered. It was as though thin air had swallowed him up once again. But I was far from being disappointed. He had shown himself to me again. In all my failures, my awkward stumbling about the swamp, and finally in my discouragement, he was telling me to push on. Never quit. Even in death's black light, go on. Fix my goal firmly in my mind and push forward, no matter what. Believe I can attain it. Make it my one center of life. And no matter what has to be done . . . do it. Keep close watch on every deed. Make sure it's right. Become the cat . . . become the cat.

What did it mean? Did I, even at that moment and with all that I had accomplished, surprising myself with abilities I never thought I had, did I know the full meaning of those words? Become the cat. That was the key to affinity with Shakespeare. How I was to do it I still didn't know. But that knowledge would come at the right time as long as I was there in the swamp ready to receive it.

Book VI

Ultimate Concealment

Good camouflage can make ambushing a
tenable technique. For predators that stalk
it can allow the hunter to close in nearer.
—*Philip Whitefield*
The Hunters

38

Top Predator

> **Swamp notes—in an oak**
> *The intelligence of a panther will probably
> never be measured. It might be impossible
> to test him. I know his habits, his behavior.
> I know that he can outsmart me with the
> flick of an ear. He plays games with me,
> perhaps his way of accepting me. He knows
> I will never harm him. I think now he is
> protecting me.*

___

In the glory of the day's dawn I parked my car and got out
with a shovel and large black trash bag. Stepping up on the
highway, I scraped up two raccoons—both fresh road kills—
and regretfully put them in the body bag and twisted it shut
with a wire. I cleaned the shovel off on the grass, looking at
the splotch of blood soaked into the asphalt.

Thousands and thousands of animals are being slaughtered every week on the highways of the world. And in the
Everglades, cutting through the middle of them like two curving swords, from Naples on the west coast to Fort Lauderdale
and Miami on the east coast, Alligator Alley and Tamiami
Trail are Florida's examples of what not to do with the only
Everglades in the world. Money, men, politics, and ignorance
form a thrashing monster that has literally set the glades on
a steady course of destruction. Both highways stop the natural
flow of water south. Both highways provide high ground for
mammals. And, in turn, both have annihilated countless numbers of animals, including panthers, over the years.

I carefully placed the bag in my trunk and drove away,
avoiding driving over the blood splotch that now looked like
a pool of red tears shed for someone else's guilt.

Within a half hour I had slipped into the north end of

Shakespeare's territory on dry ground where several oaks sat like proud Indians. Heavy-trunked and with a symmetrical crown, this tree offers a superb hiding place. I picked out the largest tree and crawled toward it. The stiff egg-shaped oval leaves that it had already shed provided a soft carpet, but its acorns scraped my stomach. A ring-necked snake poked his head up and with the speed of a racer, dashed for cover. Red ants were everywhere, and it was all I could do to endure their bites.

I opened the body bag and surveyed the area, looking for the best place for the raccoons. I found the perfect spot about sixty feet away downrange on high ground in an open area close to a cypress treeline where Shakespeare would have to leave cover to investigate the bait. I delivered the quarry and went back to the oak. If Shakespeare was hungry enough here was fresh meat, and he didn't even have to make a kill. I had taken black fishing line, tied it on the neck and hind paw of one of the raccoons, then strung it along the branches back to the oak. Every once in a while I tugged at the line to create movement, and about every half hour I would use a distress call as though the raccoon was just being killed by another predator. I knew Shakespeare was here somewhere, and alerted by the fresh blood scent, then by the call, if he was interested at all, he would come.

I had carried in a 32-foot, thin nylon rope, painted black and green, with a large shark-fishing hook on it. In one throw it easily wrapped itself around the largest trunk. As fast as I could, I climbed the tree and arranged myself in a comfortable sitting position in a crotch about fifteen feet up. For camouflage, earlier in the week I had glued oak and resurrection fern onto my camouflage utilities from my neck to my feet, so that when I lay across the trunk I blended into the contours and foliage. In this way I eliminated my shadow, distinctly disrupted my human outline, color-matched the area I was in, and, as far as I could tell, was totally camouflaged. The tree canopy offered counter shading and for all purposes I was to become an oak tree. I painted oak leaves and bark on my face, I stuck oak branches in my forest green stocking cap. My hands and boots were covered with camouflage netting.

Once settled in, I was first harassed by a red-winged

blackbird and two green herons who apparently agreed that I looked like a tree. Then a curious yellow rat snake slowly crept right over my shins and down into a hole I suspected was once used as a nesting site for warblers. Several small spiders crawled up and down my face, and one even began to spin a web on the ferns near my shoulder. I felt then that no creature knew I was there.

I stared at the raccoons. Blackbirds and crows came in first. Two black vultures soared overhead, but didn't land. Thank God for that, for they would have eaten both of the coons to the bone. Black flies landed on the open flesh. And then for a long time there was nothing.

Later in the day, a mother raccoon with four young ventured down to the kills, but strangely acted repulsed. And when I jerked at the line, bringing the dead coon's head up, they all rushed off for cover.

For more than twelve hours I lay in that oak, my back numb from my shoulder blades to my ankles. At one point there was a cloudburst that left me drenched and sticky. To amuse myself, I tugged at the line as though the raccoon were a puppet. By short jerks or slow pulls I was able to create a wounded animal desperately trying to hold on to life. And still Shakespeare did not show.

As night fell, I sighed heavily, checked the perimeter one more time in the remote hope Shakespeare might just be bold enough to show himself, then climbed down and took the line off my thumb, and began the long trek back to my car.

I hadn't walked thirty feet into a bush line when I stumbled onto panther tracks in the deep mud near willow. There was even a place in the mud where the cat had sat down and, I think, scratched himself. Dumbfounded, I snapped looks all around. Then I smiled.

Why, you son-of-a-panther!

Kneeling down in the relative position of Shakespeare, I peered among the cypress and slowly up into the oak tree to the crotch where I had lain. I got up and walked out of the bushline and checked the position, then went back to the kneeling position. I was hidden from view on ground level, as well as from the tree. Shakespeare, sometime during the day, had expertly crept up to the bushes and surveyed the situation, maybe even observed me up in the tree. The tip-off could have been an unconscious movement by me, an unnatural tugging of the fishing line, too many distress calls, my scent floating upwind on the ground. Whatever it was had told Shakespeare something was wrong.

I cursed my inadequacy and tried several times to kick myself in the backside, then started back to the bait-site, muttering something about how stupid I was.

But when I got there the raccoons were gone!

A small drag trail led back into the cypress, and on low ground, I found Shakespeare's tracks once again.

Now I felt not only stupid, but terribly embarrassed to have been outsmarted twice in one day. Shakespeare, having seen me in the tree, waited until I climbed down, then silently padded away and around the perimeter under thick cover. As I was checking out his tracks, he rushed up and stole the raccoons right out from under me.

From the oak tree to the car, tail between my legs, my pride destroyed, I walked, shaking my head. I had learned still another fragment of vital knowledge about his infinite adaptability. At times I wondered if Shakespeare was an omnipresent panther. I was beginning to appreciate his extreme intelligence, his ability forever to outsmart me. I acknowledged my own human limitations.

39

Midnight Visitor

Swamp notes—in a cocoon
*Each close contact I have with Shakespeare
is a step beyond contact with human beings.
We are having little affinities along the way.
Flash shots of the Oversoul, then nothing.
That's what Shakespeare is teaching me.*

I had been tracking all day, my feet and legs soaked through with swamp water, my face sunburned over tan, my camouflage shirt torn in several places from a small war with a thorn patch that also left long gashes on my forearms and fingers.

I had come up on an old trail originally cut through the swamp by Seminoles, later used by pioneer hunters, and still more recently by lumber companies and modern hunters with their swamp buggies.

I lost track of time and before I could stretch out my jungle hammock across the trail and tie it to two large maple trees, that wondrous black silence surrounded me, took me to its bosom, and occasionally broke itself with those echoing wild sounds of the night.

Under a quarter moon, I repaired the mosquito netting on my hammock, struck a small fire, and had a cup of coffee with honey. Before long the day's tracking got to me, so I rolled into the hammock, sighed deeply, munched on a granola bar and drifted into a lazy half-sleep. My hammock swayed across the trail in a warm winter breeze like a cocoon on a small branch. A cool breeze came through the netting.

In my dreams I thought I heard a distant, high-pitched, alpha scream, humanlike, with a sorrowful moan at the end. As I jerked up, the sound still came across the water. Again, and again, and still again, it shattered the swamp.

I had been searching for Shakespeare for three days,

and before that for six months, without a sighting and I was beginning to believe he really had gone extinct. But that night, when I heard that scream that sent a chill up my spine, I knew it was a panther, a plea, a means of communication for us.

From that point on I felt something out there, moving, creeping. My sixth sense was working overtime. I was sure Shakespeare was near, and that scream verified it.

Even though the scream would have driven most people from the swamp, I strangely felt secure. So many times before Shakespeare could have killed me, and didn't.

I kept one ear and one eye open. Suddenly, I felt very vulnerable lying in the hammock, across the trail, zipped up inside the skeeter netting, cradling a flashlight on my chest.

Fronds on baby sabal palms rustled. Slowly, I raised the flashlight and pointed the beam in the direction of the sound. The red eyes of a spider glistened, masses of skeeters passed through the beam.

I sighed, relaxed, and closed my eyes, feeling small rodents scamper across my hammock's tent top.

Again, the sound.

This time when I shined the light, a shadow stole off into a wall of fern. Suddenly I was wide awake, adrenalin pumping, praying it was a raccoon, opossum, or rabbit challenging the last of the fire to get to the remains of my supper.

"Not a bear," I whispered, "not a bear."

I shined my flashlight once again around the perimeter. And as the moon came out from behind clouds, two twinkling pale-green eyes shone bright from the bushes. They reflected the moon, then lightninglike, they were gone, followed by a long jump of an animal onto leaves, accented by that black silence.

I got out of the hammock and stoked up the fire. Had I miscalculated Shakespeare? Had he grown so used to me in his territory that he decided on a midnight visit out of curiosity?

I kept looking off in the direction I had spotted the eyes and continued to imagine them there, burning into my mind, probing my soul.

Across that small space, somehow we had exchanged a recognition. It was as though I was staring at something in myself. A magnetic, mesmerizing moment. Green fire balls burned into the dark and deep and into my heart. For that second we had shared an ancient common bond. I did have a brief glimpse at his soul, and he at mine. I wondered what he saw.

40

Roadkills

> **Swamp notes—kneeling at a panther kill**
>
> *One moment a heart is beating; the next moment it is stopped. The blood that was pumped the moment before spills onto the concrete strip that slashes through the heart of the Everglades. The blood is bright red for a few seconds. Then it turns as dark and lifeless as the heart that no longer pumps.*

I was speeding down Alligator Alley about ninety miles an hour headed toward Route 29. I had just received a call that a dead Florida panther was lying on the road a little north of Alligator Alley, about three hundred yards. Apparently it had been hit by a car sometime during the night. My heart pounded and I had trouble holding the steering wheel because my hands were wet with sweat. God, was it Shakespeare? Had the worst happened?

When I got there I found just what the caller said, a dead panther. A car had collided broadside with a Florida panther, turning its insides to jelly, crushing bones, smashing the life out of the big cat, probably before it knew what hit it.

I was stunned, sick. It took me a while before I recovered enough to check the information I had to have. It was a female. Ideas raced through my mind. How old was she? Was she pregnant? Did she already have cubs? And were they wandering around the glades, helpless, lost?

I weighed and measured her—approximately seventy pounds and six feet long. Considering the condition of her paws and teeth, I put her right at around two, maybe three years old.

Beside the road I found tracks in and down into the ditch. And peculiar smaller tracks as well. Cubs. She had cubs out there. My mind turned off all other thoughts except those cubs. I could see them, streaked and spotted, ornery and kittenish, but now lost and hungry, prey to a thousand dangers. I spent the rest of the day searching the area, a two-mile radius, and then in a five-mile radius around that mother cat now lying lifeless in the ditch where I'd pulled her. But I could find no cubs.

When I turned the panther over to the Game Commission Panther Recovery Team leader the next day, it was the first time he had ever seen a female Florida panther from the Everglades. And it was the first indisputable physical evidence other than tracks and scat that the Florida panther still roamed the glades.

I went home but couldn't stay there. I went back out in the glades but didn't know where else to look for the cubs. I sat down on a log and put my head in my hands, more frustrated than ever. In all this time I had never gone public with my panther project, had kept Shakespeare totally secret, never once revealed to anyone what I had accomplished in my tracking. But a decision had to be made then and there, before Alligator Alley claimed any more of the precious few panthers left. If I did go public, would it help? Maybe I was just as helpless as those cubs out there.

I hadn't felt this frustrated since I was aboard ship in 1966 doing amphibious landings along the coast of South Vietnam. As I sat on the log I felt that old flashback feeling coming over me. I knew I'd have to see it through to the end. Why now, damn it? I didn't have time. But I had no choice.

We had already been on two operations against Viet Cong to the south. But our third operation was on the DMZ.

DMZ. Just looking at the coastline sent fear through me. Indian country. Territory of the North Vietnamese Regular Army. Crack shots at seven hundred yards with new AK-47 rifles. Skilled in jungle warfare. And to top it off, they knew the countryside; it was their jungle. They wore uniforms and pith helmets, cartridge belts, canteens. They were the elite fighting warriors of Ho Chi Minh's force. They were the ones kicking asses all over the DMZ.

A whole Marine company went in by beach, while another was dropped in by helicopter. It was the idea of the brass to box the NVA in and then drop a ton of bombs on them. Our platoon, a support unit for I Company, was held back on ship as a reserve unit.

But on this particular war day, under a blazing sun, I Company, USMC, was going to make tragic history. By mistake the captain had taken the entire outfit eleven miles into North Vietnam. When he discovered his mistake, he turned the unit around and went running back toward South Vietnam the same way he had left. It was the biggest mistake of his life.

On high ridges overlooking a deep valley an entire NVA regiment was lying in ambush.

I was standing at the back of the ship, sweating in the heat, staring aimlessly at the silent coast when a sailor came past and announced, "I Company's getting annihilated." The words pounded against my temples. Those were the guys I'd gotten drunk with on liberty in the Philippines and at that moment they were getting blown apart with mortars, sniped at, wounded, knifed. I wouldn't let myself believe it. No way. That was impossible.

But when our lieutenant called a formation on the helicopter pad and I looked into his eyes, I knew it was true. His eyes were wide, bugged out, as though he had just seen a bad car wreck. He said the last transmission from the captain of I Company was, "Stay where you are, we're getting wiped out. . . ."

The next step was to send in a unit and rescue those guys. We were it. But the ambush had happened so fast and furious it was already too late for us to go in. All we could do was sit there, sweating, frustrated, waiting, wondering, unable to help in any way, even though we were trained, experienced in battle, and ready.

I sat on the log, sweating, frustrated, waiting, wondering. I was now experienced in the ways of the swamp, but for what? Had my goal of affinity with Shakespeare been smashed by some hit and run idiot on Alligator Alley? Was that dead panther Shakespeare? Could he have been a she all this time? And where were those cubs? I tracked furiously in Shakespeare's territory day and night for over a week, but found no recent signs of him/her. My heart and hopes began to sink. After all that Shakespeare and I had been through, would it end like this, both of us cut off from our destiny, from our cultivated affinity to come? I prayed with every step I took: Please don't let it be Shakespeare, please. . . .

At the end of ten days I still had not found as much as a track of Shakespeare, and had to face the tragic reality of death. And all this time I had thought Shakespeare was a male. But she had been a female. And now, now she was gone. My whole life fell out from under me. All my goals were falling apart.

Yet, during days on end of analyzing the situation, I finally chose to rely on some very obvious facts. Shakespeare's tracks were bigger than the paws of the female. Though she had been in close to Shakespeare's territory, his was a little farther to the south. I decided not to give up hope.

When the Game Commission performed an autopsy on the female, they found her to be sexually immature and only two years old. That put more hope back into me. It was even more unlikely that the female was Shakespeare. There was no way she could have had cubs. The smaller tracks must have been those of a bobcat.

A week later, on an early morning in deep mud above bear tracks, I found a fresh crystallized track of Shakespeare right in the middle of his territory. Breaking totally from ultimate concealment, I screamed out in joy. He was okay. We were together again. He wasn't dead or harmed in any way. He was alive and well and in the Everglades! All that time he had probably been farther south in his territory. If he had been there at that second I would have run up and kissed him. I said a prayer of thanks and tracked the rest of the day. My life had begun once again.

But my happiness was short-lived.

On February 7, 1980, one month after the female panther was killed, a man called me and told me he had accidentally hit a panther the night before on Route 29. Again I raced to the area and searched up and down the road and into the bushline. The site was right in the middle of the Big Cypress Swamp and not more than seven miles away from where the female panther was killed the month before. At the bottom of the ditch, three hundred yards away from the accident site, the panther lay motionless in the grass and mud. When I knelt down and touched him, his body was cold, and had been for hours.

His right hind leg had been broken and the skin on his spine was cut open. Blood was dried on his muzzle. Vacant, half-lidded eyes stared out at the grass and mud and sky.

It was a male Florida panther about eight feet long and approximately a hundred and twenty-five pounds.

The second one killed in a month. Male and female. A potential mating couple. When the Game Commission Panther Recovery Team leader came down to pick up this panther it was the first time he had ever seen a male Florida panther in the Everglades.

But was this one Shakespeare? It was big enough to fit in his tracks. Could I go through all the heartache again? I had to. I could do nothing but search his territory now. I had to find another fresh track. The odds were a lot longer this time.

41

The Tracker Tracked

Swamp notes—on an old logging road
I keep getting this empty, sinking feeling in my guts, as though life has gone out of me as surely as it has out of those panthers I found on the road. Every day that I track without results increases the odds against finding Shakespeare alive.

I had driven down an old logging road at the south end of Shakespeare's haunts in the early evening. I had been tracking all day and every day since the second kill. When I parked my car and got out, skeeters assaulted me, almost turning me back into the car, making me wonder what I was doing out there at a time when they were at their worst. I looked down at my legs covered black with them and looked back to the safety of the car. But I knew what I was doing there.

I pressed into the swamp on a trail reclaimed by the swamp after the hunting season was over.

There was that glades quiet, as though everything alive decided to halt in mid-stride and pay silent adoration to the reason for its existence, a distinct time in the swamp when I usually feel I am intruding on a rapture with God. That day the silence only seemed to bode death and emptiness.

Suddenly, up ahead, was the biggest water moccasin I had ever seen, slithering across the trail. At first I thought it was an escaped python because of its length, probably a good six feet, its thickness, probably eight inches round, and the reflection of the brown-gray patterns in the setting sunlight. I stopped dead, still as an oak tree in frozen ground, but he had already felt my vibrations on the ground under his scaled body. I wondered what it would be like to hold such a creature in my hands, a creature that could instantly send me into agony, my flesh swelling a deep black-purple, as I turned into a dead man, baked and bloated in the sun. But wondering was as far as fantasy went. I wasn't about to get any nearer than I was. He turned toward me, and with an authoritative stare, continued across the trail and into the water.

At each low, washed-out area thereafter I found small tracks of snakes, raccoon, and opossum. There were huge alligator tracks, wading bird trails along the edge of a slough, and near one pond the old, bleached remains of an adult otter. Overturned in the water was a three-foot alligator with a missing tail and a bullet hole right between the eyes. A poacher's quarry. His stomach was soft and partially opened, emitting a rotting stench only the swamp could harbor.

But there were no new tracks of Shakespeare, not even a hint that a bobcat had been on the trail since the last rain.

I grew weary of the mosquitoes but not of my goal of finding Shakespeare's tracks in that part of his territory. Usually, at that time of year, he was in that area. He may well have been there but left no signs of it, playing that cunning game of concealment. Or maybe he hadn't been there since that day a week ago when . . .

I was in about a mile and a half when I stopped on the other side of a low, muddy area I had just slopped through. I looked up the trail to my left, then to my right. Dejected, I turned and slowly walked back.

Though I had my head down, swatting skeeters off my neck, I really wasn't looking at the mud. But suddenly, like a hawk rushing toward prey, a panther track jumped out at me from the mud. In fact there were several tracks walking right into mine, the ones I had just made seconds before! They went across the trail and into the trees.

Shakespeare!

I looked in that direction, now feeling him in his most intense wildness. He was right next to me, but I couldn't see him, hear or smell him. Slowly I went to the edge of the trees and peered in. I could see more tracks leading down into a ditch, then up the side into cut grass. My heart was pounding against my chest. My hands trembled.

Peering back continuously, I back-tracked his paw prints across the trail and into the other side, down along the ditch, all the way back to the treeline where I had parked the car. Not only had he outsmarted my normal senses again, but, due to his immeasurable secrecy, he had easily gone undetected by my sixth sense. Even today he had tricked me, even now when I had never been more feverishly eager to find him.

Reconstructing the experience, I figured he had been in the treeline when I pulled up, dropped in behind me along the trail, and, well covered by the vegetation, simply, curiously, tracked me from about thirty or forty feet back for more than a mile. And in all that time, not once, with all of my swamp-proven skill and knowledge, did I detect he was anywhere near. He could have ambushed me at any second, leaving my bones to the vultures. But he didn't. When I stopped to turn around, he didn't have to walk across the trail. He could have remained under cover as I passed him, then gone his way.

But he chose to leave a few tracks in the mud, maybe to let me know he was still there. I couldn't help but think of that Bible passage—how does it go?—"That which you are seeking, is seeking you."

42

The Hunters

> ### Swamp notes—at a check point
> *It is hunting season and I am feeling as hunted as the deer. Though most of the hunters are careful, there are some crazies out there who have no business in the swamp. When hunting season opens, my fears of Shakespeare getting killed are even stronger.*

The first day the men began to arrive, it was like being back in Viet Nam forming a perimeter around a free-fire zone. I was among hunters with high-powered rifles, pistols, and semi-automatic weapons, and they were wearing camouflage utilities, gun belts, and ammunition clips. They pulled into the park ranger check station at dawn in four-wheel drives, trucks and jeeps. Roaring swamp buggies rolled off trailers, belching heavy exhaust.

Running through the crackle of portable radios and the nervous conversation was the anticipation of a six-point buck on the fender at the end of the day. As old hats were pulled on, old jokes were exchanged between curses. Cups of coffee were gulped down and warm beer was sipped from cans in dirty hands. I heard laughter and the heavy metallic clamp of shotgun chamber bolts going home. I saw the flashes of cigars being lit and of chrome-plated knives sliding into sheaths.

But the most extraordinary thing about these hunters was that universal expression of death. From within unshaven, sunburned faces, eyes probed other eyes, as though silently trying to assure each other it was okay to kill. In this case it was a four-footed animal. In Nam it had been a living human soul. The irony of it all was that over a period of time, both acts would cause man himself to become an endangered species.

In the bush there was already the sickening, shocking sound of rifle fire cracking and echoing across the now troubled swamps. The stale smell of used gun powder drifted into the clearing. Overhead, a county helicopter hovered, its rotor blades slicing sun rays into fragments as it patrolled the region. The muffled heavy flutter of the chopper brought on memories of med-evac missions in Nam trying to get into a hot landing zone for wounded.

Far across the horizon, a firestorm raged with red flames and smoke rushing across a dried-out prairie, marking the beginning of a dry dry season. I could just make out small toylike figures skirting about, a few on bulldozers oddly noiseless at this distance, the rest wielding tiny shovels along the edge of the line of flames.

In all of this I resigned myself to roam Shakspeare's territory among those hunters to keep an ever watchful eye out for the panther only I knew was out there. As the hunters embarked on their yearly ritualistic endeavor, I too entered the swamp on foot.

I really wasn't sure how I could act quickly enough to stop a hunter if he mistook Shakespeare in the distance for a deer, which could easily happen, but I knew if I could spook Shakespeare out of the area he would be safer.

I introduced myself as a writer in search of a story to a group of hunters who more than gladly took me along. They all wore red bandannas around their heads, camouflaged bush hats and large Bowie knives, and carried rifles that were well cleaned and oiled. One had a large hunting slingshot, and as we started down an old hunting trail now cut open and gouged out by swamp buggies, he expertly inserted a black steel ball in its pouch, stretched out and aimed at a cardinal sitting in a maple tree not more than twenty feet away. Her brownish-red color identified her as a female; very possibly the bright red mate was in a bush to her left. So quick was the shot that all I saw were red shiny feathers exploding. He had hit the male. He laughed loudly saying he was off just a little to the left. Next time he would improve on that. No sense wasting a ball if he didn't have to.

I turned my head in anger, listening to the female cardinal twit about and fly off. I wanted to turn on the hunter, take the slingshot and wrap it around his neck. But I had learned long before that violence does, in fact, breed more violence until it is out of control. Had I detected even a second before the shot that he was actually going to shoot the bird, then I would have tried to stop him. But it was too late. I knew for sure this hunter wasn't out for a swamp stomp just for the fun of it, and he wasn't out to get himself a deer. He was out for the pure pleasure of killing. I suspected most of his black desires would be taken out on small animals like the cardinal. Totally defenseless. Unable to skirt off before death would slam into them.

I could see it in his eyes. Kill. There is some strange emotion in people like that. They may not hunt for months, then, like craving for a fix of liquid snow, they will rush to the swamps and kill everything in sight. For them it is as orgasmic as having sex or tripping out on drugs. The eyes go wild, glaze over, and for a second they look like they might pop out. Then that troubled calm rushes over the face. These guys are only at peace when in war. This hunter was going to be on a killing spree for the duration of the hunting season.

As we walked down the trail, two of them lit up joints and passed them around. I declined, declaring my lungs were half rotted as it was. One told a joke and all laughed, retold the joke and laughed some more.

My first conclusion was that I would put these guys in the "wowie" category. They were dangerous with their weapons. To begin with, they broke all the basic rules of safety. Their attitudes were wrong and they weren't concerned about other hunters in the area. They could easily be responsible for an innocent hunter getting his head blown off. These boys were not the type anybody wanted to be with—and I feared were the perfect candidates to take a shot at Shakespeare.

I decided to stay with them a while longer to see what effects the joints would have on them, then, keeping their direction in mind, to excuse myself for a bodily necessity, slip off and find some other hunters.

But as we walked along I began to detect fresh deer tracks. One buck. One doe with a fawn. They cut across the trail in mud where it looked like they had stopped to drink.

But these hunters were too busy throwing their knives in the mud ahead as they walked, playing that stupid game of chicken with the knives to see how close to each other they could throw them. They didn't see the tracks and I wasn't about to call their attention to them.

These deer had walked the trail at daybreak, probably heard the first shots of the hunting season and run off to safer ground south on the other side of Tamiami Trail.

Also in the mud, on top of, in, and alongside the deer tracks, were Shakspeare's tracks! Each one I saw I stepped on. The hunters didn't notice the tracks of either animal. Their attention now was on a huge gator, one I had seen so many times in the area that I had nicknamed him Bruno. They were throwing sticks and pieces of bark at him, harassing him to see how long it would take before he sank out of sight.

One of the hunters kept aiming in with his rifle, and for a second I thought he was going to pull the trigger. I was on the balls of my feet, inches away from jumping him and throwing the rifle to the highest trees. But he let up and laughed, saying he could make a hole between the gator's eyes that a truck could run through. I wondered what they would have done to me had I jumped him.

What was so unusual about these four hunters was that they all acted alike. Each had a different name, looked different, but they all smiled together, laughed together, told dirty jokes together, talked about how much they loved their rifles. Finally it did come out that they were all in the army together in Vietnam, stationed at Cam Ranh Bay, then in support of the AmeriCal Division up north in the DMZ. They were probably a group of guys that the army had simply turned loose at the VC and allowed to do almost anything they liked as long as they came back with a good body count.

One of them asked me if I was a draft dodger during the war, and did I run off to Canada or Europe. I answered his question with a question: Do I look like I ran off, and if I did, would I be in the glades now? Yet I didn't tell them I was in Vietnam.

It puzzled them except for the one with the slingshot. He was a pretty perceptive guy, and though his mind had been warped by the war, and probably his life before that, he was smart. He came right up to me, face to face, stared hard, then with the slightest crack of a smile on his lips, said, "You were there. . . . Whatever yer name is, you were there. I been watchin' you out of the corner of my eye. You might be a writer, but nobody moves like you do if he spends half his time behind a typewriter."

"Maybe he's workin' with the rangers—you know, seein' if we're shootin' up things," one of the others said. Now they were all looking at me. I just sighed.

"Relax. Yeah, I was in Nam, just like two million other guys. Put my time in and got out."

"How come ya don't carry a weapon?"

This was no time to explain why I had given up that silliness, and to give them my philosophy on killing would have put them in an even uglier mood. "I shoot with words now. They're my best offense."

"That's heavy," the one next to me said.

One of the other hunters up ahead waved his hand,

then came back. "Okay, the huntin' boys are comin' down on the north trail. Let's take a chance, set in, and see if we can ambush a deer."

They all crouched, eased off the trail, picked out big enough trees to hide behind, and looked up the trail. I got down in the ditch and covered myself with leaves and dirt.

I kept asking myself what I could do to spook this deer off, if there was one. I decided to make some kind of a sound, something that would alert the prey to run for cover.

My plan was carried out by the hunters themselves. Each one chambered a round and the loud clamping of dull metal echoed about the swamp. It was definitely an unnatural sound, something no animal could make. If I had had a hundred dollars in my pocket I would have bet it all that the deer was long gone from the trail, had braved the water and was now seeking out high ground.

I decided feelings between those wowies and me were not the best, so it was time to ease out of the picture myself. I waited until they decided to walk farther down the trail, then got up muttering I was going off to look for a hole to pee in. They didn't pay any attention to me, just started walking up the trail, and I stepped backwards into the trees.

43

On Patrol

Swamp notes—among the hunted
*I walk the glades in thick swamp, praying
for tranquility, praying for this violence to
cease. There is no need to kill wild animals
anymore—except to satisfy that black abyss
in our souls that craves death. These hunters
at peace only in violence remind me of myself on patrol in Nam, carrying an M-14 rifle,
wondering if a VC sniper on a hillside would
crank off a round and tear my head off,
knowing I could do the same for him. I
needed that violence for survival then. Here,
now, I find no trace of it left in me. Is this
the same person?*

I had all but lost those hunters, except for occasional hideous
chatter of laughter punctuated by periodic cracks of rifle fire.
I eased back in the mud of what was possibly an old Seminole
Indian mound. When I found oxidized fragments of pottery,
I was sure of it. I mentally recorded the mound as a landmark
in Shakespeare's territory, possibly untouched up until that
moment by a white man. I had already pledged to myself
never to relay to anyone the location of other mounds I had
found, and now I included this one. I vowed never to dig so
much as a bone fragment from it. So much that Indians hold
sacred has been dishonored. I hoped that at least these small
mounds could bear the spirits of a proud people, hidden and
protected by the swamp, their swamp.

Lying there, I tried desperately to keep my concentration on what was around me, every movement, every sound.
What sound might mean Shakespeare's presence? An alligator
slid into the water and slapped his tail, spooking a great blue

heron who ascended through the cypress, excreting large white droplets that spattered into the water forming ghostly, deformed figures with bubble heads that burst at the gator's approach. But interrupting these wild sounds were the winding of swamp buggy engines and the clatter of steel tracks on soft mud.

In spite of those occasional man-sounds, it was the swamp that engulfed me, the swamp in all its intensity: the infinite dampness, heat, hovering insects, thick treeline, thick air. Was it again just the place, so like that other place, that made my mind begin to wander back to Vietnam, to dwell again on that never-forgotten war feeling? Or was it the man-sounds, my recent escape from men out to kill that triggered the intense memory I knew was coming, that I knew I had to see through to the end?

There I was on patrol to save the panther in the Everglades, but in my mind I was on patrol in Nam.

It was a weird, exciting challenge in the middle of a killing zone to snap a magazine into my M-14 rifle chamber, let the bolt go home to push a round into the barrel, tape an extra magazine upside down on the magazine already in my rifle, click over to automatic fire, sling the rifle over my shoulder, then grab two grenades—one fragmentation, the other concussion—tighten the strap on my helmet, zip up my flak jacket, and head over to report to the CP.

We always went out in fire teams of four marines. Point man twenty yards up front, automatic rifleman to the left, the two semi-automatic riflemen to the right and rear. It was all very organized as we left the perimeter. But once out of sight of the CP, we fell into our own formation by spreading well over fifty yards apart, giving the VC less of a chance to cut us all down with one burst of fire.

We figured when we were on patrol that we were bait to draw fire from the VC so the CP could pinpoint their positions, call in a fire mission of mortars or 105 cannons, and hopefully knock out an enemy emplacement or squad or so of VC. But then nobody for sure knew what the CP was thinking, and the way the operation was going we were sure the CP wasn't sure either.

It was patrol that always blew my mind. Buck's death had never left me. I felt less powerful, more vulnerable on patrol, and the high-powered M-14 rifle and grenades felt like toys in my hands. And yet the intense effort to stay alive carried with it an element more terrifying than anything I had ever imagined. Violence. It was a perverse, distorted act of physical and mental outrage brought on by bitterness and anger that welled up inside of me, a maniacal power constantly fed by more violence. An equally frightening thing about this satanic flaw in me was that it was in me before I ever went to Vietnam. Maybe I had never recognized or admitted it until forced to in Nam, but it had always been there. The war didn't cause it.

After a while it was nothing to spray a bushline with fire if I heard a noise, never thinking it might be a child lost from his mother. Without hesitation, I could throw a grenade into a VC spider hole when maybe the only ones down there were harmless villagers desperately praying we wouldn't kill them. Sometimes I would run up and shoot into a hole, then walk away without bothering to check inside.

On patrol meant survival. On patrol meant violence. On patrol meant digging down deep inside you and jerking that hideous demon free to do its worst.

But there was another demon that crept into the perimeter after we had been in the field on an operation hunting VC. When there was a long span of no contact with Charlie, boredom would take over. You could see it happening. Marines moved at half speed. There was a lethargic slowness in all physical action. Marines sat staring at nothing. Rifles weren't cleaned and our foxholes were untidy. K-ration cans went unburied.

But patrols went out of the perimeter constantly—morning, noon and night. Patrols came back in. Then out. And in again. After a while it was like going into a factory job every day until it became unthinking, until finally the patrols were boring. But then it was more boring sitting all day in a foxhole, burning under the sun, staring out at the hill, the village, the sky, other marines' tired faces.

So I began to volunteer for patrol to break that monotony. At least on patrol I was moving around, using my senses with stronger stimulus to stay alert. But eventually even that became almost unbearably boring until I was in a kind of stupor brought on by the weather and the stress of being so close to death for so long. It is one thing to have a momentary brush with death and then to be far away from that action. But it is quite another to be constantly under the pressure of getting killed, never knowing when it may happen. That stupor was an escape from that stress.

But on one patrol I was suddenly snapped out of it and left with an even more intense desire to survive.

Though we had run all of the villagers out and south toward Saigon, still, persistently, at daybreak every day a handful of women and children would trickle back into their homes and pick up where they had left off, acting as though we weren't even there. And every morning on patrol we would run them back out, firing rounds over their heads and yelling, "Dee, dee!" (Go away.) Chattering incomprehensibly, the villagers would then reluctantly pick up their belongings and slowly move out of sight again toward the south. Then our patrol would sweep through the village, out onto a rice paddy to the river, then back around on an old road along a hill and into the perimeter.

But this time we began to pick up bare footprints in the rice paddy leading from the riverbank toward our perimeter. It was a straight line of man tracks that walked along a small dike to the first treeline about a hundred yards out from our line. I walked point, stepping into the prints and looking for trip wires until my eyes came upon a six-foot by six-foot squared-off hole fortified with logs around the walls. The prints of bare feet were all over the bottom.

When the sergeant ran up to take a look, he laughed loudly and said the VC had sneaked in during the night and were building a mortar hole, possibly to hit us that night. He then jumped in the hole and put C-4 plastic explosive on the logs, put a thirty-second detonating wire on it, and ordered the patrol up onto the road. When the hole blew, it sent splinters up like a thousand needles and the rice paddy water rushed into the hole.

Though this had added a little excitement to the patrol and told us the VC were still there but were uninterested in fighting, still it was another boring day.

That was until I saw black pajamas running along the road next to the hill. A middle-aged man with no weapon, barefoot, was trying his best not to be seen by us. He crouched down once, ran along the bushes, and suddenly disappeared into thin air. I rubbed my eyes, turned to the rest of the guys and asked if they had seen it. They hadn't seen anything. The sergeant told me Nam was getting to my head, but I should check it out anyway.

So I went up on the road and checked heavily all along the bushline. There were no tracks, and really no reason to believe any VC had passed. Had it been my imagination? Maybe Nam was getting to me.

But just to make sure, I stepped in behind the bushes under the canopy and crept along black rocks protruding from the hill. Not more than ten feet over was a neatly dug hole big enough for the average Vietnamese man to crawl into.

I took out my concussion grenade, but then decided just to pump some rounds into it. Putting the grenade back in my pocket, I went up to the hole.

In the darkness I saw something move and heard a clicking sound. By reflex I aimed my rifle into the hole and quickly squeezed the trigger. Nothing happened. I looked down at my safety and saw it was on! There I stood, totally exposed in front of the hole, and in a split second would be dead. All because I forgot to take my safety off.

Suddenly someone pushed me out of the way and I went sprawling onto the rocks and some thorns. But when I looked up, the rest of the patrol was still out on the road waiting for me. I looked back at the hole, then around in the bushes. Who the hell had pushed me? Who had saved my life? It had to be the sergeant. But he was out on the road lighting a cigarette.

Quickly I grabbed my concussion grenade, pulled the pin, and dunked it down the hole. "Fire in the hole!" I yelled and scrambled out of the bushes.

The patrol trotted out of the way, and when the grenade blew it tore a hole right through the bushes.

When I went back to check it out, I expected to see parts of black pajamas, maybe even chunks of human flesh, but there was nothing.

The sergeant laughed again and said I at least found a tunnel and collapsed it with the grenade, but that there were no VC this close to the road, anyway not during the daytime.

Maybe he was right. Maybe I was just seeing things. Maybe I was going crazy. But that incident snapped me well out of the stupor and for the rest of the operation I was always alert. I always wondered who pushed me out of the way of the hole. And why?

I heard the roar of a swamp buggy engine close by, so I collected myself and moved up on a trail and turned in the direction of Shakespeare's territory.

Book VII

Glades Nuggets

Sometimes I wander out of beaten ways.
—*Robert Frost*

44

Swamp Encounters

> **Swamp notes—under monsoon clouds**
> *So many episodes. Some of them flashing
> glimpses, others full experiences. Each of
> these glades nuggets contributes to˜ my
> knowledge of the panther. Shakespeare and
> I are accumulating a past together. But it's
> not enough. We have to fight to make a
> future.*

During hunting season there was always the distant crack of
rifle fire. A stray bullet slashing through and splitting a vine
was not unusual. Once I heard the rattle of a machine gun,
then men talking and running through the swamp, then another rattle.

I located the direction and in a dead run pursued the
sound. More talking, quick orders from a gravel voice, then
the winding of a jeep engine. By the time I got to the area all
I found were the dressed-out remains of an animal. My heart
pounded. Please don't let it be Shakespeare. Please! I prayed.

The entrails were in a heap on mud, with that inner
body wetness covering it like varnish, smelling still alive. The
colon was still pulsing, and I could see where the sharp skin-
ning knife had expertly scraped out the animal's cavity, leaving
bits of membrane about. It was a very large heap of guts, and
in checking the area I found where a deer had, in desperation,
scampered about looking for an escape, then dropped on the
spot from the machine gun blast.

There were man tracks as well, possibly as many as six
men, all crowded around the bloody spot in the mud. One
had knelt down in the mud, the curved indentation made by
his knee showing up well in the softness, the toes of his boots
sticking into the dirt. I imagined the deer's stomach opened

up and the entrails pouring out in their thick oozing presence. Then the men had picked up the deer carcass and thrown it into the back of the jeep.

The jeep tracks nearby were deep in mud and water, and when I stepped into the spot where the jeep had roared off I sank to my knees. It was beyond me how the jeep had gotten in that far, let alone had been able to get out. There was no high ground for more than a mile, and at one point, as I followed the jeep tracks, it had to have gone underwater. Somebody had waterproofed the jeep somehow, put it on extremely high custom-made lifters, maybe used oversized tires and a larger bumper. It would be easy to spot something like that parked next to a shack up in somebody's driveway, or driving down the back roads. And yet to this day I have never seen such a vehicle. The only ones close to it are the souped-up jeeps guys race in the swamp buggy events twice a year in Naples.

One late afternoon I was working my way out of the swamp toward my car up on a back road, when I noticed two men checking it out. One opened the door, leaned in and put something under the seat. They both laughed, then got in their old Ford pickup and drove down the road in a cloud of dust.

Quickly I emerged from the treeline and looked under the seat. There, wrapped up in a plastic bag were rectangular pieces of paper and a clump of marijuana. I took it out, looked down the road at the dust tunnel and the back of their car, tore open the bag and threw it into the swamp.

What was all that about? I wondered.

Ten minutes later I was driving up toward Alligator Alley when I spotted a wildlife officer's four-wheel drive. The officer, wearing sunglasses, nonchalantly waved me down and asked for my driver's license.

"Doing some hunting out of season, boy?" he asked.

"No, I don't hunt."

He looked at me as though I was lying through my teeth.

"Please step out of the car," he said.

I got out and he worked his hands over me, looking for

something. Then he leaned in the car and put his hand under the seat, right where the plastic bag of pot had been planted. He stretched and gave it a thorough search, looked up at me with a puzzled look on his face, then got out.

"What are you doing out here?" he asked.

"Bird-watching."

"Bird-watching." He gave me that you're-lying-through-your-teeth look again. "Okay, on your way."

He handed me my driver's license. Driving up onto Alligator Alley, I concluded that those swamp boys didn't want me around that area, and they had told the officer I was down there with drugs. After that I always checked out my car.

On another occasion, during the dry season, I was far south where the sawgrass meets the mangroves. I had just decided to call it a day when I noticed something coming through the sawgrass far on the other side. I couldn't see the animal, but it was big. A bear? A hog? Possibly Shakespeare?

Whatever it was, I was going to get a close look. So I eased back into the mangrove treeline, then slipped down into a watery mound of mire and camouflaged myself. If the animal had not turned away from its original direction it would pass within a few feet of the mangrove treeline where I lay.

I waited. Mangrove crabs skirted about the trees nearby. Then I heard a movement. It wasn't a panther—too much noise. Wild pigs wouldn't be down this far in water and mud. And just as I was guessing again a weird sight came into view.

Unmarked black berets swayed in the grass. Four men with green tiger camouflage uniforms eased through the grass. Each carried a small, strange-looking machine gun of a type I had never seen before. Later, by accident, I spotted it in one of those soldier of fortune magazines: a Ruger 1022 converted into an automatic machine gun.

Three of the men were Spanish-looking—dark eyes, their hair cut short around the neck and ears, clean-shaven—but the camouflage cream on their faces made them look like something out of a nightmare.

The fourth man was Caucasian, large-chested with no hips and thin legs. He carried his weapon tight to his chest and had the well-trained, proven confidence of a military man with years of experience. In fact, they all seemed to have had a lot of training. There were no awkward strides, only calculated movements, silent movements. Not one of them said a word. They didn't have to. The three Spanish-looking men imitated every action of the Caucasian, who was the leader up front. When he stepped forward, they stepped forward. When he stopped and surveyed the area, they did the same, moving their heads in unison.

When they looked toward me, I buried my face in the mud, held my breath, and prayed they could not see through the trees. When I slowly looked up, they were gone. I couldn't hear them walking through the grass, and that worried me. My mind reeled with ideas. What were three Spanish-looking men with what was apparently an American military officer doing with guns like that in the middle of the Everglades where nobody goes except me, except Shakespeare?

They weren't hunters, or panther trackers. They were man trackers. But why in the glades? What was going on?

I lay in that mud and water until after dark, until I was sure they weren't coming back.

As I lay there I began thinking about the South Vietnamese soldiers who went out on patrol with green berets and marine recon teams. Some of them were called strikers, a term given to those who did a good job with the Americans. Some of them were juvenile delinquents given the choice of staying in prison for rape, robbery or murder convictions, or joining the army and fighting the VC.

American advisors would take them out on patrol to teach them the ropes so they could take over and run their own maneuvers. But a lot of times when the patrols came back in, those strikers didn't come back. Occasionally the American advisor didn't make it back. Command was pretty sure some of those strikers were VC just waiting for the chance to get an American advisor out on patrol in the bush so they could light him up with a round squarely in his back, and then plant a handful of grenades under the body to cover up their murder. Then they would run back into the perimeter claiming they were ambushed and needed help to get the American out. When we went back out in platoon force, right in the middle of the area where the advisor got it, a VC ambush would be ready and waiting for the platoon.

It was a neat plan for infiltrating VC into the ranks of the South Vietnamese army, but more times than not the VC spies were caught. I remember talking with a corpsman at the landing zone once who had seen what the South Vietnamese soldiers did to an exposed VC. He said they would wound him in the legs and then request a med-evac to take him back to the medical center. On the way the chopper would mysteriously lose weight and by the time they got to the LZ there was no wounded man aboard.

While I was healing at the medical center after I got wounded, sometimes I would wander about the tents talking with the guys and trying to get rid of the boredom. One of the ways we would break that boredom was to go down to the inpatient tent when wounded came in, and they came in every day.

On one occasion, a marine patrol had gotten hit pretty hard by a VC sapper team and they were bringing in six marine wounded. In the jeep on the way from the LZ to the medical tent, one of the guys had died of a head injury. When I saw the body as they took him off the jeep I could see why. Most of the top of his head was gone. Anger rose in my stomach.

Then a med-evac ambulance pulled up to the tent. Everybody was standing around wondering who was inside. When the door opened we saw a wounded Vietnamese. But he wasn't on our side. Word was he was one of the VC wounded in the ambush and the lieutenant at the ambush site had thrown him on the chopper too.

He stared at us in a dazed fear, wounded badly on the inner thigh. One of the Vietnamese interpreters yelled, "Dee, dee!" The VC looked up at him and started to crawl out of the ambulance, staggering, then tumbling headfirst onto the steps. The interpreter again yelled "Dee, dee!" and pointed inside the medical tent at a table. The VC crawled slowly past us all. We stared at him with no intention of giving him a hand. All I could think about was that dead marine and what his parents were going to go through when they sent the body home.

Inside, the VC left a trail of blood to the table, then struggled with what energy he had left onto the table, whimpering, sighing heavily, looking around at us for help. The interpreter interrogated him with sharp questions and sudden slaps in the face. But the VC wasn't talking. The interpreter then started flicking ashes from a cigarette into the VC's wound. His long sorrowful moans mixed with the jeers of the guys around him. Even then the VC didn't answer the interpreter. So, nonchalantly as ever, the interpreter waved his hand at the VC and said, "Ciao." As he walked away, the VC snapped a look at him as though he was going straight out to ready the firing squad. Then he looked around at us. It was the first time his eyes had been wide open since he came in. He was in fear for his life.

A jeep pulled up and two marines got out and marched into the tent. One grabbed the VC's arms, the other his legs, and they marched back out, threw him on the back of the jeep and sped toward the LZ.

I watched the chopper take off, gain altitude, and head out toward the Chu Lai perimeter. I kept watching the chopper more out of a daze than anything, and when it was far off, I distinctly saw a small silhouette dangling out of the door, the arms reaching and grabbing air frantically, the legs kicking like a spider on its back. Then the silhouette plunged into the treeline and was lost.

Lying in that mangrove mud, in the purity of the swamp, I now felt an intense shame and guilt for that murder. I felt equally bad for the dead marine, but now I had no hate for the enemy. There had been no need to throw that VC to his death like that. Because of the condition of his wound, he would never have fired on another marine in the bush again, and at the least would have ended up in prison for the duration of the war. But in war there are few rules followed when it comes to simple humanity. I now hated the person I was then and thanked God I was spared to live and at least try to do something right. Now I even wondered about that VC's family in Vietnam, wondering if they ever found the body. Or are they still asking how he died, searching records in vain the way so many American families of MIA's are still doing?

Nam faded from my mind as I waited in the trees to make sure the mysterious patrol was well out of sight before I slipped back to my canoe. Other questions loomed in my head now. What were these characters doing out here? Spanish-looking. In top physical condition. Following an American advisor. What were they up to? The only halfway decent answer I could come up with was that something must be brewing in Central or South America, and maybe the CIA was financing another secret war somewhere out in the jungle. Wouldn't we ever learn?

45

Swamp Myths

> ### *Swamp notes—sifting glades nuggets*
> ### *from fool's gold*
> *I have encountered so many people so willing to impart their panther "wisdom." The only way I can sort the truth from the myth is by relying on my own experience with Shakespeare.*

There is the story about noted panther experts who were tested whether or not they could place the panthers geographically by the color of their skins. Six skins were spread out in front of them: tawny, brown, red, fawn-gray, chocolate-brown, and clay-red. Not one expert was able to place the skins in the right location according to color.

There is another story about how a panther hunter years ago lined up ten skins for a group of panther experts. They closely examined each one, musing over them for quite some time, and came to the conclusion that the hunter had traveled to South America twice, had been in the State of Washington at least once, had hunted for the big cat in Canada, and had even hunted in Central America in the Maya mountain range. Silently the hunter picked up his skins and left with a wide grin on his face. He had shot all the panthers in the glades.

Similarly, there is no way anyone can tell the sex or age of a panther in his natural habitat by distinguishing color markings, size and shape of the tracks, or size of the cat itself. Panthers of either sex can have the same color.

A backpacker told me he had had two sightings while hiking through the Everglades. "The first one I saw was a female about two years old. She was small and brown. The second one was bigger, and a male." I asked him if he had seen the testicles or absence of them with binoculars. He said no, but he had a gut reaction and knew what the sexes were because of the size and the fact the female was brown.

A park ranger told me once he could tell the panther he saw was a female because of the way the cat walked. "The hips swayed from side to side."

Another person said, "I could tell the cat was a female. She had this look on her face. You know, like women do when they're mad. A frown is probably what it was."

Another person smiled when he told me that he knew he had seen a female. "She was jumping over all those logs. Each time she hit the ground, the sun shone on her light fur. She was small, so she had to be female."

Once I watched someone set out three plaster casts of panther tracks in front of a well-qualified biologist who was known to have a fair knowledge of panthers. He began to study the casts with the utmost seriousness. He checked every detail on the plaster: an indentation on the toe pad, the very large heel pad, a twisted lump on the back of the heel pad. His eyes moved across the casts with a well-schooled scrutiny. This guy knew his stuff. Then he picked up one cast, actually testing the weight of it. What the weight of the plaster had to do with anything I didn't know. Finally he said, "What you've got here, Jim, is a female, about one hundred pounds, maybe as much as a hundred and ten pounds, about five to nine years old, ten years at the most."

We discussed the cat a little further, her territory, possible prey she was eating. Then he said he had to get back to the office. I thanked him for his information, and sat down at the cast he had so intricately analyzed for me. I ran my fingers over perfectly reproduced claws in one of the plaster casts and sighed. He had said nothing about those. Outside in my backyard was a hundred-pound Labrador retriever. For comparison purposes I had taken plaster casts of his prints to set up against those of the panther. The biologist had picked out the plaster cast of my dog's prints!

Panthers do not travel in packs like wolves. A rancher once told me he had found a dead buck deer under a tree that had been ambushed not by one panther but by a pack of them. He found several different-sized tracks around the deer. He figured there were at least three panthers in the pack. I explained to him it was not a pack of panthers that had downed the deer, but a female with possibly three cubs almost fully grown. The female might have made the kill, or maybe the cubs had helped. At any rate, soon each cat would go his or her solitary way. A male cub would never hunt with another cat again. A female would, but only during the brief period when her cubs would join her to learn the ropes before striking out on their own.

I met a hard-core hunter who had gone all over the world gunning down some of the most treasured animals left, including the Bengal tiger, gorillas, the snow leopard, and the black leopard. A Florida panther was one of his prize trophies. When he was younger he had put all their heads up in his den, used panther skins for rugs. But age had brought wisdom. And wisdom had taught him to put his rifles away and become a saver of the cat, not a killer.

He had an extraordinary knowledge of cats. Once he said to me, "In my opinion, panthers would never overrun the glades. Just the fact they have been hunted all these years and yet are still around will tell you something. They're smart, damn smart. They will regulate their own numbers according to the size of the area. There isn't a hunting organization in the world that can justify thinning out a population of predators, especially the panther. When an area is well-stocked with panther, then fewer cubs are born."

Many backwater swampers feel the panther is a friend of man. On one occasion, the story goes, a little girl was lost for more than two days in the glades. Search parties were out everywhere trying to find her. Finally they came across her tracks, which eventually led them to a large oak tree. Underneath was the child. Around the tree were large tracks of panther.

The little girl told them that she had gone under the tree to rest, got frightened and started to cry. The panther came in and kept the other animals away from her all night and the next day. The cat even started to fight with a big old black bear. When the men came through the trees, the panther ran off.

Man-panther (Manther) is the subject of a tall tale that came out of the swamp during pioneer days. As the story goes, there was a young mother living alone in the swamp with a baby son. Her husband had died recently and left her with no money or means of support. One late evening the baby was whining and crying with the colic. Suddenly there was heavy scratching on the door of the cabin, and in seconds a full-grown female panther burst into the room and snatched the baby from the mother's arms and ran off into the swamp. The baby was never found or heard of again. A few years later there were strange sightings of a white panther that seemed to have a mane. Other sightings were of a panther that almost walked upright, but still leaning over. Its territory was deep in the mangrove swamp, and on rare occasions it was spotted on the wild beaches or in the water, foraging.

The best sighting of it was by a hunter-guide who saw it up close. He said it was a panther with no hair on its body, twisted and crooked legs, its forelegs dangling from its shoulders. When it spotted him, it ran off in the mangroves on all fours, looking back to see if it was being followed. The guide said it struck him as more like a man because he could see the penis and testicles, yet it acted like a panther.

There was a man in the swamp who claimed he had seen the ghost of a panther—many times. Usually it showed itself during the time just before daybreak in the fog during the winter. It would float across an open prairie, melt into the trees, then about three weeks later would appear again.

When I talked with him, he was dead certain it was a ghost because its feet never touched the ground. The entire body was white, and the long tail would hang in the air like "a slanted J." Once he saw the eyes glow a transparent pink in the daybreak moon.

When the warm weather would hit, the ghost would not be seen again for the entire summer.

The first chance I got I spent a night on the other side of the prairie with him waiting for the apparition. But on this particular night, though the conditions were right, the cat did not show. The man was very disappointed and never called me again.

But the story hung on in my thoughts until one day I was doing some inhouse research and read about an albino bobcat sighted near Marco Island. If it had been proven that there are albino bobcats, then why not an albino in the panther species?

Could this so-called ghost of a panther really be a white panther, a freak, roaming his territory, unable to blend into the swamp colors like the rest? Could it be the only one alive?

If there is even a possibility a white panther does exist, then why not a black panther? It has never been proven there is such a thing as a black cougar, or melanistic mutation, and yet I have records of more than a hundred sightings of big black cats in the Everglades. It is a far-fetched idea to begin with because in the recorded history of the cougar species, even in captivity, there has not been one black cat, ever, in a litter. With all the breeding populations in zoos, one would think at least one would show up. To this day, it has not.

Many biologists feel the genetic formation of the species *Felis concolor* makes it impossible for it ever to be black, or white for that matter. But many years ago it was thought that there was no such thing as a black bobcat, and yet today there are pictures of them in the wilds.

It is believed that a humid climate close to the equator is one of the factors that can cause a black mutation to occur such as found in black leopards in Africa and Asia, which are true panthers. The Everglades are not all that far from the equator, which makes the possibility more plausible.

One of the sightings I heard about was so intriguing that I could not help but check into it. There was the remote chance this guy knew what he was talking about, but I had to have physical evidence. This person claimed to have seen the black cat in his backyard out in the swamp where he let his geese run free at night. He had lost three geese already and had seen the cat sitting in ambush on top of his feeding bin. It was crouched low, trying to shape its body to the contour of the roof, its tail dangling along the edge. It turned to him and hissed, then dove off the roof in the opposite direction and fled. The man shouldered his rifle and fired, missing the cat, but putting a hole in the roof.

He called me the following morning and even before daybreak I was out at the feeder, looking at the hole, trying to explain to him how important it was not to kill this cat. If it was a black cougar, it might be the only one in existence. I tried to make him realize it would be important for research purposes.

"He's feedin' on them there geese of mine, Jim. Can't have that. But if you want to study that critter, guess I'll leave him alone . . . for now," he said.

I tracked the whole day and came onto bobcat and fox tracks and plenty of dog tracks, but nothing even close to a large panther track that might at least tell me from what direction to expect the cat if it came back to the man's yard. The next step was to spend the night staring out at the geese and feeder from this man's house, which I did in the interest of saving panthers, though I was weary from a whole day of tracking.

We sat there in the doorway, drinking beer, whispering, making bets on when the cat was going to appear, telling wild swamp stories, and lying a little. The man couldn't figure out why I was so bent on saving the panther, and why I had given up a great deal to sit it out at night just to get a look at one. He just sat shaking his head, saying how other people would be off making money.

But when I asked him why he was living out in the

swamp away from money and people and society in general, he became very quiet and mumbled something about how he was in jail at one point in his life for something he didn't do, and when he got out he didn't like people after that.

As we were talking about all of this, the geese began to chatter as though they had some animal cornered somewhere in the trees and were pecking the tar out of it.

I didn't move an inch, just sat there listening. If it were the big cat, then he would be growling at all those geese, maybe about to ambush one and carry it off.

"Right on time! He's gonna take one," the man said and jumped up and ran out toward the noise.

I was right on his heels with a flashlight, and when we got to the pine trees, we saw feathers strewn about and one leg of a goose dangling from torn flesh. I shot the light into the trees back and forth, but whatever it was was long gone. I dashed into the trees and stumbled over something under a small bush. When I looked I saw the mangled head of the goose, and nearby the rest of the fowl's body opened up, torn out. None of it had been eaten. The predator had made the kill without a sound, and because the sandy ground was thick with pine needles, there were no tracks.

"See, I told ya he was here," the man grumbled.

Reluctantly I had to tell him there was no reason to believe it was a black panther that had done this, and not so much as a track had shown up. The black panther was still as conjectural as ever.

The man didn't take it too well and was about to order me off his land when I promised him I would track the cat for the rest of the week and do my best to get a sighting to verify his claim. Disappointingly, I never had that sighting.

There could be many explanations for what he saw out there. It could have been anything—a bobcat, a feral cat, a wild dog, maybe even a tough full-grown male fox. Possibly a great horned owl. It may even have been an exotic jaguarundi, a small weasel-like cat that has a black phase. At the most, it could have been an escaped black leopard or jaguar.

I will admit that the pure idea that there could be a true black cougar roaming the Everglades, a species still unproven, undefined, was enough to keep my mind on it. To search for an unknown animal is the very essence of a swamp adventure. But my life was pledged to Shakespeare now. Maybe, just maybe I would someday get onto a black panther just as I was onto Shakespeare now. But for now Shakespeare was my life.

46

Old-timers

> **Swamp notes—near a campfire**
> *Of interesting creatures in the glades, second only to the panther are the old-timers—grand old fellows of the swamp that sit with silent thunder in their eyes. What comes out of their dried, cracked lips and into my brain are some of the most electrifying stories I have ever heard. To them it is commonplace. To me it is a chance in a million to listen to unwritten swamp tales that feature the panther.*

A camp fire, surrounded by hunters with a pint of whiskey and plenty of beer on ice in an old cooler, draws out the best stories, especially when it comes to the panther. There is a breed of hunters in the glades who were born and raised in the swamps, know them like the back of their hands, but hardly ever boast about it.

They are the ones who know how to pick and choose their shots when deer season rolls around. There is no mistaking a doe for a buck in the distance. Some of these hunters can even tell if the doe is carrying a fawn.

They are the ones who know what a panther looks like

in thick cypress, and rather than take a chance on firing, would let the animal go, figuring that if the panther is bold enough to get that close to a rifle he has the right to stay alive, maybe even spook deer toward the hunter.

On one occasion when I happened at night on flickering flames, saw shadowy arms passing a bottle around for a shot and heard the serious conversation over burned-up pieces of chicken, I knew I was among these swamp men.

"Hello, hunter," I said.

There was a sudden silence, and the arms stopped moving. Then a voice. "Clear yer gun and come in."

"Got no gun." I walked toward the fire and old torn hats, Stetsons that had been curled up, sweated in, covered with mud. I came upon gray-black beards, deep wrinkled faces, wrinkles that told of many years in the swamp. Their eyes were old and red, and their skin was blotched with tan and a thin film of swamp dirt. Some had suspenders attached to old green or gray trousers. No shoes. And those who had them had no laces in them.

I had stumbled onto a unique experience. These men were third generation old-timers. All had to be over seventy. A couple looked well past eighty. Their hands were cracked and the fingernails held dried-out mud caked in deep for years.

"Looks like we got ourselves a woodscolt," one of them said. I had no idea what he meant. Later I found out it meant a young person just learning the swamp, growing up to it, thriving off of it. I guess I qualified.

"Got a name?"

Quietly, almost in a whisper, I said, "Jim."

"Well, Jim, ya be drinkin' a beer?"

I stuck out my hand. A cold wet can hit it.

"Got yer buck yet?" the old man next to me asked.

"No, I'm not hunting. I watch a lot, but I don't hunt."

"I betcha yer one of them there bi-o. . . ."

"Biologist," a voice out of the dark volunteered.

"No, not really." How could I tell them what I was doing? "I'm a writer." Usually when I said that stories started to roll.

"What do you write about?"

"Mostly animals. Snakes, deer, alligators, panthers." I tried to slip the word in matter-of-factly, like it was just another animal to me.

"Panthers. Shit. There's no panthers left in the glades. Time was when ya always heard 'em at night. Female in heat cryin' and carryin' on. The males fight over her. But now. . . ." A bearded face looked into the smoke.

"No, they're still here. What's his name down in Copeland saw one cross the road."

"If there's any left there, they cain't be but a few. There's no room for 'em."

"They're endangered," I said.

"Endangered, are they? They always were."

How could I argue with that?

A particularly old swamp man crossed his bare feet near the fire, feet that looked more like clubs with the healed over white scars on the soles. One of his large toes was knotted and crooked, as though it had been broken and hadn't mended exactly straight. "I remember the time when there wasn't but seven families livin' out here at one time. My dad bought me my first rifle. It was a .22 bolt action. Panthers were competin' with the bears an' coons for gator eggs in these parts then. We had a big ole cat, prob'ly a tom, that'd pass right by our cabin. My dad got the rifle for me to protect my sister and family when he warn't there.

"Well, one night the panther come walkin' through an' prob'ly heard us inside an' decided to take a look-see. 'Member my sister seein' these eyes at the window lookin' at her like they was ready to jump right in the cabin. I didn't see the eyes, but I heard scratchin'. Went for my rifle and bust out the front door to take a shot." He fell silent. I was hanging on the edge of a sip of beer when he stopped.

"Tell me the rest of it."

The old man smiled. "When I got outside, black as ya please, no moon, dark as hell itself, there, maybe ten feet away was this here panther walkin' towards me on his hind legs like a man. I didn't know what to do. So I fired a wild shot, hopin' the cat would drop to all fours and light out. But he didn't. He turned on his hind paws and still walkin' like a man made it all the way to the bushline some forty feet nearer to the river. It didn't seem like a panther 'tall. More human than anything else. Next mornin' my dad, he checked the tracks and couldn't figger it out. A clean set of hind paw tracks all the way to the river. Not once did that ole panther drop to his front paws. If I'd a had more in my head about shootin', I could've leveled him with one shot. But it was the way he walked like a man. I couldn't pull the trigger again."

That story stuck in my head for days after, and as I listened to the others talk about the great cat, even more information came out. It was a known fact that once you got onto the tracks of a panther, you could always go back to that territory. He would always be there. They started giving out where they had seen panthers. One had been spotted as far south as Cape Sable. They all knew about the cat nearby, the one that stayed well into the cypress heads. Not one of them had seen him, but there were plenty of signs. I knew they were talking about Shakespeare. Could they hear me screaming inside my head: HE'S MY CAT! I guess not because they just passed the bottle and went on talking.

One talked about the state of Florida claiming there were only twenty cats left. "Maybe there is," he said, "but if that's true, how come they've seen 'em way up north towards Lakeland when those twenty are supposed to be in the glades only?"

I stayed most of the night with those relics of the Everglades, pioneers in their own right. When they finally drank the last of the beer and went to their truck campers, I slipped away, my brain electrified by what I had heard.

47

Swampman

Swamp notes—in giant snake slough
I have come upon this swampman who was born and raised in the wilds of Florida. Seminole blood runs in his veins. With skills learned in the glades he imitates owl sounds, catches rattlesnakes with his bare hands, creeps up to deer feeding on prairie grass, walks barefoot in waist-deep water among alligators. He is a wilderness being and my teacher of swampmanship in the glades.

I met Swampman under a blood-red sky among exotic Australian pine trees. When I shook his hand, I felt calluses and a strength in his tattooed, scarred, muscled arm I had never felt before in a man. It was like grabbing hold of a solid oak trunk. He smiled at me with a swamp-wise expression of immediate friendship, that kind of friendship only the swamp could engender in hearts that loved her.

Dust covered his ruddy complexion. His slightly graying moustache flared out like eagle wings. A jungle of gray hair pushed out from his chest at the top of his faded green swamp shirt. The deep creases in his thick-stalked neck reminded me of panther slash marks on trees.

His most intriguing features were his vigilant, clear, ice-blue eyes. They reflected the sky above the Everglades, and their expression told the story that had helped shape my quest for affinity with Shakespeare. I read those eyes constantly, and the power of the swamp stared back at me. I wanted that power, for they were always examining the wilds, accepting, rejecting, smiling with a deep ancestral commitment of protection that the average environmentalist knows nothing about. Those Argus eyes had witnessed great things in the swamp, for they were able to discover and recognize the slightest movement in the thickest bush at a glance. They had scrutinized a doe's suddenly uplifted head, identified distant birds by their silhouettes, flashed to the escaping tail of a black racer snake looking for cover, discovered hornets stinging an enemy at great distance. Swampman's eyes could lift up at the night sky and read the weather days in advance with intelligence born of an entire life spent in this wild place. He calculated his every glance, his every thought. Then he kept still until he was sure what his next move was, and in taking that move he did it with a Zen-like consciousness, using only that degree of energy needed to accomplish the action. In all, he had the eyes of a panther. I wanted those eyes. I wanted that control.

Swampman never set out to teach me anything about the glades, but by being the man he was, he taught me things about swampmanship I would never have known otherwise. He carried within himself those mysterious elements that merged with my desires to track Shakespeare.

For several months Swampman and I roamed the Everglades. We camped out at the water's edge, canoed through moonless nights, puddle-jumped for largemouth bass, and tracked nameless ponds for frogs and snakes. I would often meet him in the middle of the swamp at dawn and we would sit and watch the sunrise, drink a cup of coffee, and then, with me following his lead of quick-sighted, resigned calmness, move about the wilds in search of knowledge. At camp in the evenings, Swampman would stare into the fire with a hand-rolled cigarette between his lips and describe images I could almost see, tell me endless stories about himself in the wilds, and in between sips of beer, relate Calusa and Seminole Indian history to me like a walking archive. Over a smoking piece of deer meat, we would discuss the skills of survival and indirectly, Shakespeare, talking of which animals panthers ambush and why the cats have territories of different sizes. But I never once mentioned I was tracking Shakespeare.

If ever there was someone to pour my heart out to about my experience so far with Shakespeare, it was Swampman. I was bursting with excitement and had convinced myself on several occasions that Swampman should know it all, that he would then join in my efforts. But even with Swampman, at

the brink of telling him what I had done so far and why, I
always stopped short. What made things worse was that he
knew the panthers quite well and talked about them. I listened
intently, wanting to jump into the conversation and add my
own facts. But in all the time I was with Swampman, I never
said a word, even though, considering his swamp-wisdom, I
strongly suspected he knew full well what I was doing. But
he never once pushed me to tell him anything. It just wasn't
his way.

Swampman was an important link in my chain of events
to attain my goal. I will always remember his ways, his vast
knowledge of the Everglades, and that among the thousands
of things I learned from him, he taught me panther-eye, the
ability to see beyond just physical actions. Panther-eye looks
out, sees far, looks in, sees deep.

48

Gentle Breeder

> **Swamp notes—in front of a cage**
> I am always searching for better ways to
> track Shakespeare. Affinity is still my goal,
> but how to achieve it is still not certain to
> me. Maybe by studying captive panthers I
> could learn more about my wild one.

In Bonita Springs, Florida, Bill and Les Piper have a zoo called
Wonder Gardens. I went there for a specific reason. They
were trackers of the panther in the Everglades in the thirties
and forties, well before the big cat went on the endangered
list. They are the world-famous brother team who captured
panthers before most people knew what a real panther was.
Concerned men that they are, they breed the cats in captivity,

raise them to adulthood, and let them go back out into the swamps. Bill and Les are royalty among backwater swampers, know the glades inside out and are respected deeply by the people who know them as wild animal handlers. They are two of the few men who have the best interests of the panther at heart.

At their zoo there is a small population of panthers still in captivity after four generations. There they are among exotic animals from jungles around the world—Central America, South America, Africa, India. The day I first went there, I found the panthers in a long row of black steel-barred cages with concrete floors. Their growls mixed with the insane cry of the cockatoo, the low grunts of the Nile crocodile. Coming upon them, I stopped instantly. They were living, breathing replicas of Shakespeare. The strong memory of that first fleeting glimpse of him rushed through me, the cinnamon fur, the long graceful J-shaped tail, the low sleek body. I stood looking at a young male that kept looking back at me. He had put his ears up at my approach and cocked his head. For what seemed like hours, I stared at the cats until my eyes burned and watered.

Though they were confined in cages, they moved in that unmistakable cat way. I imagined Shakespeare moving like that. Closing my eyes, I walked his territory—past cypress trees and up onto the old trails, over a wet prairie, back into dense brush, all the time placing the real cat out in front of me. Each time I opened my eyes I saw new characteristics. The paws were incredibly large; muscles flexed on the floating shoulder blades; each whisker ended up on a black spot on the muzzle.

Time and again I went back to those cages, studying each cat. But just to stare at them through cage bars and wire was hardly what I had in mind. I wanted to be with the cat on the most intimate level I could, to share my emotions and dreams with him. A captive-bred panther could teach me things about Shakespeare I could never learn in a book.

Somehow I was going to raise a panther cub to adulthood, count every hair, measure every tooth, study every inch of that panther inside and out, to learn the soul of the panther.

I began to hear stories about a man in the swamp who

was known as the gentle breeder of the panther. I heard that years ago he took the panther to his heart and began to breed them in captivity in order to save them. He thought the best place to do it was in the middle of the Everglades, the big cat's home. From the wild tales I had heard about him I was sure that when we met it would go one of two ways: we would hit it off like long lost friends, or he would run me off his land with hot lead from a shotgun.

On one of those brisk, cool mornings I followed a broad-winged hawk down Alligator Alley in search of this gentle breeder's ranch. The hawk, with its broad bands of gray and almost white on the tail, soared overhead beneath black vultures. He could easily have been mistaken for a red-shouldered hawk, or even an immature red-tailed. But the wings were more stubby, instead of having that thinness to them.

When I turned north on Route 29 toward Immokalee, I came to a mailbox that read FRANK AND ELLEN WEED. As I turned into the gateway, it opened a chapter in my quest to track Shakespeare that has lasted to this very day.

Among Australian pine trees, next to a large man-made pond, were some of the most magnificent panthers I have ever seen: cougars born and raised in captivity to save them from extinction. They were healthy cats with glowing tawny fur, long sleek bodies. Some were large, heavy, with massive heads; others were smaller, more wary, moving gracefully around their cages. Their eyes, glazed over in the sunlight, glittered as though they possessed some magical power from nature, a power I had yet to discover, a power I knew I was destined to experience before my life was over.

Among those big cats stood Frank Weed, tall and strong as a cypress, his muscles as solid as the muscles of the cats themselves. His face was ruddy, aged by the glades weather. He had kind, probing eyes that had a wild animal wisdom in them. Standing among the panthers, he seemed to be as much a part of them as they were of him. He called them his children, and could boldly approach even the biggest males and play with them. I saw him coax many of the cats to put their paws around his neck and, without opening their claws, hug him. Indeed, here was finally a human that seemed to know the intimate reaches of the panther's world.

He was quick to shake hands with me, and at the same time seemed to be deciding whether to kick me off his ranch or welcome me with a smile. Fortunately for me, the smile spread across his face almost as quickly as the handshake was initiated. It was strange, but even though I had never met Frank before, I felt I had known him for a long time. Later I figured it was our mutual goal to save the panther that drew us together, and the fact that in the near future we would together oppose powerful forces in order to save the big cat's habitat.

I immediately sensed confidence and a strong will in him that would defy anything or anybody who would wantonly disturb his way of life. This quality also prevailed in his wife's personality. Ellen Weed not only loved the panther, but in a very direct way she was the mother to the newly born cubs. She helped raise them with a passion only a panther-mother could know. She had already become an important force in the preservation of the Florida panther species. She knew as much as Frank did about the wild animals. She had something rare in a human being that the race should take heed of: a true desire to help others without ever expecting anything in return. She reminded me of my own mother.

Among the giant pythons and boa constrictors, eastern diamondback rattlesnakes and water moccasins, Frank's son, who is also named Frank and is my age, was completely at home. He knew more about gators, lizards and snakes than anyone I'd ever met. He could pick up rattlers with his bare hands and milk them, handle giant iguanas as though they were puppies, wrestle a ten-foot alligator to exhaustion and then let him go. He could read snake movements in the swamp and pinpoint where they were at any moment, most of the time smelling them well before he saw them—especially rattlers. He was easy-going, willing to help out whenever he could, but made it plain that he wouldn't be taken advantage of. A formally educated herpetologist could envy the young Frank's expertise, and I said so.

In all three of these swamp beings was an overlaying quietness that produced a solid, unwavering gentleness. It drew me to them the way I was drawn to the cat. They took me into their family almost as another son, and Frank became my teacher for breeding panther in captivity as well as providing a deep insight into what goes on in the field. In turn, I offered information from my tracking in the glades. Frank's great concern about the panther in the wilds was reproduction. Could the panther continue propagating his race in the face of man's encroachment on the swamp? If not, could an experimental relocation program train captive-bred panthers to live in the wilds? Frank was determined to find out.

During the following months, I spent a lot of time among the big cats at Frank's ranch. I crouched next to their cages and scratched their backs. I studied them, their every movement. I took photograph upon photograph of those cats: tails, ears, eyes, the massive muscles, the paws. I compared their tracks with those of panthers in the wilds, with Shakespeare's, and found they were pretty much the same.

Then I began to enter the cages and put my hands on the stiff fur, the concrete muscles, the soft underside, and the tops of the paws. The cats, especially the females, looked at me strangely, wondering what I was up to. I worked at gaining their confidence, and eventually became friends with most of them. Frank always kept an eye on all of this. After a year he finally said, "You need a cub, Jim. You need to raise one yourself. Make it your own."

I had been wanting to say that for months. It had been my goal since the second I walked into his ranch. What I didn't know was that Frank had read my mind, but hadn't thought I was ready until then.

49

Thunder Run

> **Swamp notes—in the alley**
> *Alligator Alley slashes across the top of the*
> *Everglades cutting off the natural flow of water*
> *to the south and creating a dangerous bar-*
> *rier for every sort of wildlife—including the*
> *panther. And yet I use it nearly every day,*
> *appreciating the ease with which it deposits*
> *me near my entrance to the swamp. All*
> *these trade-offs add up, though. Sometimes*
> *they add up to extinction.*

I was driving down Alligator Alley toward the ranch, counting maple tree seedlings close to the canal and trying to contain my excitement about the phone call I'd just had from Frank. Suddenly my eyes saw streaks of camouflage racing past like a huge green snake. Blinking, I realized that a National Guard truck convoy was moving down the highway from the opposite direction toward Naples. I pulled off to the side of the road and stared at those trucks, jeeps and soldiers as they too pulled off for a road check of equipment. It struck me that a convoy like this, on a highway next to the swamps would just happen to go by when I was on the road. For some reason, I'd been thinking lately about thunder runs, the convoys that snaked their way up and down Highway 1 in Nam. In particular, my mind had been going over a convoy we took from Chu Lai carrying supplies and troopers to an artillery fire base. But what happened in that three-hour convoy these soldiers would never know—I hoped.

I sat riveted to my seat, my eyes roving over their bright faces, the newly painted trucks, the large tires. A jeep was moving up and down the line, and suddenly I was in the midst of a bulldozed roadline off Highway 1 in the Chu Lai desert looking at an ancient, war-ruined pagoda temple glossed over and steaming from a monsoon rain-rush. Huge jagged chunks of the decrepit gray walls had been blown out by artillery fire and riddled with bullet holes. Inside the doorway a fresh bouquet of flowers, a small bag, and a photo of a beautiful Vietnamese girl lay on an old altar swept clean of battle debris below a small Buddha statue that had an arm missing. To the right of the altar hung a buffalo hide rope roughly cut off at the end. Below it was a sandal made out of a tire.

The Vietnam morning sun blazed through monsoon clouds over the pagoda and atop lush hills farther out, rippling the skyline and those emerald humps until they looked like virescent ovals on the verge of disappearing. The hills were pockmarked with bare spaces made by napalm dropped from jets diving in pursuit of VC seeking refuge in the jungle.

Sitting in one of those trucks on top of ammo boxes under that cremating sun, I watched a pulsing stream of Vietnamese refugees winding sluggishly up Highway 1 to Chu Lai village next to the river where a temporary camp had been set up. I stared down at old men with mud-covered, stringy legs, their veins popping out like battery cables. They carried bulging sacks slung over their shoulders, while their calloused and wrinkled hands pushed wooden carts spilling over with more possessions—a chair, a table with no legs, a bundle of wood, blackened cooking pots, clay bowls, and clothes bunched up in balls. Young women dressed in mud-splattered pajamas shouldered boxes and carried bags, their babies tied to their chests with old cloth. The children were burdened with pulling wagons or carrying water or smaller brothers and sisters. Every last oriental face had that sad, drawn expression of weariness and despair that seemed to reach back centuries.

It was one of those hundreds of wartime exoduses taking place all over Nam. People came up the road to escape the destruction of the coming battle. We went down it on a thunder run to engage the Viet Cong, bring the fight to them, in the hope of rooting them out for good, only to go down it three months later to still another fight with freshly trained VC.

Forty trucks packed full of wooden ammo boxes and C-rations lined the highway, engines revving, lights on. Two

M-60 tanks at the point and rear guard with .50-caliber machine gun double mounts led the way and cleaned up the rear. In every fifth truck there was an M-60 machine gunner with an assault ammo pack half-hidden in the boxes. A platoon of grunts were up front crammed into two trucks. Rifles stuck up between them, and each wore a camouflaged helmet with a black rubber band holding the ace of spades card. All had cigarettes in their mouths except for the lieutenant who chewed on a half-smoked cigar.

I was a lone guard in one of the trucks about halfway down the convoy, ordered to protect what I was sitting on. "No VC is to get near it," a corporal said as he walked the line and stretched up to me. Then he added, "Grunt, if one sniper round hits those boxes you won't have time to even pray." Then he smiled widely with more gums than teeth and walked off.

I looked under my legs at the wet wooden boxes, then up at the corporal who was now laughing. What the hell was in them? It had been two weeks since I had gotten out of the medical center, my wounds healed, but my nerves had not yet adjusted to combat again. This thunder run was my introduction back into the war. Then and there I decided the first time we took rounds I was diving headfirst off the truck and into the ditch without the slightest concern for what else was on the truck.

I sat loading my M-14, seething in the heat under my rubber poncho, chewing on salt tablets, wiping the thick red layers of mud off my face. That red mud was on everything and everybody, making us look like we had been in a rain of blood. The guys in the truck in front of me lit up, inhaled deeply, and soon the sweet smell of marijuana hung stiffly in the air. One of them held a joint up for me, but I shook my head and ran a towel over my rifle chamber.

Then a jeep sped past winding around the people with short honks. The captain was in it, surveying the formation, stopping to talk to certain marines, standing up to see if the convoy was combat-ready for the run. The captain's driver was a thick-chested marine sergeant with a belt of ammo across his chest and a grenade launcher cradled on his lap. In the back seat a flame thrower sat on top of two backpacks and a seabag. Then the jeep sped back up to the front and the captain gave the order to move out.

We slowly started down the road just as another cloud-burst hit hard and heavy, trying to disintegrate the sun and turning the mud into slippery slush which caused the trucks to swerve as they surged ahead up onto the road itself.

Huey choppers and two loaches hovered overhead, then floated up and down the convoy, suddenly banking out and dropping down toward the paddies and hammocks to check for VC snipers and ambush sites. Then they swooped back and halted in midair, their gunners leaning out of the opened doors, throwing empty beer cans down on the people. It was odd how the people would take that abuse and act like we weren't even there.

Sitting, I put my rifle butt up on my lap, clicked the safety off, pulled off the hood of my poncho, and took off my helmet. The people had moved to the other side of the road, but it would have been easy for one of them to lob a grenade out of the crowd onto one of the trucks and split the convoy in half with one explosion.

I took my rifle and trained it over at the people, gaining the attention of several of them. A teenage boy carrying two naked babies and a makeshift pack on his back smiled oddly at me with far-off eyes. I couldn't define the smile, not even the eyes, but he made it a point to look into mine, and even then I couldn't come up with a meaning to the fleeting en-counter. Instead, I moved my rifle barrel back and forth along the line of people, trying to detect a VC in it ready to give up his life for the death of one of us. But then I realized I was a bit too jumpy, and I eased my finger off the trigger and took a piece of gum I had been saving for a day and pushed it into my mouth. Looking up over the truck in front of me on Highway 1, I saw far in the distance a village, then a stretch of open country.

Highway 1. An unsecured free-fire zone ever since the marines hit Chu Lai in 1965. Highway 1. A haven for VC land mines that could put a gaping hole in the bottom of a tank and blow a man in half. I'd seen one take a whole cab of a truck and bounce it into the rice paddy. Highway 1. The perfect place for VC ambushes, and you heard about one every other day. Highway 1. The most important road in Viet Nam, and it had been traded back and forth between the VC forces and the marines many times. For the present we had a good stretch of it south of Chu Lai to Outpost 14. After that it was up for grabs. Even with marine posts on most of the bridges, it was a constant duel. Nobody really owned it for any length of time. And here we were thunder running a convoy right through it. We had fire power, but so did the VC. Recently Communist self-propelled rockets and RPD's (7.62-mm. Communist machine-guns) had been taken off some dead VC ambushed by marines. That meant they were getting good supplies from the north.

As we passed Outpost 14, we saw that the hill ahead had been so battered with enemy mortar rounds, rain, and track vehicles that all of the vegetation had been sheared off it. Sandbag bunkers reinforced with logs lined the top like a fort. In between each bunker was an amtrac or tank. The CP bunker in the middle of the perimeter was blown out in front and a poncho was loosely spread over the hole. Part of the barbed wire defense down the hill was blown up and pieces of clothing were snagged on it. Marines were busy cleaning up and it was obvious they had been hit the night before.

After we passed the outpost I got a queasy feeling in my guts, a familiar feeling that I was getting tired of but could do little about. I found myself slipping down to the floor of the truck rather than sticking up there on the bench like a sitting duck for some wild VC sniper.

Then it started, almost on cue, almost as though some famous analyst was writing the great American book on the Vietnam war, and it was now time for the chapter on combat action to begin.

One of the choppers was grass-topping the rice paddies to my right, rifling right toward small islands of trees, then suddenly shooting up over them, riddling the islands with rounds, and not even bothering to check them out first. It was assumed that in one of them there was going to be a VC. On the third run a Huey caught return fire. The pilot swooped it up over the trees and somehow turned instantly around, putting the open door to the island so the machine gunner could point straight down on it. I watched the dual M-60 machine guns smoke and spit rounds into the trees, snapping branches and bushes to bits. I could also see VC rifle smoke on the island, which was no bigger than a baseball diamond. The chopper moved around the island. I saw a cannister fall out of the door and, a second later, a huge red cloud furrow up below it. As the chopper swerved away and climbed up and over the convoy, a jet was suddenly over the island and as suddenly gone. The island exploded, sending trees and mud splattering out into the surrounding rice paddies. Shouts and cheers bellowed up from the convoy, and I found myself standing up with my rifle in the air yelling "Yaaaaahooo!" with the rest. One marine called out, "Charlie, you bought the farm on that one!" Another yelled, "You can kiss your ass goodbye, Charlie. Your soul's in hell now!"

When we came to a village, the convoy stopped and the grunt platoon up front got off the trucks with a mine sweeper and walked up in front of the tank, slowly pacing us through, listening for that high-pitched peeping sound that would put them onto a VC mine. We couldn't afford to have a mine blow up the tank and maybe hold us up until nightfall. As the marines probed for mines, an even thicker column of people nonchalantly riding bikes and motorbikes came almost up to them, then veered off and around the convoy, undaunted by the fact a mine might destroy them. Or did they know where the explosives were?

A squad moved off the road to clear the people out of the way and wave them down into the ditches on both sides in single file, even starting to check inside their wagons and sacks for weapons. The captain was out of his jeep with his hands on his hips, slowly walking the ditch as the mine sweepers progressed. He seemed to be enjoying the convoy, periodically looking back at the smoke from the island we had blown up, then at the people complaining in Vietnamese to the marines as they were searched. He looked at his watch a couple of times, then went to a PR-6 radio in the jeep. He seemed to argue about something, looking at his watch, then put the microphone down stiffly. He yelled something at the platoon on line and the mine sweepers. They all filed back and got into the trucks again.

What he did next was either pure stupidity or worthy

of a bronze star. With his driver he sped down the road on the right side all the way to the outside edge of the village. Then he raced back in the middle of the road. Then he went back down on the left side of the road and came back once again alongside of the tank. He waved the driver onward. The tank lieutenant on the turret was shaking his head and laughing. I couldn't believe it. The captain felt we were wasting time looking for the mines, so he decided to find out the fast way if there were any there. If he had hit one it would have sent the jeep in one direction and what was left of him and the driver up on the village hut roofs in the other direction. Stupidity? Probably. Valor? In the eyes of the Marine Corps, yes.

I caught several villagers looking up and down the road, their faces revealing expressions of disappointment, as though they were trying to figure out why the captain's jeep hadn't blown up. I leveled my rifle right on the back of one villager's head. He somehow knew I was on him and turned around and looked up at me, surprise mixed with fear in his eyes. He knew I had caught him red-handed, and I was sure he was a VC or at the least a VC sympathizer.

I put my finger on the trigger and squeezed gently, taking up the slack until I felt the slightest resistance. Then I held it there, not moving my rifle barrel a tenth of an inch. I was going to kill that man. That's all I had on my mind. It wasn't bothering me at all. I squeezed that trigger the rest of the way . . . but all I heard was a click. I rushed to push my bolt back and no round popped out. I had not chambered a round to begin with! I snapped a look up at the man, but all I saw was that crowd of people now moving along the ditch again. I quickly chambered a round and jerked to my feet to survey the crowd. He was nowhere in sight.

I sat back down on the bottom of the truck cradling my rifle and for some reason I was breathing hard. It had begun to rain again and I let the rain beat on my face, while I put my hands on my rifle as though fondling it. I had a weird feeling in my stomach. I had actually pulled the trigger on a man that had no weapon exposed to shoot at me. I'd done it in plain sight of everyone around me. If I'd killed him, no one would have said a word, though. They would have counted him as a VC kill, buried him in a mass grave with other VC, and that would have been the end of it. And I would have gone on with my life. But what frightened me the most was the fact that I had calmly pulled that trigger. There was no question in my mind about what I wanted to do with that bullet. Even though he could very well have been a VC, I would never have known for sure. There was no justification for that action. If I had had a round in my chamber I would now be a cold-blooded murderer.

In other operations and on perimeter guard I had fired back when fired upon. When I was wounded in that ambush I had fired back to stay alive, to help save the others. In skirmishes with VC we had fired first to gain fire superiority fast. But this. This was murder. Jesus, I thought, looking into the rain, what the hell is happening to me? I started pulling the magazine out of my rifle. But I stopped. I couldn't do that. What if we were ambushed? Then I would be back to survival. I held onto my rifle and wondered what I was becoming.

We pulled into another village, larger than the one before. The red slushy mud not only dropped off the trucks but splattered up over the ditches and onto hooches and people. Rounding a dogleg turn, we suddenly met an ARVN convoy at least twice as big as ours. Every truck in it was filled tight with South Vietnamese soldiers standing up in clean new uniforms and boots and helmets with no camouflage covers. They were carrying M-16 rifles, and grenades were neatly attached to their backpack shoulder straps. It was obvious they had been airlifted up from Saigon and had probably never seen an hour of combat in their lives. I was willing to bet not one of them had ever fired a rifle at an enemy.

As their trucks rounded the turn one by one, the villagers were waving at them, throwing little packages up to them, smiling and laughing. The soldiers in turn stretched down and shook hands, waved at the young girls, threw scarves down to them. After about twenty minutes their convoy rear guard turned the corner and gave us the road to continue toward our destination.

When we started down the road again, the villagers suddenly had other things to do. Some of them briskly walked off between the hooches. Children stood there with blank

looks on their faces. The stream of refugees bent their heads
down once again and plodded on. I looked down the road at
the ARVN convoy now almost lost in the drizzle and mud.
Some of the older children were still running after it, hollering
and laughing. By the time I looked back at the village, the
people had all gone about their business and acted like we
had never even been there.

Resentment for this treatment came from our convoy
in an explosion and a rattle of machine gun fire at one of the
hooches. The front wall of the hut caved in and toppled over
into the ditch. Our truck stopped and I hit the floor, training
my rifle up and down the line of refugees who had started
jumping for cover and dropping to the red mud. My heart
pounded and I could feel my trigger finger squeezing again.
A scream came from the hooch and a dazed old mama san
staggered out holding her head with bloodied hands.

The grunts in the truck up front were jumping out and
surrounding the hooch, pushing the people away with their
rifle butts. The captain leapt down off his jeep with his .45
pistol in hand pointed up, yelling at the grunt lieutenant,
"What in the hell are you doing?"

"Sir, we thought we saw a VC rifle in there," the lieutenant said, his face as earnest as if he were saying "I do" to
his hometown sweetheart. Then he smiled, turned to two
marines and ordered, "Check it out."

Without hesitation the marines dove into the hooch,
their rifles out in front cowboy-style. There was some more
yelling inside, and then a rush of black pajamas and olive skin
rolled out into the drizzling rain in front of the captain. Behind
came the marines carrying an old French-made machine gun
with a clip in it.

The captain was so surprised he dropped his pistol down
to his hip. The mama san was still holding her head, pleading,
"No VC. . . . He no VC. . . . No VC. . . ."

The Vietnamese man on the ground looked around
through the rain at everyone with a bitter expression of defiance. If he isn't a VC, I thought, then nobody is.

The grunts tied him up and dragged him out behind
the hooch to a clearing and called in for a chopper to pick
him up. Then we continued on with the thunder run. We had

been on the highway for about two more hours when far off in the distance we could see Cessna planes and helicopters taking off from the airstrip we were headed for. But before we got there just about the worst of what could happen on a convoy like this happened.

We were out on an open stretch, passing two bridge marine bunkers fortified with sandbags. The marines inside were waving at us. One of the marines was particularly trying to attract our attention. He was shirtless and shoeless, wearing only trousers, an old jungle hat, and something around his neck. When we got a little closer we could see what it was. He sported a necklace of three VC ears and was holding them up so we could all see. On his left pectoral muscle was a tattoo of a monster marine holding a small VC by the hair with a long knife tucked under the VC's neck.

Suddenly there was a loud "Varooooom!" and behind it a whooshing sound followed by another "Varooooom!"

I felt myself leave the truck and in midair was already spreading out so that I hit the ditch with a belly flop. By the time I rolled over everybody was out of the trucks taking cover. The drivers were jamming gears and brakes and opening doors to dive out the other side. The marine with the VC ears had grabbed his rifle and was running down the ditch toward the front of the convoy, trying to get across the bridge to another bunker. I was up on my knees tearing my poncho off and looking around for the ambush, for something to shoot at.

Then I heard several pain-filled screams, a lull, then more screams. Marines were on their feet running up front to the tank. Smoke was coming out of it and the tank cannon barrel was off to the side. The tank had hit a mine, maybe two.

One of the choppers swooped past, then circled the area preparing for a VC ambush. But it never happened. They'd set the mine and disappeared.

I found myself up, carrying my rifle on my hip, slipping on the side of the ditch, running across the bridge, slowing to a walk, approaching the tank. Two marines were up on the tank at the driver's hatch prying at it with pipes, while inside the driver was screaming with pain. Another marine was sprawled halfway out of a hole in the middle of the front of the tank. The back of his head was gone and his whole right side was opened up. A corpsman was asking for help to get him off the tank and onto the road. When he got the wounded man down, he plunged his hand right into the blood trying to get hold of the arteries to stop the red flow pouring out on the road. The marine was shivering in a way I had never seen before. I shouldered my rifle with the strap and helped carry a stretcher off one of the trucks. The marine trapped in the tank was still screaming, "Oh my God. . . . Jesus, I'm dying. . . ." Everybody was looking at him as wide-eyed and frightened as he was. Then finally they got him free. The chopper landed on the road and both the wounded men were carried to the open door. In seconds they were in the air racing to Chu Lai.

The captain ordered the rear tank up to push the first one off the road. Then the convoy sped all the way down to a T in the road, turned right and sped down the right side of the airstrip.

We drove into a war hive of battle activity. The entire airstrip was full of planes coming in and going out. Choppers were landing near a temporary CP next to a 105 howitzer cannon fire base. A medical tent fifty feet off the strip was taking in wounded. Some were able to walk in carrying their rifles and packs, some walked with help from other marines, and others were carried in on stretchers. An ROK battalion of marines from Korea were boarding Chinook helicopters. A long line of Viet Cong POW's were being unloaded and lined up. They were blindfolded and were being tugged along to a POW camp close to the airstrip by a rope around their necks. A mile away the battle raged. I could see jets going in for bombing runs, trees blowing up. Miniature helicopters dotted the skyline. Smoke and fog mixed with fire.

Everybody moved in double time. And there was always something that needed to be done. We were assigned to perimeter guard around the 105's, then turned over to med-evac, then switched back to the perimeter, then once again to med-evac. Then there was a call for extra fire power on the choppers bringing the wounded out, so we were it, but within minutes we ended up back at the perimeter.

There I was, just out of the hospital, working furiously. Everything was happening so fast around me all I could do was kneel on perimeter guard, look out at the distant battle and say, "Hello, war."

The convoy had passed. The highway was left to me and a few cars speeding past where I was still stopped beside the road.

I shook my head. How could I have stopped so long? How could I have forgotten where I was going that morning? Only Nam could have taken my mind away from Frank's ranch and what might already be waiting for me there. I started the car and moved on down the road, grateful to be on Alligator Alley, Florida, U.S.A., instead of on Highway 1, Vietnam.

Book VIII
Tracker

A cougar is not a precocious species. The young are helpless when born in a cave or hollow log and are fed and nurtured and trained by a mother that will defend her young against all enemies. It is at his mother's side that the young cat plays and is reprimanded and learns.

—*Roger Caras*
The Forest

Book VIII

Tracker

50

Natural Born

Swamp notes—at birth
Who better to track a panther than another panther? Only another supreme natural tracking machine could track the supreme tracking machine. It is time for this breakthrough to happen, to jar loose still another path to my goal, to lead me to the soul of Shakespeare.

In the small oak hammock on the other side of the skin-smooth pond at the ranch, a red-bellied woodpecker called out in his cantus song. The air was pierced with his rolling chiv-chiv-chiv-chiv-chiv. I glanced over and located him flitting about on one of the larger trees. With his black bands, he is sometimes called the zebra woodpecker. Again he sang chiv-chiv-chiv-chiv.

Even though this bird had caught my interest, my concentration was on something more important and precious. I darted my eyes back to one of the panther cages, a female's cage. A thin stream of blood seeped out onto the cement. Riveted to the spot, I stared into her dark den. Inside, partially camouflaged in the shadows, curled up in fuzzy black and faded white balls, were three brand-new panther cubs—squirming, squeaking, nuzzling, trying their best to press against their mother, who, in turn, wrapped her hind legs around them.

The mother was extremely protective of them, a good sign, always keeping a wary eye on me with her ears half down in a defensive posture. With whispers and soft purrs, I tried to assure her I was a friend, that I would protect them as well. But she had a great deal more confidence in her powers of defense, and I quite agreed with her. A female panther defending her cubs is no cat to mess with. With those claws and fangs, she could easily kill me if I entered the cage, and that I wasn't about to do.

Using a small flashlight, I carefully surveyed each cub. Eyes were closed. Paws were curled up into fists, small creamy-white claws partially exposed. The tails were short. Each small body pulsed with life. They all looked healthy. Frank had said it was a good litter, two males, one female. Mother panther looked exhausted, head sometimes drooping. But she still finished her duty of cleaning one of the cubs with her tongue and nudged it toward one of her teats.

I was deeply disappointed at having missed the actual birth which occurred only minutes before I arrived, but was now drinking in every moment, every movement the cubs made. I thrilled to every whimper with goose bumps on my arms.

It was a rare event indeed. Here were three cub-panthers natural born, surrounded by their wild environment, the Everglades. And even though they were in captivity, still they were as natural born as cubs born in the wilds because they could now easily adapt to their surroundings, be trained to live in the wilds, be relocated right in the habitat near which they had been born and would grow up.

There was another important reason why I was watching this litter so closely. One of them was going to end up in my arms. One of them was going to step into the wilds with me. One of them was going to be as close to me as my own soul.

I wanted the female. Frank had pushed the idea as well, and I figured he knew best. And it turned out he did. Later in the swamp, in Shakespeare's territory, the fact that my panther was a female would be far more important than I realized at that moment. It would be the key that would unlock the final door.

As I looked at those cubs I saw Shakespeare's beginning. I saw his mother in season, walking her territory, crying for a mate. I saw four male panthers answer that cry, fight for her, one of the males triumphing, claiming the privilege of helping to bring another litter into the swamp.

Then for ninety days, as her belly swelled, Shakespeare's mother roamed the cypress swamp in search of high ground and dense undergrowth for a well-hidden den site. Above the bushline she found a hole facing the east where the sun would shine in the morning on the litter to warm them after the cool night.

When her time came she crawled into the hole and over a period of hours her litter was born. I imagined Shakespeare emerging from his mother's womb, wet, easing out onto the soft ground. Though exhausted from the trauma of birth, he immediately heard the wild sounds of the swamp. His education had begun. I visualized him pumping his legs and grabbing for his mother's milk. Shakespeare was a panther born wild to remain wild for the rest of his days.

Now, in that cage, in those cubs, and especially that female, I saw the birth of a new way for me to prove Shakespeare's role in this wild swamp once and for all. In those cubs I saw the rebirth of myself.

51

Vigil

**Swamp notes—observing the
female cub**
*I race to the ranch every day and sit in vigil
over the cubs' progress. I can't take my eyes
off the female cub. We are already closing
the gap between us.*

Every morning at dawn a marsh hawk showed up for a breakfast of chicken necks and liver at the ranch. Sometimes running off black vultures from their perch, the hawk would descend onto a bare pine branch and sit proudly waiting for the handout. She would glance at the vultures as they flew low in aggravation, then whistle a sharp nasal call that sent rodents scurrying under saw palmetto. From her long brown streaked tail to her sharp eyes and curved beak, all two feet of this hawk was a presence of pride and nobility. The food she took was not charity; it was an offering.

This master of flight and control in the white sky had become my companion in two days of vigil over the newborn cubs. We would peer into the den until we saw movement, then settle down to long wonderful hours of observation.

Mother-panther never left the cubs unattended in the den. Frank left food for her, usually raw juicy fresh chicken, in her cage a few feet away from her, but I never saw her leave her cubs unattended even to move that short distance. Instead she would stare intensely at me, then up at the hawk, her ears darting at his whistles. Instinct told her the cubs in the wilds would make a good breakfast for the hawk. But the security of the cage, and perhaps my being near, put her more at ease. I found a long stick and took on the duty of pushing the chicken right under her nose. On the second day she trusted me enough to grab off bites of it—never taking her eyes off me and the hawk.

After throwing chicken necks to the hawk, Frank would walk over to the cage, study the cubs, then without a word, walk away with smiling eyes. He knew panther birth, had watched it often, and each time it was a new experience for him. I knew this experience of birth was one of the reasons for his deep love of the cats, and he understood my love for tracking them. Though I had kept secret my reason for wanting to raise a cub, I suspected he knew.

On this second day of life the female cub was about eleven inches long and weighed close to seven ounces. The other two were slightly smaller. The female seemed to be more active in the den, always tugging at her mother's under-fur, nudging her head against the others for a better position to feed. She would stretch her legs out stiff and long and bare those miniature claws. On occasion she squinted her eyes as though she were desperately trying to see. They were partially open, but her sight had not been fully activated yet. I also noticed she would lie on her side and maneuver herself toward the den door. Was she looking for space, already plotting territory? The mother-panther would then bounce her back to the warmth and security of the fur on her massive side.

Ever since I knew I was going to raise one of the cubs, I had been racking my brain for a name. Many had suggested themselves, but I had turned them all down. There was Kitcat, but when she was full-grown she would hardly act or look like a kitty cat, so I dropped that one. Then I thought of calling her Panther, a realistic name, but it was hardly creative and didn't really fit what she was going to do with me.

Out tracking one day it came to me. The female cub was going to track wild panthers with me. Quite simply, then, she would be a tracker like me. Therefore I would call her Tracker. It had a nice ring to it and really told the whole story about my plans for her. So Tracker it was and I hoped she would live up to her name.

My vigil on this day took me well into the afternoon. Frank was just starting to feed the rest of the big cats, so I went to help out. I took one more look at Tracker and one more look up in the pine to see if the hawk was still there. He had long since flown to another feeding ground, but I knew that promptly the next morning I would hear that whistle, then see that flapping, soaring silhouette moving through the morning sky as though suddenly appearing from another dimension.

I was eager for Tracker to grow up, at least enough to get out in the swamp. I wondered how long it would be before her mother was willing to give her to me.

I drove to Shakespeare's territory that evening to track for a while, and at my first step in I couldn't help but smile. It was beginning to hit me what I had planned with Tracker.

52

Mother's Milk

Swamp notes—under the east wind
I've often pondered, objectively, the pros and cons of intervening in nature's course in order to save a species—or an individual member of it—from extinction. My objectivity has been blown away in the wind.

A warm bracing east wind floated unseen around us in silent motion near the cage. Lisps of wax myrtle leaves quickened. Small gusts shook wet wild butterfly orchid buds. Creeping through pores of palm fronds and flowers, over pine tree needles, through low sedge grass, and across the quiescent pond water, the wind came to us from the direction that the sun appears each morning and the moon each night. It seemed to be a good omen. This visitation of earth's life-giving element blew swamp odors across the glades eons old, bringing to Tracker and me a fresh new beginning, strength, and a power from wild windy places across the world. It swept into the den and over the cubs, ruffling their cotton-soft fur and causing them to curl up even more. But mother panther didn't immediately react by enclosing them in her large paws. Instead, she lay there uninterested in their welfare and movements. There was cause for concern.

Tracker was three days old now, a critical time when she needed all the care and attention and nourishment she could get. Yet her mother was suddenly making moves away from the cubs, once even batting Tracker away when it was time for suckling. I could see that mother panther's nipples were red and bleeding, which meant the cubs had been gnawing and pulling at them.

But mother's milk was the all-important ingredient for Tracker's growth into that supreme adult creature she could become. It was necessary for her to build up her body weight from all the elements in this perfect food until she was ready for weaning. Mother's milk would give her all she needed before she could transfer to a diet of chicken and liver and raw eggs, which would then give her what she needed to grow to a healthy adult female ready to carry and nurse her own cubs someday.

But none of this was going to happen if her mother openly rejected her now, at this critical point in her life.

I stared at Tracker's plump body, the small paws slightly clenching every now and then, the stub of her tail throbbing in cadence to her pulse, her ears still small against her head. She suddenly seemed so very helpless, so vulnerable to death by neglect. I knew that nature was never intentionally cruel, however destructive the situation seemed. I knew that nature would help us make the right decision of what to do about the cubs, about Tracker. Should we risk leaving the cubs in there one more day in the hope that mother panther was going through a temporary lapse of responsibility and would snap back to motherhood? Or should we enter the cage and bring the cubs out and care for them ourselves?

Frank and Ellen were more than willing to take the cubs out, for they knew full well what would happen if something positive didn't occur soon. There could be permanent brain damage, respiratory malfunctions, bone deformity, low resistance that would open the way for a virus or pneumonia. None of the cubs would be normal if left alone for any length of time. If left too long alone they would die.

It seemed so incongruous to me that such a powerful, highly adaptable creature could be so fragile and conquerable when young. Yet at birth Tracker could do nothing but lie there on her side, squirming, pleading with high-pitched squeaks for a swallow of milk. Right then those ounces of milk were no more than a whisker's length away, but they might as well have been a million miles away.

I watched Tracker struggle forward, trying to stretch out her neck, putting her nose close to the nipple, laying her head back and closing in on the nipple with her mouth, only to fall back weakly. But she tried once again, failed, once again, and again failed, falling back in complete exhaustion.

She lay there almost motionless. I was about ready to tear open the cage door and rush in to jam the nipple into her mouth regardless of those powerful claws of mother panther. But Frank, with his vast experience and patience, was going to give mother panther just one more evening. He said the cubs would be okay until the next morning. If the mother did not respond by then he would get the cubs out.

When I left the ranch the east wind was still with us, blowing in that steady invisible way, offering tranquility. A good omen? If it was, it meant nothing to me by then. I was anxious, frustrated, irritable. What if by some freak accident Tracker didn't make the night? What if the cubs got to the nipples and the pain of their gnawing drove mother panther into a rage? What if . . . what if . . . what if? . . .

I lay for hours that night staring up at the ceiling, on the verge many times of calling Frank. I paced the living room floor and watched a stupid movie on TV. I ate a whole jar of crunchy-style peanut butter with a knife, and stared bug-eyed out the back window to the east directly in line with the ranch, with Tracker's cage. I stood there praying for dawn to crack that treeline wide open, and when it did I was already in the car on Alligator Alley heading toward the ranch.

It must have been the sleepless night, the exhausting stress and vigil of Tracker's birth, trying to keep data on Shakespeare in the swamp—all of it rolled into a critical time in my life—that stirred a deep-rooted war guilt that I had been suppressing for almost ten years. Without warning, the war memory spilled over into my consciousness as I was driving that morning.

I began to think of the war children of South Vietnam. Their lives were filled with machine gun fire, mortar attacks, napalm strikes, watching their mothers and fathers killed, their brothers and sisters carried off, their grandparents left for dead in a leveled village. They were the ones who knew pain and death on its most gruesome level. They were the bewildered, never truly understanding what the war was all about. I'd never been sure myself.

I remember the village children crowding around me, pulling at my arms for more Kool-aid and Hershey bars, unable to understand why I kept my eyes on them and a rifle on my shoulder. I could hear them calling out, "Maline, you give me sweet water. . . ." The words echoed in my mind while the sun edged up over the swamp.

I saw again those large, pleading brown eyes, lined with mud from hiding in a hole for days, reaching out for a fragment of pity, only to be closed abruptly by a stray 105 cannon round.

Then one particular memory overtook me. I was lying in the Chu Lai medical center healing when a corpsman brought in a beautiful three-year-old girl-child who had been wounded. The story was she was a VC's daughter found tied to the back of her mother who was caught in the middle of a night ambush by a marine patrol. I spent a long time considering the kind of commitment that would mean carrying your own child into battle. It made me wonder to what extent the VC would go to win.

She lay on the operating table screaming with pain, her side opened up from an M-60 machine-gun blast, her eyes wild with fright, tears streaming down her bloody checks, desperately trying to reach out to her mother on the other table, who lay motionless under a stained sheet.

She screamed like that into a rainy night and not one of us could close our eyes. It was as though those screams echoed across all of South Vietnam, representing all war children caught in the middle of a strange war waged by adults who should know better. Those screams were pleading for peace and reason. I tried walking to the far side of the tents, but those screams came up along the sea wall and across the parade deck like creeping ghosts tearing my guts out. I prayed for them to stop, and when they did I knew she was finally free of the war.

Rolling along Alligator Alley, I knew I still wasn't. I knew I bore the burden of keeping the daughter of a pair of swamp cats from the murderous hand of extinction. If death has a point, it is to show us the importance of life.

53

Saved from Extinction

Swamp notes—under fire
*Do I imitate the weather or does it mimic
me? Out here in the glades, a strong case
can be made for the latter.*

As though born from volcanic fire, the red morning sun was
suddenly obliterated by oncoming, white, serrated flames blasting through an austere indigo sky, crowded by black churning
mountains at each flash ahead of me. Surflike clouds swelled,
foamed, and crashed against those vapor ridges on one side,
while on the other a shawl of sparkling glacierlike mist over-
shadowed cormorants wheeling downward away from this
storm, using their part of the sky as though it were a snowy
slope to slide down. Under this stern vista of electrical storms,
rain haze lingered and hid a tall cypress covered over with
vines, making it look like an angel's face, lost and lonely in
the swamp. Enveloped in fog that curled tightly and deceptively around them, two deer browsed in wet grass, oblivious
to the storm far off. It was a spectacular scene of nature on
the verge of going insane at one end of the sky while keeping
a strong steady hold on stability at the other.

My mind was like the stormy end of the sky, filled with
the swirling events of Tracker's birth, her immediate instinc-
tual sense of survival, then the sudden turn of events that put
her on the verge of extinction. My mind was filled with questions, uncertainties, frustration, and anticipation of the worst,
while my body drove the car and my eyes searched up ahead
for the turnoff to the ranch.

When I got to Route 29 and made the turn north, I did
it at more than sixty miles an hour, just missing the steel guard
rails next to the canal, swerving over into the left lane, going
off onto the shoulder, then crossing back into the right lane.

Thirty seconds later I was at the ranch entrance, sliding over the gravel and slipping through the mud around the pond. When finally I pulled up near the cage, I slammed the gear into park and flew out of the door, striding to the cage door.

Breathing heavily, as though I had run the entire distance from my house, I stared into the den. But to my horror not a single panther was there. No cubs. No mother panther. Behind the den, up on the shelf near the scratch pole, mother panther was spread out in repose with a curious look on her face, probably trying to figure out why I had raced into the ranch. I stared into the den one more time, thinking the cubs might be in one of the corners, but they weren't.

I couldn't let myself believe what my eyes were telling me.

In thin fog coming off the pond, Frank walked toward me. His feet slowly shuffled. His eyes were red and drawn with dark trenches under them.

"Been up all night," he said.

I couldn't talk.

Then Frank motioned for me to come into the trailer.

With weak legs and my stomach feeling empty of emotions, I followed Frank up the wooden steps of the embankment and into the trailer. Ellen was making coffee. She, too, looked like she had been up all night.

"Coffee, Jim?" she asked in that mother-kind voice of hers.

I still didn't say anything as I shook my head.

As Frank was walking through the kitchen he half-whispered in a cracked tired voice, "Let me show you something."

Staring at Frank's back, I went down the short hall to the bathroom. Frank pointed into the tub. Clamped onto the side of the tub was a small bell lamp pointed downward. I peered over the edge and into a large towel that had been shaped into a nest. Inside the towel black stripes and spots glowed under the lamp. A distinct musky scent came to my nose. Panther scent. I was staring at throbbing, wiggling fur with stumpy legs and squinting indigo-blue eyes. Three sets of each!

I flashed a look at Frank.

"Things weren't looking good after you left last night,

so I took the cubs for our own. They're on formula now."
Frank's face turned into a wide grin.

"Fantastic, Frank. Fantastic."

I knelt down and leaned into the tub. Tracker, who was
between her brothers, was only inches away. I carefully stroked
her side and felt the warmth with my finger. At first touch
she flinched. But I stroked her one more time and blew across
her face.

"Twenty-four hours a day, every four hours, she's taking
milk. Healthy cat. She's yours," Frank said.

When I went back out, in the distance I heard the
thunder of the glades storms rolling away across the swamp.
In the sunlight where I stood vegetation glistened with dew.
Breathtaking. In fact, the swamp and pine trees around the
ranch looked great. All of the Everglades looked great. Tracker,
Frank and Ellen were great. Everybody in the world was great.

I looked off in the direction of Shakespeare's territory.
Soon, Shakespeare, soon enough, we'll be there.

54

Meat-eater

> **Swamp notes—feeding Tracker**
> *Tracker grows and changes so fast. Not more
> than a week ago she was a blob of fur,
> bones, skin and organs, struggling in her
> cub way to orient herself to her environ-
> ment. Now look at her—a meat-eater.*

In the cypress, the sun looked like a large silver eye trying to
see through dawn into the wonderful gloom of the swamp
where I lay in my hammock as though I was some sort of
weird creature that had yet to be identified. I watched it

twinkle among the etched tree limbs for a while before it was momentarily blotted out by a passing flock of wading birds. Perfectly outlined on a tall maple was a great horned owl that flicked his long tufted "ears" and turned his head in the direction of prey. I glanced back at the re-emerging sun, and then when I looked back at the owl he had silently disappeared.

I lay in my hammock watching heavy dew beads weep from wet deer-hoof vine leaves like tears from a forgotten wild world. Underneath me a newly formed stream percolated over spongy logs, creating small niagaras, siphoning themselves along a shallow trench into a still-water fish pool. Small bass had already sought out the only cool shadow that cast itself upon that wallow, which had probably been thrashed out by an alligator. The evening before I had caught the bass in the canal with a floating rapala plug and dropped them into the pool before setting up camp. Now, seasoned with bay leaves and cinnamon, they would make a fresh breakfast.

I remembered how my father taught me to catch bass when I was a boy. Then it was digging and handling wet, sticky worms, walking muddy river trails, casting large artificial plugs, and keeping my fishing line from getting tangled in the reel. It was taking the hook out of a wiggling bass and gently putting him back in the water, watching him dart to cover. He loved to teach me about things he loved. He was the person who kindled in me my passion for the wilds. He loved to be out in it fishing, boating, just being out there. Sometimes I would catch him out of the corner of my eye staring at birds in flight or fish movement along the bank.

When I got in high school he took me on fishing expeditions to Minnesota, Wisconsin and Michigan. Then when I was ready for the big time, we went on an expedition to Canada—the real northern wilderness. I was overwhelmed by the cool, crisp Canadian mornings, the thick forest and untamed mountain ranges crowding the vast freshwater lakes fed by winter snows. Deer flashed in shadows in the treeline. I saw a bear drinking in a brook. Once our Indian guide talked about a mountain lion who had crept in close to our cabin during the night. Even then the cat was on my trail.

In all those years my father's instructions were simple,

basic, but had a great effect on my life. He would talk about how the wilderness should be left alone, how people should appreciate it, not ruin it. There were things out there people needed. And they could only have them if they left them alone. Not until I came to the Everglades did I understand how important that thought was. Then, with a smile, he would dip his hand into the water and drink it—crystal clear water born in the wilds for man.

I rolled out of the hammock, placing my bare feet into the cool water that sent a shock up my legs. Squatting, I threw some of that water up in my face, cleared my eyes, then went to find the driest of fallen palm fronds and twigs and logs.

I was in Shakespeare's territory, trying to keep as much contact with him as I could while I worked with Tracker in her early days. I had come onto his tracks in two different locations not far away, and it felt good to know he was near.

When I got the fire going well enough, I dipped a metal cup into the pool and put it close to the flame. After pouring a little honey into it, I dropped in a bouquet of shredded blackberry leaves, eleuthero ginzeng root, roasted chicory root, orange peel, rosehips, ginger root, lovage root, licorice root, panax ginzeng and tea leaves—a combination of ingredients that dated back two thousand years in Chinese history. It combatted illness, stimulated vitality, and most of all, created energy for me.

The Chinese say that the ginzeng root is a tonic that can quiet animal spirits, establish the soul, allay fears, expel evil, brighten the eyes, open up the heart, develop understanding, and if taken regularly for some time, invigorate the body and prolong life. Even if just some of it's true, it's worth trying.

After that I crowded one of the bass into a corner of the pond, shoveled it up onto high ground, and quickly filleted it, leaving the skin and scales on it. Putting the sides on a Y-shaped stick above the fire, I took my cup from the heat to let it cool a bit.

I was eager to get breakfast done, break camp, and get to the ranch. Just a week ago when Tracker was close to the end of her second week, she had already opened her eyes and begun to see objects moving in front of her. Quite often she saw huge man-eyes an inch away, blotting out the light, probing her eyes. I wondered what she thought as I held her in the palm of my hand looking at her. Once she told me quite clearly by reaching out and scratching my nose with those inexperienced claws. She tore my skin and drew blood. Already she used those claws expertly by pushing them out for an attempt to grasp my nose, and then pulling them back into the sheaths when rubbing her face or licking her paw. It had to be natural instinct. No one had ever taught her those things.

Now it was the end of the third week. She had done well with the formula and I was going to mix raw chicken livers into her diet. I was sure that before long she would be a full-time meat-eater.

I gulped breakfast down, put out the fire and slid the smoldering coals into the trench, covering them completely. Then I went over to the pool where the other two bass were still lounging and with my hands opened up a small channel into a large devil's pool and chased them into it. I wondered if they could find their way back to their own stream in the canal through the underground cavern systems. At the least, they would do all right where they were now, and might even provide another breakfast for me.

Emerging from the treeline, I jumped into the station wagon and sped to the ranch. Frank was already up walking the cage line, checking out the cats. He had another mating couple that were making no secret of how much they enjoyed each other's company by displaying for both of us in their rare feline form an early morning intercourse. I walked the line with him and then went into the trailer and checked Tracker. She greeted me with a whistle and purred. I wasn't sure whether it was meant for me or just that I happened down into the tub at the same time she made the sounds. But I returned the whistle and did the best I could to mimic the purr.

I carefully took her up in my hands and we gently bumped foreheads. It seemed to be some kind of a physical sign of recognition for her, a panther touch that meant friendliness. Later those little bumps turned into head slamming, and, of course, Tracker always got the better of me, though I still enjoyed the fact that she knew who I was by it.

With the utmost tenderness, I gave her a small swallow of milk from a baby bottle, then pulled it free. She wanted to go on and drink all of it, and issued a half-hearted squawk to let me know. But I was determined that on this day she was to take another step toward maturity.

I carved up little tiny bits of raw meat from the breast of a chicken mixed in with the bloody liver and pushed it into her mouth. For a second she couldn't imagine what it was and what exactly she was supposed to do with it. The blood trickled down the sides of her mouth. Then she caught on, and with sloppy mashing of her jaws, did her best to eat it down. When I pushed in the next morsel, she took to it fast and easy. And by the time she received the third morsel, she was taking in my fingers as well. I chuckled and marveled at this moment we were experiencing together. There was survival of the fittest in its most basic infantile form. Here was a three-week-old panther acting in a direct natural response necessary for her own continued existence and that of her species. She left no doubt that she wanted life, and that nothing was going to stand in her way. She was a survivalist: good news for the Florida panther.

I let myself imagine for a while how similar it must have been for Shakespeare in the wild. I could just see his mother making a deer kill in a prairie in a fall dawn, then quickly pulling the carcass up into a cypress head, efficiently opening up the stomach and going for the liver, half chewing it to predigest the meat, then maybe going to the hind quarters and biting out a portion of muscle. With the quickness of her breed, she then dashes back to the den, crawls inside, and sets the meat out in front of the cubs, nudging them to it and depriving them of her mother's milk in order to interest them in this first solid food. I could just see Shakespeare muscling for a good position, devouring the meat as Tracker had just done, then lying back contented and proud of himself for having a full belly. I could see Shakespeare doing all of those things. In Tracker's movements and eyes, I saw the few remaining panthers struggling for survival. I also saw the slaughter of deer and the destruction of the Everglades by man, and knew we were not learning those basic survival skills from the wildlife, the panther.

Now that Tracker was on solid food, it would soon be time to begin pursuing another stage in our relationship. But now it would include Shakespeare.

55

Swamp Baptism

Swamp notes—a born-again morning
It is a glorious day for me, for I am giving birth to a new way of tracking Shakespeare. I will introduce Tracker to Shakespeare's territory, a grand experiment in itself.

It was a genesis morningtide, and a new beginning for me. There I stood in that vast wet prairie where I had sighted Shakespeare for the first time. Floods of melted gold oozed over the high grass. Ground fog that never seemed to sleep among small islands of dripping mist looked more like icefalls. Every tree, bush, blade of grass was growing with life. Wild voices filled the sky and treeline, echoing and dissolving and transmitting onward.

Near me an apple snail deposited her tiny white eggs on a stem, each looking like a finished pearl able to withstand the crushing of feet, the battering of rain, the stifling heat.

An American egret, with its long swordlike beak used for catching fish, aquatic insects, frogs and baby alligators, stood in its white plumage camouflaged against the intense brightness of the sun, and only the flash of his beak told he was there.

I had come back to this prairie many times, off and on, and each time I saw it in a new light. It was never the same. It was never boring. It revitalized my spirit when I was down, heightened my goals when I was looking for more meaning.

It was my foundation of knowledge, of that first true contact with Shakespeare. For me, this place meant everything that the love of the wilds could bring to a human being, because I knew that it was Shakespeare's miry sanctuary. This swamp held a wild predator who had grown accustomed to my presence. And it held the divine flame sparked by our respect for each other.

On this particular dawn I had come back for a special reason. In my backpack, making whistles like a blackbird and squawks like a parrot, was a female panther. Eighteen inches long, weighing under twenty ounces, she sat in my pack awed as I was at the scene before us, staring at it as though touched by the triumphant spirit of Nature herself.

I wondered if Shakespeare could see her at that moment, smell her. Was he somewhere near trying to figure out what I was up to this time? Did he take this creature as an intruder? Or had he accepted her immediately because she was one of his own species?

I took Tracker out of the pack and held her high in the sunlight over my head. Feeling her warm body now blending with the swamp sent electricity through me. God in heaven, bless this panther. *Nam Yo Fara On.*

Looking into her dark, indigo-blue eyes, I could not yet conceive what this she-cub was going to do for me. She stared back at me deeply, so deeply that it was hard for me to keep my eyes on her. There was a power in those eyes. Panther power. Would she give it to me? Or would I have to beg her for it, tease it from her, or just steal it away from her? I was prepared to follow her lead.

At that moment Tracker became my swampmate until her adulthood.

We slipped into the cypress treeline on high ground and over to an old trail. The usual animal trails were there, and a small, lounging moccasin shot its head up and quickly crawled for cover under high grass. A pair of red-shouldered hawks signaled our presence with that unequaled high-pitched whistle of warning that sounded like a trumpet. Then they circled overhead, taking a good look at me and I suspected an even better look at Tracker. Their hawk silhouettes seemed to halt momentarily in the smoky blue sky between clouds that looked like ancient stone walls from a far-off, unknown, extinct civilization. I knew the hawks well, and in the coming months Tracker would also become accustomed to their songs and ways. To my knowledge theirs were the first wild sounds she paid attention to inside the trees. But I also realized she probably was still a bit bewildered with all that was going on around her.

So I got down on my knees, sat back on my ankles, took my pack off, and put Tracker down between my thighs. Sitting down herself, she slowly backed her hind quarters up until she was fitted firmly in my crotch. That seemed to give her security, for she was relaxed, and even looked around at me as if to say, "I'm hot stuff, huh?"

I couldn't help but smile, and I was sure that a wild-born cub venturing off from the den with its mother did the same thing. As long as she was under the protection of another sinew defense, she was "hot stuff."

We sat there for quite some time and as I had done with Shakespeare, I mentally threw away the clock. Though I wanted everything to happen with Tracker and me that second, excited as I was, I knew I could put no time limit on whatever was going to happen from that point on. I really had no idea or set plan as to how to train Tracker into actually tracking Shakespeare or any other panther. The question uppermost in my mind was, could it be done at all?

There were two advantages out here in the swamp that Tracker had to begin with. She was born in the Everglades as her mother had been. And she was a female. That fact alone sent my mind reeling with possibilities. If in fact Shakespeare was a male, then what would happen when Tracker became full grown two to three years from now? Would she, when in season, be able to call him in? Would she mate? Would she want to leave me and go off in the swamp with Shakespeare, then find a den site and raise her cubs in the wilds? Was any of that possible? Or would being with me and being oriented to man's ways all her life kill off those instincts? Would she reject him? Would she even be interested in tracking the wild panther?

Yet at the same time, going with me, she would know the Everglades, the other wildlife in it. Like me she would know both worlds, civilized and uncivilized. Maybe when the time came I would give her a choice. Maybe I would give myself a choice. Or maybe neither one of us would have anything to say about it.

All of these thoughts burned across my brain like a racing train sending sparks off the rails, and those thoughts worked to the surface, shooting out of my eyes in an intense stare at Tracker, this little butterball cat covered with grayish fur already striped with black and dotted even blacker with large splotches to camouflage her in the shadows, making her almost invisible. This baby predator, who huddled next to me on the edge of panic if I moved so much as an inch away, was my salvation. I could feel deep in my heart that Tracker was going to be a giant step toward Shakespeare. But I also felt she would be more than that. And yet, even then I had no idea what it was that could produce for me, and those around me, a true sense of meaning—and in the final analysis, a means of survival for mankind. I wondered, if I found the meaning I was searching for, was I capable of communicating it to other people?

Maybe I would start writing a book, taking all my swamp notes, evidence, feelings and dreams and compiling them into a volume for people to read. And then a movie producer would seek it out and mold it into a dramatic film for international distribution. Maybe Tracker would be the star. Maybe, sitting there under a sleeping barred owl, I was going totally nuts.

I put my pack on, picked up Tracker and cradled her in my arms and walked down the trail to the north. For the present I abandoned ultimate concealment and concentrated fully on acquainting Tracker with this wild place.

I went tortoise-slow, moving on to each new experience as Tracker saw fit. She dug her claws into my shirt and held on tightly, scratching my chest. Then she hid her head in my armpit, and I realized how afraid she was of the whole ordeal.

I kept stroking her, scratching her neck gently to reassure her that this wild swamp was her home, that her ancestors thrived in it and she could, too. But it was an overwhelming place for her: the thick smells of vegetation, an occasional wind bending the treetops, the scattering of small rodents in front of us as we pushed through the brush, frogs bouncing off logs into water, the outcry of a great blue heron as we came close and spooked him, then the silence as the swamp adjusted to our presence. All of it was a harrowing experience for her, and I was surprised. I had thought she would adjust immediately to her wild home.

Maybe a little wilderness shock therapy was in order. With Tracker's best interest at heart, I decided to baptize her into her environment. I stopped and placed her on the ground, turned my back and walked away about twenty feet, then stood still, looking at her.

At first she stood stiffly, her tail drooping, ears in a cowering position slanted down and outward. Then those ears shot up at a bird sound and her head jerked in the direction the bird was flying.

But then the realization of standing there alone, cut off from safety, rushed upon her. She looked for me and, locating me, looked up with pleading sorrowful eyes as though begging me to please put her back in the pack, protect her, shield her from the treachery of death by unannounced attacks of larger predators such as bobcats, rattlesnakes, indigo snakes, red-tailed hawks or black bear.

Suddenly she was scampering up to me and attempting to crawl up my legs. Laughing, I picked her up with both hands and she furiously gave me a scolding with those parrot squawks, then licked my face.

"Okay," I said, "we'll stick to a little at a time." Together we walked out. But when I got to the edge of the prairie I looked back over my shoulder as though by some freak occurrence I might get a glimpse of Shakespeare. There was none.

56

Panther Eyes

Swamp notes—probing wild eyes
I am beginning to read Tracker's reactions and even her intentions in her eyes. The size of her pupil and her eye movements work as telegraphs. She seems to be touching my inner world with those eyes, and I wonder what she sees.

It was at a winter dusk that I first began to notice Tracker's eyes taking on a quality known only to wild things. The dry glades vegetation rattled in a vibrant wind born from the north, swamp airflows that whispered and blustered into small green gusts wafting through bare cypress trees, exotic pepperheads, laurel oaks and willow. While sleet, rain and ice storms raged in the Northeast and Midwest, the Everglades received cool ointment from the Gulf of Mexico and dry east winds from the Atlantic Ocean. There was never any rain this time of year, and this watery wilderness would drop to drought level, crack open like thin, fragile egg shells, and dry up under wheezing expirations.

In the midst of this Tracker would sit statuelike in that erect cat posture on her buttocks, forelegs straight, head slightly up, hind legs and paws coiled underneath her body as though she could suddenly spring up into the ashen clouds above.

Now she was about eighteen to twenty pounds, twice the size of an average domestic cat, still with her heavy camouflage coloring on her fur, the black splotches and stripes on her forelegs. But I had begun to notice the slightest fading at the very edges of those markings, for at this weight she was just beginning to become a formidable predator.

Her disposition had become extremely temperamental and seldom now could I actually pet her without receiving a

278

scratch or quick bite on the hand. For the most part, she wanted to be left alone, untouched. Yet she stuck close to me wherever I tracked, never once leaving my sight.

When we would sit at dusk like this, in the middle of the glades, cut off from all human sound, I would watch her eyes. They would dart left at a cormorant taking off, then right at the movement of fire flag leaves on the edge of a slough rubbing together like stiff paper, then up at the heavy traffic of white ibis flocks flying toward their roosts in the mangroves, and then in an almost one hundred and eighty degree turn, they would look behind at an American egret hurriedly pursuing one more fish before dark.

Tracker's eyes would then come around, glance at me, blink, then look straight forward. And all the time those panther eyes were probing, evaluating, calculating, wandering, maybe wondering, studying intricately every movement detected. They taught me about Shakespeare's eyes. I was sure that while I tracked him, he would sit somewhere nearby, totally hidden in the swamp bush, his eyes following every one of my movements in front of him. And as slow as I tried to move, straining to keep sound down, straining to stay in the shadows—all the time the stretching of my leg, the reaching of my hand on a limb, the very bent crouch I constantly tried to stay in, were relaying to him visually my forward crawl. And when I got too close to his invisibly marked danger perimeter, he would instantly dash off. One of my many quests was to outsmart his eyes, and that I was determined to do with the help of Tracker.

For hours on end Tracker and I would stare at each other. I decided to learn everything there was to know about panther eyes, and I remember spending a whole week that winter doing nothing but staring at Tracker's eyes. Literally, from dawn to dusk, for seven days, I stared into those lagoons of strange light that dominated her face and stuck out in the green of the swamp like two large beacons. They glowed and glittered, twinkled and moved in the sunlight. While I stared at those eyes a line of one of James Whitcomb Riley's poems that I had learned as a child rolled around in my head: ". . . great big eyes ablazin' in their head, glittn' 'long the timber line— shine out some, and then unshine, and shine back. . . ."

In Tracker's long, steady, confident gazes, I saw lightning energy, defiance, pride, and a true mastery of the wilderness. Captive or not, she was a microcosm of all panthers. I began to take on her confidence. I began to feel sure that no animal with eyes that show such intensity to survive will ever go extinct. This was when I developed a true and lasting optimism about this great cat. I began to understand that thinking of the panther as doomed would contribute eventually to his destruction. But to be infinitely positive would mean success in developing a viable population in the Everglades once again.

In the beginning of that week of staring, it was hard to maintain direct eye contact with Tracker because she was irritated and was giving me a threatening sign to stay away. Oddly enough, I always felt Tracker's eyes on me whenever I would look away. Then when I looked back at her she would look away, and out of the corner of my eyes, as I turned my head, I could see her eyes returning to me.

And there were times she would look right through me, as though I wasn't even there.

As the days passed, more and more she kept her eyes on me until they slowly would come across my chest, up my neck and onto mine. I became so possessed by her eyes that I had dreams of them at night staring at me through the blackness. I kept asking myself where did such extraordinary eyes come from? How do they work? More important, how were they like mine? Could I have eyes like Tracker?

They were her primary sense and had developed for millions of years from that tiniest insect-eater to the present. They were round, large, protected by her skull, controlled by six muscles and an optic nerve. Just like man's, like mine.

When you think of a cat, you think of pupils like slits. But the panther has round pupils that when they expand and contract do so in an even round hole—just like man's, like mine. But as it turns out, though this is an aid to man's visual acuity, it actually hinders the panther's aperture control. Could I think of a way to use this against my friend Shakespeare in our ongoing competition to outsmart each other?

As a newborn cub, she had had indigo-blue coloring in the iris and pupil for camouflage, but now that had changed to yellowish brown. As an adult she would have a fiery yellow iris and an emerald-green pupil.

At any age, the true color of a panther's eyes can be hard to determine. Their reflection of a sunny or cloudy day can seem to change the color. And the intense color of Tracker's eyes seemed to change according to her emotions. When she was angered, they seemed to flare deep green. In her calmer moods they were a tranquil faded yellow. When she paced in frustration they changed to a dead pale gray. This was also due to the contraction and expansion of the pupil. Like panther, like man.

With this beautiful prism of colors in her eyes, it is ironic that Tracker cannot see in color herself. Rather she sees in shades of gray, like a black and white photograph. Unfortunately she has no color cones to transmit color to her brain. In this way we differed. Perhaps I could somehow take advantage of my color vision in tracking Shakespeare.

But in place of the cones, a panther's retina is packed full of sensitive rods that react to extremely low level light, giving her extra night-vision. Along with this ability to see at night much better than a human being, Tracker also has what I call "panther quick-blaze." In Tracker's eyes a special group of cells on the retina called *tapetum lucidum* reflect any glimmer of light back to her retina so that she can detect minute detail and slight movement, day or night.

Also there is a constant involuntary tremor in her eyes. This tremor causes anything she sees at night to reflect back and forth on her retina until her brain figures out what she is looking at. As in panther, not so in man. Shakespeare has the edge here.

Just as important as night-vision is her day-vision. She can see equally well during daylight hours, with stereoscopic vision from the outer perimeter of her eyes. But because of an underdeveloped fovea in the retina, she cannot look directly through the center. This "gaze into space" helps her detect movement, but gives her trouble when she is looking at stationary objects. Man has the ability to do both. Ah, I can use this one on Shakespeare.

Learning all of this was a step in unlocking those gateways to Tracker's soul. But I wanted to push beyond what science had proven already. I wanted to figure out how to use the facts of science in a new way. I wanted those facts to become a means to an end. I wanted to use them first to contact Tracker's inner being, for I felt that there, and only there, would I find my way toward Shakespeare.

I understood that science meant dividing things into tiny steps and then analyzing each one in many different conditions. It meant time, patience, concentration, dedication, willingness to give up some cherished notion when I hit a dead end with it and go back to start over again. But I believed I had inside me all it would take to follow this road I had set out on to its end—whatever that might turn out to be.

I proceeded then to classify Tracker's eye contacts with me in various categories. When our eyes were not locked together, I found that a direct stare from her in a bad mood meant a threat. But I found that my stare could offer the same threat to her if she bit me too hard or if I didn't want her to do something. Most times she challenged my stare, as though she was telling me she was sorry or she wanted to be friends again.

When going out to the ranch to pick her up, I made it a point always to greet her with a wide grinning face and round open eyes. I was telling her I wanted to play, and she would show her agreement by jumping on me and running around until she could come up behind and playfully ambush me, though her playful bites on my neck were getting to be almost too much to stand.

But it wasn't easy to understand Tracker's moods or her reactions to mine. She was able to trick me in her mysterious cat way. Once she had that wide-eyed look of fun time and play, but when I got close to her I received a crushing bite on my arm and hand. I was never sure what she was trying to tell me. Maybe it was to always be wary of the unpredictability of panthers.

Through trial and error, I invented a way of searching for Tracker's soul through her eyes. Why not, I thought, enter them, probe the very eye itself. The only way I knew of doing that was to use the time-proven techniques of meditative yoga positions and the ancient methods of relaxation. I found myself not only relaxing my physical body, but also my own soul—and Tracker's too, it seemed.

I began sitting comfortably in front of her Indian-style, forearms resting on my thighs, spine erect, eyes serenely on hers, relaxed, no squinting, forehead free of wrinkles, head centered on my shoulders. Slowly, evenly, I took four deep breaths, filling my lungs, then in an even more relaxed fashion, letting the air out. All the time I watched her eyes, concentrating on those pupils as the sun would momentarily flash in, flash out, making them appear greenish-brown flames from a fire deep within her soul. They never danced, but rather vibrated in slow motion until there was a strange rhythm to them, a pulsing fluency that could only come from such a magnificent big cat.

The longer I probed those eyes, the more I wanted to venture into that inner sanctum. So I would study each flash of color, the widening of her pupils, the wetness as she blinked, until all I could see in front of me were her eyes. And I would tell myself silently I was going deeper and deeper into them, into their microscopic center, so small only my own pupil could enter.

It was a fascinating experience, but several times Tracker broke the mood by scratching or changing position. And it was hard to get her settled enough to continue.

Those seven days triggered a direct means of communication with Tracker, though I fell far short of my purpose. It wasn't until almost two years later that I truly did find the key to the gateway to her soul. And in that period of time panther eyes were redefined for me and Tracker and Shakespeare. When Tracker was close to an adult, able to live in the wilds if she had to, she did reveal to me her soul in a way I had never expected. It was not until then that I finally realized what I had to do to reach affinity.

57

Domination

Swamp notes—challenged by Tracker
I am beginning to realize that if I let Tracker dominate me in any way, physically or mentally, all of my dreams, aspirations, ultimate goals are over. My very relationship with Tracker is over. I will have to show her who is boss.

Tracker and I began to wrestle and run, more for training for her stamina than for fun, though we always had a ood time. She was always up for it and always beat me but good in a wrestling match. The problem was she never knew when to quit—gnawing my neck until it bled, wrapping her forelegs around my chest and squeezing the breath out of me, then falling on her back and letting go with all four paws on my face and chest at once.

Our wilderness jogging always turned into a sprinting race, and I have never yet been able to keep up with a panther going about thirty-five miles an hour. It became a real question of who was training whom to stay in shape. She could jump up in a tree twenty feet high, bound over a ten-foot wide channel of water, and go flat out on a straightaway for more than two hundred yards.

But in long distance I had her beat, usually passing her up after the two hundred yards. She would sprawl out on the grass, exhausted, growling at me as I jogged past. It was the only thing I could beat her in.

In all of this I was beginning to realize how strong and powerful she was going to be at full growth. At forty pounds she was as strong as three men, had reflexes like a striking rattlesnake, and could jump and be on my chest before I knew what she was up to.

If I didn't do something quick, I was sure Tracker would take over. It would be her show, not mine.

I have never ever hit Tracker with a closed fist. I never will. Only once during the entire time we have been together have I hit her alongside her head as hard as I could with my open palm. It was necessary. I had to bluff her into thinking I was faster, stronger, and tougher. In delivering that blow I had to catch her completely off guard. I had to launch a surprise attack that would imprint forever on her mind that she couldn't overtake me, that I was the boss.

I arrived at the ranch early, opened the cage door and went inside. Tracker was on top of her den musing over a small blue heron feeding near one of the ponds. She had watched me come in out of the the corner of her eye, and I made every effort to walk nonchalantly about the cage as though I was looking for something. She picked up on it, jumped off the den onto the floor and walked toward me with no special interest other than wanting to see what I was looking for.

I turned, gave her a direct eye-to-eye stare, and as she got within range I swung with my left hand all the way from left field as hard and fast as I could. My palm landed squarely on her right cheek. It was like hitting a solid cement wall. To my amazement, she didn't even move. Then, stunned, bewildered, she looked at me, totally disoriented, turned her back, ran back and jumped up on the den.

If I had hit a man with that punch it would have crushed his cheekbone, knocked his teeth out and sent him slamming to the ground.

I stood there for a few more seconds, feeling like a beast for having done it, almost on the verge of crying and taking her in my arms. But I kept my guard up, still acting like I was going to eat her alive—even though there was pain and numbness up and down my hand and arm. Boldly, I walked closer, stared down at her, opened the cage door and walked away without looking back.

The next day when I went out to the ranch it was as though we were long lost lovers meeting after ten years. When I entered the cage she came up to me, put her paws on my stomach and started licking my face. I knelt down, put my arms around her and licked her back. From that point on she has never challenged me for domination, and I have never had to raise a palm to her—ever.

This reconciliation gave rise to consciously staring at each other close up, and when I did that I always petted and slowly stroked her belly, giving her pleasure, showing tenderness and affection. She loved it, keeping her eyes on mine as though at any second she was going to go into an orgasmic fit of ecstasy. At times she would also slowly open and close her eyes as though enraptured by each gentle touch.

On occasion, without my initiating it, she would begin to stroke my belly—or sometimes lower—with one of her front paws or the top of her head in a slow, steady, cat movement. When she used her paws, I was glad the hooks had been trimmed from the ends of her claws so that I wouldn't suddenly gain a strange reputation in the swamp. I could just see myself as the mad tracker of the Florida panther in the Everglades, the only man alive running around the swamp with claw marks in an embarrassing place—if I got off that lucky.

It was becoming clear that I was developing a lasting relationship with Tracker, and we were beginning to find new ways to each other's souls.

58

God's Own Ears

> **Swamp notes—reading fire**
> *I open up all of my senses to absorb all I can
> in the swamp. Tracker does the same. But
> she absorbs much more. Her eyes and ears
> are on constant vigil. Her ears move in direc-
> tions that seem to have no sound, attentive
> to vibrations I will never hear. Or will I?*

The moon's image gyrated on the broken surface of black water disturbed by wind from the east, that part of wild earth where sunrise and light come from. In the water, blue gills sucked surface film for freshly fallen mosquitoes. A black-crowned night heron, his deep red eyes piercing the darkness, balanced himself on a low limb and caught freshwater shrimp off hydrilla.

Tracker and I sat close to a campfire near a slough. She was lounging on her side, licking a paw. She was quite contented and looked up at me, purring loudly, then leaned back in the shadows swiping mosquitoes off her forehead. Her ears shot up and turned in the direction of the slough.

A night-crying limpkin sliced the dark cypress silence with a shrilling wail that sounded like a woman screaming, echoing over the water and bouncing off dead oak trees. I glanced away from the fire toward the sound. This odd bird's brown plumage with white spots and streaks hid him in the moonshine against cypress knees. But his long beak stabbing apple snails in the water gave him away.

Tracker and I had been there well to the north of Shakespeare's territory since 4:00 a.m., waiting for sunrise. I had heated up a cup of coffee and eaten a hard-boiled egg, while Tracker had a raw chicken wing and thigh.

I pushed up to a squat, arms dangling over my knees, head between them, and read the fire. I was sweating from the heat given off by these smoldering maple tree twigs and two dry pine logs. To me this fire was much more than flames dancing up into darkness. It was ever-changing, primal. It held within it a reflection of my own will power and deep-rooted passion for life. It refused to die. There was so much energy in that small fire that it was almost frightening.

I squinted, mused, wondered, staring hypnotized at those flames. The shifting colors, intense heat, and flashing light awed me. Flashing in. Flashing out. Flashing in once again. And flashing out. Light, heat, and color, all blending into energy.

I began to see human arms and hands stretching up toward sparks, narrow vertical eyes that blinked at me, yellow birds flying into blackness. For a second a red horse pranced across the tips of flames and a blue-skinned lady waved.

It was mere friction and flint from nature power that brought fire to mankind, producing a world-wide eternal flame that has never gone out, a natural magic that can be produced with the scraping of stones or the constant pressure of wood on wood.

In all those fleeting flames I felt purified, protected, cured of man's sins to nature, including my own. When I looked over at Tracker I was surprised to see her staring into the flames as well. What was she seeing with her pupils almost closed? Could she see her ancient cousins roaming this swamp when there were only wild animals here? Or was she seeing the evolution of her species a thousand years from now?

Gradually our gazes were broken by the white misty glow of thick banks of dawn fog curling tightly around us until even the swamp was cut off. I was reluctant to leave the fire, but I was eager to get started, and so was Tracker, who got up and tested the air with her ears. I was certain she could hear even the sounds bats produce.

I extinguished the flames, then carried the pine logs to the water and slipped them in. The hot, smoldering wood boiled the water and singed floating willow leaves. I went back and put my pack on, took off my boots and slung them over my shoulder, then knelt down on one knee. Tracker came over and brushed up against me, then looked off into the trees, her ears sticking straight up, then scanning, exploring the swamp. Her keen sense of hearing is so unique, so necessary for a predator. To hear the crack of a dry branch among hundreds of other swamp sounds was no great feat for Tracker or Shakespeare. The crack of a branch may tell them something large is afoot—a bear, another panther, possibly a man. Suddenly they are alerted, distinguishing the reason for the sound and perhaps choosing to disappear.

I looked at Tracker's ears, inches away. They were cup-shaped, rounded and funneled, with flexible cartilages, covered with skin and fur and attached to muscles that aim them in the direction of sound independently or together, sometimes sweeping almost 180 degrees.

White fringes of hair on the inner part of the ear, plus what appeared to be small tufts, kept her ears clean and acted like antennae to catch sound waves. Tracker's ears were extremely specialized mechanisms which she used for balancing her body as well as for hearing. Having researched panthers' ears, I knew that the interior mechanism below these rotating antennae not only sent sound signals to her brain but signals indicating her position in space. There lay the secret of the perfect balance of this sleek and perfect body.

Within the inner ear the auditory nerve packet has some forty thousand fibers or more, compared to my thirty thousand. That means that while I can only hear sounds at twenty thousand cycles per second, Tracker can hear them at up to a hundred thousand cycles per second. Scientists know little of how that inner ear transfers sound to receptors for recording in the brain. Even the receptors themselves are unknown. Still another mystery in the panther. What other secrets were in Tracker?

We waited a little longer until there was more light in the swamp. Then I put a 15-foot black nylon cord around Tracker's neck, loose, but with enough restraint on it to let Tracker think she had to stay by my side. We moved off the island and onto an unused trail, heading south.

She was more than forty pounds now, strong for a female at this weight. And she had some of the most beautiful camouflage markings I had ever seen on a young panther. They were more than black splotches and streaks, more than merely a means to hide her in shadows. Evolution had created a pattern of color that surpassed the greatest artistry. Each splotch along the back and sides lined itself perfectly behind the other, evenly spaced apart with the tawny white between them like cream poured into a mold. The circles on her tail grabbed at shadows, and the stripes on her forelegs dissolved her forward movement. The long black lines on her face that extended over her muzzle and under and below her eyes painted a perfect mask of disguise. She was a solid physical creature that could disintegrate into nothing by merely positioning herself in shadows and light.

For a long time we walked the trail along the places I believed Shakespeare would plot his territory with urine and scat heaps. I was attempting to teach Tracker to detect that chemical scent, to come onto it, sniff it heavily, maybe even thrash it up and build her own territory by scraping up debris and urinating herself. If I could find it, Tracker could too.

Several times she came onto raccoon scat, and she found two piles of bobcat droppings. At both bobcat sites she got excited, dropped to her stomach and crawled forward, then cautiously inhaled the old bleached-out plugs. It was a question of whether she was smelling the bobcat scent or what he had eaten. When I broke the droppings open I found opossum fur and small rodent teeth and rib bones.

Then Tracker scratched around the site and urinated right on top of the scat. In a direct sense she was now claiming this for her own territory. I wondered what Shakespeare was going to think of Tracker's intrusion into his domain.

More than ever I was watching Tracker's movements. While I constantly scanned the trail and the swamp around us, looking on the side of the trail for hidden water moccasins and the rare possibility of Shakespeare up ahead, I studied Tracker. It was my aim to transform myself into a panther and Tracker was my teacher in this, as I was hers in finding wild panthers. If this experience was ever going to happen at all it would be out there in the middle of panther territory among the wilds, surrounded by crawling wonders. Tracker was going to catapult me into developing a specialized skill that nobody else possessed. To track in the shadows of Shakespeare. To be a cat.

At midmorning when the swamp always dropped into a cryptic silence, Tracker revealed to me an ability in cats seldom recognized by humans. We had moved off the trail and onto high ground among seedling maple, popash in solution holes, and small custard apple trees. In the soft mud our feet sank to our ankles, and as we roamed up to the higher ground the leaves stuck to our feet like glue. Suddenly Tracker stopped in mid-stride, her tail dropping, her eyes and ears pointing at something in the trees. I heard nothing, but I was sure Tracker was onto an animal. My heart pounded. Shakespeare. It had to be Shakespeare, I thought.

I dropped to my knees next to Tracker and followed her stare. Her ears were slowly moving back and forth, then going back to the trees again. She heard something all right, something significant to send her into this state of vigilance.

In the slowest possible motion, Tracker eased down onto her stomach, wrapping her tail around her side and perking up her ears even more. Those ears, those magnificent tools of nature, were evaluating some sound in the treeline

I could not hear. I had never felt more inferior to Tracker than at that moment. If it was Shakespeare who had come to our long-destined meeting, then I was ready, but I felt as though I was missing out on an important chapter in this experience. What sounds was Tracker recording? Were they talking to each other? Were they making sounds to each other no human would ever hear? It was my misfortune to be a human.

Now Tracker edged ahead, left forepaw slightly forward, right hind paw pushing her body, ears more intensely up and straining.

Though bird sounds echoed through the swamp, a gator honked, and turtles plopped into the water off floating logs, Tracker was oblivious to it all, for she was "gating."

It seemed to me that she was so intent on finding out what was in the trees that she switched to this super-mode of using her senses. She had probably closed the gate to her sense of smell and all other outside sounds, concentrating totally on the sound in the trees. Soon she would close the gate on sound as well and rely on her eyes to take her to the animal. And that she did immediately. Though I kept calling her name, Tracker rose off the ground just enough to crawl ahead in a steady motion until she was closer yet to the trees. And at that second she shot her head up and a dismayed expression spread across her face.

An armadillo scurried out from the trees, sniffed the air, stood up on its hind legs, then, like a wound-up toy, turned and ran as fast as it could backwards toward cover, bumping into trees and rolling over roots.

I couldn't help but laugh, but when I looked at Tracker she was more disappointed than anything. I patted her on the back and told her she had just learned the scent of a swamp animal that was potential prey for Shakespeare, and maybe even for her.

She didn't seem to accept this as an adequate explanation, but it would have to do for the present. I was disappointed as well, because it had not been Shakespeare, but then it was early in the experiment with Tracker, so I had to accept it as a lesson learned. More important, I began consciously developing that ability to gate. I realized that I might

very well have been missing out on data by allowing everything
to come into all my senses at once. When I was looking I was
also hearing and smelling. Even when I was concentrating on
one sense, still I could take in other information. I felt the
key was total concentration on one sense. When I heard the
slightest sound in the swamp, I tried pushing my powers of
concentrating further and further to that one sound, cutting
off sight and smell.

I was learning from Tracker. My experiment was working. And I sensed that down the line what I hoped to accomplish with Shakespeare would produce sounds no human had
ever before hoped to hear on this earth. For I was beginning
to hear through God's own ears.

59

Unknown Sense

> **Swamp notes—on panther trail**
> It has become a quest in itself to know
> Tracker's senses on the most intimate level.
> Each one seems to be a separate part of her
> powerful body, a direct channel for incom-
> ing information for the animal who stands
> at the top of the swamp food chain.

White wings curled up into a hole in the tree canopy. Below,
a small pool became a maelstrom of miniature tidal waves.
Garfish snapped their tails. Loud croaks signaled all was not
well.

Tracker and I had come out of a treeline and disturbed
a flock of snowy egrets. An unforgivable act, for now all the
mammals in the area knew we were around, and for sure
Shakespeare knew it too. But I figured Shakespeare had picked

out Tracker's scent well before we got to that freshwater pool anyway.

I was familiar with this place, Devil's Pool. I could still feel the cold water rushing down my throat, and the rough rocks as I clawed at the sides, my backpack acting as an anchor, then the vomiting of sour water, delirium, and a prayer of thanks that I had been saved.

We walked to it, drank the cold water under an intensely hot sun, looking at each other's reflection through the swirls of baby fish. I wiped my face clean of mosquitoes and sweat, gave Tracker a pat as she moved to the shade, and then we crept along willows to an old barbed wire fence lost in the swamp, covered over with layers of vegetation. On the other side of the wire was another high trail.

It was now early afternoon and in my swamp estimation Tracker hadn't been doing too well. Maybe I was being too hard on her, expecting the world in a day. After all, she was young, still considered a cub, inexperienced, and had a long way to go to become that Master Tracker of the Everglades. But the least she could do was to come onto some sort of plotting Shakespeare had left.

I was betting my new hat Tracker's sense of smell was going to do the job. Her nose would be the main factor on this trail. It could lead her to a pile of scat, maybe a heap with urine sprayed on it, maybe even a kill.

Her nose was pink, small, and was made up of numerous layers of durable, thick skin. All those thousands upon thousands of odors in the swamp Tracker was picking up, measuring, identifying, were caught inside the nose by thin fragile bones. And inside the nasal cavity toward the upper back region were close to 65 million olfactory cells called "smellers." Man has only five to twenty million smellers.

It was fascinating to watch Tracker as she ventured down the trail. She sniffed every leaf, every palm frond. She was wary of the fallen, dried fronds, gingerly stepping around them, sniffing, then quickly dashing down the trail a few yards, abruptly stopping to sniff at an oak tree's bark near the roots. Had an animal urinated there? Or had Shakespeare slowly eased his body across it not long ago, leaving that temporary body scent? Or had some insect left a chemical trace there, a curious little smell that was tantalizing Tracker but that I would never know?

At specific areas the size of a half-dollar, she would spend a long time sniffing, putting her nose almost upon the leaf, the dead tree, or the branch, sometimes licking it as though she could bring the scent out more. Or was she testing it for roughage food? But, time after time, just when I thought she was onto something, off she would go to another spot.

Once she suddenly became frightened of something along the trail. When I got in closer I saw a large water moccasin that had already bent its head back, showing that cotton mouth and fangs. We were beyond its striking range and I surmised Tracker had smelled the snake's scent before she came near it. There was no way she could have seen it from her position, and I doubt she had heard it because the reptile was holding perfectly still.

Tracker's sense of smell was one sense I knew I could never measure up to. For millions of years, evolution had fine-tuned this sense so that, for example, a particular poisonous snake's scent could be detected just beyond its striking range. I imagined all of the millions of scents of the Everglades floating, intermixing, fading, coming alive again. Strong fresh ones, faint old ones. The smell of newborn animals. The stench of dead things. Scents of man. My scent. Tracker's scent. Shakespeare's scent. I had already tuned my nose to many swamp smells and probably could learn many more yet, but I knew that this kitten's nose had inborn abilities I would never be able to train into mine. Well then, I'd learn how to use her nose as an extension of mine.

Through weeks and weeks, Tracker and I walked these trails in Shakespeare's territory, some of them many times over. Oddly, we hadn't found any of Shakespeare's scat. Had he abandoned this part of it and moved to a richer place where more prey was available?

I pushed Tracker on until she became used to walking those trails, until it was second nature for her to spend a whole day in the swamp looking for her counterpart. At least I knew that was her goal. She had yet to learn it.

Her sense of smell had homed her in on a baby alligator

hidden in a hollow log near water, a stink bug that produced a stench that even I smelled as Tracker batted it around with her paw, a ribbon snake that propped itself up in the grass and then saw this monster cat coming toward it and darted under a limestone rock that Tracker couldn't budge. Once she sniffed at a badly injured black-crowned night heron, its wing broken and most of its feathers in disarray. I could tell that it had but minutes to live. Tracker approached the bird cautiously but then, seeing the condition of it, simply stood up, turned and looked at me as though to ask, what do I do next? She didn't bolt to it in ambush as I had expected. Maybe she thought it wasn't worth it.

I crouched close to the bird, looked it over, said a prayer, and tugged at Tracker's long black nylon rope to move back on the trail. A little farther down the trail, just at the moment a red-tailed hawk streamed silently overhead, Tracker began to act strangely. She usually kept well ahead of me, but now she backed up, and when I tried to pull her ahead, she sat down and resisted stubbornly.

Her nose was in the air and the pink on it was moving back and forth. She stretched her neck and pushed it forward down the trail, and I could hear her sniffing the thickness of scent. Animal scent. Something was up ahead. But rather than pursue the scent as she usually did, she widened her eyes, stuck her ears up like antennae, and pointed her tail straight out backwards. She even started backing up, pulling me away from whatever she was smelling. Now I resisted, jerking the rope and letting her know we were going forward. She fought me and finally lay down, hell bent on winning this tug-of-war in the swamp.

I kept looking down the trail, encouraging her to come with me. "Come on, Tracker. Let's find out what it is down there. Maybe you will meet Shakespeare. Come on, girl. Let's do it."

But Tracker would have none of this. She wanted out of the swamp. There was fear in her eyes, fear I had never seen in them before. She had been overwhelmed by the scent of whatever it was.

Maybe, in fact, she was smelling Shakespeare. Maybe

he was lying in ambush for her, or for both of us. Maybe he was fed up with all I had done so far and was going to put a stop to it.

Tracker was still small by panther standards and could hardly defend herself against a wild, full-grown male panther on the prowl. Tracker could be Shakespeare's next kill. I was tempted to tie Tracker to a tree nearby where she could still see me and venture boldly down the trail to take a better look. But it would be easy for Shakespeare to circle around and jump her on the rope where she wouldn't have a prayer in the world of escaping. I abandoned that idea, knelt down next to her and began patting her and stroking her stomach. "Take it easy, big girl. We'll solve this problem. Take it easy." I could feel Tracker shivering in the heat. The fear had now brought on the panther shakes. She leaned against me for protection.

I calmed myself and let my sixth sense take over. Why wasn't I feeling that fear? I was just as vulnerable to Shakespeare, yet if there was any danger for me up ahead, I didn't feel it. I felt so confident of my sixth sense by now that I put myself at ease, sure that at least I wasn't to be sacrificed yet in the swamp.

We sat there in silence and vigil for more than an hour, staring up the trail. The swamp would breathe through the trees now and then, its hot breath brushing across the water in pools and irritating lazy green bass near the surface. Through those long silences, a single bird song would occasionally pierce the air and then be swallowed up. Tracker was lying down on her stomach, still leaning against me, but had stopped trembling. She was more at ease, even licked her paw and rubbed her ear on my leg to brush off mosquitoes.

The animal up ahead was gone. My curiosity was pushing me to get down the trail and check it out now. I rose and pulled the rope. Tracker jumped up and followed, eventually edging ahead. We had worked our way down almost a hundred and fifty yards when Tracker began to walk in a straight line toward something on the trail in an open part of the grass. I gave her all of the thirty feet of rope, and before I could tie it to my wrist, she came up to a large pile of scat. Fresh scat. Hot scat. Panther scat. Shakespeare's scat!

She crouched halfway and pulled toward the scat. As she got closer to it her nose went into action in a way I had never seen before. It vibrated almost out of control. She growled. And the closer she got the more she began to hiss in that defensive sound to ward off close-in danger. In effect, she was hissing at Shakespeare, not just his scent in the scat, but Shakespeare himself, because that scent was as much a part of him as his very teeth.

Tracker sniffed closer yet, inspected the hairy, wet scat and long plugs. Her eyes danced, several times darting up and looking around. Her ears rotated, using that wonderful sound-tracking method. She continued to evaluate the scat almost to exhaustion, as though she was going to make sure she would never forget his scent. From that point on, if he was miles away and that odor swam through the air to Tracker's nose, she would know it and would be able to turn in his direction, and if need be walk right up to Shakespeare.

I imitated Tracker's actions, trying to enter into her world of smelling. I got down on all fours, put my nose to the very edge of Shakespeare's scat, breathed in deeply, trying to implant his scent in my nose and brain, that peculiar strong stench that only a panther could produce. At that moment I was very close to Shakespeare, and it was Tracker that had found this prize. She was going to be a good cat. She would continue to teach me about Shakespeare, his ways, his faults, his accomplishments. She was surely going to teach me to be a panther.

Now Tracker was on to Shakespeare as I had been the first time I found scat. But she was mixing her scent with his similar scent, a scent I could never produce. But I would work on that idea. How could I make my scent animal scent? How could I create panther scent? How could I merge myself into the swamp to become like Tracker, like Shakespeare? If ever I could answer these questions, develop the method, prove its worthiness through a success of drawing Shakespeare to me, I could become the Master Tracker.

Staring at Tracker, who was sitting calmly next to the scat as though she had claimed it as her own, I smiled. "You did good, big girl. You did super good," I said.

As I finished those words, Tracker performed an animal

ritual. She scratched around the scat several times, inspected her scratch marks, and then crouched, bottom down directly over the pile, and urinated on it heavily. She was erasing Shakespeare's plotting post, a part of his territory, and beginning to plot her own territory, right in his, challenging him with her scent. I would work on that idea as well. Maybe that, too, was another step to Shakespeare: plotting my own territory in his.

60

Beehive!

Swamp notes—in fall calm
To be enraptured by the swamp with Tracker by my side, to be alive, well, vibrant, able to continue my search, is dream made into reality. I have never taken for granted my good fortune, but sometimes I am overwhelmed by it all. It seems so infinite. Every time I reach out and grab a thread of knowledge, I have to reach out farther for the next fragment. Other times it comes to me in rushes.

The prairie was still heavy with morning bridal-veil fog and the rallying sun hailed the earth, reflecting through millions of water crystals, making this prairie look like a frost-covered icefield. The region was devoid of trees except for a long narrow stretch of baby cypress. Surrounding the entire area was a lemon halo of green cattails sporting their new fall growth. In the middle of the prairie was a saw palmetto oasis that looked like an Indian village crowded with chickees.

Shadows of those bronze glades people walked about, and I knew their memories would never leave this swamp.

In all of this calm, a silent storm of the last of summer's mosquitoes blew past Tracker and me. Then, suddenly, off a hidden pond to the east, a winged multitude of mallards exploded in a brown fury, washing the gray-blue sky with a spray of swamp droplets that blurred the flock and made them look as though they had taken on spirit bodies.

In this display of glades power I realized how important it was to track Shakespeare with the help of Tracker. Before, it was just concepts, my ideas conjured up to do a more intensive research project, always trying to answer my own questions. How can I do it better? What way can I simplify things? How can I be the cat? Now it was beginning to take on much more meaning. I knew I was embarking on a tracking project in the swamps of my inner self, to push myself beyond all human limits to see what was left. So it was more than Shakespeare, Tracker, the glades. It was my own human adventure to turn myself inside out—to touch holy nature outside of me with all that is holy inside myself. With Tracker by my side, I knew we were tracking God.

On such days as these I dispensed with my rigid step-by-step objectives with Tracker. In the wild spirit of Shakespeare, I decided to let Tracker wander, giving her the full length of her thirty-foot leash as though she were wild, by herself, in her selected territory, roaming the glades in search of solitude, food, water, high ground, and a good shady place to rest until dark. But she never wandered far from me, and every once in a while she tugged at the leash just to make sure I was there. I was very much her anchor to security. And young as she was, I am sure if she had been born in the wilds, she would be doing the same with her mother.

It was a time of letting Tracker continue to get accustomed to the wilds, to let her put her nose in the air and smell those scents, to probe the high grass and distant treelines for movement, to listen for those extraordinary sounds I couldn't hear but longed to. Tracker took full advantage of the "free" times to push her sensory horizons farther each time out. Had she sensed my goals and taken them on? Or was she simply being a panther, and this is what it took to survive in a panther territory?

Every movement she made, every darting glance, every time she stopped, put her nose in the wind, turned her ears, cocked her head, moved with the ease of grass brushing her whiskers, I imitated her.

Sometimes she would sit with her head just above the grassline, not moving an inch, waiting for a breeze to part the blades for a look far off. I studied her posture and, slightly behind her, tried to get into it exactly. She would look back at me as if to say: No, not that way, get your head down, pull in your feet, put your knees on your chest. Then she would be off on her own again, walking a little farther across the prairie.

I was learning from her all right. And as I did, I could see how inadequate my tracking had been before, even though I had been using skills learned in Nam. My efforts had been rewarding, of course, but this swamp education with a panther was so beyond what I'd done before that I could understand what the problem had been. I had been tracking Shakespeare with the thoughts, actions and habits of a human being. The premise from now on would be to think like a panther. That expression, "be the cat," hadn't really sunk in before. But being with Tracker in the glades made me see clearly what it meant for the first time.

Even though it was cool and a nice breeze flushed over us often, I sweated furiously. My back ached. My eyes periodically blurred. My legs became numb. My arms felt like dead weights filled with lead. But I kept watching Tracker, moving with her, imitating, trying to match her.

As a teacher, she never let up, never rested, and when she was standing still, she was teaching even then. There was no time when she wasn't doing something I needed to try myself. I had to put my nose to the ground, smelling raccoon and rabbit scat. A bear grass bed had to be checked out thoroughly, circled several times, then urinated on. I didn't urinate, but I acted it out, and got a look from her as if to say, Who are you trying to kid? But you're learning.

We made our way like that across the entire prairie until we came to a waterhole. Tracker wasted no time in getting a drink in her cat way by crouching down near the water close enough so that her muzzle wasn't touching as her tongue lapped up the water easily. I found myself doing that, and was amazed at how easily I could get a drink like a cat, forming my tongue into a flexible spoon like Tracker, then scooping up a swallow of water.

I was hoping that after the drink she was going to find high ground nearby and take a rest, but she didn't. Onward we went toward the cypress treeline. Tracker had it all over that sergeant at boot camp who had pushed us further than we ever thought we could go. And this cat did it with guile. When I saw in front of me those beautiful muscles flexing under her fur, I wanted muscles like that more than I wanted rest.

But there was a vast difference beyond that. In the Marine Corps in Vietnam, we were always in a fire team of four, a squad, platoon, maybe even a battalion-size force. When moving out on an operation, everybody in Nam knew who we were and where we were going. Never were we able to camouflage ourselves in platoon force and hide. The Viet Cong always had a good fix on our position.

But a panther and a man alone together in the swamp, well, that was an altogether different experience. Creeping, using the swamp more than ever for ultimate concealment, learning to move like the panther, noiselessly, indeed it was a different endeavor.

Exhausted, I finally tugged on Tracker's leash, and she came back to me, lay down beside me and put her head on her paws. I sighed long and hard, wanting to go back to that waterhole but too tired to make the trek. So I spread out on the wet grass of the prairie and stared up into the sky, and then away from the sun to the south, at the long bush trail we had left as we passed through from that direction. Far on the other side we had left two distinct trails, leading out into the prairie itself, but halfway across, where I had followed Tracker, I noticed our trails had begun to merge into one, forming an almost perfectly straight line to the waterhole and beyond. I must be learning something, I thought, if I can match her track for track.

As I was watching the wind blow the grass over our trail, my vision was interrupted by one, two, three, four, then a mass of flying insects. I focused on them. Tracker had already gotten up on her feet to see what was going on. I sat up too, and when I did I saw that we were encircled by a buzzing force of bees. They were gradually closing in. One, two, then three bees left the ranks and buzzed us, twice bumping me in the head.

Then I heard Tracker cry out. She'd been stung. I jumped to my feet, pulled at her leash, and started running right through the encircling bees. Tracker took the hint and ran alongside me. It was everything I could do to keep up with her as she got stung two more times.

Then I was feeling them on my own back and neck, and the stings were excruciating. I swatted at them, ran up alongside Tracker and swatted at the ones on her back, neck and ears. In anger, she turned around and snapped at me, but we kept running for the car. The bees were swarming around us when I caught sight of the car up on high ground near the old oil pad. I was breathing in hoarse breaths, and Tracker's back was a mass of crawling bees.

I was on the verge of panic. "God, get us out of this!" I screamed, running my hand over Tracker's back and getting stung in the process.

When we got to the car, Tracker jumped for the window, but it was closed and she sprawled out on the ground. She was going crazy with pain and anger. It was everything I could do to hold on to the leash. I opened the car and she rushed in, almost getting crushed as I slammed the door behind her. But the bees had followed her in.

I did the best I could to swat off the bees on me, and then I jumped into the car. Inside, Tracker's face was covered with bees and she was clawing at them, crying, whimpering. I dove across the seat and tore the bees off, crushing them in my hands, taking more stings. Then I started on myself and got them off, stamping them on the floor, swatting more off my chest and face.

Finally there were no more bees, and I lay there in a free sweat, dripping as though I had jumped into a river. I could hardly breathe and I felt sick to my stomach. Tracker was looking at me and licking her paws and chest. Then she sniffed one of the dead bees.

As I watched her, feeling her pain and my own, my stomach rolling, the words "beehive, beehive" blotted out everything else in my mind. And I began to remember a night in Vietnam that I had not allowed myself to think about ever since I had found the peace of this swamp.

I could still remember sitting in that foxhole, sweating furiously, my face sticky from mosquito repellant and salt from my body. I remembered all right. A piece of my life I thought would never come to the surface again. But those bees conjured it up in all of its horror.

On that particular night, surveying the perimeter, watching shadows of trees turn into hallucinations then back to just shadows, my eyes worn out from no sleep and too much sun during the day, we caught small arms fire on our north flank. It was common enough to be harassed by these little fire-fights that never amounted to much, sometimes only lasting a few minutes. Then it would die down for the rest of the night, and the most we expected would be a sniper round at daybreak, perhaps some young VC who was trying for a kill to impress his leader so that he could maybe get an extra bowl of rice for his mother and sister.

But this time the fire-fight kept up, even catching a small mortar from somewhere on the upper part of the hill. By then our captain was fed up with everything in the area. The brass back at the ship had tied his hands on a killing zone designation in the area, saying that the villagers weren't ready to leave yet. Too many innocent people would get hurt. So we had to deal with the hit and run fire-fights as best we could. But the brass had said nothing about not taking the 105 howitzer cannons and cranking them down to point-blank range and attempting to level the whole section of the hill where we were getting the worst of the firing from. So the captain vaguely reported to the CP that we were into another harassment night attack, and then turned off the radio and ran over to the 105 emplacement. Everybody wondered what he was up to.

The howitzers inched down into the blackness out of sight of the rest of us. The captain passed the word to cease fire and let the VC come in a little closer. When they opened up again, there would be a surprise for them.

Charlie did come in closer, in fact right up to the barbed wire before they cut loose again.

All of a sudden somebody yelled, "Beehive! Beehive!" and the cannons all opened up in unison with an ear-splitting explosion.

Never had I heard a more sudden silence, once my ears stopped ringing from the explosion. No more small arms fire, no more 105 cannon rounds, not so much as an order was issued. Just a very quiet night. In the morning a patrol went out into the area where the VC had been. When they came back their faces were white and drawn in the intense sun. One of the guys said he had never seen anything like it. Another marine immediately put in a request to be transferred to a unit in the rear, a request that was refused.

I climbed out of my foxhole and walked over to the 105 emplacements and looked out over the wire. Where once there were bushes and trees, now there was a gap in the earth. It looked like some huge knife had come in and sliced it out.

"Beehive, beehive." The phrase came back to me. I asked one of the 105 cannon crew what it meant. He smiled, then said, "It's like a giant scatter gun, a sawed-off shotgun, so to speak. We all jammed a round in last night under the skipper's orders. There ain't nothin' left of Charlie out there, just some hunks of flesh and stuff. You know, it's kinda like a swarm of killer bees. That's why we call it beehive."

I was sitting in the car, thinking about that, grateful that I had never been on the receiving end of a round of beehive in Vietnam. Though my stings ached and I heard Tracker whimpering at hers, these angry glades bees had just given us a few welts and left us with our lives. We must have been close to a hive out there on the other side of the prairie, and the bees decided to teach us a lesson.

The stings on my arms and face were sore and aching. I looked back at Tracker, who was panting hard in the hot car. I started the motor, drove away, opening the window for ventilation. At the other end of the road I stopped, got out and went to a mud hole and packed the cool soft mud on my welts. I took Tracker out and let her drink the water.

I looked off in the glades. "Beehive." It was the first

time I had ever been attacked by bees. Tracker and I would both know better next time.

61

Cry of the Panther

> **Swamp notes—rare dusk**
> I heard it again tonight—the cry of the panther! I know very well what biologists say it is supposed to mean. But anyone privileged to hear it out here in the wilds comes away knowing it means more. It is a sound that cuts straight to the bone, changes your life.

A sky-washed dusk assaulted the swamp with gold-lined clouds tinged with saffron forming enigmatic red figures against a fiery descending sun that illuminated treelines and stained a solitary pond. A steady wind tormented lanky royal palms and bent them eastward, causing their thatched fronds to pierce the sky like hundreds of sabers. And in that sky, fringed by those clouds, the first stars looked like proud eyes of an unknown species. Nearby gray smoke billowed from a burn-out and filled etched vales in the sky, while maple trees were ablaze with late fall's touch. In all this glades grandeur, an inch-wide stream of inky water ambled in lazy loops and twisted underneath a grass bed, while distant pronged hardwood hammocks, looking like careening sea vessels, seemed unaffected.

Tracker seemed unaffected by it as well, weaving through slash pines on the high sandy soil. She seemed to be thinking more about where she was heading than what splendor she was going through on her way. But I was staggered. I drank up every detail, every changing of a cloud formation, the last sway of a palm frond, maple leaves falling. It was a miraclelike place to be in, and I felt myself selected to be in that spot at that particular turn of wilderness events when all of this came together for just a few seconds, a few moments of a part of heaven revealed. It brought tears to my eyes and a swamp prayer of thanksgiving to my lips. It also brought a fear to my heart, a fear that man wasn't ever going to understand his mistakes against wildlife, and one day I would walk out to this same place and it would be gone with absolutely nothing on the horizon but black skyline.

Then I looked at Tracker, and I imagined Shakespeare out there, and knew that for me they were the key to understanding all of this. Could I make them the key for others—all the many others who had to understand the importance of preserving wilderness and wildlife? All those others needed this swamp. They needed to know how it was their lifeblood, how without it they were nothing more than prey for themselves, feeding off themselves, gouging out the very elements of survival they needed to exist. How to show them, how to show them, how to show . . . the words echoed in my brain. Why are people so blind? I asked myself. Why are they so bent on destruction for the mere purpose of money? Why do they choose to treat greed as a virtue?

It took a little while for me to calm down and take up the business at hand, but soon Tracker and I were involved in an interesting phase—communication. I had been searching for more ways to relate more directly to her, achieve an ever closer communication with her, submerge myself in her world. And the next step would be to "talk" with her, use her means of expression to understand her, and for her to understand me.

Tracker was smart. There was no doubt about that. She comprehended me and her surroundings quickly, adapting just as quickly, harmonizing patiently, seeking out her own advantage. She could do it with ease once she knew what she was confronted with. She would size up a situation, evaluate it in terms of how it affected her, then decide what she was going to do about it. There was no conscious effort on my part to invent or set up situations for her to test her abilities.

Rather, I began simply by observing her reactions to me, the swamp, the wildlife, the scent markings of Shakespeare, and so on. At no time did I try to construct a scientific experiment to evaluate her under controlled conditions. But at the same time my motives for taking her out in the swamp to track Shakespeare, to learn from her the instincts, actions, and characteristics of panther tracking, created their own controlled conditions. The fact I had her in the swamp with me presented us with a natural experiment that would have gone on anyway had she been a wild-born panther in the glades. The difference was she was next to me, adapting to me as a human being while she dealt with nature. As for me, as I let myself go into her world, I found myself many times losing contact with my own kind. It was often only through the greatest effort—my own and that of some higher force—that I was able to return to my human ways.

The most masterful trait Tracker exhibited was that world-famous independence that any cat has. She always wanted to do exactly what she wanted to do, and only through a great deal of prodding on my part did I get her to change her mind on occasion. This independence I preferred to label "solitary adaptation." What it meant was that in order for Tracker to survive, she had to have a sense of complete freedom, as all panthers in the wild do. She had to know that she could rely on her own abilities to make it in the world she lived in, a world of man and animals.

In comparison with Tracker—a comparison I began to make constantly—I found that I too had these qualities. Basically, I wanted to be left alone to do my work. I hoarded my panther project and kept almost all of the information to myself. I always tracked Shakespeare alone, under his conditions, and, in effect, adapted to his environment. But I also knew well man's environment. So, obviously, I had adapted to it. I detested human gatherings of any sort, but like Tracker, put up with them, learning patience from her I never thought I had. I too had to know I had complete freedom to do as I pleased, relying on my skills of survival in dealing with life in general.

There was no doubt that Shakespeare had those supreme qualities of independence to have outlived and outsmarted man under such adverse conditions. The three of us, a strange combo to begin with, a panther-man-panther world, were very much alike. That likeness I cultivated and developed to such an extent that I found myself sometimes wondering where all this was going to end.

But the three of us were subject to a basic law of survival. I chose to call this axiom "glades dependency." In spite of our "solitary adaptation," we were all three still at the mercy of those elements that would keep us alive. Without prey, Shakespeare would starve to death. So he was dependent on the deer population and the general mammal count throughout his territory. He depended on water and air, and enough cover to hide in.

Tracker depended on me to bring her food every day and provide her with a dry place to sleep at the ranch.

In turn, I relied on both of them for my means of survival. Shakespeare related to me vital information on the panther in the wilds. Tracker was always with me when I gave wildlife lectures—the means I had finally struck upon to make enough of a living to keep me going, to give me swamp-time. The wilderness around me gave me water, air and food. And I had come to rely almost totally on Tracker to teach me how to be a panther in the glades so I could track and attain an affinity with Shakespeare.

So, as the months passed, I began to communicate with Tracker. It began with her body language, facial expressions, and tail gestures.

Tracker's body language was an explicit means of communication with me. The very position she put her sleek form in told me things about her overall mood, her likes and dislikes, her fears and joys. She did this with the way she walked, displaying her attitudes, bending her head, hiding her eyes, turning upside down. Some of this panther action was done unconsciously, while at other times it was clear that she knew exactly what she was doing.

My impressions of Tracker's body language were immediate. I labeled her an achiever because of the smart way she carried herself in the swamp, around people, or at the ranch. She behaved like a leader and she was most definitely that. Sometimes I wondered who was leading whom when we were out in the swamp. She would stride out with her head up straight, eyes leveled ahead, tail perfectly in the J-shaped position. I got the impression at times she was like one of those stately Arabian horses prancing in front of the tribe chieftain. When in this attitude she always took on an air of superiority, making me feel inferior next to her.

But, panther that she was, she could also skulk, even cower into a position of almost total submissiveness. She could roll over on her side and contort herself into a position with her head curled under her neck, or even down to her stomach, splaying out her paws to me and wrapping her tail unnaturally under her crotch.

What fascinated me the most was her stalking routine. While in the swamp, she would be moving along nonchalantly, when suddenly she would stop, look around, zero in on whatever she suspected as being out of place in her world, then crouch halfway down, stretching out her neck toward the direction of the problem, ears dropping halfway down too, head now level with the straight line of her back, tail at the ready. Then she would slowly work her way through the grass, pausing, rising, stalking a little farther, constantly narrowing the gap between her and the object up ahead.

This routine I took for my own. I studied her and practiced it constantly. It seemed to be the single most important set of body postures I could use to track Shakespeare. It covered all of the necessary concealment requirements and then some. It gave me the edge on Shakespeare's prey, being able to stalk closer to them. It also gave me the physical quality of a panther. My success using these stalking postures gave me great pleasure. I was becoming the cat. My experiment was working.

I came to recognize Tracker's facial gestures as even closer than her body movement to the center of her emotions. She attained all of her facial expressions with the combination of her skin, fur, lips, tongue, nose, eyes, ears, whiskers, and manipulation of the colors on her face. With her face, she related to me boredom, alertness, deep concentration, sadness, affection, wariness, joy, anger, and other less easily recognized emotions.

The most exciting facial gesture to me was a full snarl,

which was sometimes a warning and other times the action before a good bite. It seemed all of the gesture mechanisms came into play when she snarled. It might appear suddenly and last for only a few seconds, or it might come on her face slowly, as though she were playing with my growing fear. The snarl and my fear interplayed, fed off each other.

First she would show a blank expression; then the facial muscles would go limp, her eyes losing all of their emotion. Then, slowly, the jaws would open wide and her black lips would pull back exposing and framing the white canines and a pink wet tongue. Then the whiskers on her cheeks and the fur over her face would fan out and up, her face suddenly appearing to be bigger than it really was. The white fur on the muzzle below her nose and under her eyes and on her lower jaw would bristle, presenting as a focal point her mouth with those bared teeth.

The skin and brown fur on top of her nose up to the middle of her eyes would wrinkle, and when it did, dark brown lines appeared. There was always a deep vertical groove between her eyes that ran all the way up over her forehead, darkly colored, forming another line blending with the wrinkles on her nose. Now the eyes would slant and the black color around her eyes blend with those wrinkles. Now her ears would flatten, and she would appear to be a streamlined attacking machine.

When Tracker didn't want me near her, or when I was bothering her, she would show this snarl accompanied by a strong hiss, spit and growl. So every time she did this to me, I immediately did it to her as menacingly as I could, to let her know I was not showing any fear of her and that I still had the upper hand.

Tracker's tail gestures were another means of communication, but one I was at a loss to imitate. That powerful appendage gave her a means of performing some of those impossible jumps and acrobatics while she was running, leaving me behind, standing stupidly.

Her tail was in constant motion, even when she slept. It could communicate emotions such as pleasure, fear, anger, anxiety, or simply nervous tension or stress. When she was eating raw chicken, she began with her tail on the ground, occasionally moving it back and forth lazily. Then it would move into action in slashes as she progressed in her meal, as though she were enjoying the meat with her entire body.

Once I tried to take her food away and her tail turned into a cobra snake, sweeping back and forth as I approached, standing a fourth of the way up as I got in closer, then going rigid as she growled when I put my hand out, then suddenly dropping dead when I moved away.

I noticed when she was still a cub playing in the litter that she would take her tail and wrap it around the neck of another cub or snap it back and forth in front of them like a whip, displaying dominance.

When she held her tail in an almost upright position, the tip swaying back and forth, I knew she was in an aimable mood. But I also found that when she held it stiffly, she was more alert to things, but still docile toward me.

It seemed that she manipulated even the fur on her tail, standing it out more for displaying apprehension, wariness.

During the intensely hot summer when mosquitoes and flies were abundant, she used her tail for a bug swatter, and in the cold night of winter she wrapped it around her to keep warm.

Combined with body language and facial expressions, the tail expressed to me Tracker's uncanny ability to learn how to manipulate me into just about anything she wanted.

Tracker's means of communication with me, and mine with her, took on a whole new dimension when we began touching. It was mysterious the way we began to "talk" through physical contact, sensitive to each other's soft spots of communion, developing an even closer bond.

Tracker's greatest pleasure was when I groomed her fur on the sides and back, scratching her vigorously, then smoothing out the fur and then starting all over. She loved it, and would drop into a languorous mood, purring loudly, returning my touching by rubbing her solid body against mine, or wrapping those powerful forelegs around my chest and squeezing tightly. It was a panther hug I much enjoyed, and always returned with a human hug.

There were times when she would come up alongside me and roll over on her back, exposing that beautiful underside of creamy soft fur. I would scratch her under the chin and on the stomach, and she would go to sleep.

Licking was always a most comforting touching session. From it she received enjoyment, and it was her time to give me "ultimate affection" by licking me up and down my arms and all over my face. To reciprocate this, I licked her on the face and neck, biting as a male panther might do. Though I enjoyed this because I was giving her happiness, I always ended up with a mouthful of fur.

In our touching we formed a pleasure bond, and I found myself experiencing a rare communication with a powerful animal that most of the time wanted to be left alone, and yet, Tracker would close the gap herself by coming to me to "touch."

But there were times when she would have no part of touching encounters, when, if I grabbed her tail, she would snarl and lash out furiously with paws, missing my face by inches with those canines. Whenever I attempted to shake paws with her, the same violent reaction was evoked. Those areas were off limits, too sensitive for even me to touch. Her tail and paws were critical parts of her life support system. Grabbing them made her fear I would hold on and inhibit her. It was a sudden confining action that she was not accustomed to and could not and never did adapt to.

But every other form of this touching channel of communication did break down barriers between Tracker and me because we were directly transferring emotions back and forth much as man and woman do.

Next to touching, communicating with Tracker through sound was by far the best. It gave us an insight to each other's emotions and desires that seemed to put me in touch with her soul.

Tracker, like Shakespeare and all panthers, is a feline soprano who produces high-pitched sounds by passing air over a U-shaped bone (ossified hyoid) located at the base of the tongue, causing the soft part of the palate to vibrate. By this means she can purr, scream, cry, mew, growl, hiss, spit, whistle, squeak, call, trill, moan, and probably make sounds my human ears will never hear.

She could purr like a domestic cat to express contentment and friendliness. Several times I heard her purring when she was sound asleep.

She would growl at me when defending her food or herself, or when for some reason she wanted to threaten. While fighting me even in play she would growl in that menacing way.

Her faint or loud squeaks that sounded just like mouse-squeaks were her words of greeting when she saw me coming toward her.

She could whistle like a blackbird, and she used this whistle for locating me when she could not see me. I suspect that this whistle is used quite often in the mother-cub relationship. The cubs probably use it constantly when mother panther is off hunting. When the whistle stops, it alerts her that the cubs are in trouble.

Tracker could make a hideous ear-racking screech that sounded like a parrot's scream. She used this on me to scold me or tell me she was not pleased with some situation.

She always filled the air with a steady low moan when I approached her with nice, raw, fresh chicken.

I began to learn about the many other kinds of cries a panther makes, both from Tracker and the other cats at Frank's ranch. One is the ambush cry. At the exact moment a panther leaps from ambush onto the prey, there is a short, guttural cry before the kill.

There are a number of mating cries. The female will hiss and snort as the male approaches her, then at penetration there is a continuous high-pitched cry as of ecstasy, followed by whining shrills. At the moment of orgasm for the female there is a quick, high-pitched violent cry followed by slow exhausted growls.

During mating, the male growls in low, steady moans, picking up cadence at penetration. Then at orgasm there is a deep, violent screeching growl.

But of all the sounds Tracker made, and of all the sounds the panther makes in the wilds, what can only be called the "cry of the panther" is by far the most phenomenal. Few humans have ever heard this sorrowful scream floating across swamp water in the glades, an unearthly wild wailing that pierces to the bone.

It starts with a faint low mew, climbing up to a long

trill, and gradually increases in volume until it fills the swamp and stops the heart of every listener. Then it loses strength, descending the scale slowly to a whine. It is a female's cry while in season screaming for a mate. It is the cry of all past generations of panthers to carry on their race and it is the cry of all future generations of panthers to be born. It is the cry of survival. It is the cry of all living things to exist, to be. It is the cry of the panther.

Whistling, squawking, squeaking, whining our way through barriers until we both understood each other, Tracker and I communicated.

But it was the cry of the panther I wanted to perfect, to someday be able to take it with me into the glades for Shakespeare. For now I had something very special in mind. I listened to the cries of all the female panthers at the ranch, recorded their sounds, and carried the tape around with me listening to it for days on end.

I knew I was going deeper and deeper into Shakespeare's world.

62

Paws

Swamp notes—following Tracker
*Tracker can sneak up behind me without a
sound, without so much as breaking a dry
leaf. I'm going to follow her, study those
paws, until I figure them out. Then I'm
going to become panther-footed.*

Tracker and I walked the trail, and while I stumbled on cypress knees and broke small twigs of gumbo-limbo trees, she floated as if on a cloud across the ground in her awesome panther stride.

For days on end I had been watching her paws, those efficient tools as sensitive to the wilderness floor as an indigo snake's belly. How could I have paws like that?

They were highly specialized sensory organs that could detect every minute object on the ground beneath them from the bent-over blades of grass to the scurrying of a roach. Their physical structure had become so highly adapted to their environment I wondered if they would ever have to evolve any more, for they seemed perfect. God must be somewhere beaming that he had already created the perfect panther paw.

Sometimes I would stop and let Tracker walk ahead, studying intensely each paw, the last hair that touched the edges of grass as it was gently placed on the ground, then raised just high enough for the next stride, conserving that valuable energy.

Each forepaw has four toe pads in front of a thick, smooth, calloused heel pad. Located farther up the foreleg is another toe called the carpal pad, used for anchoring her claws in the flesh of kills. It is never detected in a mud track, although I had a swampman tell me he had seen the groove of the carpal pad where he found tracks in soft mud some twelve inches down. Most of the time the heel pad of the forepaw is three-lobed, but I have seen tracks where the three lobes seemed blended into one. Each hind paw also has four toe pads and a three-lobed heel pad. But the hind paw is slightly narrower and less flexible than the forepaw. All four paws are built to withstand a great deal of punishment in the swamp. At birth, Tracker's paw skin was tender, soft, smooth. But as she grew older and walked the swamp, it developed thick, hard calluses. I could only imagine Shakespeare's giant paws and how thick the calluses were.

What struck me even more about Tracker's paw movements was that they all seemed to be raised up off the ground. Tracker was walking more on her toes than on the whole foot. That meant the bones in the foot and legs were constructed to be more compact and fused together to withstand a great deal of pressure from her body and the torture she could put her paws through in all her maneuvering. And yet they were also built for grabbing and ripping prey.

Tracker's toe pads were egg-shaped and rounded off.

When I touched them I found that they were not stiff or stationary, but rather she could wiggle them individually, flare them out, twist and fold them under if necessary. There was also skin webbing between each toe covered with fur.

Watching her steps even closer, I saw the way the fur around her paws would ease down, around and over the ground, and then I understood why such an action was taking place. There is a reason for every physical characteristic on Tracker, and that fur was no exception. Every time she placed her paw on the ground, that fur was helping muffle the sound of any branch breaking or leaf snapping, giving the panther still another edge on the prey when ambushing. How could I have feet like that?

I also found out that there are sweat glands packed into the paws. That constant perspiration fluid being emitted as the panther moves through his territory could well be temporary chemical scent marking. So as Shakespeare was out there just walking his territory, he was plotting it for all wildlife—especially all panthers—to know it was his.

I observed Tracker's gait, her exact form when placing each paw on the ground. Sometimes her paws looked like they were entities apart from her body, thinking by themselves. The forepaws would reach out and attempt to pick out the absolutely best spot so that she could move forward a little farther. When making that stride, she would then bring her hind paw up and, more times than not, place it in, or almost in, the spot where the forepaw had landed. In this way only one spot on the ground was tampered with, and it was usually the one spot around where there was no debris that would make sound.

Above each of her toe pads, Tracker had still another set of precisely constructed tools with a specific purpose: the claws, razor sharp, curved back toward the body, retractable and deadly. They are about one inch in length and can easily curl up and under the skin of their prey once they prick the skin. No prey could expect to walk away from such an attack, and if one did, he would be marked beyond repair. The claws retract above the toe pads into fleshy sheaths when not needed. Strong elastic ligaments with flexor muscles stiffen out the toe bones and expose the claw when the time is right. Like my finger nails, Tracker's claws are made of protein, constantly supplied with new material as they wear down or break. There is also another claw on Tracker's foreleg toward the back which is not retractable. It is called the dew claw, and it acts like an extra locking tool for holding prey. I knew Shakespeare was an expert with his magnificent paws and claws, chasing prey, running from hunters, fighting bears, climbing trees, and doing things my human eyes would never see.

63

Panther Nap

> **Swamp notes—in swamp light**
> *I almost never bring "foreign" things into the swamp. But today I've brought these newspapers because I wanted to think hard about what they say while I'm here in the swamp light. Others will read the news in buildings under artificial light, and there catching and collaring panthers might seem sensible. Out here it seems as foreign as these pages, mostly ads. As a matter of fact, right beside the panther article is an ad for a housing development crowding the swamp, crowding Shakespeare.*

I sat down on soft earth in swaying prairie grass under one of those large rain clouds that don't seem to fit in the sky, and spread the two newspapers out before me.

One was a few months old. I had saved it because it announced the state's panther radio telemetry project. True, radio telemetry is probably one of the fastest ways to gather information on a roaming animal. But it is also risky. The process is quite simple. Using dogs, they chase the panther until he is exhausted and runs up a tree. Then, with a tranquilizer gun and dart, a biologist shoots a chemical into the cat which causes the cat to go to sleep, and hopes the cat will not fall out of the tree. Then someone climbs the tree and ties a rope around the cat and lowers him to the ground. After checking the cat for ecto-parasites, they take a blood sample and weigh and measure the animal. Then they fasten a thick collar with a small battery radio around the cat's neck and check to make sure it works. After the panther wakes up, the biologist can sit in a truck or plane and track the cat without ever going out in the bush. Seemed easy enough.

Then I picked up the other newspaper. I'd already read the headline, so I knew. But reading the details, even dressed up in journalese, made me sick.

I lay back on the grass, exhausted both from too many late nights out tracking and from what I had just read. A panther nap was coming on, but even as I closed my eyes I could see the horror of what I'd just read. Soon I slipped off into sleep.

Deep in a huge cypress swamp a female Florida panther steps slowly out of a hollow log and peers at the new dawn filtering through the winter trees in dim, gray shafts clouded with fog. She hunted well the night before, ambushing a young doe before full moon. She stuffed herself with more than ten pounds of fresh venison from the deer's flank, then spent the rest of the night in the log under a rainstorm. Before full light she feeds again, savoring every bite, then roams to the north.

Ever since she was born in a bush den seven years before, she has wandered the glades as one of the few panthers left in this area. She knows the swamp like she knows her own soul—every animal, every sound. Nothing escapes her senses. And for the most part, she has gone unharassed, except for the two horrible times a year ago when dogs chased her. She felt a sharp pain, and then when she woke up, felt a thick, uncomfortable, tight collar buckled around her neck. She has never gotten used to it, and has tried time and again over the year to tear it off. Once when she was chasing a raccoon she even got it caught on a low limb and almost strangled herself, but luckily the limb broke.

Now she yawns, licks her muzzle, stretches panther-style, then ambles toward the prey she has hidden next to a fallen sabal palm tree under leaves and dirt about two hundred yards away.

But in the middle of her third stride she halts with the alertness of her kind. Strange sounds have entered her domain. She cocks her ears toward abrupt, explosive cries. And in a blurring burst of speed, untouchable by any other animal in the glades, she sprints out over paw-deep water up onto and down the trail, pivoting expertly around each small tree, bush and vine. She broadjumps logs and lounging rattlesnakes, passes gator holes and bounds headlong into a thick Brazilian pepperhead patch, coming out the other end in an explosion of leaves and branches, putting as much distance as she can between those cries and herself. They are the same horrible sounds she heard a year ago, just before that collar was put on.

A hundred yards down the trail an old red pickup truck pulls up to a treeline and stops. A lean man with a darkly tanned, weather-beaten face, and wearing an old Stetson cowboy hat, gets out and goes to the back of the truck. On the truck are five steel wire cages, each holding a barking dog. One by one, he takes the dogs out, fastens a leash on each collar, and with sharp commands, orders the dogs down the trail. He looks up through the trees and sees the airplane that has given him the panther's approximate position obtained by radio telemetry tuned in to the beeper on the panther's collar.

The dogs pull the man along as though he is on a sled, their noses to the ground, sniffing, snorting, growling back and forth and up and down the trail. Then suddenly, as though all of them catch the scent at once, they stop, point their noses toward the treeline and go into a barking frenzy.

"You're on 'em," the man says, straining to see down the trail that is partially covered over with bushes. He snaps the leashes off and the dogs race away, yelping and barking and stumbling over each other to take the lead.

The panther hears the dogs coming toward her as she

keeps on running. But after another three hundred yards she has to stop, panting heavily, her legs now turning to jelly. She hurriedly laps at the water, gulps some down, and is off again.

The barking gets closer and closer and she knows if she doesn't shake the dogs soon she will be overtaken. She cuts across a clearing of high sedge grass, then alongside a custard apple tree slough into more water, then up on a trail that has not been used by man in more than ten years. But a hundred yards down the trail she feels her muscles so weakened she doesn't know if she is running or not. She stumbles, regains her stride, stumbles again, tries to get up but finally collapses on the mud, gasping for air. Her body is just not built to run long distances.

The barking draws closer yet, and when she looks back she can see the dogs running toward her in a close wild pack of flopping ears, growling teeth and paws digging into the mud and water.

With what energy she can muster, the panther rises and jumps onto the trunk of a large oak tree, then climbs up more than thirty feet. Now, down below at the base of the tree, the dogs crowd around yelping, barking and trying to jump up into the tree themselves.

In desperation for a final escape, the frightened panther tries climbing across one of the limbs to another tree, but the branches are too small, and when she puts her weight on them, she almost falls off. She is trapped.

There is the roar of the truck, followed by another truck, a jeep, and a four-wheel drive blazer, all sporting Florida Game and Freshwater Fish Commission insignia and all speeding down the road, then stopping as close to the old trail as they can get. Doors slam. Excited voices mix with the thrashing of bushes as they approach the tree surrounded by the dogs.

The man in the Stetson hat gets to the tree first, grabs the dogs and puts their leashes back on, then pulls them back over to the truck where he jams each dog into a cage. Then he trots back to the tree, looks up at the panther, and smiles.

Five other men, dressed in khaki shirts and green trousers, are busy setting up. One has a backpack on and another is carrying a rifle. It is a special kind of rifle. Calmly he inserts a large tranquilizer dart into the chamber and snaps the bolt shut. Cradling the rifle in his arms, he walks up to the tree. Easing the rifle up on his shoulder, he unclicks the safety and peers over the sight. It is a hard shot because he is trying to put the dart into the panther's large hind-leg muscles. When he is sure the panther is not going to move, he takes up the slack of the rifle trigger and holds it as long as he can. Still the panther doesn't move. He squeezes the trigger and a streak of metal that looks like a miniature missile projects through the air.

At first the panther feels nothing. Then the long, piercing needle of the dart penetrates her tough skin and well-developed posterior muscle and approximately a tenth of an ounce of combined ketamine and protamine tranquilizing chemical squirts into her backside.

Her hind legs feel numb, tingling, as though all of the blood is oozing out of her body. Then she feels tired, as though she weighs a thousand pounds. She has trouble moving her paws, and her head trembles. By now all of her coordination is gone. Then her head begins to swim and her eyes grow watery, vacant, and finally her whole body goes limp. Balancing on a small branch, she makes one last effort to hold on, but before she realizes it, she is falling downward, slamming onto the swamp floor. The tranquilizing dart has hit the femoral artery and sent the chemicals directly through the bloodstream to her brain. She is dead.

I woke up in a free sweat, cold from the coming storm, disoriented. The dream had been so vivid—as if I had actually witnessed the panther kill I had just read about in the paper. A female panther gone from the glades forever. A potential litter wiped out.

It was hard to accept. Surely there would be a public outcry now. People would never stand for the continuation of a project that put the few remaining panthers in even graver danger, would they? Accident or not, the panther was dead, and nobody could bring her back.

A fine drizzle had started, so I got up and headed back for the ranch. As I was striding across the prairie, my face, hair and shoulders dripping with the rain the drizzle had now become, I came across tracks, Shakespeare's tracks. I stood there staring at them, watching the rain rapidly dissolve them into the earth. Then I snapped my head up, a question shooting through my mind. What if they got Shakespeare and collared him? What would be his fate then? I won't let it happen, I told myself. I won't let it happen.

64

Call of the Swamp

Swamp notes—fire on the horizon
Tracker's spots and stripes are fading now,
blending more into a tawny coat of fur
brushed over with brown. The creamy white
of her underside is accented by a white fleck
on the back of her neck. She's growing up.

It was an hour before dawn, and Tracker and I were sitting on the edge of a prairie staring at the mystifying presence of a swamp fire far on the horizon. It poured into the entire stretch of trees like a long, shimmering, orange-red river, and filled the dark sky with streamers of torchlit halos that made me think of small aurora borealises. The darkness fought that flood of flames with livid murkiness, but the bloodhot tempest returned with sunbursts of glittering tree explosions that formed arches, spreading the burn-out even wider.

I looked into Tracker's eyes and the flames danced in her pupils devillike. But when she glanced at me there was only a wild animal's excitement of witnessing such a spectacle.

We watched the fire rage for more than an hour until dawn flushed the sky and caused the fire to turn to smoke. It was so reminiscent of the B-52 bombing runs in Vietnam. So many times I had sat on perimeter guard at Chu Lai, staring off to the west over the rice paddies toward the hills, watching the thunderous five-hundred-pound bombs blow out huge craters, level whole tracts of jungle, and wipe Viet Cong off the face of the earth. Then the fires would start up, burn all night, ooze down the sides of the hills like lava flow, and eventually turn an entire hillside into cinders and black rock. And the very next night the B-52's would go back to that same target and do it all over again.

Tracker and I still sat there musing, scanning the nearer swamp in the first seconds of dawn. The sun was up, but the white moon still held to the sky with its chiffon shadow. The glades sat quiet. The earth was still asleep.

A little time after that a large oak, overworked by beetles and time, creaked and fell to the ground somewhere not far away from us, issuing a rush of wind and wood-crashing. Nature would feast on that bough until one day it would become just an impression in the mud. Tracker's ear went up as the tree fell, her head darting in the direction, neck stretching up. Then she looked at me, and when she saw I wasn't too concerned about it, she dropped back at ease.

She was eight months old now, about thirty pounds, slightly larger than a male bobcat. That meant she was as fast, if not faster than the bobcat, quite able to outrun a full-grown black bear, and if taught, could catch small game like rats, opossums, armadillos, maybe a small raccoon.

I noticed that the bigger she got, the harder she was to manage. On her thirty-foot leash, she now took all of it, tugging me along. When she wasn't satisfied with my progress, she would sometimes come back and try to bite the leash off or take a swipe at me. And as she grew older, she began making circles around me. The older she got the bigger the circle became. I concluded she wanted more and more freedom.

As an experiment, I took the leash off that day, and her whole attitude seemed to change. That leash had been a direct connection to me for her protection. Now that it was off, she stuck even closer to me. In effect, she had to learn about freedom, independence, relying on her own abilities to survive, rather than me as her anchor to life. Freedom was not all that easy for her to attain, even when it was freely offered.

She had taken some important steps already. She was

born outside in the Everglades environment and taught to eat only raw meat and wild sedge grass, and to drink swamp water. I had introduced her into the swamp as a small cub, giving her the opportunity to see and touch her real world. It hadn't been too long before she had developed true panther eyes, ears, and nose to sense the world around her.

Freedom. What did that mean to Tracker? Did she hear the call of the swamp? Did freedom mean complete release from me, on her own in the swamp to fend for herself, to learn and stimulate her own natural instincts, to rely on those instincts for survival as all panther do in the wilds? Questions crowded my mind. How could I teach Tracker freedom? Should I? Did I have the right to plunge Tracker into the swamp on her own? And if so, what would be accomplished?

It had not been my intention to train Tracker to live in the wilds. But as she grew up before my eyes, in the swamp tracking Shakespeare, she began to own that swamp. She plotted territory by leaving urine heaps and scat, by rubbing up against trees, scratching and biting on fallen logs, destroying bobcat droppings and then replotting the territory with her own.

Off the leash, that circle she made around me got bigger and bigger, and I began to get the feeling that more and more she wanted to be left alone, and didn't really regard my presence as all that important—except for food. When it came to raw chicken she stuck pretty close to me. I always carried a plastic bag of it in my pack.

For several days more we walked Shakespeare's territory, often with Tracker unleashed and on her own. We had found large fresh scat and his tracks in soft mud. Once we walked across a highway to get on low ground on the other side to find more of his tracks on the east bank of a shallow pond. Shakespeare had not gone around the water. It looked like he had walked through it. The water was teeming with mosquito fish and crayfish, and there was an especially deep hole in the middle.

Maybe he was cooling himself off, I thought. But on looking around the high grass and willows on the bank, I saw small fish bones, probably bones from blue gills and bass, up in a cool shady area. In the sand were rapidly dissolving toe pad prints, large ones, Shakespeare's. He had been fishing, probably standing near the deepest part of the water, maybe even dropping the tip of his tail into the water to attract a fish, then, with those blinding reflexes, batting the fish out of the water and snagging it with his claws.

Tracker inspected the bones closely, sniffing, wetting her nose and sniffing more. Finally satisfied with whatever she had perceived, she walked away. And she kept on walking as though I wasn't even there. I turned in her direction and followed, but when I did, she suddenly dashed off into the saw palmettoes and disappeared in that thick entanglement.

My heart jumped. She was gone. This was the first time she had ever left my sight, the first time she didn't look back to see if I was close behind. Was she testing me, or her own sense of freedom?

I came close to screaming out her name and running into the bushline, but that would have been the worst thing I could have done. It would have been out of character for me to react to her like that. She had never seen me do that, and it could have spooked her to run off forever. So I remained calm and started whistling in that short, high-pitched sound, the location call that panthers use, cubs to mother.

I stared into the palmettoes. "Come on, Tracker, come on," I whispered. I got a piece of raw chicken out of my pack and waved it in the air, then laid it on the ground at my feet. "Come back, Tracker."

When I looked up, there was Tracker at the bushline, staring at the chicken and me as if to say: What were you worried about, anyway? She came over to me with a low, steady moan, and when she got to the chicken she growled heavily, mouthed the morsel, and backed off a little to sit down and eat it, gorging herself on the fresh flesh. When she was finished, she looked up at me and purred loudly, as though to say thank you. I smiled.

In the most cautious way I maneuvered my way close to her with the leash behind my back and quickly put it around her neck. That she didn't like at all, and told me so with hisses and spits and a snap of her jaws.

I took her back to the ranch, and went back out to the swamp to check for tracks before dark. Tracker had now left my side, and though for only a very brief time, had felt the call of the swamp. I now knew that if I continued to take her out like that, someday she would run off and never come back. It was a tough decision, but I backed off from teaching her to live in the wilds. She would go back on the leash for as long as she could help me devise a system to track Shakespeare on my own, as long as she could help me become like her.

65

In Season

> **Swamp notes—in swamp mist**
> *Even now the Everglades seem a strange
> and fantastic place to me. They whistle,
> breathe, in a way no other wilderness can.
> I wonder about Shakespeare in all his glory
> here. I wonder if he has ever thought about
> an affinity with me.*

A revelation of water, sky and flora created a swampscape with a thin haze produced by high humidity and hydrocarbons emitted from the lush vegetation. It hung from invisible hands, while cypress and willow in full bloom draped low to the water and lapped at it as a breeze passed. Snowy egrets lost themselves in clouds too large for the sky. Black-tipped sulfur butterflies massed on a single night-blooming cereus as it slowly closed before the coming of day. And light reflected from a pool flashed up at cackling crows. I wondered how long God had contemplated all of this before he gave life to this small heaven.

I knew Tracker and I were in a special place, a place I

hoped would bring to me some sort of deep insight into a skill Tracker possessed that I could then develop for myself, claim it as a rare ability, then use it for tracking Shakespeare on my own. I was beginning to believe Tracker might even steal my affinity with Shakespeare. For she was a rapidly maturing female panther, two years old now, who would soon throw her in-season scent up into the swamp air in Shakespeare's territory to lure him. Maybe she would soon even give the cry of the panther, calling to him directly.

I was near a decision that tore at me from both sides. Should I now include Tracker in my quest all the way to my goal? I had already used her for that purpose all along, learned from her panther ways. Did I have the right to suddenly dismiss her from the project? Without her I would never have gotten as far as I had. Without her I probably would have wandered about the Everglades and maybe by sheer luck might have occasionally stumbled onto something that would help me make a stride toward Shakespeare. But again, it had been Tracker, that cat next to my legs, who had catapulted me this far along toward my destiny.

I knelt down next to her and rubbed the soft white fur under her chin. She closed her eyes and stretched out her neck, leaning toward me as I scratched harder and harder. Then she began to lick my arm, getting the dried salt with her rough tongue.

I looked into her eyes inches away, probed them as deeply as I could. "Do I have the right to claim a victory with Shakespeare without you, Tracker?" I asked.

Tracker looked back at me and probed my eyes, and never before had she looked so intensely at me. That stare was so strong I had trouble keeping my eyes on hers, but I made every effort to do so. Something very strange was happening. Suddenly I couldn't take my eyes off hers, not even when I tried to. Tracker had me in her hypnotic grip, as though she were going to reach out and devour me. But I still couldn't look away.

Then a pleading whimper came from her, a sound I had never heard from her before. That whimper then turned into a long, squawking cry, Tracker's powerful flanks heaving in and out. She lay down on her stomach and straightened her backbone. The cry was long and continuous, echoing all around the swamp.

What was going on? I asked myself.

Tracker then broke our eye contact, turned her body all the way around and began to cry even louder than before. She propped her hind legs up, exposing her hind end to me. I looked around at the swamp, then at Tracker as she looked over her shoulder at me. Then I realized what was going on. She had gone into season for the first time. She was calling for a mate. That cry was the same one I had heard at the ranch when other females were in season. And the same cry of the panther I'd heard in the swamp. That was plenty to shake me up. But it also dawned on me just what she was trying to tell me. She wanted me as her mate!

This in itself was a small affinity. Here I was being selected by a female panther as her mate.

I drew away from her far enough for her to see I wasn't interested, but not so far as to tell her I openly rejected her. That was not my intention. As I was doing this, it came to me the perfect way to draw Shakespeare to me. In effect, I would become a female panther in Shakespeare's territory. I would plot my territory with Tracker's urine and scat while she was in season and I would learn from Tracker how to give the cry of the panther.

There were many more skills I had to learn, to develop and perfect, before I could become a panther in the swamps, but I knew my main goal. Everything I had learned about the panther would now be put into use, every fragment of knowledge I had discovered about Shakespeare would now be used—now that I had found the missing link in the chain of events leading to affinity.

I stared down at Tracker. In her wild animal way she had given me one very direct answer to all my questions.

At that moment the Everglades, panther, myself, took on a whole new meaning. I was going to make it. I was going to transform myself into a panther. And maybe, just maybe, for the first time in my life, I would see myself as I really was. I already knew what Shakespeare really was. He was a symbol of the will to survive.

Book IX
Affinity

All are but parts of one stupendous whole,
Whose body nature is, and God the soul.
                                    —*Alexander Pope*

66

Glades Ritual

> **Swamp notes—in Shakespeare's prairie**
> It's like coming home standing here in this
> wet prairie where I first sighted Shake-
> speare—that panther body erect, solid, cau-
> tious of every movement—then the sudden
> spring away from my eyes. I put my hand
> out toward the spot and it seems so long
> ago that I entered this deep dark swamp,
> vowing promises I have tried to keep.

Nam Yo Fara On.

The Rain Giver stormed his spirit across and into this
wild land in long blue blazes of rain like sabers drawn from
ancient sheaths. The wind slanted and bent the grass into mud
and mire, filling the prairie with large, rolling, golden waves.
Mist curled up from the tops of the cypress trees like frosty
smoke. Above, the nimbus cloudbanks obscured what was
once a sunny morn and swirled the moving river into a thick
monsoon.

Everything was afloat: my spirit, the glades spirit. The
rain beat at me. Blinded me. Kept me from watching this
cloudburst overwhelm the grass, insects, lizards, and birds
shielding themselves in low parts of the trees.

It held me like that for over an hour, and all that time
I stood rigid in the prairie, oblivious even to my own being.
I kept my eyes closed, feeling the rhythmic beat on my face
and shoulders. Throughout my quest I had had small affinities
with the glades and Shakespeare, and this was but one more
I had been privileged to experience. This swamp miracle was
nothing less than another morsel of knowledge in the great
palm of Nature.

Then the roar subsided and I felt a hot sun dry my face.

I opened my eyes and stared about this swamp Eden that was now mine. But now, even more, I was the swamp's possession. I was starting over at the exact spot I had started from to track Shakespeare, but now with a rare knowledge of him gathered through our shared experience.

I had just taken a week out from tracking to review all that I had learned to that point and to devise new strategies. I looked off into the horizon toward the ranch as if to communicate with Tracker, my teacher. I now knew she was my key to open the door wide to affinity. And now much of her was in me.

I had chosen to become an invisible swamp shadow, black-hooded and panther-footed, ripe with female panther scent, and for the present, I was a big cat unseen by Shakespeare. Soaked across my chest and on my shoulders and along my legs, I had poured Tracker's urine, collected earlier for that purpose. To absorb all light and movement I wore dull black, long-sleeved utilities, black mosquito-netted gloves, and I had camouflaged my backpack with black spray paint. On my feet I had black scuba diving boots with thin soles. And on those boots was black fur to absorb the slightest sound made as I walked, like the fur on Shakespeare's paws.

I slowly descended to my knees and wrapped myself in the prairie grass shadows. Then I looked up into the sky at the sun breaking through the receding clouds. With my spine erect, I bowed my head forward until my chin touched my chest, and then I dropped it backward onto my spine, and then I returned it to an erect posture. This I did three times, each time farther than the one before.

Then I slowly twisted my head to the right three times, each time a little farther than before, each time trying to see my right heel over my shoulder. I did the same to the left in harmony with those cool breezes.

Then I loosely rolled my head clockwise, then counter-clockwise, three times. In threes I found the exercise complete.

Putting my finger to the left side of my nose, I breathed deeply through my right nostril, then switched to my left nostril, three times each, exhaling through my mouth. I now began to relax.

In a whispered monotone I chanted "A-I-E-R . . . Om . . .

Om . . . Om," until I felt a serene vibration through my mind, body, and spirit-self. I was seeking a clear state of mind, a place where my real soul could take over. I was seeking to leave my human existence behind and enter Shakespeare's world.

With the utmost concentration, I began to give myself suggestions to dwell on a single thought. "The swamp is my home. . . . The swamp is my home. . . . The swamp is my home."

I closed my eyes and imagined myself in the cypress swamp ahead of me, Shakespeare's territory. In my thought I said to myself, "Relax now. . . . You are relaxed."

I tried to relax all of my muscles in my body and yet remain erect. My toes, legs and hips, stomach and back, neck and shoulders, chest and arms—all were relaxed.

Thinking to myself, I said, "I am going deeper and deeper into the swamp, deeper than I have ever been before." I imagined trees moving past me, bushes parting like soft cream, silent water rippling, vines lifting, flowers closing, leaves changing to dew, the very air opening to receive me.

I counted backward as slowly as my mouth could move from ten to zero, still going deeper and even deeper yet into the swamp, deeper into that serene concept of tracking my soul.

I began to suggest to myself this thought: "I am a panther. . . . I am a panther. . . . I am a panther. . . . I can walk like a panther. . . . I am a panther. . . ." Over and over again, without moving so much as an eyelid, I repeated those phrases to my mind, convincing myself with all that I had learned about Shakespeare, the glades, tracking, that I could attain a level of tracking presently not touched, could cross over that threshold to panther existence. It meant to live like a panther and to know his world. And in order to do that I was to become a panther, think like Shakespeare, walk like him, *be the cat*.

As I let those words soak into my mind, crowding all other thoughts out, I went even deeper into the swamp.

Slowly, then, I opened my eyes and said, "God, protect and help me in this day of tracking."

I leaned forward and put my hands on the ground, drew

my knees to my chest. Head up, eyes forward, I moved through the prairie grass toward the cypress, those long grass blades moving across my shoulder like long, reassuring hands from swamp dwellers now a part of history.

Around me there was a rainy afterglow that crystallized in the sunlight through a fine mist. Leaves steamed as though on fire. Spider lilies drooped from the weight of the fallen rain, their long, white, featherlike petals half eaten by immature grasshoppers. An eastern hog-nosed snake slipped across a thin sheet of water, his farmyard hog-nose upturned sharply, his dull olive-brown coloring making him disappear. He didn't even bother with me, or he never saw me to begin with. My movement was so slow, so shadowlike, that I suspected I could have laid my finger on his head without his knowing until he felt me. At a basic, still minor level, I was already accomplishing the feat of imperceptibility, escaping to the unseen world. Though I was a part of the glades on the physical level, with my suit of darkness I was also a shadow completely blended into the balance of the Everglades.

I approached the belt of cypress trees and stared into the exact cleft of foliage where I had seen Shakespeare for the first time. It was a womb of the earth which had given birth to a chance of survival for me in so many ways that I had already recognized. Shakespeare was my bridge to understanding myself. Now I wanted to be his bridge in telling Planet Earth what it will take for the human race to understand itself, to survive.

I felt rain drizzle brush my shoulders, and when I glanced over my shoulder, the prairie was again being assaulted by a storm. This one fell out of a huge black cloud streamlined by the sun behind it, creating rainbow halos in a haphazard fashion as far as the horizon stretched. The rain seemed to fall in layers, more like lakes falling on top of each other. And the roar splattering up from the ground gave me the perfect edge to enter the cypress without being heard. I did that as swiftly as possible, inching my way up onto the high ground Shakespeare had chosen for his roaming this part of the swamp, now on the verge of being taken over by the ever-building waterline. I eased down and rolled next to a fallen log, smelling its young wet wood, sensing it with my whiskers, becoming that log's shadow, placing my right eye just over the edge to look into the slough. I was now in Shakespeare's territory once again.

67

Panther-footed

> **Swamp notes—into panther life**
> I am developing a panther style of walking
> that borders on cat heritage. With this skill
> of prowling perfected I will be able to roam
> the sloughs in that awesome feline silence—
> just like Shakespeare.

The black-bellied cloudscape, with its swarmy tails, now boiled into a primordial soup over my wildwood sanctuary, causing white ibis, Louisiana heron and snowy egret to exodus through vapor wreaths to another feeding range well away from this turbulence in the sky.

But in sharp contrast, near me nature's tide of life revealed remarkably strange calms. Fog nuzzled around stiff-leaved air plants. An irridescent water strider stood glued to a lily pad. On the corrugated bark of an oak, a misplaced plump, pale-green Io caterpillar with its red stripe inched upwards. Turtles, unconscious of the weather, lounged on small logs mirrored by shimmering water. I lay there in the momentary twilight, my cheeks resting on the soft wet wood of a log, watching an army of termites scurry back and forth in an opening, oblivious of the primeval violence taking place in the sky.

The storm had not only drenched the swamp, but had given it a misty gray light that stole the original green colors from the vegetation, making it look like an unfinished painting.

The rain had also beat away maple leaves and cypress needles to form new holes in the tree canopy. I noticed a bird nest hanging weakly from a branch. On the ground were two small, smashed eggs, the shells bluish-white with reddish-brown speckles, the oozing yokes mixing with the tea-colored water making it look like syrup. Chunks of black mud that looked like chocolate fell away from what was once an island and melted into the water streaming south. A small wet mouse rushed up to one of the chunks, grabbed a wiggling something from it, then rushed back to the roots of a fallen tree and disappeared in green wet moss. Above the moss was a pink round-ended feather that teetered on an exposed root, then suddenly whisked away with a breeze. Was it a nature sign for peace?

To my right was a small leaf island with a few dead maple trees. It would be my next position. Oddly, while the swamp flourished with life around it, this island was barren, as though some strange wind had fallen from the clouds and spread a poisonous gas over it killing the vegetation.

Though in miniature, it reminded me how in Vietnam thousands of acres of wild jungle were defoliated with agent orange from American planes. There would be miles of lush vegetation, then suddenly a dead barren plot in the middle of nowhere. After a while those plots began to join with each other. Agent orange was doing its job.

But now that the U.S. has come and gone in Vietnam, we have begun to understand that this chemical not only destroyed Viet Cong strongholds, exposing hiding places and sending the enemy elsewhere, but it also destroyed and deformed the humans in its path, including our own soldiers. The evidence is mounting that agent orange has left mental illness, twisted genes and cancer in its wake.

I remembered walking through an area defoliated by agent orange while I was on patrol west of Outpost Fourteen. It looked like nothing more than a recent jungle burn-out. Everything was dead down to the roots of the grass. The bushes were bare and the trees looked like old pillars ready to crumble. The lieutenant said that napalm had started a fire over the whole region the month before. We thought nothing of it and walked on. We'd been told that planes spraying this

killer chemical were only using a mild insecticide to destroy
mosquito larvae to protect all of us on the ground from those
biting critters. Maybe they were. Officially, agent orange didn't
come to Nam until 1968. But unofficial rumors of it spread
well before that.

Little did many marines know they were breathing in
slow death. Maybe I had too. I looked down at my black-clad
body. I'd kept it finely tuned. It felt as strong as it had the
last day of boot camp. I was in perfect health—so far.

A crying swamp breeze brought my thoughts back to
reality. I blinked a few times, wiped my face, and crawled
around the log and over to the island. I knew Shakespeare
was nowhere near this area at the moment because the previous day I had checked for him far north and found tracks.
If it was going to happen through the process I had in mind,
this was a good place to start my long-range plan for my final
push to Shakespeare's side.

Through an intensive physical training program I had
developed my muscles to a point where I could believe that
my thighs and calves were thick, strong hind legs with power
to rear and pounce, and that my shoulders and arms were
giant forelegs with strength to slash and tear. As reinforce-
ment, I kept saying to myself, "I am a panther. . . . I walk like
a panther. . . . my feet are paws. . . ." These auto-suggestions,
repeated over and over again to my mind, had already induced
a wilderness mode of panther behavior in me to the point
that I could believe my feet were cat paws.

Many times over, I had watched Tracker silently pad
her way through the swamp at my side, and having studied
every inch of her paw anatomy, I had decided to make my
feet paws like hers, like Shakespeare's. I had been observing
Tracker at the ranch walking back and forth, blocking out
the rest of her body until all my eyes saw were four panther
paws performing a silent wild ballet. I had watched her so
often and so long that when I closed my eyes or slept, those
paws padded back and forth in front of my eyes. In my mind
I tried to slow up the movement, stopping them in midair,
checking them for a position, then letting them stretch out.

I had been taking Tracker for long walks on a leash,
staying two to three feet away, trying to copy her. Her paws

floated through the air in perfect coordination with her body, taking the short distance between each step with mystical action. Then her toes landed first softly and silently, even on the roughest ground and in the rockiest places, followed by the front edge of her heel pad.

Soon I was raising up on my toes and the balls of my feet, and with pain and frustration, mimicking her gait for short distances. I noticed immediately how much that reduced foot noise.

I had practiced that over and over again, walking man-style, then raising up on my toes and going as long as I could before dropping down on my heels. I was surprised how long I could stay up on my toes, and eventually began to cover a good distance on tiptoe. But even though I had reduced the noise considerably, still I was crunching twigs and wincing from the pain of jagged rocks.

So, observing Tracker closer yet, I had found that she would sometimes stretch out with her paws, feel for debris such as a rock, and brush it aside with her toes, then carefully pad on. It seemed she was consciously figuring out ways to do away with noise.

Wearing thin-soled scuba boots, I began walking old gravel roads and doing the same thing Tracker had done. Soon I was able to eliminate even more sound. Then I took off the boots and walked barefoot to see how sensitive my soles were. It was an excruciating experience. Jagged rocks, pebbles, bits of sharp seashells, and an occasional sandbur punctured and sliced my feet, which were hardly conditioned for such punishment. But after a while, using my toes as fingers, I learned to brush the impediments aside and make a smoother path. Time was immaterial. If it took me forever to become panther-footed, then so be it, I thought.

It became a pure joy, stepping forward, probing, holding, raising my other foot and holding it in midair, then gently placing it down on the ground, then moving on. I began to experiment with all kinds of ideas.

When I wanted to make movements past a tree or bush-lines, maybe get to a waterline fast, I invented another step. The process was simple. After I put the toes of one foot down on the ground with full weight on them, I quickly brought the other foot up and down to the ground, and, seconds before that action was completed, I jerked the first foot up. There was less time that my toes were on the ground and less chance of breaking a twig.

In all of this I had a slight advantage over Shakespeare. He had four paws to manage, while I had only two to train to reach out, feel for the best place where I would make the least noise, place my toes down and move forward. Even though he would sometimes place his hind paws in the tracks of his forepaws, still he had to perform that action. I didn't.

The swamp, too, helped me in my panther-foot program. Rainy season had softened the ground, made the leaves pliable, the twigs spongy. At this time of year sound was at a minimum anyway.

Unnoticed at first were the unprecedented, unexpected swamp experiences I began to have as a result of this skill. When I melted into tree shadows, bushes, overhangs, or stood next to trees bending my body into the contours of cypress stumps, things happened around me that never had occurred before. Or at least I had never noticed them before. But gradually they made their way into my consciousness. Had I really attained invisibility sooner that I thought? At dusk I could stand inches away from sleeping butterflies and camouflaged moths on trees without disturbing them. A female opossum with a litter hanging on her had ambled right past me. I had stood next to a gumbo-limbo tree five feet away from a great horned owl and hadn't bothered him in the slightest.

Panther-footed I moved soundlessly across the island, reserving the silence for whatever sounds the swamp would bring to me. The swamp complied. I began to hear strange, liquid, reverberating sounds. Sounds that dug deep into the swamp and my ears. I had never heard them before. They drew me to the water around me. I floated to those sounds and found myself at a pond where the aquatic serenade was coming from.

Rup,rup,rup,rup,rup. It was harsh at first; then as I drew nearer, it became high-pitched and rhythmical in a murmuring sense. Suddenly it went back to rup,rup,rup,rup,rup.

I checked for gators, saw none, and so slowly eased into

the water—treading along the edge where giant fire flags stood like wrinkled sentinels. And the watery harmony kept up, steady, sometimes abrupt, but always with those strange wild lyrics—rup,rup,rup.

I didn't spot the source of the song until I was in the midst of it: several schools of catfish swirling about at the surface, turning their bellies to the sun, then flipping their tails and losing themselves in the blackness. But it seemed as though they all moved on cue to break the surface, turning their bodies to the sun, then flipping their tails and issuing their contribution to the symphony.

Those musicians I called disco catfish. The deep rup,rup,rup came from the vibration of the thin bladders that throbbed through their bodies, making the noise that was then carried across the water, as smoothly coordinated as an orchestra. I took it as a musical tribute to my debut as a cat in the swamp.

I floated to the edge of the pond and slid out and into the bushline, looking one more time at the ripples and listening to the songs of the disco catfish. I shook the water from my feet and then, panther-footed, I was on my way to high ground once again.

I knew I was ready now to begin my final plan. This barren island was the launching pad for the tactic that would bring me to Shakespeare, or more accurately, bring him to me. We'd been on a collision course for much longer than the few years I had been tracking him in the swamp. But now, as impact drew near, I could hardly contain my excitement.

I had very little control over my obsession now. It was like wearing heavy leather blinders around my eyes, like those that were put on plow horses in the fields years ago. I could only look forward, plowing my way through barrier after barrier.

68

Plotting Territory

Swamp notes—Signpost Alpha
Being the animal of the shadows tells me so many reasons why there are panthers. One is to relay to man the mystery of the wilds—those surrounding and those within him—to stir in him his own meaning of life.

The Everglades entranced me into an ever deeper spell as I watched the hypnotic, serial sweeps of an immature red-shouldered hawk—back and forth, back and forth. I stared at crystal droplets streaming down a tree with prehistoric slowness over thick white webs of lichen. One drop merged into another to form still another which continued down to the next droplet, again and again . . . and once again. Before me a slate of water was suddenly disturbed by a falling leaf, and the endless trancing ripples furrowed on forever, each one more perfect than the last. I was traveling deeper and deeper into my soul, letting myself go to a place I'd never been before.

It had taken me more than a week to decide on the exact three-inch spot where I would begin plotting my territory in the midst of Shakespeare's. After searching many miles, I had found the location to the west where a moonflower sat in the green like a lacy chunk of ice in early morning sunlight. The spot was between a healthy laurel oak struggling with a strangler fig wrapped around it like a climbing spider and a cypress tree split halfway down by a powerful lightning flash. Sap oozed from the split and mixed with red fungi as though it were thick blood from a knife wound.

I knelt between these trees. On the ground was a small open area with swamp grass, leaves, bits of bark and small branches lying as they had fallen. A good place for a panther to defecate, I thought. I designated the spot Signpost Alpha. My first plotting as a panther, for a panther, because of a panther.

I had collected some of Tracker's scat and urine earlier, wrapped it in a plastic bag and frozen it. I now carefully opened the bag and let wet plugs roll out onto the ground. The steamy, frosty spoor melted and I smelled panther stench hover in the air. I could almost see it whisked away into the swamp toward Shakespeare's nostrils.

A thrill went through me. I was into my territory. I had taken another step toward pantherhood. For most swamp purposes I was a panther who had just crossed Shakespeare's territory, felt at home in it, and started plotting. I had begun a new chapter in tracking. My human scent was gone.

Disguised in Tracker's scent, I was banking on the strong possibility Shakespeare would be curious about it, wonder exactly who had wandered into his range with the nerve to set up a territory right in his. Shakespeare now had a scent trail—and a new incentive—to track me down, fulfilling his half of the quest. But for some reason I had the feeling he would do much more than his half.

I sat back on my heels, stared at the wet scat where flies now hovered, then off into the swamp. I then stared into the hot sun beating on me. Signpost Alpha was more that just a plotting. It was the start of a unique means of inter-species communication. Or, if things went the way I was beginning to think they might, one of us would cross that arbitrary line between us. I looked back down, rubbed my whiskers, then rose and began searching for my second plotting site.

I padded through the swamp, keeping on high ground. I stopped to watch blue gills in the water expose their thick, fishy lips to lure mosquitoes. I felt a faint hunger, and momentarily considered slapping one of those fish out of the water, tearing it open and enjoying its rich, cool flesh. But other goals sent me on.

Questions played in my mind as I crept on, panther-footed. Does Shakespeare move through his territory only when he is on the prowl for prey? Thinking like him, I thought: If I were hungry, I would move; if satisfied, I would rest in hidden shadows. But there were other things that would cause me to move. I would avoid other panthers, men, bears. During the rainy season I would move to high ground. During the dry season I would move to avoid fires. Or was it in Shakespeare's brain, created through long evolution, that he should walk his territory to let prey know a predator was lurking so they could keep their senses alert, and so that the healthiest of them all stayed healthy?

The intense heat had sweat-soaked my utilities. I poured more scent on me. The black hood, with only an opening for my eyes, boiled my head. I knew I was driving myself too far too soon too fast in the heat. I couldn't afford a heatstroke or a mirage. Too much was at stake. I had to keep my concentration solely on the quest now. I splashed water from the nearest pond on my face and rested until my temperature dropped.

I was on the move again through willow shadows, then higher onto a trail, over it and into cypress once again. I calculated that a mile or more from Signpost Alpha I would plot Signpost Beta.

When I had gone that distance I checked for landmarks: a hidden pond with bladderworts floating on it, a popash slough to the south, high ground and two trees that formed a cross.

This time it would be a urine heap. I took out a small bottle with an eyedropper in it. Extracting a full load, I dropped Tracker's urine onto the ground and let it pool on several leaves. The heavy, musky odor dominated the air. I got down on my knees, stretched out my hands like paws and scraped leaves, needles, and other debris back toward my lap until I covered the spot. Then I put several more drops on top just to make sure. Signpost Beta was the second brightest star in my wilderness constellation of plotting for Shakespeare. I sat down to rest and contemplate my position—a cat in my own territory, a man on his way toward his goal. I began to think about a chance meeting I'd had recently with another man on his way to his own goal.

He was South Vietnamese and about my age. He had been in the ARVN as a rifleman, and when Saigon fell he quickly gathered his family and fled to the United States. His father, a doctor, stayed in South Vietnam with his grandmother who refused to leave.

What was so strange about meeting this man had to do with where we met, a quiet park in Naples, Florida. I was watching some children playing on the swings when I spotted this Oriental family nearby. Immediately I knew they were Vietnamese. I maneuvered my way to them and began a conversation. He was cordial, outgoing, talkative. He looked robust, a little too robust for a Vietnamese, but that was because of an American diet. His wife was a typical Vietnamese lady, remaining silent and watching the children.

Without my saying a word he knew I had been in Nam. We sat and talked and his three sons sat around us. Naturally the conversation got around to the war. But it wasn't the war itself, rather the open-ended results of it. I saw no bitterness in his eyes that the United States had pulled up stakes and left. And he saw none in mine that I'd had to fight in a war where I didn't belong.

As he was telling me a story about his times in Da Nang, I noticed his two older boys were hanging on every word he said. It was as though they were hearing for the first time about the war, about their homeland. They seemed so out of place in America, there in Naples, Florida, thousands of miles away from rice paddies, mountains and small villages. They would never experience those places.

At the end of our conversation he stood up and shook hands and said he would like to go out with me in the swamps. He had driven across Alligator Alley and to him it looked a little like the lowlands of Vietnam. I smiled, knowing how right he was. But he took me by surprise with a statement that hung on my mind for days after. As he walked towards his car, he said, "I'll tell you, Jeem, when we go back to South Vietnam, to my village to live, I never want my children to fight a war like we did." I was completly taken aback by that. Did he really expect to go back in his lifetime? He seemed confident that would happen. But how? I had no answer to that, and really didn't expect to get any. It was his dream of affinity. I had my own.

I called my mind back to the present, sighed with a smile, and moved farther into my territory.

As the days passed I continued plotting my territory, working feverishly, under Shakespeare's spell. But in the midst of my intensity was a certain calm center born of the assurance that I was becoming the cat. As I moved through the swamp seeking out the best spots for scat and urine heaps, making signpost after signpost, alpha to omega, I felt at home. I was in my territory.

Then I began to check, revisit, replot every post from alpha to omega. I checked to see if Shakespeare had torn mine up and reestablished his. So far he had not been to one of them, and it would soon be a month since I began this operation. Once I found tracks of a bobcat at Signpost Alpha. The bobcat had ventured in close, smelled the scat, and then probably in a burst of speed put his tail high in the air and dashed off before the owner of this territory could come close to him. But even the bobcat had not disturbed my plotting.

To say the least, it was disappointing. I began to wonder if I was doing it right or if I should be using that strategy at all.

How else could I plot my territory, I asked myself. I began picking up roadkill raccoons, opossums and rabbits. I placed their opened bodies in key places in my territory as kill sites, always dropping some of Tracker's scent on the dead animals. I placed them on logs, or half buried them under leaves and dirt near fallen logs. And still there were no signs of Shakespeare. Either he was being cautious or he just didn't care to play the game.

On the road I came onto a bobcat killed minutes before, threw him into a plastic bag and carried it to a chosen spot in my territory. There I spread his intestines out on the ground, took some of his blood and made a trail from an ambush site into the treeline. It was a male bobcat, so I sliced open his bladder and let what urine there was in it blow up into the sky. Then I piled two inches of soft dirt all around him and left. Three days later when I checked the site all I found were vulture tracks and the carcass drying in the sun. Most of the fur had been pulled off to expose red muscles. Not one panther track was anywhere within a hundred feet of it.

I talked a hunter into giving me steaks of a deer he had butchered and frozen the previous hunting season. At another kill site, I spread the venison out in chunks all over mud.

Surely Shakespeare would check that out. But he didn't. In fact, a few days later I found hawk claw marks in the mud and not one piece of the deer meat was left.

A queasy feeling came into my stomach. A thought I had rejected many times before refused to be dismissed. Was Shakespeare gone—forever? Had the law of averages caught up with him on one of the highways? Not now, when we were so close! I couldn't accept it.

To make sure, instead of plotting my territory, I struck out for a week of tracking Shakespeare once again, and as the lords of the swamp beheld, I found him far north, nowhere close to all of my signposts and kill sites. He was staying clear of me—of this female panther I had become. He wanted nothing to do with me. Was it a law of the swamp for males to stay away from females unless the female is in season crying for a mate? Was that possible? Maybe that was truly the key, as I had thought before. Get urine and scat from Tracker when she went into season again, plot it heavily all over the swamp, and cry for a mate.

I had waited this long. I could wait now until Tracker came into season again. And when she did I would seize the opportunity. Until then I would continue plotting my territory as the female panther I had become.

Every day in the swamp brought me nearer my own cat-being. I had begun to realize that my imitations of Tracker were coming from within. No longer was I imposing cat actions on myself. They were erupting from deep within me. I could be the cat because at some distant, distant time I had been the cat.

I felt I was just learning what Shakespeare had known all along.

69

Man-Cat Creature

Swamp notes—pantherhood
*When I come here now—my swamp, my
territory—I leave the man in the car. Here
I am the cat, nothing more—and nothing
less now. The Breath-maker sends wind and
I sniff it in through my long elegant cat
nose. I move over the earth and through
water on cat paws. My ears and eyes are
cat-sensors to this whirring, blurring world
where hunger guides me to my prey.*

Pale moon, pale stars, pale sky—all sat above tallow clouds
disappearing into black pigments well before dawn. I had
been deep in my territory for hours already. "*Nam Yo Fara
On* . . . I am a son of the swamp," I whispered. Slowly, patiently, I performed my glades ritual. Then I whispered, "I
am a panther. . . . I am a panther. . . . I am a panther. . . ."

I let myself go, opened my mind, body, and spirit to
my catness. Then I added a panther exercise I had observed
Tracker and the other cats at the ranch do quite often. It
always dropped me deep into the peaceful inner place where
wildness is born.

I placed my hands on the mud and pushed my midsection up until it formed an arch, my feet shoulder-width
apart, my arms and legs straight. Then I slowly dipped my
midsection straight down to the ground, pushing up with my
hands only, until my arms were straighter yet. At the same
time I stretched out my legs and back and reached up and
back with the back of my head as far as it would go, imagining
I could touch my heels with it. Every muscle in my body
stretched—this time more than ever before. It seemed at any
second they were going to tear off my body.

I did it again, and again, and once again. I felt a primeval fire smoldering somewhere deep inside me. I felt like I could tear trees up by their roots, but I also felt like a tree—tall, straight, grand, rooted. I continued on with this panther exercise, undulating, stretching, undulating and stretching in one continuous motion, more and more like a panther, flushing my body with rich, hot blood. I pushed my muscles beyond all limits, straining more and more, fascinated with myself as panther. Finally I collapsed on the mud and spread my cat-body out, whispering, "Now . . . now . . . I . . . am . . . a . . . panther."

A wave of knowledge swept over me. Everything took on new meaning. I pulled off my black hood and licked my paws, then rubbed them over my face until it was as clean and bright as my soul. I knew my eyes gleamed, reflecting the pale moon, its white fire now centered on me. I ripped off my black utilities, turned toward the full glow of the moonlight, and cried out in a long, piercing primeval scream that echoed through the swamp, its black water and blacker mud fluorescent beneath the silhouettes of trees.

Panther-squatting, I eased my face down into this creamy, rich muck, caressing it with this swamp bottom where medicinal elements dwell. I took whole handfuls, smearing it on my face, neck and hair, sculpturing deep, oozing creases with my fingers. In kisses of peace I smeared this sacred earth on my shoulders, chest and arms, coating my legs, pressing the slime deep into my skin, into my soul. The man disappeared. A black cat lurked in mud-shadows.

Then suddenly I was on my feet in a panther crouch, darting looks about, listening, smelling the wind. Then I was on the move toward Shakespeare's territory, swiftly prowling through the swamp, feeling every leaf, twig, cypress knee, jagged fallen branch, piece of bark, seedling, empty apple snail shell, vacant snake egg with my bare feet. Rising up on my toes, I leaned forward, stealing shadows from trees and bushes, stumps, fallen logs. I slipped into shallows, then leapt up onto high ground, feeling every vine, branch, leaf, flower flick across my chest and shoulders. I moved away from, toward, and under swamp avenues that never existed for me before.

I pushed myself on as dawn arrived in a rush over the swamp with a strange red glow that flushed the cypress like a huge meteor crashing to the earth. My body was red, then yellow, then red again.

This was Shakespeare's territory, near one of my signposts. Now I could smell the sign I'd left for his nose. But something else was familiar. Jagged rib bones stuck up from the ground like the fragmented hull of a rotted boat in tall grass in a clearing. To my right was a cypress head. To my left was Shakespeare's deer kill site, my first physical evidence of his presence. The dry brown blood that had flaked on the grass blades had long since been washed away by hundreds of rainstorms. Had it been so long? There were no vultures feasting. No black flies swarming. No more heavy carcass stench. The scavengers had had their day.

Approaching slowly, I ran my finger over the smooth, fragile bones that splintered at my touch and blew away in a breeze. Kneeling, I dug at the earth—like a panther, with my front paws—and found what was left of the skull. No antlers. Probably a hunter's souvenir by now.

This buck. That Buck. The first time I came on this kill site had been one of the first times I'd let the swamp take me back over the worst and let me clean my mind of its war-filth. This buck. That Buck. This buck had now reentered the earth, its cycle complete. That Buck, too, had gone his full measure in my mind to haunt me no more. Not that I'd forgotten. But I'd let go of all of it, shaken its hold on me. And when the hold had broken it had propelled me to the point where I now found myself. A cat in the dawn.

Deeper and deeper and deeper yet I prowled Shakespeare's world, repeating my glades ritual, "I am a panther. . . . I am a panther. . . . I am a panther. . . ."

A sky temple for the orange sun formed around it with cavernlike chambers in a smoke storm from a huge swamp fire. Yellow fire geysers shot up from the steaming forest floor, sighing as they were sucked back into hot cinders. Scorched saw palmetto roots lay exposed like masses of dead snakes. The strong smell of wood burning to white ashes singed my nostrils. Charred pine trees, their green needles turned to auburn in the rush of flames, stood naked. The fire itself had long since marched south like an army in pursuit of the enemy, destroying everything in sight.

I moved along the edge of this blackened oasis for dead things, using the thick smoky shadows as camouflage, letting them curl around me. My eyes watered and my lungs ached from the poison fumes as I prowled on, muffling coughs. Finally, with summer winds, the smoke began to thin. I stopped and curled up into a black ball, dissolving my human outline. I became a large black limestone chunk. Scanning with panther eye, I could see no movement. With God's own ears I could hear nothing out of place. But I waited anyway to see if Shakespeare would venture by for easy prey or test my panther sixth sense.

He didn't, so I meandered nearer the burn-out through a maze of vapor curtains, passing scorched cabbage palms and cremated turtles, their carapaces already looking like ancient pottery. The burned grass and immature pine cones crushed and crackled beneath my feet like brittle bones.

Then I stepped out of that dead world and again into brush vegetation. At the nearest pond I pushed my hot feet into the cool soft mud at its edge. I knew this place. It was a landmark for Signpost Omega. Checking, I found the scat had hardened and bleached out, but there were still no signs Shakespeare had visited it yet. I went back to the pond and slipped in up to my waist, lapping at it catlike, cooling my body inside and out from the fire walk that had left me all but dehydrated.

Revitalized, I moved back up to the edge and forward, knuckled fist to the ground, wrist rigid, knees working like paws. Letting mud muffle the sounds, I twisted through a beautiful Guzmania enclave. Each long razor leaf of the air plant sliced the sky with its green and dripped a single star tear from its point.

Entwining myself in fire flags, I smeared more mud all over my body, momentarily taking on the shape of a cypress stump hung over with a head of swamp ferns. I was roaming now as a panther should—prowling, in command of my space on earth, wild, free.

Before long I was on muddy high ground, and before

my eyes were tracks. Panther tracks. He was here. I dug at the tracks with my paws, smeared them on my body and face. As I began to move on I heard the single sound of a branch breaking under a heavy weight. I put my nose in the air searching for scent, slowly turning until it was at its strongest.

On that high ground among oaks and pepperheads, I scanned for the right tree. Not far away I saw an oak leaning almost to the ground, on the verge of snapping its buttress. I slid over to it and climbed as far up as I could, turning in the direction of sound and musky scent. Hiding behind the trunk, I looked across the pond, and on the other side saw three deer watering: a buck with full antlers and two does. While their bodies remained stiff, their necks and heads stooped just enough for their tongues to lap up water. The buck kept a wary eye open, and the does would dart their heads up at any sound, then back down to the water.

Quickly I slid down the tree. Here was my chance. I made a wide circle around the pond, making sure the wind was blowing over and behind me away from the deer.

I kept well into the trees, making my trail as far away as possible, yet slowly moving toward the deer. I could feel the tension suddenly take hold of me and wondered if Shakespeare felt the same way at those moments. Mustering all of my energy and patience, I moved slowly, peering with one eye around a bush, slipping forward on wet leaves under a blanket of vines, holding that position for more than five minutes, then crawling a few inches forward. Through a one-inch opening in leaves, as a breeze parted them, I saw the deer move away from the water. It didn't seem like they were getting ready to run, but as if they were merely finished drinking and looking for tender leaves to feed on. The buck was sticking close to the does, and all three out of habit looked around, always covering their rear.

I panther-footed closer, on my toes, brushing twigs aside with panther ease, closing the gap a little more, confident I could get to a good ambush site.

Now I was back down on my hands and knees pulling my knees up under my chest and lowering myself to my elbows and forearms. Inches turned into miles. I did not flex a muscle or eyelid unless I was absolutely sure I wouldn't make a sound.

I surveyed in front of me for debris, then moved a little farther. I gated my eyes and nose so I could hear. Then I gated my ears and probed with panther eye ahead, always keeping that fawn-gray fur in sight.

It was in the interval between moving closer and stopping that I found myself totally obsessed with but one thought. Ambush. Pick out the deer least prone to bolt first. Decide which one was a second slower or didn't look as healthy. Were ribs showing? Were there ticks on the back of one of the deer? Did one limp? All were considerations for a clean ambush and fresh meat.

I watched every movement the deer made. When they were busy snatching grass and leaves I crawled closer, stopping in mid-stride when they looked around, then moving a little closer yet. I knew I had to get within at least ten feet to make a good bound toward the destined prey. That would be the most critical moment of this man-cat ambush.

I was bursting with excitement at being able to stalk in as close as this without being detected by the deer. I was twenty-five yards to the west of them and so far the wind was playing the drama out with me. It had not changed direction, not even died for long minutes. I waited for swamp sounds, then moved a little closer.

Unaware I was even around, the deer moved closer to me in pursuit of more leaves. Twenty yards. Fifteen yards. Only forty-five feet away. I had a long way to go, but I was doing it with the ease of Shakespeare and the help of the swamp.

Crouching lower yet, and only able to see the deers' legs, the hooves sometimes stamping at the ground, I attempted to close the gap. Within fifteen minutes I had shortened it to about twenty feet, still without alerting the deer that a predator was near.

I studied the swamp around us and tried to calculate their next moves. Maybe, as before, they would move toward me. And that was exactly what one of the does did. Though watching the buck and other doe closely, she pranced a little to another small tree, and suddenly her scent was in my nose, her hide emitting that musk smell of a wild deer. Surely when Shakespeare smelled that he went wild with excitement. I sensed his mouth salivating, pushing his claws out, taking his hind paws and crowding them under his body, tensing for the great leap that would bring him onto his prey.

I moved my feet into position, raised my head up to about two feet off the ground, waited until the doe was busy pulling leaves off the tree . . . and then . . . with all the strength, energy, desire, commitment that were in me jammed into one all-important second, I leapt out of the swamp, up into the air toward the doe, screaming at the top of my lungs, landing on my feet inches away from her.

The doe was so shocked she didn't even bolt for a few seconds. I could easily have run up and put a rope around her neck. Then, with blurring stride, she dashed right past the other two who had already leapt for freedom and were melting into the trees.

I screamed again and again and began to laugh. I laughed loud and long, rolling on the ground until my sides ached. My cat patience and concentration converted into man-laughter, so pleased was I with myself.

Exhilarated and filled with renewed energy, I swept through the swamp toward my starting point. I ran on high ground, on an old trail, and seeing the pond near where I had left my clothes, I jumped through the trees and dove into hydrilla and water. I had never felt more alive, more important, more confident I was near something big, something right.

I washed myself clean of the mud, emerging from the pond upright, standing like a man. I could go no farther on that day, so I sprawled on leaves among popash, naked, totally exhausted, happy.

70

Night Tracking

Swamp notes—in dark shadows
*Like Shakespeare, I am a creature of the
night, swift, invisible. Like him I move with
the wind, pass through shadows that are
alive and breathing, taking in the full embrace of pantherhood.*

I darted from tree to tree, hot-footed, high-tailed, panther-
low, a shadow without scent, picking and choosing the darkest
shadows of moonshade. As lightning flashed from a coming
thunderstorm I froze in my position, checked the swamp,
decided on my next position and streaked to it when it was
dark. I sprinted to trees, under bushes, behind logs, moving
during the thunder as it trailed off down the coast like guttural
groans from a dying panther, drowning out my sounds. Sweat
stung my eyes, blurred my vision. The ungodly thick humidity
plastered my black utilities against my sweltering body.

With rapid leaping strides I hastened to high ground
where soft mud was created by a night rain already fallen,
oozed through it, then bolted to a huge oak shadow. I spied
a limestone rock, waited for the interval between lightning
and darkness, then shot to it, turning around, surveying, evaluating every movement.

Then I was on the move again, peeking over the edge
of a bush into misty shrouds of wet swamp overhang that
brushed my back and momentarily snagged my head, lodging
my shoulders in crooked vines, shaking insects onto my back
that competed with thick layers of mosquitoes already covering me. An aerial whirlpool of gnats hovered above my head.
The black water close by looked like thick granite slabs. Above,
a leaden flush from the nightly cypress glow eclipsed dark
images in pulsing leaf shadows that melted into a strange light

that reminded me of fading aerial illumination rounds over a free-fire zone in Vietnam. Through the arching branch ribs of the trees the winged silhouette of a night heron rode the sky under rotating star clusters inlaid with astral ether, space wind and black voids.

I looked off into the trees. I had never seen the swamp look more beautiful under that night shroud with moon glow and flashing lightning. I adjusted my breathing to the night sounds around me, holding my breath at every sudden silence, breathing low, long and steady during the noisy times. In watery obbligatos, barking frogs searched for cover at my presence. Cone-shaped grasshoppers, twig girdlers, weevils and click beetles chirped, squeaked, snapped and ticked. Bass bumped hydrilla with their stiff tails and slurped on the water's surface for fallen insects. There was a searching series of hoots from a great horned owl, a screaming wail from a limpkin, gators honking, warm breezes slipping willow leaves across bark.

Among these silent cries I pushed off that soft mud and started to cross a seemingly endless branch of water. The night smell of that water was an aquatic aroma composed of over-heated, ripe, steamy vegetation now drenched with fog and humidity. It filled my head, tempered by a hot breeze that left skeeters feasting on my eyelids.

The night swamp was a completely different world from daylight glades. I had to learn all over again Shakespeare's territory and it took me weeks to do that and another month to be able to enter water like this where gators fed and water moccasins roamed searching for frogs and rats. But after I learned to be at ease in the water I could cut across long stretches of swamp and be that much closer to his tracks.

Now, like Shakespeare, I cat-kicked just below the surface, never once letting my hands or feet break or splash the water. I moved with my chin just above the water level, spitting out mosquitoes and vegetation. When my hands clawed into a hydrilla bed, I slowly maneuvered up on top, keeping plenty of air in my lungs all the time, and liquidlike, pulled across the floating exotica like a snake, submerging in open pockets, then doing it all over again.

At loud splashes of gator tails I tensed and stopped and

treaded water until the danger had passed. I kept close to the banks, giving myself about twenty feet of swimming room to get out—but I had never had to resort to that. Not until this one particular night.

It had always been my objective to move as silently in the water as on high ground, like Shakespeare. I knew splashing would attract gators anyway, so I tried to slip through the water like a fish, under the surface. I perfected that skill in night tracking maybe too well.

On this night, on the other side of a hydrilla patch, I found myself hitting the broad side of a log. It was a log that suddenly moved with clawed hands and a sweeping powerful tail that raised up in the air off the surface of the water, slapped down and propelled a huge, scaly body down into the black water. So surprised were both the gator and I that we turned in opposite directions and made for safety. Terror of getting pulled down from behind by the jaws of that gator clamping on one of my legs caused me to move like an otter. All I could see was this gator jerking and twisting in the water and pulling me under to drown me. That one thought put me up on the bank in seconds.

I had never moved to high ground so quickly, so efficiently as at that moment. And when I looked back I saw the dark outline of the gator cruising in the moonlight among hydrilla, in total command of his element, and I wondered if I had scared him at all, or whether he thought I was just another gator competing for a fish.

Gaining my panther composure once again, I quickly moved to the side of a trail and into the trees. As I moved through this black world it reminded me of a legend in Vietnam that made the rounds through Da Nang and Chu Lai in 1966, a legend about a recon marine they called the Prince of Darkness. He moved only at night and never saw the light of day, or so the legend went. He had completely adapted his eyes to nocturnal vision and could easily low-crawl up to VC camps, count the enemy, and ease back into his perimeter without once being detected. In 1973, Stateside, in college, and years after I had left Nam, I talked to other vets who just got back. I told them about the Prince of Darkness, half joking.

But with serious eyes they told me he was still there in Da Nang operating in the Central Highlands, alone as always.

Sometimes I wonder what I would have developed into in the Marines if I had gone to Vietnam knowing what I know now. Maybe I would have volunteered for night patrols like that. More likely I would not have gone at all, for I could no longer apply my skills for killing.

But now I was a man-cat creature to do *good* things, swiftly creeping through a cat creature's territory, seeing, hearing, smelling his world, feeling the intensity of the midnight glades, night tracking. By day I knew Shakespeare's territory like I knew my own soul. Now, night tracking, I could move through a full moon, pad among dark holes just like Shakespeare, live in a world of shadows and be accepted there to seek the unknown in the unknown. With night tracking I was making a long and lasting stride toward Shakespeare. He was nocturnal, a night feeder, a night tracker. So, to experience every side of his life, I would be nocturnal as well. At first that was my only reason for doing it. But after blending my spirit with the night, I found that night tracking was also the challenge of learning all over again why I was in the glades tracking Shakespeare in the first place. I would stop at nothing to learn something more about panthers. I would risk everything to do it. I would challenge the challenge itself. And in every way I would succeed. I kept reaching out and grabbing for Shakespeare's spirit. But he was always a step ahead of me wondering if I would come on. When I did, he would move on himself into another phase to put me through. In order for me to attain affinity, I needed to know what it was like for Shakespeare in his swamp at night, so I followed him.

I also found out that though I had to develop my senses in a different way for night tracking, it was still the mysterious sixth sense that would take over most of the time. Shakespeare, with his sixth sense, was the conquering master at detecting my presence, and after studying Tracker all that time, I realized that for me to outsmart any cat, especially Shakespeare, with this soul-deep quality, I had to develop it far more than I already had. It was a composite of all my senses, plus an extra something that made me more aware of more than I would have been aware of without it. It worked in daytracking, and I knew it would prove itself at night. I relied on it more and more. It was one of the keys to night tracking. It was also a means of attaining more invisibility.

My black attire and mud smeared over my face and hood blotting out all color (even though Shakespeare was color-blind) gave me the advantage of a dull-black secrecy that absorbed light and reflected nothing, which meant I was able to become a one-dimensional object with no clear outline. Distortion became an ordeal in itself. In a hiding place I twisted and stretched myself to become that place—tree, bush, or shack wrecked by time. It was my quest then, night tracking, to obliterate all my human sound, movement, even my shadow until I was . . . invisible.

Scanning this swarthy wild chasm with trained off-center vision, I looked for moving silhouettes at ground level. In Nam on night perimeter guard, I'd sit and stare out through the night, suspicious of anything that moved, changed shape, even though the shape might in the morning prove to be nothing more than a bush in the wind. After being in this swamp for more than two hours, my eyes had already adjusted to extremely low level light, so it was easy to observe an object off-center by looking slightly to the sides of it, pausing above and below it, distinguishing its shape in relation to where it was standing among other shapes. But this was good for only fifteen seconds. After that fading occurred and the object dissolved into altered images and was lost. I had to keep shifting my eyes to continue to see and believe what I saw.

Once in a while I saw floating amber dots, radiant shining rubies, beguiling pearls, and blinking ivory globes appearing in the blackness, winking out, hovering, winking in, disappearing, then floating once again. Some were spider eyes. Others lightning bugs. Still others snake and mammal eyes.

At each flash of those jewels in the night, I remembered VC night sniper rounds erupting in the treeline outside our perimeter. I could still feel the rush of wind past my face from an incoming bullet as I huddled in my foxhole, and hear the crack of a rifle or pistol at close range, then bare feet running off in the sand to another position, followed by the heavy slam of M-14 rifle bolts going home and then the staccato chatter of fire power that was so thick nothing could escape.

I wondered how many times the whites of my own eyes were reflected in the swamp, what they looked like and what other eyes saw them. How was I to camouflage them? All I could do was close them momentarily during lightning flashes, or when the moon would peek out between clouds, to block off the reflection at least for seconds.

Where trees danced in the dull flashes I saw their trunks form crouched thin men with no heads, a large raven, and a Buddhist monk bent over in prayer. I could almost hear the reverent petition murmured into the call of the yellow-crowned night heron. "Om . . . Om . . . Om . . ."

I worked my way through the low overhangs snagging myself on newly formed root buds, getting my feet entangled just when I thought I was free, sinking down into freshly decayed leaves and pulling up the earth's excretion with my hands, attempting to prevent that echoing, sucking sound, doing so, then starting all over again.

As I advanced slightly, I came onto what I thought was high ground. I drew my legs up under me, conformed my black silhouette to look like an arched tree by squatting and curving my back over my knees and putting my head between them. I began to practice shallow breathing, peering over my knees to detect movement. I glimpsed a small bobcat slipping into a shadow.

Suddenly my feet began to sink and I could feel the weight under me start to give way slowly. Was I dreaming? Or was the swamp floor starting to disappear? What was happening?

Before I realized it I was waist deep in rapidly expanding and sucking quickmud, a dread of the swamp I had never before come onto in all my tracking. It was like huge hands grabbing at my waist with a power I could not combat, pulling me down into mud which was already up to my chest. I stretched out desperately and grabbed a branch, trying to pull myself free, but I only sank farther down in the mud. The branch stretched and I could hear it start to crack.

"God, help me," I murmured. "Please."

Suddenly the mud sank down off my body and an unnatural sigh came up around me as the mud sifted downward into a gaping pit below me that looked like the mouth of a giant beast. I held tight to the branch and pulled myself up and out, then stared down into what was left of the swamp floor.

Quickmud. A natural element in the swamp that had built up inside a limestone hole for maybe centuries. Rain water, swamp debris, maybe even dead animals had filled it in. Little by little the weight built up to an unbearable degree beneath that thin crust on top. If a raccoon or rat—or panther—had happened to walk through it and caused it to give away, the animal would be sucked down under the mud now, at peace in his swamp grave. Only a creature with upright stance and hands to grasp could have survived; that is, only a human. I was momentarily glad I was still a man-cat, not yet a full cat.

I thought about that for a time as I stared into the blackness of the hole. If Shakespeare had roamed over it he would probably be lost forever down in that bottomless grave. I had done both him and myself a favor by sinking it, even if only by accident.

I wondered if Shakespeare had heard the commotion and run off to the other end of his territory. I even seriously contemplated aborting that night and coming back later in the week. But I felt time was on my side. So, with cultivated perseverance, diligence and determination, I went on. Fifty feet more and I hit even higher ground. As I crept I could feel the cypress knees bend under the balls of my feet.

Farther on, the ground was heavily woven over with swamp debris. Saw palmetto bushes, with their daggerlike leaves, sat on the edges like so many assigned protectors. If I got through them I was in good swamp. If I was pricked, my blood would be left on the tips as scent signs for Shakespeare. With the ease of the lightest of breezes I crouched alongside the swamp swords, let my arms hang at my sides with my elbows out like receptors, and brushed up against each plant. With most of the spines pointing upward, I easily deflected the stiff spikes, brushed past them and finally moved out of them.

I could then see what appeared to be a familiar passageway that wound itself into blackness. Hunched sturdy wax myrtle bushes thickened the vegetation. It reminded me of paths and trails on the outskirts of the villages near Tuy Hoa close to the rice paddies. I remembered walking down them on patrol just before sundown, all nerves. The paths were perfect places for bushline trip wires, grenades and pungi traps, and even worse, they were custom-made for VC ambushes. Marine squads and whole platoons were ambushed and annihilated in seconds on trails like those, their bodies mutilated and left for the morning patrols to find baked in the tropical sun, their fatal wounds infested with flies.

But when I started down this glades passageway, the happiness and joy of each step brought tears to my eyes. I could have closed my eyes and walked it backwards if I chose, made all the noise I wanted, and still be certain there was no Charlie up ahead in the bushes with a crossfire ambush set up. I could scream at the top of my lungs and there would be no contact, no nerve-shattering ear-deafening clatter of rifle fire. Here was serenity. I was as safe here as I was at home in bed.

But I kept my joy behind my smile and shrank even further into my silhouette. I began to move sideways along the side of the trail just inches away from the foliage, not down the middle, just as I had learned to do in Nam. Crouching, I pointed my front foot in the direction I wanted to go, stabilized my position by flaring my back foot, and began crossing each foot over the other. With my palms down and facing backwards, I was able to feel the bushes when I got too close to them. I was moving like a side-winder snake and a cat at the same time.

I had learned that like this I could cover a lot of territory undetected by even the day-feeding wading birds sleeping in the trees. I came onto a tree loaded with about twenty white ibis resting on the higher branches. I sidewound through the leaves below them which were white-washed by their excrement, coming very close to one ibis on a lower branch. He was resting with his head almost buried in the feathers of his back, one eye peeking over his wing. What would he have done if I had reached out and grabbed him by the feet? He didn't even know I was there, and I saw how easy it was for Shakespeare to sneak up and snatch one.

Out of curiosity I inched up a feather's distance from him and looked right into the eye that was showing. Still he didn't move. Either he didn't see me or he was playing that game of utter stillness, gambling that whatever was standing next to him might not see him. I almost laughed, but eased away and continued down the trail.

As I did so what walked out in front of me far down the trail both stunned my senses and my body and sent my mind reeling. A queer shivering went up my spine. A low, black, long-tailed cat silhouette with its head facing me crossed into the trees. I dropped to my knees and curved my back. There was that buzzing sound in my ears, the intense exhilaration of my entire body flushing and sweating freely. Though I wanted to get up and race toward the spot, I stayed low, and with my panther feet, ears and eyes, I moved slowly at first, then a little faster along the trail, keeping to the bush shadows.

"Shakespeare, Shakespeare, Shakespeare," I whispered. This was it. . . . This was it. . . .

I wasn't sure what was going to happen, but with so much sudden excitement and with Shakespeare so near I felt sure something was in the making. But when I got to the spot, staying down, looking about, whistling catlike to draw him to me, I couldn't detect the slightest flick of a leaf. So, like Shakespeare, I swiftly eased into the treeline, using the still flickering lightning to flash out scenes in low level water and islands. No panther.

I knew there was no hard reason to believe anything had walked past there. It could have been another apparition. Had I pushed my senses beyond the point of exhaustion so they were again playing tricks on me? It was a real, clear-cut affinity I wanted. Not one that could be a figment of the night shadows. Not one that would melt off in my mind like so much slough algae in sunlight. No, I wanted it to last forever. I didn't know how I would feel when my affinity occurred, but I knew this event wasn't it.

I knew night tracking had drawn me closer to Shakespeare, but I decided to get back to daylight tracking and pursue affinity. Then when I saw Shakespeare again it would be as real as Tracker standing next to me. A real panther living and breathing.

71

Affinity

> **Swamp notes—under an owl**
> *I am now tied to Shakespeare just as water is to a river. We are blood of blood. My blood and his blood run from the Greatest River of All. This is why I know I will attain affinity. I will do it with his blood in my veins.*

On this glades morning two slow-motion American egrets shared a freshwater seance among willows with an alligator, three cooter turtles on a log, and a banded water snake. At the egrets' feet the mud looked like chunks of chocolate crystals. A kingfisher streaked across the water, its harsh high-pitched rattle piercing the early calm.

On this day the sun filtered through peculiar cloud overhangs that rushed past like herds of white deer, their dusty trails forming tiny valleys bordered by serrated highlands. I scanned this swamp horizon, the sky above it now a reverberating belt of glistening aqua jasper that trailed off into a blurred emerald haze mixed with topaz crystals that prismed drowning sunlight.

As long as I could keep coming out to this untamed swamp that stands in defiance of civilization, I would see new wonders and learn more of its existence, understand more of its meaning, but never all of it. As long as the swamp remains bewildering, perplexing, a mysterious labyrinth of azure trailways, connecting, non-connecting, between and through dense tropical hardwood hammocks, and long crooked cypress heads reaching out in a sprawling, seemingly endless maze, it will be one of man's links to survival. Shakespeare had taught me that over and over.

On this day I was to embark upon the most important moment of my entire tracking experience with Shakespeare. I could almost reach out into the swamp then and there and touch Shakespeare. It was that close. Spiritually, I had been doing just that for weeks. I had been out in the swamp most of the time, day tracking and night tracking. Whenever I was not in the swamp, my mind was there centered on my goal. And I was praying that all my research would bring me to that final moment of accomplishment.

Physically, I pushed myself relentlessly, doing more and more panther stretches, running the swamp trails, adding more weight to my pack and straining to gain more wind and endurance.

But on this day I carried with me the most important gift ever given to me. Tracker had gone into season. The second I pulled into the ranch that distinct rasping cry of a female panther in season played across my ears with swamp intonations that stirred in me as much excitement and anticipation as I knew it would in Shakespeare. Rushing to Tracker's cage and going inside, kneeling next to her, I watched her raise her head, open her mouth in a smiling attitude and cry out again and again for a mate. I burst out with laughter that brought tears. I knew that all I had done as a human being to lure Shakespeare was insignificant compared to the natural powers of attraction of this lady here in front of me, twitching her tail and crying out for what she had yet to experience.

I waited. I stood vigil. And as Tracker urinated and defecated, I gathered it all onto cotton balls and into plastic bags, trying to make sure I would have enough to replot my territory with in-season scent. It seemed to me Tracker knew what I was doing. When I would dab at her urine pools, she would walk over, sniff it, then rub her muzzle against mine. When she defecated, I would rush to the spot and roll it into the plastic bag, reach out and pat her on the head. She would turn and look at me with a contented expression and usually lick my arm. During the time she was in season, I collected specimens and froze them, desperately hoping I would have enough when her cycle had run its course.

Now back out in the swamp, I opened one of those precious bags and poured and spread its contents over me until the swamp air was filled with a scent that would surely lure Shakespeare. Standing there in my territory, I soaked my black utilities with her urine, slipped into my scuba boots and pulled on my black hood. Playing the odds, I eased into a spot where I had found hot tracks a day before, knelt and did my glades ritual, then took my first step inward. I was now a female panther in season on the prowl for a mate.

I had also recorded Tracker's in-season cry and tied a portable tape recorder to my side intending to turn it on once I was plotting. But the clicking and snapping turned out to sound so startlingly unnatural in the swamp that I had begun to listen to Tracker's cry, trying to imitate the tones, wails, raspings, all blended into one echoing song. Eventually, I got it to where it was beginning to sound like her, or as close to it as a human could get.

Signpost Alpha had now become a swamp monument to Shakespeare. It had been plotted, plotted again, then re-plotted with scat, urine heaps and kills. Several times it had been disturbed by raccoons and a bobcat, and I also believed a human being once. But now it was to become the final plea to Shakespeare, a distinct connection, the scent marking that would draw my liberty to his. I chose to use a urine heap this time, carefully stretching out and dipping into the soft smelly earth and piling up debris. Then I took the cotton ball and squeezed fresh-thawed urine onto the dry parts and let it soak into the heap. I could smell that thick musky scent come up and lose itself in a breeze. I sucked the scent in through my nostrils and blew it back out again into the breeze and whispered, "Go."

Then I padded to Signpost Beta and rolled fresh scat out onto the swamp floor. The scent was much stronger and I figured it would be the first one to draw Shakespeare in.

For three long fantastic days I roamed about my territory, slipping by deer and birds, into sloughs of gators and up on high ground where swamp rats scurried about. I dropped to my belly at strange sounds, straining to hear paws padding, looking with panther eye to detect that brown fur, a long tail in the bushline. Each time I went to a new signpost I checked the ones before it. Each time I replotted my scent just to make sure. Then one morning I dipped my hand into my pack and there were no more urine cotton balls or plastic bags full of scat. I had used up my supply. But my territory was completely marked.

Now I waited and it began to dawn on me that this was it. Everything was riding on this time around. Tracker was well out of season now, and I didn't know when she would cry again, when she would drop that musky urine for me again. I began to worry. What if Shakespeare drew away completely from these plottings as he had done before, practicing his avoidance strategy? But if he were a healthy, red-blooded Everglades panther, the second he caught that scent he would be on it. But what if he didn't? What if . . . what if . . . what if? The what-ifs were bugging me more then than at any time in all of my tracking. So I decided to do something about it.

I started wandering about my scent markings crying for a mate. At long intervals I would sit in a tree wailing, rasping, crying, lying in shadows and scanning for him as I cried more. After a while I grew hoarse and my throat felt like raw meat. But I discovered that my raw throat made me sound more like an in-season female panther. It gave me the gift of the cry of the panther. It had to be the air passing over a rougher throat that did it. I pushed it harder and harder until I lost my voice completely. Then I began my worrying again. So I went back to the method of the tape recorder and wrapped a black towel around it when I had to click it back to the beginning, wrapping my body around it as well, to muffle the click sound as much as I could.

I constructed make-shift blinds in oak trees, went back to the pond and nighthawked, eased through cypress to get to the far side of some of my plotting and sat in ambush.

I knew that the second I put my scent out it began to fade. I prayed it would not rain. I worried that a burn-out would sweep through my territory and destroy it all. I worried and prayed about more things then than I ever had in Vietnam.

And that was my biggest problem. I wasn't being wholly positive. I was thinking negatively. I was thinking more about what might go wrong than about what I should have been doing to make things right. A positive way of thinking had been the basic ingredient that had seen me through all of the worst times, both in tracking Shakespeare and in Vietnam. It was that gut-proven edge that could make the difference. If ever there was a time to be positive, it was now.

So I switched my whole way of thinking around. Every movement, every sound I made was interlaced with positive thought. "Do it to win," I told myself. "Do it for Shakespeare."

When my voice came back I started crying again and promptly lost it within two days. Back to the recorder.

After more days and nights of failure, and with the scents growing fainter, I finally faced up to an idea that had been at the back of my mind all along. I knew I was good at ultimate concealment and could slip and slide through the swamp undetected by man and most of the animals with relative ease. I had, on rare occasions, even come close to outsmarting Shakespeare. But I finally faced up to the fact that even though I had attained pantherhood, very possibly I should just sit it out in camouflage at the strongest signpost. Be the ultimate ambusher. Be a panther in season at an ambush site. Be passive. Avoid the urge to be doing something. Tap my cat-patience. Let Shakespeare come to me.

My choice of an ambush site had to be a place undisturbed, in its natural state. At the criss-cross of where my territory intersected his was the place. Signpost Omega.

When I got to Omega there didn't seem to be anything obvious I could use. But just off the ditch, on high ground level with the trail's embankment, was an old oak tree that had been uprooted and knocked down by a storm. The roots stuck up and out like a monster squid. Leaves had already fallen on the dirt, and armadillos and raccoons had dug up the scurrying insects and worms. It was a nice cool place for a rattler to crawl up onto or under the dry leaves during the hot part of the day. So I checked every inch and came up with a little population of poisonous scorpions. I picked out each one and sent it on its way to better sleeping quarters, then began to experiment with the best possible way of concealing myself as close to the trail as possible and still be unseen by Shakespeare. I lay stomach-down on the leaves and dirt and wiggled my way below the leafline. I threw the leaves over me until I was completely covered by them and until my head was covered with dirt, only my eyes visible. Then I dug my hands into the soft dirt until the outline of my arms disappeared. By being totally still I became part of the swamp floor. And while I lay there smelling the fresh dirt, some of the baby scorpions came back and crawled over my head and into the leaves. I rationalized that they were better companions than a five-foot rattlesnake.

I forgot about time, everything around me, and what I had to do to push on to Shakespeare. I just let happen what was going to happen. Was I wrong to sit still now after spending years developing my skills to move about the swamp as a panther? No, I would have never known Shakespeare's swamp or his every habit had I not put myself in his place. Had I never become a panther I would not have been at that moment at that place where I knew our paths were destined to cross.

For a long time I lay there, more comfortable than if I had been home in bed. Maybe it was being that close to earth, feeling it, smelling its fragrance, seeing insects crawl about, listening to the leaves crackle underneath the scorpions. I felt drawn into the earth, more a part of it than ever. I had become a son of the swamp. I made a mental note to pursue that idea as soon as I completed this.

Before long my mind began to wander from subject to subject. Keeping my eyes and ears open to the swamp, I let my mind rove over friends' faces, my family, crowds. Then I reviewed on the most detailed level Shakespeare's territory, my plotting, all the experiences I had had with him. Maybe it was enough already. Even then, I could have stood up, walked out of the swamp, clocked out of the wilderness business, and would always have known I had done something in my life no one else could put a claim to.

But I didn't. Rubbing my chin on the dirt to free it from

a crawling scorpion, I just stared out at the trail. Shakespeare's going to walk down there, I said to myself. I know he's going to walk right down there . . . soon.

My mind kept wandering, moving in and out of experiences. What was so peculiar was that I wasn't plunged into a Nam flashback Though those livid horrors would be in me for as long as I lived, I had found that by facing them squarely while out in the wilds, they seemed to have found their rightful place in my mind now. They were staying put on their memory shelves instead of jumping off to grab my whole attention whenever they could cause the most trouble. Those days were over.

Another scorpion on my chin brought me back to my present situation. I brushed it off and waited. Nothing happened on that day. So before full dusk I checked some of the other signposts for evidence. A heap had been stirred up, and an old kill I had dropped urine on had been dragged out from a bushline. But nothing definite to indicate that Shakespeare was close. And yet, all the time I knew he was there.

That night I had a crazy dream of being able to track Shakespeare visually, close enough so that I was actually seeing him make kills, walk his territory during the rainy season, come on to a female in season, copulate. Then I watched the cubs being born. It was a crazy dream all right. No human being would ever be able to do that with his own eyes. So the mystery of the panther would never be fully penetrated, no matter if we did gain my goal of momentary—yet eternal—affinity. For some reason I liked that idea.

I kept returning to the site, kept digging in, keeping vigil on the trail. After three days I worried that Signpost Omega had lost its scent completely. And yet I could feel Shakespeare's presence, almost as though if I jerked around and looked into the swamp his eyes would center on mine. So why didn't he boldly walk down this trail he used so often? Why didn't he destroy Omega and replot his own signpost?

I strongly suspected now that he not only knew I was in his territory, but maybe was, in fact, watching my every move. Had I been naive to believe I could outsmart him in the final moments? There was one way to find out. For another three days I furiously tracked him until I came onto fresh tracks at the north end of his territory. Whan I saw the first one I was so excited I almost grabbed the mud and ate it. But instead I beat a path back to my car and raced six miles south to where I could go in the back way through two small sloughs lined with cypress and then crawl to my hiding place near Signpost Omega. The odds were that if he stayed in that direction that day, heading south and keeping his pace, he would walk right past me not more than ten feet away.

Once in the dirt and under the leaves, my mind settled, I began to meditate, praying it was going to happen. I had calculated everything down to the last detail. He had to walk down that trail.

But he didn't. More dejected that ever, I rose from my hiding place, brushed off the dirt and leaves and clambered up onto the trail and over to the signpost. With a swift kick I demolished the entire marking. Then I stomped my foot down on it and twisted it back and forth.

Maybe that was what it was all about. It would just be an ongoing tracking project for as long as I lived. I would find tracks, scat, and on extremely rare occasions maybe even by accident I would get a glimpse of that magnificent panther. Maybe that was the affinity I was reaching for—a neverending pursuit with no conclusion. Maybe I was missing the whole point of what Shakespeare, either by accident or design, was telling me.

More troublesome than ever to me was the fact that I really had no idea what affinity meant to me on the physical level. What did I expect Shakespeare to do—walk up and put his paws around my neck and give me the biggest, sloppiest kiss a panther could give a human being? And then take his massive paw and pat my head and say, "Jim, you did a great job tracking me. Here's a medal for your trouble"? Even then when I was feeling so discouraged, that was such a comical thought that I turned around and began to laugh.

I pulled off my hood and stuffed it in my pocket, went to the water's edge, got a drink, washed the mosquitoes off my face and lay back on the trail staring up into the blazing sun. At that moment I knew I truly loved the Everglades, Shakespeare, Tracker, all wildlife. I would do my part to help protect what is left of it to my dying day, and all that I have learned I would use to that end.

"God, thank you for all of it," I said, then got up and started down the trail and over to the slough.

But I had walked no more than ten feet when the hair on my arms stood up. I got this familiar feeling in my stomach, and I was immediately sure someone else was there in the swamp with me. I never broke stride, never let on I suspected. But casually, I looked out in front of me and to each side. I bent over and picked up a small stick and threw it in the water and turned around and looked back up the trail. I froze in stride. My heart suddenly drummed, then started pounding against my chest.

There in front of me, frozen in stride himself, was the panther Shakespeare.

I squeezed my eyes and looked again. He was still there standing in the sunlight staring right back at me a little more than fifty feet away close to Signpost Omega. It was no apparition. No ghost. He was flesh and blood, solid muscle poised in the noonlight. He was as real as I was standing there in that intense heat of the swamp under a wild sun. I was in two worlds. One had swamp sounds and sweat; in the other I was engulfed in a moment of my personal history that would change my whole life.

Shakespeare held his head high and a little cocked to the side. He was much bigger than Tracker—at least eight feet long, including his tail, and no less than a hundred and fifty pounds. No ribs showed. A healthy panther. His coloring, in the sun, was a light brown, blending in with that fawn gray trailing across his back almost to the base of his tail. The creamy white of his underside almost glowed. His paws were huge and I could imagine them stuffing into the mud as he roamed.

Both ears were aimed at me. Even though a bird chirped, a turtle plopped into the water, he didn't glance away and he never flicked an ear. He was gating. I was the most important thing in his life right then. I was gating, too, keeping my eyes riveted on him.

Our eyes locked. And as they did, something unlocked.

The gates spun wide open. Our long journey had come to an end . . . or a new beginning.

Behind him the sunlight slashed through the trees brighter than any phosphorus flare or fire-rush or napalm drop. It was as if the sun had moved closer to this favored spot on earth.

The more I looked into those eyes, the more I wanted to be engulfed by them. The yellow irises glowed and danced like the sun above. The deep green pupils weren't pupils at all. They were pulsing lights of liberty. There was no bitterness, no hatred of mankind in them. Only that pure wild glint that pierced through to my soul. I welcomed it, wanted it, and realized that I had been craving it for a long time. He burned into my soul an infinite commitment to fight to save his home. He was a mysterious messenger, but his message was absolutely clear.

I was in his world completely, and I never wanted to leave. I was experiencing an intenseness in my life I had never felt before. There was divinity here in realistic forms of wilderness, panther and man. Small explosions of realization were missiling back and forth between us, the spiritual meeting the material, the material dissolving into the spiritual. I felt an overwhelming sense of God right next to me, around, in me. There was joy and happiness, but I wanted to die—because, I guess, I knew even then that the rest of my life could not measure up to this moment.

I wanted to reach out and run to Shakespeare, to embrace him and feel that panther power wrap around my soul. But that would have violated what I had already learned as the only way to save these cats. Protect their territory and leave them alone to procreate their own species.

But without realizing it, I had stepped toward Shakespeare and broken the trance. He stepped back, looked at me strangely, and as fluid as the air itself, turned and bounded off into the high grass until he disappeared into the trees.

I ran after him, harder, faster, and longer than I had ever run in my life, until I could run no more. I didn't want the moment to end. I wanted it to go on forever. But it was Shakespeare who had come to me, had brought on this moment, this affinity, and it was Shakespeare who then called it off, let it go, let it be.

I lay there panting, gulping for air, thinking how naive I had been all the time I was tracking Shakespeare trying to forge ahead to a destined final meeting of affinity. His message was as clear as the water I lay next to. Life itself is an affinity if we only choose to accept it. Wilderness is how it is. It took the swamp and Shakespeare to get me to see it.

EPILOGUE

On that day I left the swamp. But I went back and I started tracking and counting other panthers in other places in the Everglades. I found five, seven, eleven, fifteen, eighteen, twenty-one, twenty-four. I conducted a feasibility study outside the Everglades and found forty-one different sites where a panther could survive, or was there to begin with.

My work became known, and I was contracted by conservation organizations to track and find panthers in critical habitats in Florida. And when I did so the reaction was vehement, because more often than not these critical habitats for the panther and other endangered species were already on the drawing boards of developers eager to expand their private profits at the expense of wildlife, and thus at the expense of the common good.

The biggest reaction came when the Ford Motor Company decided to build a car test track right in the middle of panther territory in Collier County. I had found one panther with territory in the midst of their site and had reason to believe that there was a mother with at least one cub in the same area. And the Florida Game and Freshwater Fish Commission had already verified yet another panther in the region.

Though to date there have been many concessions on both sides, the fact still remains that Ford is going to put the test track in the same site where these panthers live. Ford is still disregarding state and federal endangered species laws.

These people have yet to realize how important wilderness is, have yet to meet their own wilderness affinities. Ford Motor Company has an opportunity to become an example of how large companies can decide to help save a species on the verge of extinction. I hereby invite the president and chairman of the board of Ford Motor Company to come out tracking with me in the glades.

After that meeting with Shakespeare I went back periodically to his territory to monitor his movements and make sure he was okay, that he was still with me in my commitment. At times I could find no sign of him for weeks. Then, out of nowhere, he would leave something to let me know he was there and safe. The very fact he continued on with his mysterious elusive behavior gave me a positive attitude he would be okay.

Then, out of the swamp, in town, at gas stations, I began to hear more and more stories about the panthers in the swamps. Some people still believed none were left, and I never denied that notion when it came up. During the tourist season I was called time and again by photographers who wanted me to guide them into the swamp to get the last picture of a panther. I always refused, though it would have been harmless enough and the odds were quite against the possibility of sighting one anyway. I still protected my right to Shakespeare or any other panther I had found.

But then the stories began to take a different turn, as though the swamp had begun to breed an evil element. One tale was about hunters in full camouflaged utilities and jeeps lining up at one end of a cypress strand and walking the length of it to flush out a panther and gun him down. These individuals, if they were real to begin with, carried smoke bombs and M-16 rifles. What was even more appalling about the story was that they were reported doing this right in the middle of state and federal government parks and preserves. I roamed the back roads and alerted the dispatcher in West Palm Beach for the wildlife officers to be on guard, but I never came onto any such people.

I heard authentic stories about a percentage of the population living near the Everglades who were much more concerned about deer than panthers. In fact they believed the panther were destroying the deer population, which of course is not true since a predator and his prey must remain in nature's balance. But these people were often heard muttering, "If I see a panther, I'll shoot that son of a bitch." These were glades people who were born and raised in the swamps and who had always relied on the deer population for food and income, whether it was deer season or not. Poaching had been a way of life for a long time, and if it meant money and soup on the table, very little was going to stop them from bagging a panther pelt.

I heard a wild swamp tale that kept me roaming the glades constantly for more than three weeks, both day and night. It seems there was this highly skilled professional big game hunter who was under contract to hunt down the Florida panther with a scope and starlight scope at night in critical areas where there was a strong possibility of commercial development. Secretly he would kill a panther and bury it well out of sight—all except the tail. The tail was to be evidence for him to produce a fat check from his client.

It was hard to believe this sort of thing could go on, but when I thought about it, it did make a lot of sense for this character to exist and be out there efficiently going about his job. Why should any huge multimillion-dollar development that would breed more millions of dollars be bogged down in court battles and conservation fights and bad publicity when all they had to do was make the problem disappear and nobody would be the wiser? An endangered species protected by state and federal laws was a big stumbling block creating unnecessary difficulties and draining the budget. With a game hunter who knew his stuff all that could be avoided. I was praying I would come onto this idiot so I could have him arrested and drag his client into court for the media to have a field day on both of them. But as time went on, and no evidence came up, I began to believe less and less in the tale, yet it lingers.

On an August afternoon I went to a place in Shakespeare's territory where he had spent a lot of time. There were kills made there, even a resting site among cypress on a leaf island. I liked that spot just as I liked my first sighting spot of Shakespeare and Signpost Omega. There was that wildness about it that never seemed to be tainted with civilization. It was a good place.

On that afternoon I found no evidence he had been there for quite some time. No hot or cold tracks. No scat. No heap. And no reason to believe he would be headed toward that spot, because there was no evidence nearby.

Just to make sure he was okay, I put out urine heaps from Tracker, scat on dry ground. I piled it up over and over again. And in a period of two weeks no tracks showed. With all those stories around, my stomach was queasy. But I laughed it off. Surely, I thought, he's probably down near the prairie chasing buck deer. And before I completed the thought I was already heading back to my van and then leaving a dust rooster tail on the gravel road heading south. I worked the area heavily, making all the noise I could to get him to move and leave evidence. But none appeared. I kept at it for over a week. Then, exhausted, I went home and shrugged it off. All he's doing is playing that silly game with me again, I thought. But in conversations with other people, or at a lecture or school program I was doing, the question would creep into my mind: Where was Shakespeare?

The following weekend I jumped back into the swamp, gathered all of my resources and tracked until I dropped. Shakespeare was being his old self all right. But enough was enough. I would have settled for one scat plug bleached-out in the sun for days. One toe pad in shallow mud. A scratch on a log. Anything. I found nothing.

I began to rely almost completely on my sixth sense to pick up Shakespeare's presence. I didn't have to see him physically, I kept telling myself. No, just that feeling he was close by, that would be enough. But months passed and it never happened.

I fought off the obvious conclusion, but finally one day at Dead Man's Slough it overwhelmed me. Shakespeare was missing. I had begun to understand how the families of MIA's must feel. No coffin comes home, there is no official time to mourn and get it over with. There's only just enough hope to keep wondering if maybe one day he'll turn up and you will

all say how you never gave up hope. You won't say how
sometimes you wanted to give up hope just to get it out of
your mind.

I forged ahead in the swamp and broke through a treeline. Egrets exploded into the air from a pond. Gators plopped
underwater.

"No!" I screamed. I sank to my knees. I felt sick and
I wanted to die. I wanted to plunge into that pond and be
lost in there forever. "Shakespeare!" I yelled. His name echoed
across the water and off into the swamp. But there was no
sound of him rushing off in trees.

More months passed. It took me a long time to accept
Shakespeare's disappearance. I rationalized for a while. I surmised he had heard a female in season far off in another section
of the glades and after mating with her built himself a whole
new territory over there. I thought maybe he was an old cat
who had put in his time in the swamp and it was time for
him to move on. Panthers don't live very long anyway. I could
handle that. What I couldn't handle was him being hunted
down as in my nightmare, being killed and carted off like so
much raw meat and fur. Or he might have wandered off onto
a road and been hit by a truck.

There could be many reasons why he wasn't in his territory. And as I write this I still have not found any evidence
he is there. Hope lingers. I went to look for him this morning.
I'll go back out tomorrow.

I would like to think Shakespeare is still out there, more
elusive than ever, more mysterious than mankind could ever
imagine a panther to be. I would like to think he has truly
outsmarted me this time, letting me believe he no longer exists.
Maybe that final trick is what it will take for panthers to
survive.

Nam Yo Fara On.

APPENDIX

Notes on the Natural History of the Florida Panther

The Florida panther is one of some thirty subspecies of the cougar, the big cat of the Western Hemisphere who is also known by a number of other names including mountain lion, puma, and catamount. Cougar still roam throughout the Western Hemisphere, though their range has been steadily reduced, notably during the past fifty years.

The Florida panther became different enough from other cougars to be considered a subspecies by adapting to the subtropical environment of the extreme southeastern United States.

Name

The word "panther" comes from the Latin *panthera*, which in turn derived from the Greek word which refers to the tiger's black stripes. Big cats around the world have long been commonly called panthers, and today the word is often used loosely to designate a number of big cats, especially pumas, leopards, jaguars, and other cougar subspecies.

Most often "panther" is used to mean a black cat like the leopard that lives in Africa and India or the jaguar of Central and South America. A mutation has been shown to be responsible for the black cats among these two species, just as the mutation known as albinism may produce white cats.

So why is the tawny cougar of the Everglades called a panther? "Panther" is only one of many misnomers that have been applied to him. The various names evolved as knowledge of the cat itself evolved.

In the year 1500, Amerigo Vespucci, a European explorer who gave his name to two great continents, was probing the coastline of Venezuela when he saw what he reported as lions because they looked to him like the African lions he knew of. So, without recognizing it himself, Vespucci was the first white man known to have sighted and recorded a cougar in the Western Hemisphere. Vespucci's report reached another European explorer, Christopher Columbus, and in 1502 Columbus, on his fourth voyage to the New World, saw Vespucci's "lions" along the beaches of what are now Honduras and Nicaragua. Columbus was thus the first European known to have sighted cougar in Central America.

But it is Cabeza de Vaca who gets the credit as the first European to sight a cougar in North America, and he saw it in the Florida Everglades in 1513. He, too, however, reported "lions," not cougars. A few years later, Hernando de Soto verified Cabeza de Vaca's report, noting in his journal that "there are many lions in Florida."

In 1565, Sir John Hawkins, an English sea captain, reported "lions and tigers" in Florida. His "tigers" were probably cougars young enough to still have their camouflage stripes and spots. Much later, in 1598, Rene Laudonnierre wrote of a "certain kind of beast in Florida that differs little from the lions of Africa," perhaps indicating that he had some doubt as to whether they were in fact lions.

Pioneers settling in the Everglades referred to the cougars as "tigers," even up through the 19th century. Here again the confusion probably resulted from sightings in the distance of young cougars still wearing their blurred stripes.

In the 19th century, famed American naturalist, writer and artist Ernest Thompson Seton visited the Florida Muskogean Indians and wrote that they used the names "Catsa" and "Coot-ot-a-cho-bee," both meaning large wild cat, for the Florida cougar.

At about the same time people were reporting having seen what they described as black cats in the shadows of the swamp at night. They described these black cats as "ornery," and about the size and shape of panthers, and began calling them panthers. The name spread far enough to become engrained in Floridian minds, and ever since the Florida cougar has been burdened with a misleading common name. And since the Florida panther is not a black cat, a color most people associate with panthers, the name is doubly misleading.

But a cougar is a cougar is a cougar, whatever he may be called, in Florida or anywhere else in the Western Hemisphere. However, a commonly accepted name is sticky, and it would be foolhardy to try now to change the name by which the Florida cougar is commonly known, so Florida panther let him be.

Over the last eight years I have collected quite a few other names by which he is known, for example: swamp devil, swamp screamer, night screamer, white lion, silver lion, red lion, American lion, swamp lion, brown tiger, red tiger, deer tiger, deer killer, southern panther, southern lion, king cat, tall grass creeper, slough walker, night crier and swamp crier.

To scientists, the Florida panther is *Felis concolor coryi* Bangs, of the cat family Felidae, Mammalia, order Carnivora. *Felis concolor* is Latin for cat-with-color. Cory and Bangs are the names of two scientists who described this cat as a subspecies.

The Latin name *Felis concolor* was first applied to the cougar in 1771 by Carl von Linne, the Swedish botanist better known himself as Carolus Linneaus, the father of taxonomy, who devised the binomial system for classifying plants and animals. Half a century later, in 1834, Sir William Jardine, an English natural historian and sportsman, declared the name should be *Puma concolor*. The word "puma" means a powerful animal in Quechua, an Inca language. But although the biologist, J. A. Allen, calls the panther *Puma concolor* in his 1868 book, *On Mammals and Winter Birds of East Florida*, and even today the term occasionally turns up in textbooks, *Puma concolor* was never generally accepted and the name *Felis concolor* is now regarded as standard.

In 1896 biologist Charles Cory distinguished the Florida

cougar from those in other regions of the hemisphere by calling it *Felis concolor floridiana*, to indicate that the Florida cat was a subspecies. Although he did not describe a type specimen, he did record the distinguishing features of *Felis concolor floridiana* in his 1896 book, *Hunting and Fishing in Florida*.

Then in 1899, Outram Bangs, a New England zoologist, decided that the Florida cougar population was a separate species and should be called *Felis floridiana*, but noting that this name had already been given to the Florida bobcat, he proposed the designation *Felis coryi* in recognition of Cory's work on the cat.

Nelson and Goldman solved the problem in 1939 by deciding the Florida panther was indeed a subspecies, not a separate species, and gave it the now widely accepted name of *Felis concolor coryi*.

Distribution

The Florida panther is known to have once roamed throughout Florida, Georgia, South Carolina, Alabama, Mississippi, Louisiana, and as far west as Arkansas and eastern Texas. Information gathered during the past few years indicates that this panther's range is now far more confined. In the southern third of the state, the panther is known to be in the Big Cypress National Preserve, Collier Seminole Park, Fakahatchee Strand, Everglades National Park, the Big Cypress Indian Reservation, the Miccosukee Indian Reservation, and the Loxahatchee National Wildlife Refuge. Sightings have been reported in the panhandle in the Appalachicola and Osceola National Forests. On the peninsula panthers have been seen in the Ocala National Forest, the Kissimmee River Valley, around Lake Okeechobee, and in the Highlands Hammock and Myakka River State Parks; and in the southwest portion of the peninsula in Desoto, Charlotte, Glades, Lee, Hendry and Collier Counties. However, many of these sightings have not been accepted by all authorities.

Territory

The territory of a panther is his home range, his specific domain within a wider wilderness area. In the Everglades, a panther's territory might be as small as 36 square miles or as large as 400. In open country, a panther's territory is larger than in a confined region such as a cypress stand.

Female panthers seem to have smaller territories than males. In some cases, panthers' territories overlap.

Under normal conditions, the panther stays within this territory, but there are many factors that control his roamings. He might stay in an area for a day or a week before he moves on. He might cover 20 miles in a day, or in two days, or three.

Size

The Florida panther is the largest unspotted cat in North America.

An adult male weighs something like 150 pounds, is 7 to 8 feet long from nose tip to tail tip, and stands 20 to 33 inches high at the shoulder.

An adult female is slightly smaller and weighs approximately 60 to 100 pounds, measures maybe 6 or 7 feet, and has a shoulder height of 18 to 24 inches.

Two instances of much larger panthers killed in Florida have been recorded. The largest on record was a cat shot at Elbo Creek near Eau Gallie in 1875. It was 9 feet 4 inches long and weighed 240 pounds. Another, killed near Estero in 1939, weighed 200 pounds.

Color

The Florida panther's color ranges from chocolate brown to cinnamon or even light to silver gray.

The tip of the tail and the back of the ears are either dark brown or brownish-black. Bordering and inside the ears, the fur is grayish-white to brownish-white. The lower chest, belly, and the inside of the legs are grayish-white in sub-adults, creamy white to brownish-white in adults.

Reports of black panthers have never been substantiated.

Sprinting and Endurance

The panther is a sprinter, not a long distance runner. He is said to attain a speed in ambush of up to 35 miles an hour, but he cannot sustain such a speed or anything like it for long. This is because his blood has more "sprinter cells" than "long distance running cells." Sprinter cells supply a high yield of oxygen for a short time, while the long distance running cells supply oxygen steadily for long periods. The cheetah, which must catch its prey on the wide open plains of Africa, is noted for the long distance running cells without which he could not have survived, but because of the heavy vegetation in his territory, the Florida panther is much better served by sprinter cells.

Although they cannot maintain high speeds for long, Florida panthers have plenty of stamina. They roam their territories constantly, seldom staying in one place for more than a day or two.

Jumping
Panthers are adept at both the high jump and the broad jump. I don't believe any other cats on the face of the earth can equal them in spring action, ease and agility. I have seen a panther jump more than 15 feet high, and others have reported seeing them broad jump a distance of almost 40 feet.

Patience
The panther is a lone hunter, and patience is essential to his success. He can sit almost motionless for hours in a treeline with deer grazing nearby, waiting for the exact moment to spring on his prey.

Swimming
Panthers take to the water and swim, although they are not known to stay in it for any length of time. A panther may swim a canal and several sloughs to get to high ground; or during the rainy season, a panther may make his way through the water in his territory without even looking for high ground.

Prey
The panther will eat almost any creature he can efficiently kill. His diet includes wild pigs, turkeys, quail, opossums, raccoons, rabbits, wading birds, small alligators, frogs, turtles, bobcats, snakes, fish, squirrels, mice, armadillos, deer, domestic chickens and geese, and occasionally cattle.

Solitary Nature

There is no evidence whatever to support reports of a pack of Florida panthers. No two full-grown Florida panthers have ever been known to travel together as a team. A male and female will stay together temporarily for mating, and a female with cubs takes them with her for training until they are capable of going off on their own, but otherwise the Florida panther is a loner. The reported sightings of panther packs are almost certainly of a female traveling with her almost mature cubs.

Mating

When a female screams day or night for a mate, males hearing it answer the call. If there are several males, a furious battle is likely. When the fight is over, the loser drags himself off, and the winner escorts his prize in the opposite direction.

Panthers' den requirements vary, but females heavy with young seek out secluded spots in which to deliver their young. In the Everglades, the site could be a hollowed-out log in a remote custard apple swamp, in a thicket of bushes, under a massive oak tree uprooted by storm, in an abandoned man-made culvert or an old hunting cabin reclaimed by the swamp, or possibly on a small island. What she looks for is a site where she will not be disturbed and where the litter will be safe from harm.

The gestation period is thought to be from 84 to as many as 120 days. A litter may include from 2 to 8 cubs, but usually no more than 4. New-born cubs usually weigh between 8 and 14 ounces, and measure from 7 to 12 inches long. Their claws are fully developed and protrude from the paws. Their eyes are closed at birth but open 12 to 16 days later. During the blind period they can crawl short distances, but do not move about. Suckling lasts about 6 weeks; then the cubs' teeth develop and the mother starts feeding them raw meat. Cubs grow slowly at first, but after 8 to 10 weeks they may weigh 7 to 10 pounds. At 5 months the growth rate is rapid and a yearling may double his weight and grow to 4 feet long. When the cubs are old enough to walk, their activity centers in and around the den until they start walking the territory with their mother. From her they learn how to set up territories of their own, find fresh water, and kill prey, starting with small mammals such as mice and rats.

Life Span
Panthers in the Everglades have an estimated life span of perhaps 15 to 20 years, but there is little hard data on this. In captivity, they can live for as many as 20 years.

Ecto-parasites
Ecto-parasites are insects or arachnids that live on the panther outside of the body. Panthers are not free of fleas, ticks, mites, etc., but because they are continually on the move, and because the female probably does not use the same den site for successive litters, panthers have less difficulty with these pests than might be expected.

Ticks are more dangerous to panthers than fleas. The tick is an arachnid, not an insect. It's bite can transmit tick fever infection into a panther's bloodstream, which may bring on paralysis and death.

Ticks are found normally on a panther's neck and ears, since it is almost impossible for a panther to rub ticks in those locations off with a paw, or to roll them off in grass or mud.

Eno-parasites
Recent autopsies of panthers killed on the roads through the Everglades and blood samples from temporarily captive panthers have augmented the meager supply of information about the internal parasites of panthers. They have produced evidence of round worms, tape worms, and even heart worms.

Natural Mortality
Like most wild animals, panthers both young and old are threatened by fire, flood, and starvation. In the panther's case, the danger from flood is less of drowning, since panthers can swim, than of starving for lack of prey.

The weakest of a litter can be pushed away by the stronger siblings and die of starvation, and if the mother panther is disabled, all the cubs are doomed. Birds of prey can swoop down on cubs, or a black bear could eat them while their mother is out hunting. Even adult male panthers have been known to eat cubs.

Young panthers on their own but not yet skilled in the intricacies of predation may not be able to catch enough prey to feed themselves.

The worn-out teeth, cracked canines, or splintered claws of an old panther may become inadequate.

A panther leaping on his prey may impale himself on a jagged branch, or crush his skull on a limestone rock. If he is ambushing a buck deer, he may miss his target and be gored to death, or sliced by the deer's sharp hooves. Merely while roaming he risks being dragged to his death in a gator hole, and there are, of course, plenty of poisonous snakes in the swamp and rattlers in the high country, to threaten his life. A wild boar can sometimes gore a panther to death. And there is always the possibility of meeting death from another panther in a fight for a mate.

Man-made Mortality

Pioneer settlers regarded the Florida panther as a livestock killer, and a nuisance to be slaughtered ruthlessly. They laid traps for him and hunted him with dogs. In 1832, before Florida had become a state, the federal government instituted a reward for those who killed panthers. In 1837, John Lee Williams, who was a Florida assistant of John James Audubon and so could be expected to have known better, restated the erroneous general idea that panthers are a menace to livestock.

By 1884 panthers had become scarce enough to foster the assumption that they had been totally eradicated, but in 1887 a law authorized a $5 payment for panther pelts, just to make sure.

Early in the 20th century, President Theodore Roosevelt did the panther the greatest injustice of all. Roosevelt probably did as much as any president to preserve the country's wilderness areas, but he was also an avid big game hunter and led a crusade against the cougar. He pronounced the panther "the big horse-killing cat, the destroyer of deer, the lord of stealthy murder, facing his doom with a heart both craven and cruel." He led his loyal followers by the thousands into the forests and swamps to kill them off.

During the 1930's two new threats to the Florida panther emerged. Panther meat was exploited as a substitute for pork, and an attempt to rid the area of tick fever by poisoning and hunting down the deer on which the panthers preyed left the panthers, along with some other species, to face starvation.

As their numbers dwindled, the Florida panther became a prized trophy, and big game hunters from around the world turned their attention from the lions, tigers and leopards of Africa and India long enough to trek in the Everglades.

By the 1950's a panther sighting had become rare indeed, and again popular opinion concluded the big Florida cat had become extinct. However, a few were seen, and some measures to protect them at least partially were adopted.

In 1968, the Florida panther was put on the state and federal endangered species list. At long last, he was finally removed from the list of game animals, and awarded the full protection of the law. Florida was the first state to take these steps, but others have since joined in.

Now it is destruction of his natural habitat that is edging the panther toward extinction. Today the most serious threat to the Florida panther is development in the areas where he roams. Developers covet that virgin land; big corporations seeking plant sites consider the panther a stumbling block to commercial expansion. Oil drilling proceeds in the Big Cypress Preserve, one of the most sensitive wilderness regions in the country.

An almost equally serious threat is from the highways that now run through panther territory. Since 1979, 14 panthers have been killed on those highways, and no one knows how many others have been hit and limped away into the swamp to die.

Counter-measures

For the last few years, the Florida Game and Freshwater Fish Commission has undertaken a study of the Florida panther by means of radio telemetry. The purpose is to gain enough information about the panther's habits to help save him from extinction. The method involves tranquilizing and capturing a panther long enough to fasten a collar containing a radio transmitter around his neck, and then setting him free again. The transmitter enables the researchers to track the panther night and day, from the air as well as from the ground.

Laudable as the objective may be, there is a serious question about the method, for out of 7 panthers collared before this writing, 5 are now dead. One was killed on the highway, a death that cannot fairly be attributed to the project, and one died as a direct result of the project in that she was killed by the tranquilizer dart. The others are less easy to attribute. One died of trauma after being collared and set free; another was found dead in a low area full of water, apparently drowned but with his skull smashed; and the cause of death of the last could not be determined as the carcass was found only after it had decomposed. Valuable lessons have been learned, but the big question is whether or not the price is too high.

Save the Panther—A Proposal

More serious than the problem of how to learn enough about the wild panther to be able to protect it is the problem of official and public apathy. On the official side, the fact is that the laws we now have to protect endangered species are inadequate, and beyond that, are not vigorously enforced. They should be strengthened and strictly enforced. On the public side, it is a sad comment on environmental education that the true meaning of a predator is still not widely understood. And it is even sadder that wildlife conservation is still viewed by many as an impediment to human progress.

It is up to the state legislature to adopt Project Save-the-Panther by resolution, to set aside critical state and federal wildlife refuges, commit state and federal funds for purchase of the needed land, and to work directly with land owners and developers to acquire this land.

A comprehensive panther management program on the state level should be undertaken immediately. State agencies, conservation organizations and private concerns have a good deal of information, but a central body is needed to coordinate goals, strategies, and tactics. An effective program will require more expertise, energy, time and money than has yet been expended on the Florida panther.

Goals, and criteria for evaluating progress toward them,

must be established and clearly set forth. The obvious goal is to increase the panther population, starting with the panthers in the existing state and federal preserves.

The coordinating body's job would be to enlist and synergize the efforts of the many state departments and agencies that can play a role. It would see that panthers now living in areas that have already been committed for development are relocated. It would find ways to reduce the appalling mortality, starting with immediate steps to:

- prohibit all hunting in panther territories;
- limit the number of hunting licenses issued and increase the fee;
- shorten the hunting season;
- limit off-road vehicles' access to wilderness areas;
- increase rewards for information leading to the arrest of panther killers;
- deter commercial and residential developers from building on land that will be needed for wildlife preserves in the future.

The next job would be to verify the panther's presence in given areas, by means such as finding tracks, kills, scat, scrapes, and other signs. Once the territory of a panther is known, that area should become the critical concern of the wildlife officers there and in the surrounding areas.

Analyzing this data by regions according to number, age, size of territory, prey, and other factors, will provide the basis for a sound, long-term program to stabilize the panther populations by protecting their habitats, and more constructive work on increasing the populations could begin.

It goes without saying that the entire program should be accompanied by the strongest possible campaign to spread public awareness of both the problems and the programs to resolve them, through the media, environmental education classes, and all other means. The Florida panther is such a truly beautiful creature that it should be easy to enlist the public support that will be essential for the program's success.

There are already signs that public concern is ready to crystallize, and perhaps the tide has at long last turned for the Florida panther. Only a couple of years ago, 600,000 students across the state voted overwhelmingly to choose the big endangered cat over the manatee and the alligator as the official state animal. In 1982, Governor Bob Graham signed the bill confirming this choice.

BIBLIOGRAPHY

Allen, R. 1950. "Notes on the Florida panther, *Felis concolor coryi* Bangs." *J. Mamm.*, 31:279-280.

Allen, R. and W.T. Neill. 1954. "The raccoon preyed upon by panther and rattlesnake." *Everglades Nat. Hist.*, 2:46.

Bangs, O. 1898. "The land mammals of peninsular Florida and the coast region of Georgia." *Proc. Boston Soc. Nat. Hist.*, 23:157-235.

Bangs, O. 1899. "The Florida puma." *Proc. Biol. Soc. Wash.*, 13:15-17.

Barnett, Lincoln. 1962. *The World We Live In*. NY: Time/Life.

Baudy, R.E. 1976. "Breeding techniques for felines destined for release in the wild." p.99-108 in *Proc. FL Panther Conference* (P.C.H. Pritchard, ed.), Orlando, FL: FL Audubon Soc. and FL Game & Fresh Water Fish Comm.

Bauer, Erwin A. 1972. *Treasury of Big Game Animals*. NY: Harper & Row.

Belden, R.C. 1978. "Florida panther investigation—a 1978 progress report." p.123-133 in *Proc. Rare & Endangered Wildlife Symposium* (R.R. Odom and L. Landers, eds.); Athens, GA: GA Dept. Nat. Resour. Tech. Bull. WL4.

Belden, R.C. 1977. "If you see a panther." *FL Wildlife* 31(3): 31-34.

Belden, R.C. and L.E. Williams, Jr. 1976. "Survival status of
the Florida panther." in *Proc. FL Panther Conference*
(P.C.H. Pritchard, ed.), Orlando, FL: FL Audubon Soc.
and FL Game & Fresh Water Fish Comm.

Beverly, F. (F.A. Ober). 1874. "The Florida Panther." *Forest
& Stream* Dec. 17, 1874. p.42-49; in Tinsley, J.B. 1970.
The Florida Panther. St. Petersburg, FL: Great Out-
doors Pub.

Bologna, Gianfranco. 1975. *The World of Birds*. NY: Abbeville Press.

Boudreau, J.C. and C. Tsuchitani. 1973. *Sensory Neurophys-
iology, the Cat*. NY: Van Nostrand Reinhold.

Brown, Tom Jr. (as told to Wm. J. Watkins). 1979. *Tracker*.
Englewood Cliffs, NJ: Prentice-Hall.

Buckles, Mary P. 1978. *Animals of the World*. NY: Ridge
Press Book-Grosset & Dunlap.

Burt, W.H. and R.P. Grossenheider. 1964. *A Field Guide to
the Mammals*. Boston: Houghton Mifflin.

Burton, Maurice. 1975. *Reptiles*. London: Octopus Books.

Cahalane, V.W. 1964. "A preliminary study of distribution
and numbers of cougar grizzly and wolf in North America." *NY Zool. Soc.*

Caras, Roger. 1979. *The Forest*. NY: Holt, Rinehart & Winston.

Carr, Archie and Coleman J. Goin. 1955. *Guide to the Reptiles,
Amphibians and Fresh Water Fish of Florida*. Gainesville: U. of FL Press.

Chapman, F.M. 1943. "Everglades Islet." *Audubon Mag.* 45:19-
25.

Conner, D. 1979. *Coastal Plants of Florida*. Hollywood, FL:
FL Dept. of Agri.

Cory, C.B. 1896. *Hunting and Fishing in Florida*. Boston: Estes
& Lauriat.

Craighead, Frank C. 1963. *Orchids and Other Plants of the
Everglades*. Coral Gables, FL: U. of Miami Press.

Dahne, B. 1958. "The truth about black panthers." *FL Wildlife*. 12(6):26-27, 48-49.

Dalrymple, Byron W. 1978. *North American Game Animals*. NY: Crown Pub.

Dickson, J.D. III. 1955. "An ecological study of the key deer." *FL Game & Fresh Water Fish Comm. Tech Bull*. No. 3.

Dodson, P. 1973. *Journey through the Old Everglades: the Log of the Minnehaha*. Tampa: Trend House.

Douglas, Marjory Stoneman. 1947. *The Everglades: River of Grass*. NY: Rinehart.

East, Ben. 1977. *Bears*. NY: Crown Pub.

Eaton, R.L. 1976. "Status and conservation of the puma." Edited discussion. p.46-48 in *The World's Cats*. in *Proc. FL Panther Conference* (P.C.H. Pritchard, ed.). Orlando, FL: FL Audubon Soc. and FL Game & Fresh Water Fish Comm. 3(1):1-95.

Eaton, R.L. 1974. *The Cheetah*. NY: Van Nostrand Reinhold.

Eaton, R.L. 1973. "The status, conservation and management of the cougar in the United States." p.68-86 in Eaton, R.L., ed. *The World's Cats*. Winston, OR: World Wildlife Safari.

Eaton, R.L. 1971. "Florida panther." *Nat. Parks & Cons. Mag*. 45(12):18-20.

Eaton, R.L. 1970. *The World of Cats*, Vol.1. NY: Dept. of Int.

Elliot, Charles. 1969. *The Outdoor Eye: A Sportman's Guide*. NY: Outdoor Life Publishers.

Elliot, D.G. 1905. "A check list of mammals of the North American continent, the West Indies, and the neighboring seas." Publ. Field Col. Mus., Zool. Ser. 6:1-761.

Florida Game & Fresh Water Fish Commission Annual Report, Jul.1,1972-Jun.30,1973. *FL Wildlife* 27:9-28.

Frye, O.E., with Bill & Les Piper. n.d. "The disappearing panther." Mimeograph.

Gadd, Laurence. 1980. *Deadly Beautiful*. NY: Macmillan.

Goertz, J.W. and R. Abegg. 1966. "Pumas in Louisiana." *J. Mamm.* 47:727.

Goldman, E.A. 1946. "Classification of the races of the puma." p.175-302 in S.P. Young and E.A. Goldman, *The Puma, Mysterious American Cat.* D.C.: Am. Wildlife Inst.

Goodwin, H.A. and C.W. Holloway, compilers. 1976. *Red Data Book. Vol.1:Mammalia.* Morges, Switzerland: IUCN.

Grzimek, B. 1975. *Animal Life Encyclopedia.* NY: Ronald Press.

Guggisberg, C.A. 1975. *Wild Cats of the World.* London: David & Charles.

Hall, E.R. and K.R. Kelson. 1959. *The Mammals of North America.* (2 vol.) NY: Ronald Press.

Hamilton, W.J. Jr. 1941. "Notes on some mammals of Lee County, Florida." *American Middle National,* 25:686-691.

Hamilton, W.J. Jr. 1943. *The Mammals of Eastern United States: An Account of Recent Land Mammals Occurring East of the Mississippi.* Ithaca, NY: Comstock Press.

Henry, V.G. 1976. "The recovery plan concept of the Fish and Wildlife Service as it relates to the Florida panther." in *Proc. FL Panther Conference* (P.C.H. Pritchard, ed.), Orlando, FL: FL Audubon Soc. and FL Game & Fresh Water Fish Comm.

Hollister, N. 1911. "The Louisiana puma." *Proc. Biol. Surv. Wash.* 24:175-178.

Horan, J. 1978. "The search for the Florida panther." *Natl. Wildlife* 16(4):36-39.

Hornocker, M.G. 1970. "An analysis of mountain lion predation upon mule, deer and elk in the Idaho Primitive Area." Wildlife Monograph No. 21:1-39.

Howell, A.H. 1932. *Florida Bird Life.* Tallahassee: FL Dept. Game & Fresh Water Fish.

Howell, A.H. 1921. "A biological survey of Alabama." *N. Am. Fauna* No. 45.

Jenkins, J.H. 1971. "The status and management of bobcat and cougar in the southeastern states." *Proc. Symp. on Native Cats of N. Am., Their Status and Management* 9S.E. (Jorgenson & L.D. Mech, eds.). D.C.: US Fish & Wildlife Ser.

Jenkins, J.H. 1953. "The game resources of Georgia." *Tech. Bull. 1*. Atlanta: GA Game & Fish Comm.

Jones, A.D. 1974. "Big Cypress Swamp and the Everglades: no solution yet." *Living Wilderness*, 37(124):28-36.

Kisling, V.N. Jr. 1976. "Captive propagation and study as an integral component of a field-captive management program for the Florida panther, *Felis concolor coryi*." in *Proc. FL Panther Conference* (P.C.H. Pritchard, ed.), Orlando, FL: FL Audubon Soc. and FL Game & Fresh Water Fish Comm.

Layne, J.N. 1974. "The land mammals of south Florida." in *Environments of South Florida: Present and Past*. Memoir 2 (F.J. Gleason, ed.), p.386-413. Miami: Miami Geol. Soc.

Layne, J.M. and M.N. McCauley. 1976. "Biological overview of the Florida panther." in *Proc. FL Panther Conference* (P.C.H. Pritchard, ed.), Orlando, FL: FL Audubon Soc. and FL Game & Fresh Water Fish Comm.

Leposky, George. 1975. "Have you seen this cat?" *St. Petersburg Times Floridian Mag.*, 8 Jun: 14-16.

Lewis, J.C. 1969. "Evidence of mountain lions in the Ozarks and adjacent areas, 1948-1968." *J. Mamm.*, 50:371-372.

Lewis, J.C. 1970. "Evidence of mountain lions in the Ozark, Boston and Ouachita Mountains." *Proc. Okla. Acad. Sci. for 1968*. p.182-184.

Line, Les and Frank Russell. 1976. *The Audubon Society Book of Wild Birds*. NY: Abrams.

Long, R.W. and O. Lakela. 1971. *A Flora of Tropical Florida*. Coral Gables: U. Miami Press.

Loveless, C.M. 1959. "The Everglades deer herd: Life history and management." FL: Game & Fresh Water Fish Comm. Tech. Bull. 6.

Lowery, G.H. Jr. 1944. "Distribution of Louisiana mammals with respect to the physiography of the state." *Proc. LA Acad. Sci.*, 8:63-73.

Lowery, G.H. Jr. 1943. "Check list of the mammals of Louisiana and adjacent waters." *Occas. Papers Mus. Zool.*, LA State U. 13:213-257.

Lowery, G.H. Jr. 1936. "A preliminary report on the distribution of mammals in Louisiana." *Proc. LA Acad. Sci.*, 3:11-39.

Lowery, G.H. Jr. 1974. *The Mammals of Louisiana and its Adjacent Waters.* Baton Rouge, LA: LSU Press.

Lowman, G.E. 1975. "A survey of endangered, threatened, rare, status undetermined, peripheral, and unique mammals of the southeastern national forests and grasslands." US Dept. of Agri. Forest Serv., Southern Region.

Macgregor, W.G. 1976. "The status of the puma in California." p.28-35 in *The World's Cats*, in *Proc. FL Panther Conference* (P.C.H. Pritchard, ed.), Orlando, FL: FL Audubon Soc. and FL Game & Fresh Water Fish Comm.

McCauley, M.N. 1977. "Current population and distribution status of the panther, *Felis concolor*, in Florida." Unpub. MS thesis. Tampa: U. of S.FL.

McCormick, Jack. 1966. *The Life of the Forest.* NY: McGraw-Hill.

Mattis, George. 1980. *Whitetail.* NY: Van Nostrand Reinhold.

Maxwell, Lewis and Betty. 1977. *Florida Insects.* Tampa: Lewis S. Maxwell.

Maynard, C.J. 1883. "The animals of Florida." *Quart. J. Boston Zool. Soc.* 2:18, 17-34, 38-43, 49-50.

Merriam, C.H. 1901. "Preliminary revision of the pumas (*Felis concolor* group)." in *Proc. FL Panther Conference* (P.C.H. Pritchard, ed.), Orlando, FL: FL Audubon Soc. and FL Game & Fresh Water Fish Comm.

Morine, D.E. 1976. "Preserving the Pascagoula." *Nat. Conservancy News* 26(4):12-16.

Nat. Geographic Soc. 1979. *Wild Animals of North America.*
    D.C.: Nat. Geographic Soc.

Nelson, E.W. and E.A. Goldman. 1939. "List of the pumas
    with three described as new." *J. Mamm.*, 10:345-350.

Noble, R.E. 1971. "A recent record of the puma (*Felis con-
    color*) in Arkansas." *Southwestern Nat.* 16:209.

Nowak, R.M. 1974. "The cougar in the United States and
    Canada." *Rpt. to US Fish & Wildlife Serv.* as amended
    1976.

Nowak, R.M. and R. McBride. 1973. "Feasibility of a study
    of the Florida panther." *Rpt. to World Wildlife Fund.*

Nowak, R.M. and R. McBride. 1974. "Status survey of the
    Florida panther." *World Wildlife Fund Yearbook, 1973-
    74.* Mus. Nat. Hist., U. of KS.

Ovington, Ray. 1975. *Birds of Prey.* St. Petersburg, FL: Great
    Outdoors Pub.

Packard, Winthrop. 1983. *Florida Trails.* Englewood, FL:
    Pineapple Press.

Peithmann, Irvin. 1957. *The Unconquered Seminole Indians.*
    St. Petersburg, FL: Great Outdoors Pub.

Perry, Richard. 1970. *Bears: The World of Animals.* NY: Arco
    Pub.

Phenicie, C.K. and J.R. Lyons. 1973. "Tactical planning in
    fish and wildlife management and research." US Fish
    & Wildlife Serv., Bu. Sport Fisheries & Wildlife. *Resour.
    Publ.* 123.

Pritchard, P.C.H., ed. 1976. in *Proc. of the FL Panther Con-
    ference* (P.C.H. Pritchard, ed.), Orlando, FL: FL Au-
    dubon Soc. and FL Game & Fresh Water Fish Comm.

Rue III, Leonard Lee. 1978. *The Deer of North America.* NY:
    Crown Pub.

Rue III, Leonard Lee. 1968. *Game Animals.* NY: Harper &
    Row.

Schemnitz, S.D. 1974. "Populations of bear, panther, alligator, and deer in the Florida Everglades." *FL Sci. (Quart. J. FL Acad. Sci.)*, 37:157-567.

Schwartz, A. 1951. "The land mammals of southern Florida and the upper Florida keys." PhD thesis, U. of MI.

Sealander, J.A. 1951. "Mountain lions in Arkansas." *J. Mamm.*, 32:364.

Sealander, J.A. 1956. "A provisional check list and key to the mammals of Arkansas (with annotations)." *Am. Midl. Nat.*, 56:38-41.

Sealander, J.A. 1979. *A Guide to Arkansas Mammals.* Conway, AK: River Road Press.

Sealander, J.A. and P.S. Gibson. 1973. "Status of the mountain lion in Arkansas." *Proc. AK Acad. Sci.*, 27:38-41.

Seidensticker, J.C. IV, M.G. Hornocker, W.V. Wiles, and J.P. Messick. 1973. "Mountain lion social organization of the Idaho Primitive Area." Wildlife Monograph No. 35:1-61.

Seton, E.T. 1920. *Lives of Game Animals.* Vol. 1, Pt. 1: "Cats, wolves and foxes." NY: Doubleday, Doran.

Smith, G. 1968. "The Florida panther." *FL Wildlife*, 21(8):30-31.

Smith, G. 1970. "Mystery cat." *FL Wildlife*, 24(3):4-6.

Sprunt, Alexander Jr. 1954. *Florida Bird Life.* NY: Coward-McCann.

Sutton, Ann and Myron. 1979. Wildlife of the Forest. NY: Abrams.

Taglianti, Augusto Vigna. 1977. *The World of Mammals.* NY: Abbeville Press.

Tinbergen, Niko. 1965. *Animal Behavior.* NY: Time/Life.

Tinsley, J.B. 1970. *The Florida Panther.* St. Petersburg, FL: Great Outdoors Pub.

True, F.W. 1891. "The puma, or American lion: *Felis concolor* of Linneaus." p.591-608 in *Ann. Rept.*, US Nat. Mus., Year ending June 30, 1889.

Tucker, James A. 1968. *Florida Birds*. Tampa: Lewis S. Maxwell.

Ulmer, F.A. Jr. 1941. "Melanism in the Felidae, with special reference to the genus lynx." *J. Mamm.* 22:285-288.

US Dept. of Int. 1969. *Environmental Impact of the Big Cypress Swamp Jetport*.

US Dept. of Int. 1973. *Threatened Wildlife of the United States*. Resource Publ. 114, Bu. Sport Fisheries & Wildlife.

Vanas, J. 1976. "The Florida panther in the Big Cypress Swamp and the role of the Everglades Wonder of Gardens in past and future captive breeding programs." in *Proc. FL Panther Conference* (P.C.H. Pritchard, ed.), Orlando, FL: FL Audubon Soc. and FL Game & Fresh Water Fish Comm.

Villarrubia, C.R. 1977. "An investigation on locating elusive wilderness carnivores: particularly the cougar in Louisiana." LA Co-op. Wildlife Res. Unit. Baton Rouge: LA State U.

Walden, Fred. 1963. *A Dictionary of Trees*. St. Petersburg, FL: Great Outdoors Pub.

Webb S.D., ed. 1974. *Pleistocene Mammals of Florida*. Gainesville, FL: U. Presses of FL.

Whitefield, Philip. 1978. *The Hunters*. NY: Simon & Schuster.

Williams, L.E. Jr. 1976. *Florida Panther*. p.13-15 in *Mammals* (J.N. Layne, ed.) Vol. 1, in *Rare and Endangered Biota of Florida* (P.C.H. Pritchard, ed.) Gainesville: U. Presses of FL.

Wolfe, J.L. 1971. "Mississippi land mammals: Distribution, identification, ecological notes." MS Mus. Sci., MS Game & Fish Comm.

Young, Stanley P. 1958. *The Bobcat of North America*. Lincoln, NB: U. of NB Press.

Young, S.P. and E.A. Goldman. 1946. *The Puma—Mysterious American Cat*. D.C.: Am. Wildlife Inst.